Caribbean History
for CSEC®

Kevin Baldeosingh and Radica Mahase

OXFORD
UNIVERSITY PRESS

UNIVERSITY PRESS

Great Clarendon Street, Oxford OX2 6DP

Oxford University Press is a department of the University of Oxford.
It furthers the University's objective of excellence in research, scholarship,
and education by publishing worldwide in

Oxford   New York

Auckland   Cape Town   Dar es Salaam   Hong Kong   Karachi
Kuala Lumpur   Madrid   Melbourne   Mexico City   Nairobi
New Delhi   Shanghai   Taipei   Toronto

With offices in

Argentina   Austria   Brazil   Chile   Czech Republic   France   Greece
Guatemala   Hungary   Italy   Japan   Poland   Portugal   Singapore
South Korea   Switzerland   Thailand   Turkey   Ukraine   Vietnam

© Copyright Oxford University Press

The moral rights of the authors have been asserted

Database right Oxford University Press (maker)

First published 2011

All rights reserved. No part of this publication may be reproduced,
stored in a retrieval system, or transmitted, in any form or by any means,
without the prior permission in writing of Oxford University Press,
or as expressly permitted by law, or under terms agreed with the appropriate
reprographics rights organization. Enquiries concerning reproduction
outside the scope of the above should be sent to the Rights Department,
Oxford University Press, at the address above

You must not circulate this book in any other binding or cover
and you must impose this same condition on any acquirer

British Library Cataloguing in Publication Data

Data available

ISBN: 978-0-19-832999-2

16

Printed and bound by CPI Group (UK) Ltd, Croydon, CR0 4YY

Paper used in the production of this book is a natural, recyclable product made
from wood grown in sustainable forests. The manufacturing process conforms to the
environmental regulations of the country of origin.

Acknowledgements

The authors and publisher are grateful for permission to reproduce the following copyright material:

p6 Special Collections, University of Amsterdam, UBM NOK 95-156; p7 University of the West Indies; p8 Special Collections, University of Amsterdam, UBM NOK 95-156; p10 The Metropolitan Museum of Art/Art Resource/Photo Scala, Florence; p11 Spectrum/Heritage Images/Photo Scala, Florence; p12 David McNew/Getty Images; p18 Tessa Mcgoldrick/Corbis Images Ltd.; p21 Goncalo Veloso de Figueiredo/Shutterstock; p23 Ann Ronan/Heritage Images/Photo Scala, Florence; p32 Heritage Images/Corbis Images Ltd.; p33 Hulton Archive/Getty Images; p34l Mary Evans Picture Library; p34r Mary Evans Picture Library; p43t Rischgitz/Stringer/Getty Images; p43b Radica Mahase; p44t North Wind Picture Archives/akg-images; p44b Radica Mahase; p45tl Radica Mahase; p45ml Radica Mahase; p45br The College of Arms; p47 AAA Photostock/Alamy; p51 Mary Evans Picture Library; p52 Mary Evans Picture Library/Alamy; p54 Pack-Shot/Shutterstock; p62 Alberto Paredes/Alamy; p64 Marcus Rainsford/The British Library Board; p68 Katja Wickert/Shutterstock; p69 Heritage Images/Photo Scala, Florence; p70 Heritage Images/Photo Scala, Florence; p71 Heritage Images/Photo Scala, Florence; p73 The John Carter Brown Library at Brown University; p74t Classic Image/Alamy; p74bl Heartland/Shutterstockp; 74br The Print Collector/Alamy; p77 redfrisbee/Shutterstock; p79 Heritage Images/Photo Scala, Florence; p81t Francesca/Alamy; p81b The John Carter Brown Library at Brown University; p82 Jon Arnold Images Ltd/Alamy; p83 White Images/Photo Scala, Florence; p86 Interfoto/Alamy; p87 rook76/Shutterstock; p91 The Print Collector/Heritage-Images/Imagestate; p92 Getty Images; p93 Grosvenor Prints/Mary Evans Picture Library; p94 Hulton Archive/Getty Images; p95 Anti-Slavery International; p97 Library of Congress; p99 Ann Ronan/Heritage Images/Photo Scala, Florence; p106 Rischgitz/Hulton Archive/Getty Images; p113 Bettmann/Corbis Images Ltd.; p118 Corbis Images Ltd.; p125 Mary Evans Picture Library/Alamy; p126t Radica Mahase; p126b Radica Mahase; p137 The British Library/Heritage Images; p143 Keystone/Hulton Archive/Getty Images; p144 Dorothea Lange/Library of Congress; p147 Library of Congress; p149 Library of Congress; p151 The Print Collector/Alamy; p152 Archive Farms/Getty Images; p164 Mike Agliolo/Corbis Images Ltd.; p166 Bettmann/Corbis Images Ltd.; p170 Interfoto/Alamy; p172 Roger Viollet/Getty Images; p176 Library of Congress; p187 Vector Images; p194 Vector Images; p203 dbimages/Alamy; p204b Art Media/Heritage Images/Photo Scala, Florence; p205t Grey Villet/Time Life Pictures/Getty Images; p205b University of Guyana; p206 Simon Burt/Rex Features; p208 Franklin McMahon/Corbis Images Ltd.; p213 Library of Congress; p213r Underwood & Underwood/Corbis Images Ltd.; p218t Mahesh Patil/Shutterstock; p218b Brittany Somerset/Corbis Images Ltd.; p219 Axiom Photographic Limited/superstock ltd.; p220 Bruce Coleman Inc./Alamy; p221 Bettmann/Corbis Images Ltd.; p222 Radica Mahase; p225 American School/Private Collection/The Bridgeman Art Library; p230 Mansell/Time Life Pictures/Getty Images.

Background images courtesy of Olgapsheni.../Dreamstime; Artwork by Q2A Media Services

Cover Image: Peter Stone/Alamy

We are grateful for permission to reprint extracts from the following copyright material:

W J Bernstein: *A Splendid Exchange: How Trade has Shaped the World from Prehistory to the Present* (Atlantic Monthly Press, 2008), reprinted by permission of Grove/Atlantic Inc.

David Eltis: *The Rise of African Slavery in the Americas* (Cambridge, 2000), reprinted by permission of Cambridge University Press.

W Arthur Lewis: 'The Industrialization of the British West Indies' in Dennis Pantin (ed.): *The Caribbean Economy* (Ian Randle, 2005), reprinted by permission of the publisher.

Sam Selvon: *A Brighter Sun* (Heinemann International, 1995), first published in 1952, reprinted by permission of Susheila Nasta for the author.

Hugh Thomas: *The Slave Trade - The History of the Atlantic Slave Trade 1440-1870* (Phoenix, 1997), copyright © Hugh Thomas 1997, reprinted by permission of The Wylie Agency (UK) Ltd.

Although we have made every effort to trace and contact all copyright holders before publication this has not been possible in all cases. If notified, the publisher will rectify any errors or omissions at the earliest opportunity.

Authors

Radica Mahase is currently a Senior Lecturer in History at the College of Science, Technology and Applied Arts of Trinidad and Tobago. She would like to dedicate this book to Rishi Vidyarthi as well as all the history students at Naparima Girls' High School, San-Fernando, Trinidad.

Kevin Baldeosingh is a columnist with the Trinidad Express. He is the author of *The Autobiography of Paras P* (Heinemann, 1996), *Virgin's Triangle* (Heinemann, 1997) and *The Ten Incarnations of Adam Avatar* (Peepal Tree, 2005). He would like to dedicate this book to Farah.

Contents

Introduction　4

Section A

1 The Indigenous peoples and the Europeans　6

2 The Caribbean economy and slavery　32

3 Resistance and revolt　64

Section B

4 The metropolitan movement towards emancipation　91

5 Adjustments to emancipation 1838–76　118

6 The Caribbean economy 1875–1985　137

Section C

7 The USA in the Caribbean 1776–1985　164

8 Caribbean political development　187

9 Caribbean society 1900–85　208

10 The School-Based Assessment　225

Index　235

Introduction

> **WHAT IS HISTORY?**
>
> History is the study of past events and people. It is the recording and writing of past events relating, for example, to people, country and period. It is usually studied and written in chronological order. It is possible to write a history of almost anything – the history of a country, ethnic group, school, sports club and so on.

If the only subject you ever studied was history, and if you did so thoroughly, you would become knowledgeable about many other subjects, such as psychology, sociology, economics, politics, literature and even some mathematics.

This is because history is not only about events. It is also about how human beings behave and think. Why do we act in the way that we do? What circumstances can make some people heroes and other people villains? Do heroes and villains really exist, or is it their time and their place which create them?

These are questions which history helps to shed light on. How has history made me the kind of person I am today? The first event in your personal history was your birth. Before that, there was the history of your parents and your grandparents, as well as all the other people who may have influenced them. However, human beings all live in some kind of society. The kind of society we live in influences the kind of people we are and it is history which shapes the kind of society we have.

You can see this in common products around you. For example, the sugar in soft drinks, or the beans in coffee, or the cotton in your shirts have played an important role in Caribbean history. It was the demand for sugar in Europe which led to the trade in enslaved Africans and, later, to the coming of indentured labourers from India and other continents. Cotton and coffee also played similar roles. So when you understand that history, you will understand why your ancestors came here. Understanding that, in turn, helps you understand why our society is the way it is, with all its advantages and its shortcomings.

The Caribbean has had a turbulent history. The first islanders settled here 7,000 years ago, and lived a typical hunter-gatherer existence until the Europeans arrived in 1492. Then, for 400 years, this region was considered one of the wealthiest in the world. In that period, the European nations colonized and fought over the islands. New crops were introduced, and new peoples brought here. So our history in the past four centuries is also a history of the Western world.

How is the study of Caribbean history important to us?

- It helps us to understand how the Caribbean has evolved to the point it is at today.
- It teaches us about past events which took place in the Caribbean.
- It gives us a sense of belonging – knowing where we came from.
- It helps us to understand and appreciate the different ethnic and religious groups which can be found throughout the Caribbean countries.
- It gives explanations for the similarities and differences between people of different Caribbean countries.

What skills can we learn from studying history?

- We can learn to think critically. When we study history we are forced to look in more detail at events and ideas to see what really happened and not just look at the surface.

- We learn to analyse different events and ideas and then make intelligent conclusions based on these. We can then give informed opinions on topics from the past, as well as the present time.
- Studying history gives us an opportunity to learn how to process information and how to use our minds to think objectively.
- It sharpens our skills in understanding why people think and act the way they do, thereby making it easier for us to communicate with people.

A guide for students

How can I pass my examination?

A student who wants to be successful in the CSEC® history examination has to focus on these three things.

1. Writing a well-researched School-Based Assessment (SBA). See Chapter 10 for a step-by-step guide to writing SBAs.
2. Studying all of the core topics. This is important as Paper 1, which is a multiple-choice examination paper, covers the entire syllabus – that is, all the core topics.
3. Studying, in detail, at least three themes, one from each section, as outlined on the contents page of this book.

What does the examination consist of?

The final examination is broken down as follows.

- Paper 1 consists of 60 multiple-choice questions. **Students are required to answer all questions in this paper.**
- Paper 2 has one question on each theme. **Students are required to answer one question from each section.** This means that for Paper 2 students have to answer three questions in total.

The examination paper contains a combination of questions which require short answer responses and questions which have to be answered as an essay.

Short answer questions

- **Make sure that each section is numbered properly.** For example, each short answer question comes in sections (a), (b), (c) or numbers (i), (ii) or (iii). You must make sure that you answer the questions according to the section, otherwise you will lose marks.
- **Answer your questions according to the number of marks given for each part of the question.** Each section might be allocated a different amount of marks. For example you might get a question where part (a) is worth 2 marks, part (b) is worth 5 marks and part (c) is worth 10 marks. It is important to write your response in relation to the number of marks. For example, your answer to part (a) will be much shorter than your answer to part (b) and because part (c) is worth 10 marks, your answer to this part will have much more detail than your answers for parts (a) and (b).
- **Do not repeat your answers for the different parts.** Although the questions may seem the same, each part is actually asking you either for new information or to expand on points which you gave before. Therefore, make sure that your answer to each part is different.

Essays

- Each essay must be well planned, and written so that the examiner can understand your points.
- Essays must be argumentative rather than narrative.
- You have to get your points across in a simple, to-the-point manner.

For more on essay writing see Chapter 10.

1 The Indigenous peoples and the Europeans

This chapter will answer the following questions.
- How and why did the Indigenous peoples arrive in the Caribbean?
- What were the social, political and economic practices of the Indigenous peoples in the Americas?
- What types of Indigenous art forms were present in the Caribbean?
- Why were Europeans interested in the 'New World'?
- What impact did the arrival of the Europeans into the Caribbean have on the Indigenous peoples who were settled there and vice versa?

Migratory and settlement patterns of Indigenous peoples in the Caribbean

More than 7,000 years ago, small groups of people left the South American continent in canoes and settled in the various islands of the Caribbean. Human beings had first reached the continent between 14,000 and 35,000 years ago by crossing the Bering Strait, between Siberia and the Americas. North and South America had been colonized by the people who lived in East Asia about 50,000 years ago (an era called the Upper Paleolithic). Genetic analysis suggests that human beings first came to the North American continent about 14,000 years ago. Then there was a second migration about 12,000 years ago and possibly a third migration 10,000 years ago. It was people from the first wave who spread to South America, while those in the second and third waves stayed in the northern part of the continent. Members of the first group eventually left the mainland in canoes to populate the Caribbean islands. Although historians had long assumed that the original inhabitants of the region had migrated from island to island, the recent discovery of a ancient boat design, which had a fin to keep the canoe steady in rough waters, suggests that the South American natives could well have paddled the 563 kilometres separating the continental land mass from the islands.

Archaeology the study of historic or preliterate peoples. It is done by analysing their remains such as artefacts and monuments.

It is not surprising that historians assumed that the Caribbean became inhabited as people from South America island-hopped from the Lesser Antilles to the Greater Antilles – that is, starting from Trinidad, which is separated from the South American continent by just 12 kilometres, and continuing up the island chain to Cuba. The sea currents favour travel from south to north and from east to west. A south equatorial current, which flows across the south Atlantic sea from Africa, is deflected north along the coast of Guyana, and the Tainos' South American ancestors may have ridden this current out of the Orinoco river and into the Windward Islands. In the 20th century, this same current would carry escaped prisoners from Devil's Island (a small island off the coast of what used to be called French Guiana) to Venezuela and Trinidad. Trade winds, which blow continually from the north west for most of the year, strengthen the westward sea currents. It is possible that the Caribbean was peopled from two directions: first, by the Casimiroid people from the Middle Americas and then by the Ortoioroids from South America. This latter group inhabited Trinidad when it was still attached to the continent. Around

655 AD, or about 1,400 years ago, the Ortoioroids in Trinidad were displaced by the Cedrosan Saladoid people, who came from the Guianas through the Boca Grande or by sailing along a sea current called the Canó Mánamo, which flows into the Gulf of Paria on Trinidad's southern coast. The sea currents and wind conditions all favoured such a hypothesis. However, recent archaeological evidence shows that some of these people rowed directly from Venezuela to the Leeward Islands and eastern Puerto Rico. Although this is a considerable distance, it could have been accomplished by paddlers taking shifts. Cloud formations on the horizon would have given them an indication that a land mass did lie ahead, since low clouds do not form over the open sea. Archaeologists in Cuba and Santo Domingo have found sites 4,000 and even 7,000 years old and, because of the similarity to prehistoric sites in Nicaragua, speculate that the inhabitants came to the Caribbean directly from Central America.

We might wonder why these people settled in the islands rather than remaining on the mainland. The main reason may have been the most basic: food. The islands offered land for planting and game for hunting. Some of the settlers may have also wanted to set up their own communities, while others may have been fleeing to avoid enslavement by the powerful Aztec, Inca and Mayan civilizations. Some may have just been following the human urge to explore.

> **Roleplay**
> Imagine that you are the chief of an Amerindian tribe. Give three reasons why you would lead your people from one island to another.

As had happened all over the planet since human history began, the Casimiroid and the Ortoioroid peoples were displaced by a new tribe, the Saladoid invaders and their Ostinoid descendants. By the time Christopher Columbus sailed across the Atlantic in search of a western passage to Asia, went astray and by chance sailed into the Bahamas archipelago on 12 October 1492, there were somewhere between 750,000 and six million inhabitants on the islands.

BANWARI MAN

Let us introduce you to 'Trinidad's oldest resident' – Banwari Man. He can be dated to approximately 3,400 BC. This means that these remains are about 5,400 years old.

Banwari Man was discovered at Banwari Trace, Debe, South Trinidad. This is believed to be the oldest human settlement in the Caribbean and radio-carbon dating of the pottery at this site has placed it at about 7,000 years old. Banwari Man was excavated in November 1969 by members of the Trinidad and Tobago Historical Society. When they found him, he was lying on his left-hand side in what was apparently an Amerindian burial position. He was found with a round pebble by the skull and a needle point by the hip, 20 cm below the surface.

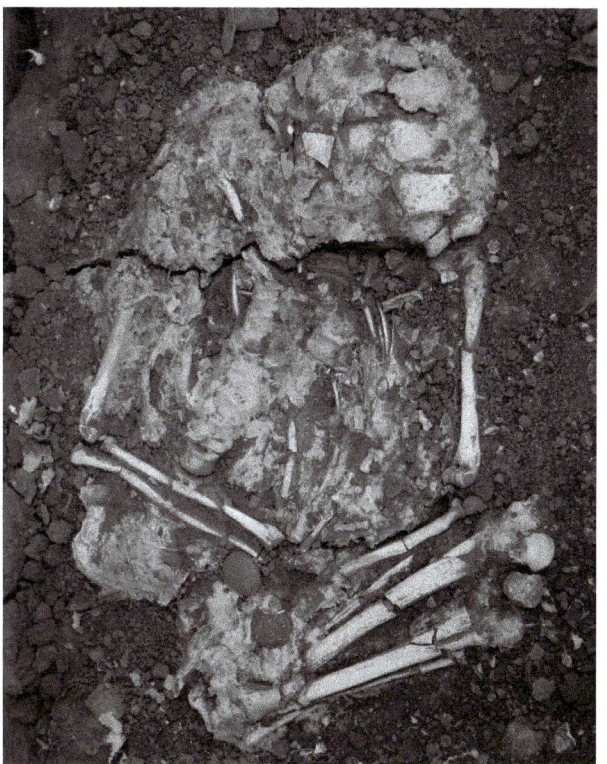

1.1 'Trinidad's oldest resident' – Banwari Man

> **Activity 1.1**
> In small groups, use the Internet to research why the Banwari Man's age holds such significance for understanding the migratory patterns of peoples from South America into the Caribbean region.

This is a very wide range, but historians do not have a better estimate because the Europeans did not make a proper tally and the Indigenous peoples did not have a counting system that went above three or, for that matter, a writing system to record any numbers.

Columbus himself had a tendency to exaggerate numbers, which led some historians to claim that the Caribbean in the 15th century had over 13 million people inhabiting the various islands.

For example, when he landed in Cuba, Columbus found only a single large village of about 1,000 people, yet in a later letter claimed that there were 'an infinite number of small villages and people without number' on the island. However, since the population of Spain in that period was just under seven million, it seems unlikely that the less agriculturally and technologically advanced Caribbean would have had a population of similar size. The largest population was on Hispaniola (an island which is now divided between Haiti and the Dominican Republic) and may have totalled about 500,000 people, while the island now called Cuba may have had a population of about 50,000 and Jamaica could have had 20,000 people. We cannot be more certain than this because most history depends on written records. When such records do not exist, or are unreliable, information has to come from archaeology and languages.

Archaeologists, by examining pottery and tools, and bones and buildings, can estimate how long ago a society existed, how big the groups were and what kind of technical skills the people had. For example, the period before the arrival of the Tainos' ancestors is divided into two ages: the Lithic, or Paleo-Indian, in which human beings created tools by flaking stones; and the Archaic, or Meso-Indian, in which stones and bones and shells are ground to create tools and ornaments. Sites from both periods have been found in Cuba, Haiti and the Dominican Republic. In Trinidad, sites as old as 2,400 to 7,000 years have been found in beaches and at the edges of swamps, though not far inland. Most of the sites have bone projectile points and barbs, from which archaeologists deduce that there were good opportunities in Trinidad to hunt fish and small game.

Linguists, who study languages, can analyse words to determine how much contact different groups had with one another. If two different languages have the same or similar nouns for certain objects, this indicates a strong possibility of close contact in the past. Even the types of words might indicate what type of contact there was – for example, if the words are for goods, this might reveal a trading relationship.

We will discuss the issue of language and history more fully in Chapter 2 in relation to West Africa.

> Extract from Columbus's diary on his first meeting with Indigenous Caribbean inhabitants:
>
> 'All the men I saw were young. They were all very well-built, with fine bodies and handsome faces. Their hair is coarse, almost like that of a horse's tail, and short. They wear it down over their eyebrows, except for a few strands at the back, which they wear long and never cut. They are the colour of the Canary Islanders, neither black nor white, and are heavily painted. Some of them paint themselves black, others white, or any other colour they can find. Some paint their whole faces. Some their whole bodies, some only their eyes, some only the nose. They do not carry arms, nor know them, for when I showed them swords, they took them by the edge and cut themselves out of ignorance. They have no iron. Their spears are made of cane, with a fish-tooth used to make a sharp tip. They are fairly tall, with fine limbs and good proportion.'

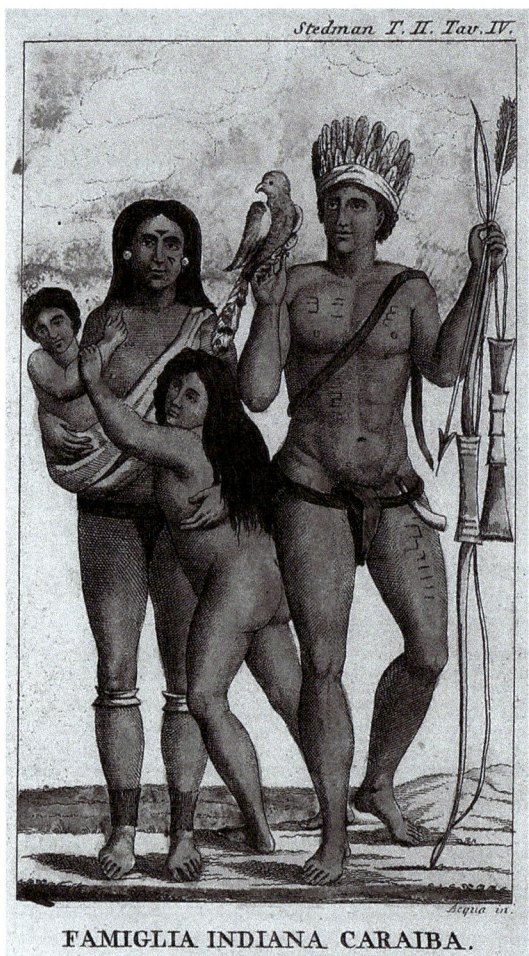

1.2 Painting of a Carib family by John Gabriel Stedman, 1818

In the Caribbean, none of the Amerindian languages are still spoken. This is not surprising, since there are now just three to four thousand Amerindian-descended people in the region. Most of the Amerindians had by the 16th century been wiped out by diseases brought by the Europeans, particularly smallpox for which they had no immunity, as well as the destruction of their crops by the Spaniards.

The information is therefore sparse. Nonetheless, historians, archaeologists and anthropologists have been able to discover significant facts about the first inhabitants of the islands.

Migration movement of people and animals from one place to another.

The first group of migrants to the Caribbean probably migrated from the Guianas in South America, while a second group came from Belize in Central America. This migration continued over a period of nearly 5,000 years for the first group and for about 3,500 years for the second group. The third group to come to the Caribbean did so much later, starting 2,500 years ago and ceasing just one century later. Over the next 1,500 years, four other groups were to migrate from the continent to the islands. Their descendants were the Caribbean natives who the Spaniards encountered when they came to the region.

Activity 1.2 Draw a sketch map showing the migration of early Amerindian groups across the Bering Strait across North America into the Caribbean. Your map should show the Americas, Siberia and the Bering Strait. Use symbols and a key to indicate the journey of the Amerindians.

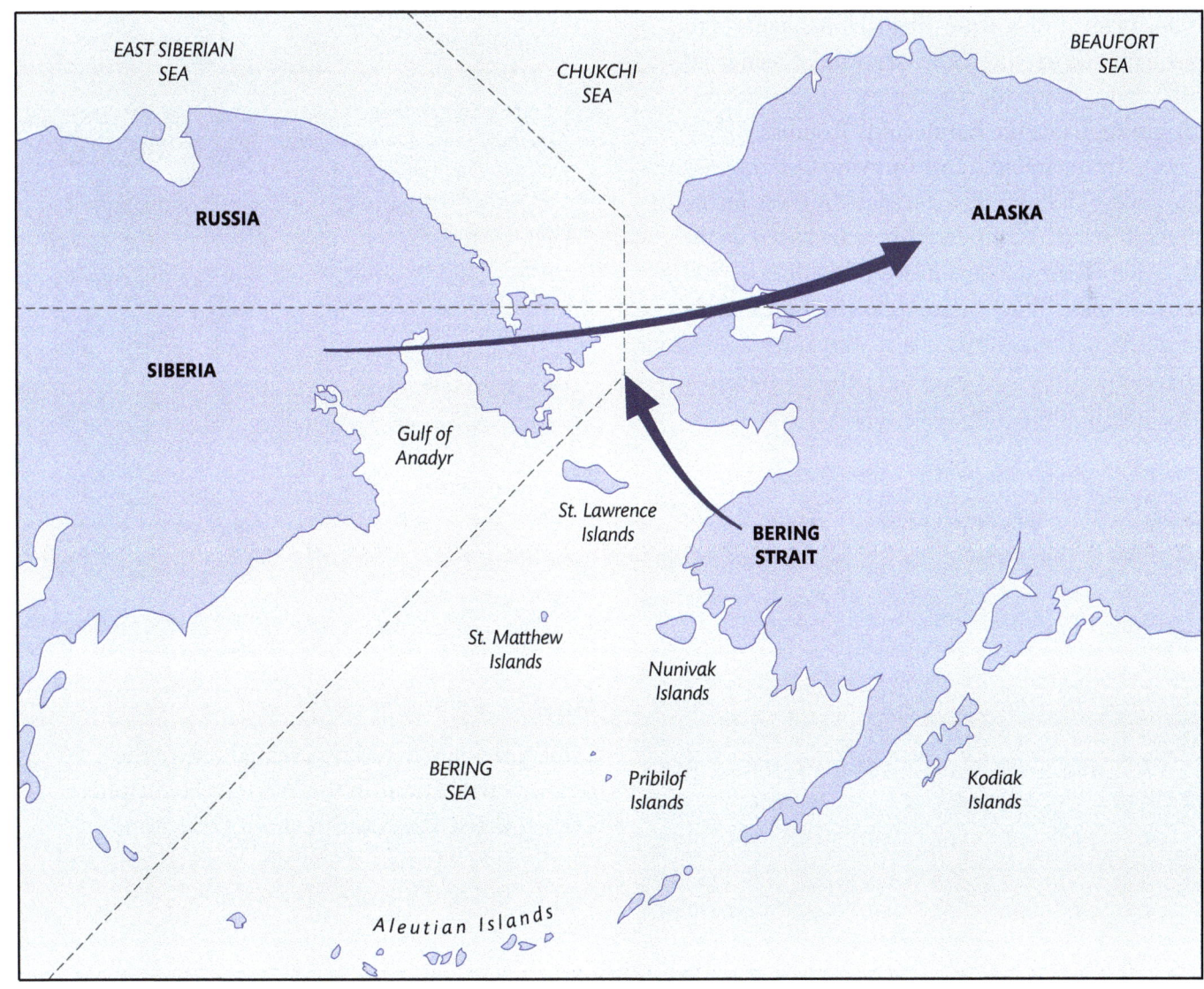

1.3 Migration across the Bering Straits into America

> **FAST FACTS**
> - Our region is named the Caribbean because one of the tribes first encountered by Europeans were designated 'Caribs' by them.
> - The other popular tribe are Arawaks. Both Caribs and Arawaks include different groups living in the islands. Caribs, for example, are really three groups: Island Caribs, Caribs from South America and Caribs from the Windward Islands (called Kalinagos).
> - Arawaks were mainly located in the Greater Antilles and the Bahamas when Columbus sailed into the region and may have been the first natives he encountered.
> - The largest group, however, were called Tainos, and they were from north-eastern South America.
> - There were also different groups in the various islands with their own identity. This would have been similar to the situation we have today; there are different groups such as Jamaicans, Vincentians and Guyanese.

Archaeologists divide the original inhabitants of the region into eight types. The Ortoiroid, Casimiroid, and Saladoid were the first three to migrate to the Caribbean. Later, the Barrancoid, Troumassoid, Suazan Troumassoid, Caribs and the Ostionoid came. The people did not call themselves by these technical names; instead, the modern labels are based on the sites where their settlements were first discovered by archaeologists. The Ortoiroid people, for example, are called this because their sites were unearthed along the Ortoire River. The Saladoid people's settlements were first discovered at Saladero in Venezuela.

Table 1.1 Original inhabitants of the Caribbean region

Group	Migration period	Sites
Ortoiroid	5000–200 BCE	Ortoire river, east Trinidad
Casimiroid	4000–400 BCE	Casimira, Dominican Republic
Saladoid	500 BCE–CE 600	Saladero, Venezuela
Barrancoid	350–650 CE	Barrancas, Venezuela
Troumassoid	500–1000 CE	Troumassée, St Lucia
Suazan Troumassoid	1000–1450 CE	Savanne Suazey, Grenada
Island Caribs	1450 CE–the present	Guianas, South America
Ostionoid	600–1200 CE	Ostiones, Puerto Rico

In the following sections, we will look at three of the main cultural groups, or tribes, in the region: the Maya, from South America; the Tainos, who spread throughout the Caribbean; and the Kalinagos, who lived on the Windward Islands.

> **FAST FACTS**
> - The various groups are distinguished from one another mainly by their pottery. Pottery is very important for archaeological classification.
> - Pottery shards are often the only remaining examples of settlement after many centuries have passed.
> - Pottery in itself represents a certain level of technology – it means that the people have learned to shape clay and fire it to make wares.
> - The different styles of pottery, including how it is painted, are a good indicator of different cultures.

1.4 Indigenous pottery

Maya

2,000 years ago the Maya created one of the greatest civilizations in the Western Hemisphere. They practised agriculture, built great stone buildings and pyramid temples, worked gold and copper and had hieroglyphic writing.

As early as 150 BC the Maya had settled in villages and had developed an agriculture based on the cultivation of maize, beans and squash. By 200 AD their villages had grown into cities containing temples, pyramids, palaces, plazas and ball courts. The rise of the Mayan culture started around 250 AD, and what is known to archaeologists as the Classic period of Mayan culture lasted almost seven centuries.

Between 300 BC and 100 AD, the lowland Maya had begun to create a civilization that was to become the greatest in the 'New World'. The Petén-Yucatán Peninsula lacks many raw materials and does not have much fertile land, but the area had limestone, which could be easily quarried for buildings, as well as flint for stonework. Producing cement and plaster, which were easily made by burning limestone or shells, was the basis for Mayan advancement.

The heart of the Mayan civilization was northern Petén, in Guatemala, where the oldest dated Mayan stelae are found. The Late Formative culture of Petén is called Chicanel, evidence of which has been found at many Mayan centres. Chicanel pottery includes dishes with wide-everted and grooved rims, bowls with composite silhouette and vessels resembling ice buckets.

Did you know?

The Maya also helped invent chocolate! Spouted, teapot-shaped vessels excavated in northern Belize have been found to contain the residue of ancient chocolate. The chocolate drink the Maya had, however, was not the sugary version we know today, but dried cacao beans ground to a fine powder and mixed with water, honey, chilli pepper and, occasionally, maize.

Stelae upright stone slabs or columns, which usually have a relief design or commemorative inscription.

At its height, Mayan civilization consisted of more than 40 cities, each with a population of between 5,000 and 50,000. Among the principal cities were Tikal, Uaxactún, Copán, Bonampak, Palenque and Río Bec. In this period, historians

1.5 The remains of a Mayan pyramid – Uxmal, Yucatan, Mexico

estimate that there were about two million Maya, most of them in the lowlands of what is now Guatemala. After 900 AD, however, Mayan civilization suddenly declined. The people vanished, leaving the great cities and ceremonial centres empty and covered by jungle vegetation. No one knows for sure what caused this, but the exhaustion of agricultural land, droughts and resulting wars between the cities seem the best explanations. It is also possible that climate change, in the form of global cooling that lasted from 535 to 900 AD, caused a severe drought in 899–900 and first set off this chain of disasters. Between 900 and 1519, cities such as Chichén Itzá, Uxmal and Mayapán in the highlands of the Yucatán Peninsula continued to flourish after the great lowland cities had been depopulated. However, by the time the Spaniards conquered the area in the early 16th century, most of the Maya were villagers growing their own crops and practising the religious rites of their ancestors.

Taino

Although they were the largest and most widespread of the three groups living in the Caribbean, the Tainos were virtually wiped out within one hundred years of the arrival of the Spaniards in the late 15th century. They once however occupied Cuba, Jamaica, the Bahamas, Hispaniola (now divided into two countries, Haiti and the Dominican Republic), Puerto Rico, the Lesser Antilles and the Virgin Islands.

The Tainos were descendants of the Ostionoid people (see Table 1.1) and inhabited the Caribbean from 1200 to 1500 AD. They were not Arawaks, as many historians first thought. The Tainos spoke a different language and had different cultural practices from the Arawaks. Although both groups worshipped ancestral spirits and used griddles to bake cassava bread, the Arawaks had a simpler culture than the Tainos. For example, the Arawaks practised slash-and-burn agriculture to make temporary farms, whereas the Tainos built rows of

FAST FACTS

1.6 Street corner in Chichicastenango, Guatemala

- Mayan communities still exist today. They are most prevalent in Guatemala.
- The modern Maya are basically agricultural people, raising crops of corn, beans and squash.
- They live in communities organized around central villages, which may be permanently occupied but more commonly are community centres with public buildings.
- The people live on farm homesteads, except during fiestas and markets when they go to the central village to trade and celebrate. Some keep pigs and chickens and, rarely, oxen that are used for farming.
- Just a few industries exist and a few craft items are made, mostly for domestic use.
- Usually some cash crop or item of local manufacture is produced for sale outside the region to provide cash to buy goods the villagers cannot grow or make for themselves.
- The women wear traditional Mayan clothes, but the men wear more modern factory-made clothing. Although Maya women once spun and wove their own cloth, most of their garments are now made of factory-woven cloth.
- The cultural effect of the Spanish conquest is reflected in the fact that almost all Maya are classified as Roman Catholics.
- However, their ancestral religion influences how they practise Christianity. Christian figures, for example, are usually identified with Mayan deities.
- Public religion is basically Christian, with Mass and saint's-day celebrations, but in private the native pre-Columbian religion is often followed.
- They don't make chocolate anymore!

mounds of earth, dug drains and prevented erosion in the fields to grow their crops. Different Taino groups had different levels of development. The Tainos of Cuba, for example, were once thought to be a different tribe, called Ciboneys, who were slaves to the Tainos, but new archaeological analyses suggest that they were a Taino group who lived in caves and lived mainly on fish. The Ciboney were not very advanced technologically. They did not weave their clothes nor did they make pottery. Their weapons were simple wooden clubs and stones. They got food entirely through hunting and gathering, and did not even cultivate cassava, unlike the other Taino groups.

When the Taino first encountered the Spanish, their staple crop was cassava and they gathered wild plants to eat. They also grew maize and cultivation of this crop increased after the Spanish conquest. Other crops included peanuts, peppers, beans and arrowroot. They hunted birds, lizards and small animals. Fish and shellfish were other important food sources. They ate catfish, mullets, eels, conch and oysters, as well as turtle. This diet was supplemented with a variety of other reptiles and insects.

Conuco cultivation a form of agriculture based on mounds of earth which reduced erosion, improved drainage and optimized land use.

Their settlements were as small as single families and as large as 3,000 people. They had log houses with thatched roofs and dirt floors. The chiefs lived in large rectangular buildings, while the common people lived in small circular huts. The men generally went naked, while women wore a net or a grass apron. Both men and women painted themselves on special occasions; they wore earrings, nose rings and necklaces, which were sometimes made of gold. The Tainos, however, did not have many craft works, making only some pottery and woven baskets. Government was by hereditary chiefs and sub-chiefs, and the society was not egalitarian, for there were classes of nobles, commoners and serfs (or slaves).

Egalitarian the belief that all people are equal and therefore deserve equal rights and opportunities.

The most advanced Tainos lived in Puerto Rico and Hispaniola, where they had ball courts and stone-lined plazas.

Activity 1.3 The Tainos played a ball game called batos (batu). Find out more about this game. Describe how the game is played.

The islands were divided into provinces, each of which had its own chief (cacique), and there were sub-chiefs and headmen who ruled the communities or villages within the provinces.

Settlements ranged from single units of many families to towns of about 1,000 houses and about 3,000 to 4,000 people. However, most villages would have about 150 inhabitants. Houses were often made of intertwined branches, although the chief's house would be constructed out of adobe (a yellow clay) with a straw roof.

The main duty of each chief or his subordinates was to organize the hunting and farming which the people depended on for food. When there were extra provisions, the chief arranged storage and distribution. He also negotiated relations with other villages to maintain peace. Every chief seemed to have wielded more or less absolute power over the common villager, including the power to order executions. Chiefs and their subordinates typically had more than one wife, unlike commoners, and since there were about the same number of men and women this would have meant that many young men would not be able to find wives within their communities.

1.7 An example of a Taino village

Interestingly, the Europeans recorded some female leaders among the Indigenous Caribbeans. There was a cacique named Anacaona, who ruled in Hispaniola after her brother died, and women were reported as village leaders in St Croix and in Suriname.

When a male cacique died, one or two of his wives were sometimes buried with him. Unlike common people, whose bodies were buried naked in graves or in caves, a cacique was bound with cotton cloth and buried with ornaments and prized possessions.

The religion of the Tainos was polytheistic, which means they worshipped many gods or spirits. These zemis, as they were called, were represented by carvings of wood, stone, bone and even the remains of the family's ancestors. Each household had several zemis, usually around 10, and it appears that the more zemis a person possessed, the higher that person's status was in the community. The most important gods among some Taino groups were Yúcahu, who was god of the cassava and the sea, and his mother Atabey, who was goddess of rivers and fertility. Before communing with a zemi, the Tainos purified themselves by vomiting (which they induced by sticking a special vomit stick down their throat). Using a forked tube, they would inhale a snuff called cohoba, which was made by crushing the seeds of the piptadenia tree, and which caused hallucinations. The Tainos made food offerings to their zemis and once a year the whole village would pay homage to the cacique's zemis. This ceremony began with a procession of the villagers, who would be wearing their best ornaments, carrying baskets of cassava bread and singing songs in praise of the zemis. In the larger villages which had a temple, the cacique sat at the entrance beating a drum while Taino shamans (or priests) entered and dressed the zemis. In the smaller villages, the cacique's bohio, as it was called, served this purpose. The villagers then presented themselves in front of the temple, induced vomiting with their sticks, and entered with bread for the shamans, who in turn offered it to the zemis. After this, there would be dancing and singing, with bread from the offerings being distributed to the heads of families. This was eaten and also kept as protection against accidents.

As in most hunter-gatherer societies, the shamans were also the healers. In the larger groups, where numbers allowed some specialization (that is, the priests did not also have to plant or hunt), shamans would be paid in cassava or other food. If a person fell ill, the shamans painted zemis on their bodies and performed a ritual to make the patient better. Both shaman and patient would fast before this ritual, which involved the shaman taking snuff and swallowing an herb (called gioia) to make him vomit. The shaman would light a torch and sing, accompanying himself with a rattle. This ritual was supposed to remove the spirit causing the illness from the patient's body, but shamans would generally know about useful herbs to treat various ailments as well.

> Extract from a letter written by Columbus to Queen Isabella of Spain in 1492:
>
> 'They were so affectionate and have so little greed and are in all ways so amenable that I assure Your Highness that there is in my opinion no better people and no better land in all the world. They love their neighbours as themselves and their way of speaking is the sweetest in the world, always gentle and smiling.'

Although the Tainos that Columbus encountered were relatively peaceful, compared with the Caribs, the letter written by Columbus quoted above probably reflects only the Spaniards' experience, rather than how the Tainos actually behaved, since all known human groups in pre-modern times have waged regular battles and wars with one another, and the Tainos also fought among themselves to avenge murders or resolve disputes over hunting and fishing grounds. The Spaniards themselves also had several battles with Taino groups in later voyages. In the extract, Columbus fails to realize that the spears he would have observed were not just for hunting, but also for fighting. The Tainos also used clubs, and bows and arrows. However, some groups were more peaceable than others – for example, the Tainos who occupied Jamaica, as compared with those in the Leeward and Virgin Islands, who often had to contend with raids from the Kalinagos.

The peaceable facade presented to Columbus and his crew was partly because the Tainos wanted to gain the help of the militarily superior Spaniards in fighting the Kalinagos, who regularly raided their villages and captured their women. However, the Tainos were also traders rather than warriors. Individuals, as well as groups, undertook regular sea voyages in their dugout canoes to exchange goods with the inhabitants of the other islands. Some districts were even famous for specific products – for example, the inhabitants of Gonave island, off the west coast of what is now Haiti, produced wooden bowls which were in great demand. The Tainos also cultivated tobacco, drying the leaves and chewing them or pounding the leaves into a powder which they inhaled. They also made dyes from indigo, which they used to paint their bodies and to colour their cloth. Taino cotton was skilfully woven, mainly by the women, and was used to make insect nets, fishing nets and even hammocks (this noun is itself derived from the Amerindian word 'hamaca'). The Tainos also made baskets from palm leaves and grasses.

The Tainos displayed particular skill in making the canoes which they used to travel from island to island. They did not invent or discover sails until the Europeans came, nor did they ever cut planks to make their boats. Instead, they made what are called dugouts which, as the name suggests, were tree trunks which were carved in the centre to make a hollow space for the rower to sit in. The main type of tree used was silkwood, which was light but also large enough to make canoes to carry as many as 20 men. Cedar and mahogany were also used. After the tree was cut, it was carefully burned and parts were hacked away to make a balanced shape that would sit properly in the water. This required a lot of time and effort, but the canoes lasted a very long time.

Table 1.2 Comparison of economic organization

Maya	Taino	Kalinago
The economy was based on agriculture but not conuco cultivation.	Conuco cultivation was used.	Conuco cultivation was used.
Maize was the main crop.	Cassava was the main crop.	Cassava was the main crop.
The Maya relied more on agriculture than the Tainos or Kalinagos.	The Tainos hunted, gathered and fished.	The Kalinagos mostly hunted and fished.
They had a big market economy where they traded cotton textiles, foodstuff, ceramics and gold.	They traded on a small scale.	They traded on a small scale.
They were settled people who established great cities.	They were settled but with smaller communities than the Maya.	They were still a rather mobile, nomadic group.

Like most hunter-gatherer groups, the Tainos had a relatively leisurely lifestyle compared with that of modern societies. They would have worked for about four to six hours daily, which left plenty time for other activities, such as ball games. The favourite game was played with a hard rubber ball (which was probably obtained through trade with the Maya since the islands did not have balata trees) and involved keeping the ball in the air using only the legs and hips. The Tainos had alcoholic drinks called piwari and cassiri, which were consumed in great quantities at celebrations, and the Tainos celebrated nearly everything – the birth of a first-born male child, the coming of age at puberty, clearing a field, holding a council and so on.

The Tainos are now gone, and all the knowledge we have about them comes from the ruins of their cities, pottery shards and other artefacts, and the records of the European explorers written centuries ago.

Kalinago

The Kalinagos were the last group to settle in the Caribbean before the arrival of Columbus and his crew. Indeed, when his ships, the Niňa, the Pinta and the Santa Maria, reached land in 1492, the Kalinagos had been here only for about 40 years. In the Windward Islands, they had established settlements in Barbados, St Lucia, Grenada, St Vincent and Dominica, and were still migrating from the mainland when the Spaniards came. Since the Kalinagos were latecomers, this may explain why they were more war-like than the established Tainos and Arawaks. They were seeking territory and women. They provided the fiercest resistance to the Europeans, for the Kalinagos themselves had driven out the Tainos from the Lesser Antilles. Perhaps the more aggressive stance of the Caribs explains why the region is today called the Caribbean instead of Arawakania or Tainoland.

Patriarchal a system or society which is controlled by men.

FAST FACTS

- The Kalinagos painted their bodies in red dye and pierced their ears, noses and lips.
- Their 'fearsome' appearance was emphasized by their custom of compressing the heads of their infants to flatten the forehead, so that the skull sloped back from above the eyes.
- The men were usually armed with a club and long knife, and bows and arrows.
- A high ratio, perhaps a majority, of the females among the Kalinago were Taino as the main purpose of the Kalinago raids was to acquire Taino women and food.
- The Kalinago men had captured so many women that their wives actually spoke Taino languages among themselves.
- The Kalinagos had a patriarchal culture in which men were dominant.
- Kalinago women weren't even allowed to eat their meals in the presence of the men.

Kalinago women were crucial to the tribe's diet, since they cultivated the crops such as cassava, sweet potatoes, yams, beans, peppers, guava and papaya which sustained everyone if the hunting was unsuccessful. Iguanas, snakes, birds and agouti provided meat. Kalinago men were skilled fishermen, who used small nets, hooks and line made from vines or cotton and even their bows and arrows. They were noted for their skill at making dugout canoes and, oddly enough, for basket weaving as well. It is even possible that this warrior tribe brought the technique of cotton spinning to the Guianas.

Unlike the Tainos, the Kalinago cultivated arrowroot and may also have brought certain plants to the Caribbean with them, such as sugar cane and plantain.

The Kalinagos lived in villages near a river or creek, always strategically located in case of an attack from other tribes, such as the Tainos. The huts were oval-shaped, and their living arrangements also reflected the strong patriarchal culture, since men and boys lived in the larger buildings and the females in a smaller house.

Table 1.3 Comparison of social organization

Maya	Taino	Kalinago
The head was called the halach uinich. This position was hereditary.	The chief was called a cacique. This position was hereditary.	The chief was called an ouboutou. This position was attained by the head of the largest family. Physical strength was important.
The houses of ordinary Maya were small and simple but the houses of the nobles were built of sculptured stones. Ordinary people lived on the outskirts of the temple and only went in to worship and buy their food.	Tainos built houses around the community square and living space.	Kalinagos did not have a community square but had a communal fireplace.
They lived in households containing extended families.	They lived in households containing extended families.	They lived in households containing extended families.

Maya	Taino	Kalinago
The men had one main wife but had other concubines.	They did not practise polygamy.	They practised polygamy.
They had ball courts.	They had ball courts in the community square.	They had no ball courts.

Unlike the Tainos, however, the Kalinagos had a less hierarchical society, so that their chiefs did not have as much authority but essentially ruled by consensus. Only in times of war did the chief gain obedience, since this was necessary for an effective fighting unit. The Kalinagos are said to have used drinking bouts as a ritual which they used to whip themselves into a frenzy for going into battle.

It was this martial prowess which may explain why, of all the Indigenous groups in the Caribbean, only the Kalinagos survived the encounter with the Europeans. Initially, the European invaders recorded that the Kalinagos fled to the forests and mountains when they encountered them. However, the Kalinagos soon began attacking the Europeans. The Tainos had already formed an alliance with the Spanish to fend off these attacks and the Kalinagos were no match for the Europeans' superior weapons. At the same time, the Spanish were also intent on subjugating the Tainos, so there were also later times when the Tainos allied with the Kalinagos against the Spaniards.

In the end, though, only the Kalinagos and some other small tribes would survive the coming of the Europeans. The Kalinagos in the Lesser Antilles held off attempts to subjugate them, so the Spanish and then the English and French left well enough alone. The most important consequence of this was that, unlike other tribes, the Kalinagos did not become widely exposed to European diseases. This is probably why all the living people of Amerindian descent in the Caribbean trace their ancestry to the 'Caribs'.

Indigenous art forms

With limestone being one of their major products, it is not surprising that the Maya had a tradition of sculpture and relief carving. Their visual art reached its apex between 600 and 900 AD, and seemed to have been based on the principles of painting rather than sculpture. The relief carving told a story and was detailed in a way quite unlike the simpler carvings found in other Meso-American cultures. Only the stonework has survived, although there must have been other artwork created out of wood, gourds, feathers and so on. There were probably also murals, now destroyed by the wet tropical climate. A few wooden objects have been preserved, such as the massive lintels of Tikal, which have scenes showing the Maya rulers and their guardian deities. The wet climate also destroyed their mural art.

The Maya artists also carved in jade, which was their most precious substance. The jade was mainly fashioned into thin plaques, carved in relief, or into beads. Since they did not have metal tools, the artists used abrasives and water with cane or perhaps other pieces of jade to create their works, which is testimony to just how skilled they were.

Since the Tainos and Kalinagos had a smaller and simpler environment, their art was technically less complex. We know they had jewellery, such as earrings, nose rings, pendants and necklaces, which were fashioned from bone, stone and sometimes gold. They probably also did body

> **FAST FACTS**
> - Mayan pottery intended for burial with the honoured dead was usually painted or carved with scenes of nature and, often, quite macabre visions, such as strange creatures and weird landscapes.
> - Their pottery was a bright and shining polychrome, which the Maya potters achieved by first painting in semi-translucent slips over a light background, then firing the vessels at a very low temperature.
> - To do relief work, the sculptors carved their scenes before the vessels were fired, then finished the process to set the decoration.

painting, but no images of this artwork remain and we know of this custom only from the written records of the Europeans.

Architecture

The simplicity of their lifestyle and environment also meant that the island inhabitants had no architecture beyond that of their huts. The Maya, however, built huge palaces and temples with distinct architectural styles and features. These buildings were made of stone and limestone blocks, ornamented with complex relief carvings, and have lasted for centuries.

The Maya used rubble and cement, just like modern builders. This material formed the base of their temple platforms, which were then covered with thick layers of plaster. The platform was a four-sided, stucco-covered, stepped pyramid and there were usually stone masks of gods on every side. Maya architects also used the corbel vault principle in their temples, which means they constructed arch-like structures with sides that extend inward until they meet at the top. This makes the building stronger and more stable.

Indigenous beliefs

The Mayan religion was based on nature. As we know from their writing system, which was deciphered only in the early and mid-20th century, the Maya worshipped gods who represented the sun, moon, rain and corn. This tells us that the main purpose of worship was to ensure good crops.

> **FAST FACTS**
> - The Maya had hieroglyphs which revealed that Maya dynastic rulers often waged war on rival Mayan cities and took their aristocrats captive.
> - These captives were tortured, mutilated and sacrificed to the Mayan gods.
> - The Maya believed that torture and human sacrifice brought fertility and pleased the gods.
> - The Maya rulers also practised self-torture and bleeding themselves because they believed blood was the means of communication between human beings and the gods.

Systematic explorations of the Mayan sites were first undertaken in the 1830s, and a small portion of the writing system was deciphered a hundred years later. These discoveries shed some light on Mayan religion, which was based on a pantheon of nature gods, including those of the sun, the moon, rain and corn.

Hieroglyphs a picture-based form of writing.

The Indigenous populations of the Caribbean islands had a less complex religious system, which is best described as animism; that is, the belief that nature has spirits, such as a tree god, a rain god and a sun god. This last is usually the main god in most pagan cultures. For the Tainos, every house had zemis, carved representations of gods, who they prayed to for various favours, and there was communal worship overseen by the cacique.

1.8 Mayan temple, Guatemala

Individuals also had their personal zemis. All homes also had vomit sticks, which people would push down their throats to cleanse themselves before going to worship. There was no priest caste, as with the Maya, but some individuals were considered to have special mystical or spiritual gifts. These people served the same functions as priests: to communicate with the gods to ask favours or find out their wishes, to work spells for love or luck or health, to assist the spirits of the dead, to foretell the future and so on.

Animism the belief that spirits inhabit natural objects, such as trees or rocks.

The Kalinagos are thought to have had similar beliefs to those of the Tainos, but it is likely that they prayed more for successful raids than successful crops. The Kalinagos of Guyana, for example, paid more attention in their rituals to appeasing evil spirits than good spirits, since the former were thought to be responsible for hurricanes, diseases and death. The Kalinagos were also said to have included cannibalism as part of their religion. This has been disputed by some scholars, who claim that cannibalism was a myth created by Columbus and other Europeans to demonize the fierce warriors who resisted them.

Cannibalism the practice of eating human flesh.

Indigenous science

As in all complex societies of this time, the Maya had a class of priests who were trained in mathematics and astronomy. This training was not scientific in the modern sense of performing experiments and creating theories, since the main purpose of Mayan knowledge was to calculate the appropriate times for religious rituals and ceremonies. Nonetheless, the Maya's achievements in these disciplines were impressive. In mathematics, they had a concept of zero, which only one other civilization (in India) had ever invented. Their calendar actually began from a zero date in 3114 BC, which is more sensible than the Gregorian calendar used in Western civilization, which starts from year 1. (This means that the 20th century ended on 31 December 2001, rather than 2000.) In astronomy, the Maya accurately calculated the solar year, which they summed as 18 months of 20 days, plus an unlucky five-day period. They also compiled precise tables of positions for the moon and the planet Venus and they could predict solar eclipses.

The island Amerindians, like all human groups, had a technology invented mainly for hunting and fighting. Their simplest hunting tool was a wooden club used to kill birds and other animals. They also used baskets and traps to catch fish. Their weapons included spears and javelins tipped with fishbone points. They also used bows and arrows for both hunting and fighting, and some groups tipped their arrows with poison. However, the favoured weapon was the atlatl, or spear thrower, a device with a handle at one end and a cup or spur that the spear rests against, which was used to add distance and force. The Tainos in Puerto Rico and Santo Domingo also had stone hatchets and axes.

As a migratory people, the islands' inhabitants also developed a basic boat technology. Their dug-out canoes were made well enough to ply the often rough waters between islands and they could make boats big enough to hold a large crew: between eight and 15 rowers. However, they never developed the sail or planks for boat building.

Agriculture

Agriculture was the centre of Amerindian society, since Amerindians depended on this for survival. The relative sophistication of their agricultural practices is perhaps best illustrated by their cultivation of cassava, which was grown in large fire-cleared fields and was used as we use bread today. Although easily grown, cassava is also poisonous, but the Amerindians were able to solve this problem by inventing the matapi to squeeze the poison out. The matapi is a long cylindrical basket into which the finely grated cassava is put. The basket is then twisted until its fibres crush all the juice out, thus removing the poison. The remaining dry meal was shaped into a flat cake and baked on a griddle to make cassava bread. The juice was not wasted as it was a key ingredient in casareep, which is a preservative agent the Amerindians used to keep their food from spoiling, just as modern people use refrigerators. Fish and meats were put into a pot with casareep, along with peppers, and this prevented spoilage for several days. Amerindians living in the Guianas still use these techniques today.

Pepperpot a dish consisting of stewed meat or fish with vegetables, usually flavoured with casareep.

FAST FACTS

- Maize or corn was the staple crop of the Indigenous population.
- It was bred from a wild grass named teosinte.
- The cob of that grass was originally about no thicker than a pencil and about as long as your little finger.
- Through selective breeding over 7,000 years, the Native Americans genetically engineered teosinte into the corn plant we know today.
- Corn became a staple in the USA after being discovered by the European conquerors in the southern part of the continent.

The Amerindians also cultivated yams, beans, guavas, paw-paws and pineapples, and these crops spread from the 'New World' back to Europe and, in the case of yam, Africa, where it became an important staple.

Hunting supplied protein for the Amerindians' diet. Traps, spears, and bows and arrows were the main hunting tools to catch birds, fish, and agoutis, lappes, quenks and other small game. Today the Guiana Amerindians are skilled at spear fishing – they can stand in a muddy river, detect the slight ripple on the water's surface made by a swimming fish and accurately throw their spear, calculating from the ripple what direction the fish is heading in and how fast.

Table 1.4 Comparison of religions

Maya	Taino	Kalinago
The Maya believed strongly in a spirit world.	The Tainos believed in animism which was based on the existence of a spirit world.	The Kalinagos believed strongly in a spirit world.
They worshipped Quetzalcoatl, the great God and culture hero.	They worshipped the universal Creator, Aluberi.	They claimed that Analwaea and his brother Vochi created the world.
They offered blood sacrifices and they believed that torture and human sacrifices brought fertility.	They did not give offerings to their gods – zemis.	They offered material goods such as food and water.
They had priests.	They had men called piaimer who they believed possessed supernatural powers.	They had men called piaimer who they believed possessed supernatural powers.
They worshipped gods who represented the sun, moon, rain and corn. The main purpose of worship was to ensure good crops.	They had eight classes of spirits – both good and evil.	They had five classes of spirits – both good and evil.

The coming of the Europeans
Factors which led to Columbus's voyages

Historians have offered many reasons for Christopher Columbus wanting to sail to the west in order to reach the east. Some say he wanted to prove that the Earth was round, or to discover gold or to convert the peoples of China and India to Christianity. Whatever Columbus's motives were, the real question is why the Spanish King and Queen, Ferdinand and Isabella, decided to finance his voyages.

The answer is spices. In the modern world, we can get almost any spice we want just by going to the nearest grocery store or market and we do not pay a fortune for them. However, since 200 BC, when Greek merchants began trading with India, products such as pepper, cinnamon, ginger and nutmeg were the most profitable trading goods and were so expensive that only the rich could afford to buy them. Such flavourings were in high demand among the upper class to improve the taste of European dishes. A 1,700-year-old Roman cookbook, notably, calls for pepper in 349 of its 468 recipes.

Most of these spices came from east and south Asia. For Europeans there were only three ways to reach the suppliers of spices: through the Gulf of Suez, the Persian Gulf, or around Africa's southern cape, or through unmapped seas to the west. The navigator who could find a route through the west, therefore, would also find his way to great riches, as would the sponsors who would share in the profits of any such voyage.

> **Roleplay**
>
> Imagine that you are Christopher Columbus and you are given an opportunity to meet with the King and Queen of Spain. Write a speech in which you will present your case to gain funding for your voyage.

The first Europeans to try and sail the Atlantic Ocean in order to find an alternate route to the Indies were the Genoese of Italy, so it is no coincidence that Columbus was himself from Genoa, even though by the time he undertook his voyages Portugal was the main seafaring nation in Europe. Columbus sailed south to the African Gold Coast (present-day Ghana), west to the Azores, and north to Ireland. Columbus was thus well prepared for his voyages of exploration.

Activity 1.4 Locate the places mentioned above on a map of the world.

FAST FACTS

- In 205 BC, the Greek scholar Eratosthenes calculated the circumference of the Earth, using the fact that a deep well in the city of Cyene in southern Egypt had its bottom entirely lit by the sun at noon on a certain day of the year, and that objects in the city of Alexandria cast a shadow at the same time, which meant that the latter received sunlight at a different angle.
- Using trigonometry, Eratosthenes measured the circumference of the Earth to within 3% of its actual value of 40,000 kilometres (24,900 miles) without equipment or making a voyage around the world.
- A more accurate measurement was not done until two thousand years later, in the late 18th century, by a large team financed by the French government in an exercise that took seven years to complete.

1.9 Astrolabe (a navigational instrument)

That spices were on Columbus's mind is confirmed by a letter from a famous Florentine physician and mapmaker Paolo dal Pozzo Toscanelli, who told Columbus that he approved of his fellow Italian's ambition to 'pass over to where the spices grow'. Columbus also wanted to convert the Asian peoples to Christianity. Despite the widespread claim that Columbus wanted to prove that the Earth was round, this is unlikely since few if any educated people in the medieval era believed that the Earth was flat.

Columbus' voyage was not without opponents. Scholars in the 15th century thought that Columbus' planned voyage was impossible, not because they thought the Earth was flat, but because they saw, correctly, that Columbus' estimate of the distance between Europe and Asia was too short – by about 25%, in fact. The scholars calculated that the distance between the two continents was about 12,500 miles, which meant a four-month voyage at top speed for vessels and in that era no ship could stock enough supplies for that long a time. In fact, if Columbus had not encountered the Americas, which he did not know

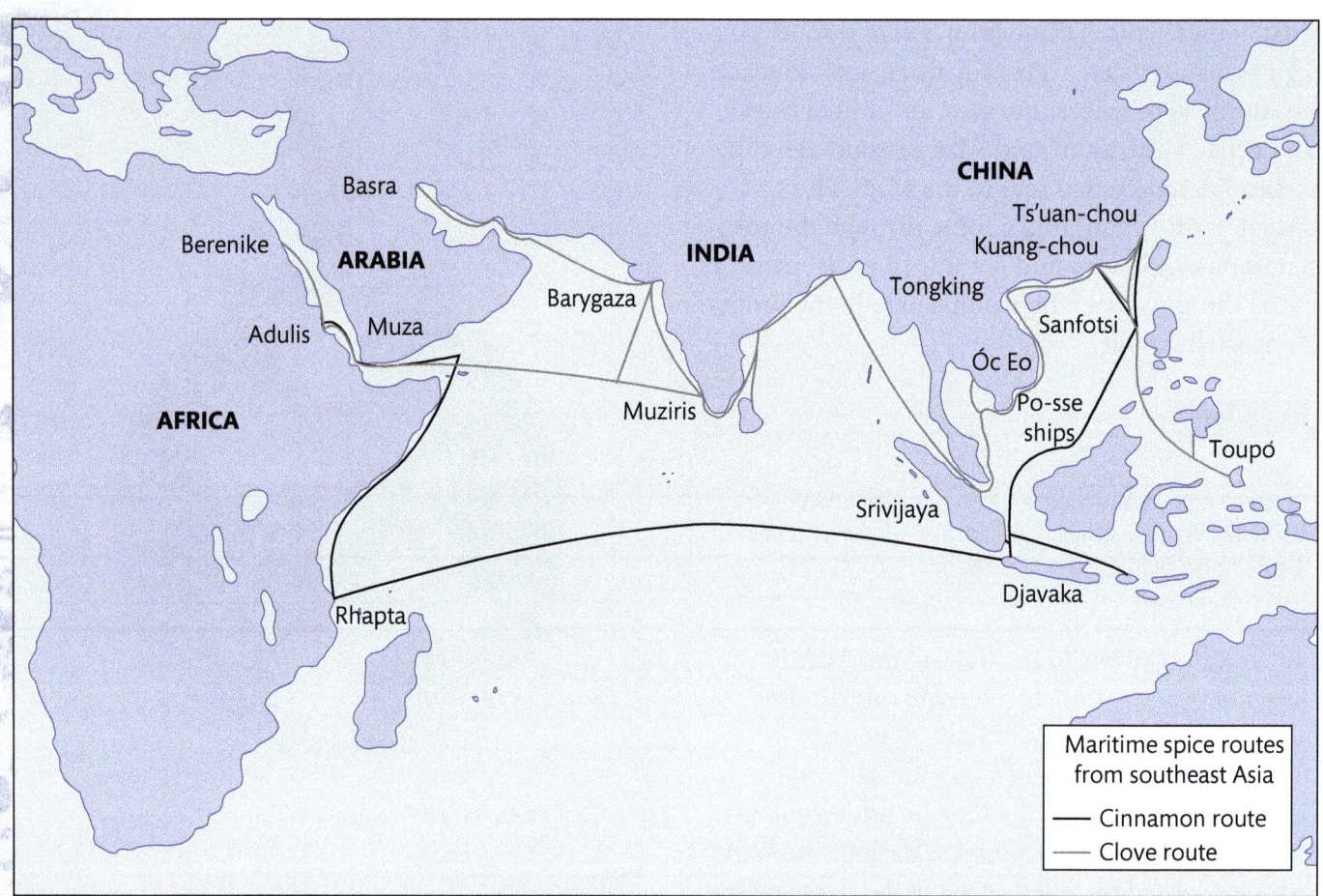

1.10 Trade routes

Table 1.5 Reasons for European interest in the New World

Desire to find a route to India, China and the East Indies	This would reduce the need for middlemen traders and increase profits.	**The Renaissance**	This was a period of revival in arts and letters in Europe. It led to a growing sense of nationalism and the search for new land to increase resources and wealth.
Increasingly difficult land routes	The so-called 'Silk road' to China and India had become difficult and dangerous with the fall of Constantinople to the Ottoman Turks		
		Mercantilism	There was a desire to increase national wealth through trade with foreign territories.
Desire to spread Christianity	Europeans wanted to establish alliances with other Christians, especially given the threat of the Moors and Muslim movement into parts of Europe.	**Glory**	There was a desire for fame and popularity in Europe.
		Breakdown in the system of vassalage	Only first-born sons were eligible to inherit properties while other sons had to establish themselves on their own. This created a group of men who were keen to acquire wealth and property abroad.
Developments in navigation	An improved compass, the astrolabe and quadrant, and portolani maps had been developed.		
Improvements in ship building	Ships were sturdier than previously and could traverse longer distances and sail against the wind and ocean currents such as the lateen.	**The emergence of a new class of merchants and traders**	These people were willing to fund voyages overseas.

existed, he and his crew would have died from starvation. However, he did not realize this and, thinking he had really reached India, he labelled the native inhabitants 'Indians' before finding out what they called themselves. In fact, it was not until his third voyage to the Caribbean that Columbus realized he was nowhere near Asia.

Columbus and his crew of 90 men first landed on an island in the Bahamas archipelago, which the Indigenous people called Guanahaní. The natives, whom anthropologists now classify as Western Tainos and who the Spanish called Lucayos, came out to the Spanish ships on their boats and by swimming. When the Spaniards came on shore, the natives offered them parrots, and cotton thread wrapped in darts and skeins to trade. The Spaniards in their turn offered them red caps, green glass beads, brass rings and small bells. Columbus wrote that the natives took much pleasure in these trinkets.

> **Roleplay**
>
> Imagine that you are an Amerindian chief who welcomed Columbus and his men to your settlement. However, some of your people are suspicious of the presence of these strange-looking men. Prepare a short speech in which you will try to convince them of the benefits of the Europeans' presence.

CHRISTOPHER COLUMBUS
(1451–1506)

1.11 Depiction of Christopher Columbus landing in the Americas, 1492 (painted c.1920)

Columbus was born in Genoa, Italy in 1451. He was the eldest of five children; son of Domenico Colombo, a wool worker and merchant, and Susanna Fontanarossa. As a boy he did not receive a formal education and he was fascinated by the sea and ships so he became a sailor during his teenage years.

In 1476, he was on board a ship when it was attacked by French pirates. He survived the attack and went to stay with his brother Bartholomew in Lisbon, Portugal.

His brother owned a book and map store and it was here he received a more formal education in navigation and map making. He was employed as a chart maker but also worked as a seagoing trader.

Various accounts note his physical gifts: sharp eyesight and keen hearing and sense of smell. He was above average height (which, in Europe 500 years ago was about 5 feet 6 inches for men), very fit, with reddish greying hair and blue eyes. He had the curious mind of the true explorer and an excellent memory. When he arrived in the Caribbean, he made observations about the geography, the behaviour of the animals and variations in temperature. His character was said to be stubborn, spiteful and courageous and he was hungry for fame. He also believed himself to be chosen by God for a special mission which would change the world.

In January 1492, he successfully convinced King Ferdinand and Queen Isabella of Spain to fund a voyage to cross the Atlantic Ocean. They gave him three ships – the Niña, the Pinta and the Santa Maria and they paid for the crew and supplies needed for the journey. He made a total of four voyages to the New World.

Voyages

1492–93: San Salvador, northeast coast of Cuba, the northern coast of Hispaniola and parts of the Bahamas.

1493–96: Dominica, Guadeloupe, Montserrat, Saint Kitts, Redonda, the Virgin Islands, Saint Croix, Antigua, Nevis, Saint Martin, Tortola, the Greater Antilles, Jamaica and Puerto Rico.

1498–1500: Trinidad, Tobago, Grenada, La Isla de Margarita.

1502–04: Honduras, Nicaragua, Costa Rica, Panama.

He renamed the island San Salvador and, after meeting the natives, took six Tainos back to his ship with the intention of teaching them Spanish so they could serve as interpreters as he sailed deeper into the region. Later in his diary, Columbus wrote:

> 'These men are still travelling with me, and although they have been with us for a long time, they continue to entertain the idea that I have descended from Heaven. On our arrival at any new place, they publish this, crying out immediately with a loud voice to the other Indians, "Come, come, and look upon beings of a celestial race."'

Whether the Tainos really considered the Spaniards to be supernatural beings is not clear. One Taino word for the Spaniards was 'guamikinas', which translates as 'covered men'. Columbus recorded that he was able to use the interpreters in most places he landed in, so it seems that the inhabitants of the Bahamas and the Greater Antilles spoke the same language, or closely related languages.

Roleplay

Imagine that you are Columbus. You have just arrived in 'San Salavador' and you have decided to write a letter to your brother telling him about the problems you encountered during your journey to the Caribbean and how you feel now that you have found land.

He landed next on the shore of Cuba, then crossed the Windward Passage to Hispaniola. There, on the north coast, he was received by the local chief, whose name was Guacanagarí. At this point, Columbus had only one ship, the Niña, left. The Pinta had broken away from the convoy, because the sailors on board did not want to go any further into the unknown seas and wanted to search for gold. Then the Santa Maria foundered on a coral reef, and had to be left, along with most of its crew, for repairs. Columbus left the men with provisions for one year, and sailed back to Spain on 15 March 1493. He would not see them alive again.

Columbus took the six Tainos back with him, and is reported to have named one Diego, which was also the name of Columbus's eldest son. This Taino youth served as Columbus's interpreter on his second voyage, which left Spain in September 1493, and which this time had 17 ships with 1,500 men, including a doctor, a mapmaker and several clerics. Diego had been baptized when he was given his new name. One of the clerics, Father Ramón Pané, studied the Taino religion on this journey, and it is from his records that much of our knowledge of the Taino's now-vanished culture comes. However, all his data was collected in one small territory in Hispaniola, so many of his findings are not necessarily true of all the Taino groups. Even the names below may not have been used by all the Tainos, since they also had different languages.

> These are the original Amerindian names for some of the Caribbean islands.
>
> Wai'tukubuli – Dominica (Tall is her body)
>
> Karukera – Guadeloupe (Beautiful water)
>
> Hamaica – Jamaica (Land of wood and water)
>
> Iere – Trinidad (Land of the humming-bird)

On this second trip, Columbus learned from the Tainos that the Lesser Antilles extended further into the Atlantic Ocean than he had thought. With Tainos as his guides, Columbus was able to shorten his journey through the region and land at more islands. He went from Dominica to Guadeloupe, where there was a six-day delay when the landing party got lost in the forest. It was here that the tales of cannibalism started among the Europeans, because the sailors found dismembered human remains which had been used in rituals by the island Caribs.

> Extract from Columbus's diary on the Caribs:
>
> 'In these islands I have found so far no human monstrosities, as many expected, but on the contrary the whole population is very well-formed… Thus, I have found no monsters, nor had a report of any, except in an island "Carib", which is the second at the coming into the Indies, which is inhabited by a people who are regarded in all the islands as very fierce and who eat human flesh.'

However, all accounts of cannibalism are based on European records, especially Columbus's diary, which has been described by Caribbean anthropologist Basil Reid as a 'litany of half-truths, anecdotal descriptions, hearsay and preconceived Eurocentric ideas about the native people of the Caribbean.' The Spanish used the term 'cannibals' to describe any native groups which resisted them, as well as the term 'Carib'.

When Columbus returned to Hispaniola on 28 November 1493, where he had left his men building a fort, he found the structure destroyed and his men dead. Chief Guacanagarí claimed that the Spaniards had been killed by another chief, Caonabo, who ruled over a region in the southern part of island. Caonabo had reacted to aggression by the Spaniards, who had stolen from the Tainos and raped the women. Columbus continued his journey on 24 April 1494, sailing to the Greater Antilles. He landed in Jamaica, hearing there was gold on the island, and, when he failed to find the precious metal, went on to Cuba.

On Columbus's fourth voyage in 1502, a sustained period of storms as well as a worm infestation of the ship's planks forced him to beach his vessels at St Ann's Bay in northern Jamaica in June. He and his crew were marooned there for over a year. Two canoes were dispatched to Hispaniola to get help from another Spanish convoy which had landed there. Columbus organized a system of barter with the natives, exchanging goods for food such as cassava bread and maize, but also agoutis and iguanas. Columbus ordered his men to stay on board unless he gave permission for them to leave, and over 100 men were crowded into huts built on the deck, forecastle and poop. After a few months living like this, some of the men mutinied.

On 2 January 1503, the mutineers left the ship and began outfitting canoes to row to Hispaniola. Just 20 healthy men, and those too sick to move, stayed on board the waterlogged ship with Columbus. The mutineers set off on the high sea, but were soon driven back by the high winds and strong current. Having landed back on Jamaica, they began attacking the natives and stealing from them. As a result, the natives refused to supply any more food to Columbus's remaining crew. However, Columbus was able to frighten them into doing so, by threatening to kill the moon. He knew that a lunar eclipse was due in January 1504 and when this occurred, seemingly at Columbus's command, the natives promised to resume supplying food if he would restore the moon. The crew was finally rescued in the June of 1504, but Columbus was ill and died two years later. He asked for his remains to be carried to the Caribbean and buried there.

Impact of the New World on Europe

The discovery of a vast landmass, supposedly filled with riches for the taking, naturally caused great interest in Europe. Younger sons who were not in line to inherit their father's wealth, military officers who had no employment in times of peace, the outside children of noblemen and persons fleeing the law all saw the New World as a place where they could make their fortunes. The kings and queens of Europe were no less excited; they thought the acquisition of gold and silver would mean wealth and power for themselves and their nations.

Conquistador a Spanish soldier.

The most immediate conflict involved the two foremost seafaring nations of the time: Portugal and Spain. When the Niña, the Pinta and the Santa Maria left the harbour of Palos de la Frontera on 3 August 1492, this duel had already been going on for a long time. Many of the political and military disputes between the two countries were mediated by the Roman Catholic Church, for the Pope had more power than any monarch in these centuries. The trouble was, different Popes, or sometimes the same Pope, favoured Portugal at one time and Spain the next.

Pope Nicholas V, in the mid-15th century, issued a Papal Bull known as the 'Charter of Portuguese Imperialism' which praised the King of Portugal, and authorized him to conquer and convert all the pagans between Morocco and India. However, just eight days after Columbus left Spain on his first voyage, a Spaniard was installed as Pope, taking the title Alexander VI. The new Pope issued a Papal Bull giving Spain ownership of new land discovered by Spanish explorers.

FAST FACTS

The Papal Bulls – These are decrees issued by the Roman Catholic Pope on property matters.

- They gave Portugal a trading monopoly in all territories between Africa and the Indies.
- They awarded Spain possession of all lands discovered by Spanish explorers.
- They gave Spain ownership of all lands 350 miles west of the Cape Verde islands, including territory which had not been discovered yet.

Treaty of Tordesillas – This was an agreement, intended to resolve a dispute created by the Papal Bulls following the return of Columbus, between Portugal and Spain. The Treaty defined which parts of the world each could conquer and colonize.

- It was established when the Portuguese King John II decided to bypass the corrupt Pope and negotiate directly with King Ferdinand and Queen Isabella of Spain.
- It divided the world into two hemispheres, with Africa and Asia belonging to Portugal and the New World to Spain.
- It outraged the other European powers, who wanted their piece of the New World pie and who over the next few centuries would battle Spain and one another for it.

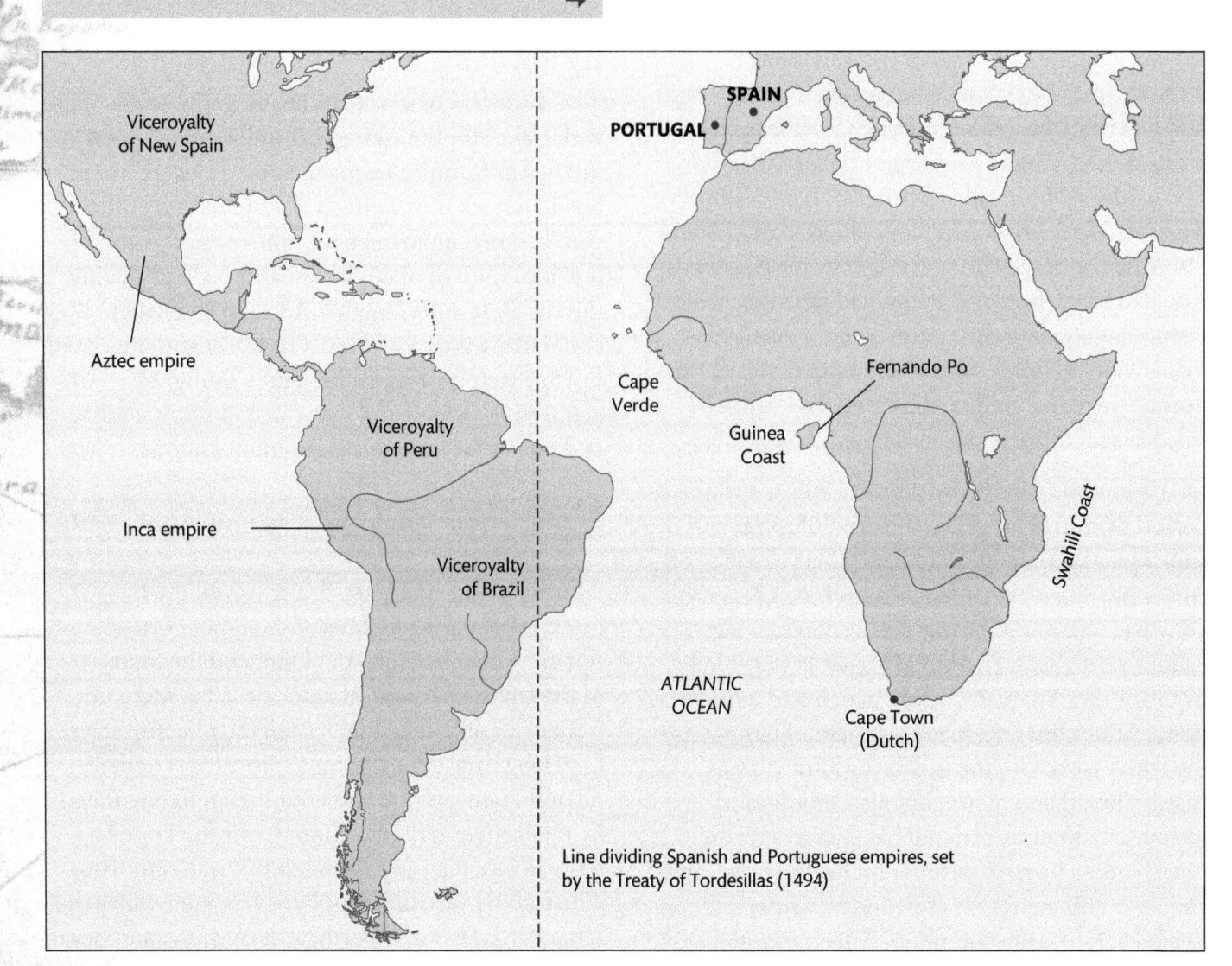

1.12 Map showing the Treaty of Tordesillas

The second Papal Bull naturally outraged the Portuguese, especially since they had been the first Europeans to explore the African coast. The Portuguese monarch John II decided to bypass the corrupt Pope Alexander VI and negotiate directly with Ferdinand and Isabella. This led to the Treaty of Tordesillas. Before Columbus's voyage, such a treaty would not have been agreed to by either nation, but Portugal had just found a sea route to the Indian Ocean and Spain had two new continents to play with.

Another effect of the New World was to increase wars between the European nations. They were already fighting one another within Europe and on the high seas, but now the arena of war was moved to the Caribbean. The British and French competed most fiercely with the Spaniards, and with each other, to seize the islands and settle colonies on them. St Lucia was conquered 17 times by France and Britain alternately. Martinique and Guadeloupe changed hands seven times, Tobago six times and St Vincent and Grenada four times.

This was the main reason why piracy in the Caribbean began. Spain was becoming wealthy from its South American and Caribbean possessions. The Spanish Crown was using this wealth to finance wars against other European powers, such as the French, the English and the Dutch, and so becoming more powerful.

> **Privateer** a private individual who owned and officered an armed ship commissioned by the government and authorized for use in war, especially in the capture of enemy merchant shipping vessels.

Since it would have been difficult to take over the Spanish colonies in South America and the Caribbean, the other European monarchs decided to attack the Spaniards at sea. The French were the first to use this strategy in the 16th century, but the French government did not have a big enough navy to overcome the Spanish ships. Instead, the government gave official letters to private ship owners which allowed the owners to capture Spanish ships legally and even take control of towns until the Spanish government paid a ransom. These 'privateers', as they were called, were pirates who were financed by businessmen who expected to make a profit from trading the goods seized from the Spanish ships or the ransoms paid for the captured towns.

In 1523, a French privateer took a very valuable cargo when it captured two Spanish galleons near the Azores. These ships were part of a fleet coming from Mexico with treasures from the palace of the Aztec emperor Montezuma. This treasure included gold masks, jewelled head-dresses, and multi-coloured feathered cloaks. When other pirates learned about this booty, they flocked to the Caribbean, centring their operations in the Bahamas where they waited to attack Spanish ships in the Florida Channel. Spanish settlements in the Caribbean were also plundered. In 1553, a French pirate named François le Clerc, with a fleet of 10 ships, attacked nearly every Spanish-occupied island in the Caribbean.

The war between Spain and France ended with the Treaty of Cateau-Cambresis in 1559, but both sides admitted that piracy was out of control and could not be stopped. However, the privateers no longer had the support of the French government, and so would be arrested and tried if they were caught. This agreement lasted until the 17th century when France and Spain went to war again, but piracy did not stop in peace time or war.

> **Activity 1.5** Find out more about the Treaty of Cateau-Cambresis, 1559. What were the main parts of this treaty?
>
> Who benefited most from this treaty?

One of the most successful English pirates was Francis Drake. In 1572, Drake raided a land convoy of mules loaded with Peruvian silver. So profitable was this raid that every sailor went home a rich man. Between 1585 and 1586, Drake stole more than £300,000 in booty from Spanish ships and towns. However, such raids became more difficult as the towns became bigger and more fortified, and set up squadrons to patrol the region. Drake's last trip, between 1595 and 1596, was defeated by the Spaniards, even though Drake now had a fleet of 27 ships. He tried to attack the town of San Juan in Puerto Rico, and was forced to retreat. Drake lost 12 ships, eventually died from dysentery, and his fleet returned to England with no profits.

Another famous pirate was Henry Morgan. He became commander of British pirates, known as 'buccaneers', in 1668. The term 'buccaneers' came from the French word 'boucan'. Pirates who settled on the island of Tortuga between raids hunted hogs and preserved the meat in strips wrapped in aromatic leaves called 'boucan'. The meat kept for months and prevented scurvy. Morgan captured the town of Puerto Príncipe (now Camagüey) in Cuba, and sacked the city of Portobelo on the Isthmus of Panama. In his last raid in August 1670, with 36 ships and nearly 2,000 buccaneers, Morgan set out to capture Panama, defeating a large Spanish force in 1671. The city burned to the ground while his men were looting it and on the return journey Morgan deserted his men and disappeared with most of the booty.

However, Morgan's raid on Panama had taken place after the conclusion of a peace between England and Spain. He was arrested and transported to London in April 1672. Luckily for him, the peace did not last, and in 1674 King Charles II knighted Morgan and appointed him as Deputy Governor of Jamaica. Morgan lived at the right time for pirates and was able to use England's conflicts to enrich himself. He lived out his days as a rich planter in Jamaica.

Spain was also at war with the Netherlands. Holland was a trading nation, so it already had many ships plying the Caribbean sea-routes, and between 1569 and 1609 Dutch privateers were also very active in the region. The Dutch were a major presence, but they were mainly there to trade rather than colonize. Even so, Dutch pirates proved to be a headache for the Spanish, and diverted enough Spanish ships and men for the British and French to colonize most of the Lesser Antilles. In a nine-year period, the British colonized St Kitts (1623), Barbados (1625), Nevis (1628) and Antigua (1632). The conflict between these various European powers was most clearly played out after the Haitian Revolution in 1791, when Britain, Spain and the USA cooperated with the Haitian forces at various times to defeat the French.

It has also been argued that the Americas helped spur the Industrial Revolution, by providing raw materials, especially cotton, to Britain and other European nations, as well as offering a place to export their growing populations. The Industrial Revolution was what allowed Europe, especially Britain, to become the most powerful region in the world.

The discovery of huge silver deposits in Peru and Mexico created a new global monetary system, in which the Spanish eight-real coin had the significance of the US dollar in the 20th century. This wealth from silver also had long term negative effects on Spain because, instead of producing goods for trade, the Spaniards could now buy whatever they needed from other countries. This would ensure that Spain over the next few centuries would lose out to other European nations, in particular England, which would become the dominant power in the world for the next four hundred years.

The most significant impact on Europe from the New World did not come from precious metals, which was the main concern of the Spaniards, but from crops. Within a few decades of Columbus's second voyage in 1493, which had 17 vessels and 1,300 colonists, the exchange of corn, wheat, coffee, tea and sugar between the continents had forever changed the world's agricultural and labour markets.

Impact of the Europeans on the Indigenous peoples

When the Europeans landed in South America and the Caribbean, they brought with them a weapon far more deadly to the native inhabitants than any sword. In their bodies the Spanish carried microbes to which they were immune, but which were deadly to the Indigenous Amerindians. Over two centuries after Columbus's arrival, smallpox, measles, influenza and typhus infected and killed 95% of the Amerindian populations of the New World. In Hispaniola, the native population may have been between 200,000 and one million people in 1492. By 1535, the majority had died out.

Why were the Indigenous Americans so susceptible to these diseases and why did New World microbes not kill the Europeans in the same way? The first reason was time: microbes co-evolved with humans in Africa, and the Europeans had a long history of animal farming, which allowed them to develop resistance to diseases (so that people who had had cowpox, for example, became immune to smallpox). Flu, typhus, tuberculosis, malaria, plague, measles and cholera are other infectious diseases that evolved from microbes that first developed in animals. The invading Europeans were not similarly killed on a mass scale by New World diseases, because the New World inhabitants over the succeeding generations probably lost whatever immunities they may have had when they first entered the continent thousands of years before. Also, they had wiped out all the species in the Americas which might have been domesticated so no new diseases evolved there from contact between animals and humans. Were it not for this, the handful of Spanish conquistadores who first came to the Americas could not have so easily conquered the empires of the Aztecs and Incas.

The Spanish also cleared the way for the Europeans who came after them, often displacing the Spanish themselves. Ten European nations fought over and colonized the various Caribbean islands. Apart from Spain, the countries most active in the region were Britain, France and the Netherlands. Germany, Sweden, Malta, and Denmark also had colonists at various times and from the 19th century the USA had economic and military interests in the Caribbean.

Although the Spanish colonies were taken over by several of the other powers, the Spanish names, as well as architectural styles, were the first European stamp put on the region. The Spanish colonial towns, for example, were built in a standard pattern. The centre had a town plaza, with a church and mayor's office and other important government buildings. Streets were laid out in a neat grid at right angles. Houses were built of stone or brick, and constructed with thick walls against hurricanes and to keep the interior cool in the tropical heat.

Thus, the villages of the natives were razed or displaced to the interior of the islands and the settlements of the Caribbean took on a European-based appearance that persists to this day. Of all the Amerindian groups, only the Caribs survived the European onslaught, and that is because many of them retreated to the mountains of the Lesser Antilles, which the Europeans did not occupy. Even so, in 1651, the French defeated the Caribs in Grenada and in 1773 the British did the same in St Vincent. Nowadays, the remaining Caribs live mainly in Dominica and St Vincent, while some persons of mixed Amerindian ancestry are found in Aruba, Trinidad and the Greater Antilles.

Activity 1.6

Research the Carib community in either Dominica, St Vincent, Aruba or Trinidad. Use the following headings as a guide.

a   Location
b   Population
c   Cultural activities.

Activity 1.7

Read the following extract from *The Devastation of the Indies: A brief account* by Bartolomé de las Casas. De las Casas was a Spanish settler and historian who felt compelled to write upon witnessing the treatment of the Indigenous people. Answer the questions below.

'... these people are the most guileless, the most devoid of wickedness and duplicity, the most obedient and faithful to their native masters and to the Spanish Christians whom they serve. They are by nature the most humble, patient and peaceable, holding no grudges, free from embroilments, neither excitable nor quarrelsome. These people are the most devoid of rancors, hatred, or desire for vengeance of any people in the world. And because they are so weak and complaisant, they are less able to endure heavy labor and soon die of no matter what malady.'

- According to the extract, what are two ways in which the Indigenous population declined?
- What is las Casas's attitude towards the Indigenous people?
- Why do you think las Casas spoke of the Indigenous people in such a favourable manner?
- Do you think his opinion reflects that of other Spaniards at that time?

The first Spanish settlement was in Hispaniola's northern coast, established by Columbus on his second voyage in 1493. All the larger islands, such as Cuba, Puerto Rico and Jamaica were also settled, which is the main reason why some Amerindians in the smaller islands managed to survive. The Spaniards first demanded tribute from the Amerindians, mainly gold from those who lived near the mines and cotton from the others. However, the Amerindians had never mined gold or woven cotton for more than their own use and many of them could not produce what the Spaniards wanted.

Impact of the Europeans on the Indigenous peoples

Genocide
- The Indigenous populations were decreased so considerably under Spanish rule only minority groups existed throughout the Caribbean region.

Forced labour or systems of enslavement were introduced.
- Repartamiento system – a percentage of the Indigenous male population between the ages of 18 and 60 was recruited to work for a Spaniard for a week for pay. However, they were hardly ever paid.
- Encomienda system – smaller groups of Indigenous people were allocated to a few privileged Spaniards (known as encomenderos). The encomendero was granted a parcel of land, with the right to exact tribute (usually in the form of labour or crops, or both) from the Indigenous people living on the land. In return he was expected to convert them to Christianity and protect them.

New types of diseases were introduced.
- Indigenous peoples were not immune to diseases such as smallpox and chicken pox.

Families were broken up.
- Adult males were moved from place to place by Spaniards. Many Kalinago males were killed in wars with the Spaniards.

Indigenous agricultural systems were destroyed.
- The production of crops by Indigenous peoples was affected. The Spanish brought animals such as cattle, horses, sheep and goats, which trampled the fields. Often these animals were placed to graze on the agricultural fields of the Indigenous people.

Infanticide was carried out.
- Many parents preferred to kill their babies because they did not want them to grow up under such conditions.

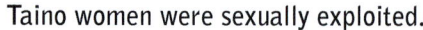

Taino women were sexually exploited.

The Indigenous peoples lost their land and their sovereignty.

There were changes in Indigenous religious practices due to the forced conversion to Christianity.

There was a breakdown of Amerindian culture as the Tainos and Kalinagos had to conform to European way of life.

When Columbus was faced with a threat of rebellion from his own men, he gave them land grants which included the forced labour of the Amerindians. This was the encomienda system. The Spanish monarchy, with no sense of paradox, insisted that the Amerindians be treated as free persons, which meant that they would be forced to work only six to eight months in the mines, be fed and retain the right to their property or to buy their freedom. Most important of all, from the Crown's perspective, the colonists had to ensure that the Amerindians were instructed and converted to the Catholic faith, since this would ensure that in return for their labour their souls would be saved.

The Americas were changed forever by the arrival of the Europeans. Having destroyed the Indigenous way of life, the Europeans then also changed the flora, fauna and the population itself. They brought pigs, which flourished in the new territory, as well as cattle and horses. They also brought new plants. Coconut trees, now an iconic image in tourist brochures of the Caribbean islands, did not grow here before they were brought from south Asia. Nor did mangoes, bananas, oranges or sugar cane.

It was to be sugar that would shape the history of the region, and beyond, for the next 400 years.

Impact of the Indigenous people on the Europeans

Given the devastation wrought by the European presence in the New World, the Indigenous groups themselves had little direct impact on Europe, save for those political and economic effects mentioned above. However, the very existence of people whom the Bible did not mention was to change the Eurocentric view of the world. The intellectual undermining of Christian beliefs, as well as the realization that Europe was a relatively small part of the planet, were the first steps toward the Enlightenment movement of the 18th century, starting in France and England. The widespread deaths and enslavement of the Amerindians also aroused intense moral debates in Spain, with the Catholic priest Bartolomé de las Casas being the best-known champion. Although at the time all such effects were confined to mere discussion, the ideas that were introduced at this time were to shape Europe in the coming centuries. That change started, in part, because of the Europeans' interactions with the Amerindians.

Activity 1.8

Find out more about Bartolomé de las Casas. Use the following headings to guide you in your research.

a Personal life
b Attitude to the Indigenous people
c Work with the Indigenous people in the Caribbean.

REVISION QUESTIONS

1 Read the passage below then answer the questions that follow.

   Imagine you are an escaped Taino (Arawak) cacique whose community in Hispaniola was enslaved by the Spaniards in 1520. Give an account of your encounters with the Spaniards under the following headings:

   a The reaction of free and enslaved Tainos to the Spanish presence in Hispaniola. *(13 marks)*
   b The impact of Taino resistance on the Spaniards and on the Tainos themselves. *(12 marks)*
   (Total = 25 marks)
   CXC Past Papers, Basic Proficiency, May/June 2002

2 Read the passage below then answer the questions that follow.

   When Columbus set out he said he was confident that his sponsors would gain great benefits from his explorations. At first, many people did not share his views but later they recognized the importance of his voyages.

   a Give three reasons why Columbus made his voyages to the New World. *(12 marks)*
   b List four crops that the Spaniards found when they arrived in the New World. *(4 marks)*
   c Describe three ways in which Columbus's voyages affected the people of the New World. *(9 marks)*
   (Total = 25 marks)
   CXC Past Papers, Basic Proficiency, May/June 2002

3 Critically examine the impact of European contact with the New World on Europe and the New World.
   (25 marks)

4 'The Mayan civilization was an advanced one.' What evidence is there to show this? **(25 marks)**

Recommended reading

- Anthony, M. *The Golden Quest: The four voyages of Christopher Columbus*, London: Macmillan, 1992
- Beckles, H. and Shepherd, V.A. *Liberties Lost: The Indigenous Caribbean and slave societies*, Cambridge: Cambridge University Press, 2005
- Coe, M.D. *The Maya*, New York: Thames and Hudson, 1984
- De Las Casas, B. *The Devastation of the Indies: A brief account*, Johns Hopkins University Press, 1992
- Reid, B. *Myths and Realities of Caribbean History,* Alabama: University of Alabama Press, 2009
- Wilson, S.M. *The Indigenous People of the Caribbean,* Gainesville: University Press of Florida, 1997

2 The Caribbean economy and slavery

This chapter will answer the following questions.
- Why was there a change from trade in tobacco to sugar and from logwood to mahogany?
- Why were Africans enslaved and how was the trade in enslaved Africans organized?
- How were the sugar plantations organized?
- How was sugar manufactured?
- What types of African cultural forms were transported to the Caribbean?
- How did different groups relate to each other on the plantations?

Before 1492 the main reasons for trade between countries in Asia and countries in Europe were food and scents. This was why spices were so profitable for Asian merchants to trade with Europeans. After the Europeans arrived in the New World, however, world trade was driven by stimulants such as coffee, tea and sugar. At first, it was mainly wealthy people who consumed these products, but expanded cultivation in the Americas brought prices down until consumption of sugar and coffee, along with tobacco, became widespread in Europe, especially in England, even among the less well-off. Before that stage came though, it was spices which, indirectly, created the trade in enslaved Africans to the Americas and the Caribbean.

As you learned in Chapter 1, there were only three ways to reach the Indian Ocean and the suppliers of spices: through the Suez or the Persian Gulf, or around Africa's southern cape, or through unmapped seas to the west.

The Europeans wanted to control the last two routes, since the Suez Gulf was already dominated by Arab and Asian merchants and rulers. Table 2.1 lists the most powerful Asian trading states from that era and the present-day countries where they are located. One of the lessons we learn from history is that even the most powerful countries and individuals may be forgotten in the passage of time. For example, Aceh, which was one of the wealthiest city-states in the 16th century, in the 21st century is just a remote underdeveloped town which became known to the world only when it was hit by a tsunami in 2004. Similarly, none of the other city-states listed is located in the world's richest and most powerful countries today.

Activity 2.1 Research the city of Aceh. Locate it on a world map and find out why it was so vibrant during the 16th century.

Table 2.1 Major 16th-century city-states

Name	21st century location
Aden	Yemen
Hormuz	Iran
Cambay	India
Calicut	India
Aceh	Sumatra
Malacca	Sumatra

Although the merchants and rulers from the Middle East and India dominated trade routes and markets, hardly anyone was prevented from doing business wherever he wanted to. Any merchant from any country, as long as he paid customs fees, gave gifts to local sultans and fought off pirates, could trade with anyone. But the Europeans, especially the Portuguese, wanted to control the high seas through superior naval power which they could use to cut off rival merchant vessels. By doing so, they would give themselves the advantage in trade.

The Portuguese became the first traders in captured Africans to Europe. Prince Henry (known as Henry the Navigator) became Europe's main patron of maritime science. He financed not only voyages, but ship builders and map makers from all countries, and he had the largest collection of navigational maps in the world. Portuguese ship builders also invented the caravel: a round-hulled ship with lateen rigging (a triangular sail set at a 45-degree angle to the mast). These ships could sail closer to the wind than other ships, which had to tack back and forth longer distances so their sails could catch the prevailing winds in order to move forward. If it were not for the caravel, the Portuguese could never have sailed down the African coast.

HENRY THE NAVIGATOR
(1394–1460)

Dom Henrique was the third of five sons of King John 1 of Portugal and his English wife Philippa. He became known as Henry the Navigator, not because he had travelled extensively to foreign lands, but because he used his wealth to promote travel and navigation. In fact, he never travelled to any of the lands where trading networks were established because of his funding.

Prince Henry had fought in battles in North Africa and while there he had also seen the wealth brought by the mainly Arab traders. Thus, his interest in Africa grew at this time and by 1418 he was sponsoring voyages to Africa. One of his explorers rediscovered the Madeira Islands and others went as far as the west coast of Africa.

Thus, Prince Henry's interest grew and he established the first maritime school for the study of the arts of navigation, map making, astronomy, ship building and maritime commerce at Sagres, Portugal. The caravel, a new type of ship, was developed at Sagres. His main intention was to find a route to the Indies, to take part in the spice trade, to sail to Africa and to spread the Christian faith. He is known in history as a pioneer in navigation and exploration – he was responsible for the exploration of Africa by individuals such as Gil Eannes, who brought the first shipload of 200 slaves to Portugal, Diogo Gomes and Alviste de Cadamosto.

In 1458, Prince Henry negotiated several treaties with African rulers, promising that the Portuguese would not steal slaves or other goods but would barter for

2.1 Prince Henry, known as Henry the Navigator

them. The Cape Verde Islands, an uninhabited volcanic archipelago discovered in 1456, were used to hold slaves from the nearby African coast.

Prince Henry never married and he died at Sagres on 13 November 1460.

2.2 A caravel

A carrack

Exploration stopped for 10 years after Henry's death, until responsibility for Africa and the Cape Verde Islands was handed over to an entrepreneur named Fernão Gomes. Gomes not only had to pay the Crown 200 réis per annum for the privilege, but he was also contracted to explore another 300 miles of new coastline every year, so the Portuguese learned more about that region than any other Europeans. In 1498, the Portuguese explorer Vasco da Gama reached the east coast of Africa. By then, the Portuguese had been capturing Africans for over 50 years.

Agricultural changes in the Caribbean

When the sailors on Columbus's ships landed on the Caribbean islands in the 15th century, they saw a landscape very different from the one which exists now. The beaches had no coconut trees, but just the bushes and twisted, bright green vines that grow in sandy soil. The only fields were small ones cleared for cassava. There were no large animals. And, of course, there were no roads, just trails, and no large buildings, just huts.

The colonists who arrived in later centuries found a completely transformed landscape. There were banana, orange and mango trees. Horses and cattle roamed fields, which had cotton plants and cocoa trees at first. Later, even larger clearings would be filled with the arrowed leaves of the sugar cane. But the most obvious transformation was human: no longer were the islands populated mainly by Amerindians, but by Africans and Europeans.

The European colonists came mainly to make their fortunes, and the crop which was initially most profitable was tobacco. Cotton, cocoa, coffee and indigo were also favoured, because they were the most profitable for the colonists to sell to Europe. The ships, even up to the 17th century were quite small, took months to travel between Europe and the Caribbean, and had no refrigeration. This meant that any goods which were perishable, such as fruit and unsalted meats, or which were too bulky, such as timber and cattle, were unsuitable for trade. So the goods produced in the colonies had to be small and aimed at a luxury market – that is, they had to be products that rich people were willing to pay a high price for. Cocoa and coffee were very popular among the rich, but tea from the East Indies began to compete with these beverages, making it less profitable for the Caribbean colonists to grow the crops. Cotton and dyes (from indigo and logwood) were somewhat profitable, but cloth producers were the only buyers and, until the Industrial Revolution in the late 18th century made weaving cheaper, there was not a very high demand for cotton or dyes.

Tobacco, however, had none of these production problems. The crop had the following advantages.

- It was not perishable once its leaves were cured.
- A good quantity could be stored in small packages for transport.
- It was easy to grow, since the landowner and his family, perhaps with a few labourers, could cultivate it.
- It did not need a large investment in machinery, buildings or livestock.
- Smoking tobacco was a fashionable habit among the aristocracy in Europe.

However, by the 17th century, sugar cane had taken over from tobacco as a more profitable crop for production in the Caribbean. This was mainly because tobacco in the US colony of Virginia was cheaper and of better quality than Caribbean tobacco. Sugar had all the same advantages as tobacco listed above, except that it required more labour and more investment. Before the Atlantic slave trade provided a cheap source of labour, honey was cheaper than sugar to use as a sweetener. However, even honey was becoming expensive, as tea and coffee became more popular.

THE ORIGIN OF SUGAR CANE

Sugar cane was one of the first crops domesticated by human beings. It originated in New Guinea, growing wild in the forest. It was a giant member of the grass family, with a stem as thick as bamboo but filled with a sweet juicy pith. The New Guineans who first cultivated it grew the canes low on mountain sides. The canes were later carried to India, where a hybrid variety was cultivated, and where it is likely that the juice was first boiled to make sugar crystals. Eventually, the canes reached Brazil, from where it was brought by the Dutch to the Caribbean.

African enslavement
Reasons for enslaving Africans

Early in the morning of 8 August 1444, in Lagos in Portugal, 235 enslaved Africans were off loaded

THE SUGAR REVOLUTION

This term was used to describe the change from the cultivation of tobacco to the cultivation of sugar. This change was pioneered by the Dutch, who provided capital to establish sugar plantations. They also taught the British and French planters how to manufacture sugar and provided a market for the sugar which was produced.

There was a decline in the price of West Indian tobacco which meant that tobacco produced in the West Indian colonies could not compete favourably in the world market. This led to a decline in the production of tobacco.

The sugar revolution was influenced by the rising demand for sugar in Europe. Sugar was used more and more as a sweetener for tea and coffee. Consequently, there was a change in the size of landholdings as the plantation system required large-scale cultivation of one crop (monoculture).

The change to the large-scale cultivation of sugar for export to Europe led to the need for labour and, subsequently, enslaved Africans were transported into the West Indies.

from six Portuguese ships. This was the first commercial transportation of captured Africans to Europe. Their arrival was recorded by Eannes de Zurara, a courtier to Prince Henry's brother.

> 'Some kept their heads low, and their faces bathed in tears, looking one upon another. Others stood groaning very dolorously, looking up to the height of heaven, fixing their eyes upon it, crying out loudly… others struck their faces with the palms of their hands, throwing themselves at full length upon the ground; while others made lamentations in the manner of a dirge, after the custom of their country.'

So began four centuries of slave shipments from Africa. However, this was not the beginning of slavery itself. Since the Agricultural Revolution 10,000 years before, farming communities and pastoral tribes had become more numerous than hunter-gatherer bands. Such large human groups, settled in one place, allowed the development of architecture, writing systems and extensive trade.

The large settlements also made it possible for individuals to specialize in one skill or task. So, for the first time in human history, there were different classes of people who did specific tasks: aristocrats, priests, soldiers, merchants and slaves.

Once there were nations, from Europe to China to India to Persia, there was also slavery. In fact, the word 'slave' comes from 'Slav' (people from Yugoslavia), which was the main group enslaved in Europe. But why did Africans become targeted for labour on the plantations of the New World?

Activity 2.2
Find out more about the presence of slavery in different parts of the world such as China, India, Persia and Europe before the 19th century. What was slavery like then? How different was it from slavery in the Caribbean?

In the past Africa was mainly inhabited by hunter-gatherer bands who survived using stone-age technology. By 900 AD, one tribe, the Bantu, had developed wet-climate crops, such as yams, and had added iron tools from the Sahel zone to their arsenal. They also had genetic resistance to malaria. This combination gave them an advantage over the other tribal groups. Eventually, the Bantu were able to conquer the other tribes, or inter-married with them, and the Bantu tribe became the main one in the sub-Saharan region. However, agricultural productivity in Africa never flourished, because the soils were poor and techniques such as crop rotation, irrigation and fertilization with manure were not practised. The plough was invented only in Ethiopia, and there were no wheeled vehicles, watermills or windmills. The main tools were digging sticks, iron hoes, axes and machetes.

The region which mainly concerns us is West Central Africa, since this was the area from which most Africans were brought to the Caribbean. Human beings first appeared in the area over 100,000 years ago. By the late Stone Age, which is 10,000 years ago, these humans' tools and rock art could be found throughout the region in many archaeological sites. We know how these preliterate people lived by studying their stone tools, which do not decay, and by their food remnants, such as nuts. The ancient West Africans hunted game and gathered plants for their diet. Women were the main gatherers and knew which plants were edible, where they could be found, which were good for medicines or for making clothing, and how to process them. Edible plants included tubers which were dug out of the soil using digging sticks; fruits and nuts; melon, squash, pumpkins and calabashes; and the seeds of a few grasses, which were crushed using grinding stones. Tubers were the most important plant, because they were the main source of high-energy carbohydrates. In the drier areas, pumpkins and melons were also important because of their high water content.

Around 400 BC, or 2,400 years ago, migrants from the tropical rain forest of western equatorial Africa came to the Lower Congo and into the northern part of West Central Africa. These groups brought ceramics and root crops, along with Bantu languages. This created a cultural shift in the region, and by 800 or 900 AD the region had a unified culture. Women were probably the crucial agent in this process – because they married between communities, they chose which languages to teach their children and they carried technological and even cultural innovations from one community to the next. The main languages in West Central Africa today are from the Njila language family, because this came to dominate all the other Bantu languages that were originally spoken. The adoption of cereal foods was also a key factor in unifying the region.

Before the 16th century, West Africans ate mainly rice, millet, African yam and bananas – a diet that provided only minimal nutritional needs. When cassava and maize were imported from the Americas, the West African population began to increase, since these crops allowed more people to be fed. However, this increase only ensured that West and Central Africa's population did not dramatically decline as the European slave traders took millions of people to the New World over a 400-year period.

The slave trade changed the relationships between rulers and the ruled in Africa. Most groups in Africa were chieftainships. The chiefs ruled over particular territories, and the larger the territory the more powerful the chief. Historians estimate that these units first began about 900 years ago, although it is impossible to be certain. But linguists can estimate when the first words for 'chief' began to be used, such as ohámba (which means 'he who surpasses all others'), soma, sobá, and homphá. The size of these chieftainships increased dramatically after the Atlantic slave trade got underway in the 17th century. By the 1750s, the network of slave merchants within Africa covered the lands of the upper Kasai and Lwena basins to the upper Zambezi River.

Wherever there were friendly chiefs along the caravan routes, their villages became way stations where food, slaves, ivory and wax could be bartered for cloth, beads, guns and other European goods. These chiefs became very rich from this trade. By the 1850s, each of the capitals of the four main Cokwe chiefs contained over 1,000 inhabitants. The Atlantic slave trade also resulted in tribal laws being undermined, since the purpose of punishment was no longer justice, but to get slaves. Wars were also fought in order to acquire captives to enslave and sell them to the European traders. As a result, powerful chiefs became tyrants who displayed human skulls on their houses in order to rule their people through fear and intimidation.

2.3 West and Central Africa, the areas from which Africans were captured and brought to the Caribbean

We can divide the factors that made Africa an attractive source of labour into four categories:

- geography – the physical features of a landscape, such as rivers, mountains, as well as the climate
- ecology – how humans interact with their physical environment, including its animals and plants
- technology – the kinds of tools and machines a society uses
- economics – the goods people produce to consume and to trade.

Each of these factors affects the other, since mountain barriers, rivers and climate determine ecology; how humans interact with their environment shapes technology; and technology influences the goods people produce for trade.

Geographical factors

- Geography meant that Africa was well placed for cheap trans-shipment of slaves by Europeans to the New World.
- The triangular trade – of coffee, cotton, sugar, rum and tobacco from the New World to Europe; manufactured goods from Europe to Africa; and slaves from Africa to the New World – took only a few months and the Atlantic passage did not have winds or currents which made the journey too perilous.
- Africa's rivers had many rapids and waterfalls, so it was not possible to travel on them for long distances. West Africans therefore never had any reason to build boats.
- Even on the coast, the heavy surf and 200-mile-long sandbar along the 'Slave Coast' of Dahomey and Togoland had stymied any development of advanced boat-building technology.
- Only light well-built canoes, used mainly for fishing, were common.

Ecological factors

- Ecology, which has to do with the relationship between living things and their physical environment, also made Africans suitable for labour in the tropical climate.
- Africans were accustomed to heat and resistant to yellow fever and malaria.
- They were experienced farmers, who knew how to use ploughs and hoes. At the same time, poor soils in Africa limited their own agricultural productivity.

FAST FACTS

- The factor of disease also prevented Europeans from travelling far beyond Africa's coast, since white people had no resistance to African microbes.
- As the Europeans could not invade and settle within Africa, they had to depend on African rulers to supply them with slaves. The rulers therefore had a profit motive, which made them capture more slaves.
- If farming in Africa had been more advanced, a farm labourer would have been more valuable than a slave, so there would have been less reason for rulers to sell a labourer to European slave traders.
- Before the invention of machines, advanced farming required large domesticated animals. The equatorial Africa's tsetse flies, which carried trypanosomes to which African mammals are resistant, were deadly to Eurasian and North African livestock, such as cows, horses, sheep and goats. Disease therefore also had a second effect: it prevented the spread of livestock, which could have improved farming techniques in African societies. Large African animals, such as the rhinoceros and the zebra, were too fierce to be tamed.

Vaccination an injection which gives immunity to a disease.

Parasitic referring to an organism which lives in or on another organism and gets its nutrients at the other organism's expense.

Main diseases prevalent in Africa in the 15th and 16th centuries

- Malaria is spread by mosquitoes and thrives in tropical climates.
- Yellow fever is also transmitted by mosquitoes and therefore also prevalent in tropical climates. An infected mosquito spreads yellow fever from one person to the next. There is no cure for yellow fever and vaccination is the main way of trying to reduce outbreaks.
- Anklyostomaisis (hookworm) is an infection of the intestines by parasitic hookworms. These worms live in the intestine and ingest blood, thereby causing internal bleeding.

> Schistosomiasis is caused by parasitic worms. It is also called 'snail fever' as freshwater snails may be a carrier of the parasite. It is spread through contact with water.

- Disease also affected the demand for African slaves. In the New World, as outlined in Chapter 1, Amerindians were struck down by European diseases for which they had no resistance. After the Amerindians began dying out, Spanish colonists wrote to the newly elevated King Charles asking for black slaves. In 1518, Judge Alonso Zuazo sent a letter to Charles V suggesting that a general licence be given for the 'import of negros, ideal people for the work here, in contrast to the natives, who are so feeble that they are only suitable for light work' (Thomas, 1997: pg 97). Permission was granted, and the slaves were supplied by Portuguese traders.

FAST FACTS

- It took some time for other Europeans to start buying African slaves. In the colonies owned by the English Crown, for example, Africans were not the first choice of labourers for the New World. The first workers in the Anglophone Caribbean were white servants, and by the late 17th century most of them were English prisoners brought to the New World to finish off their jail terms.
- Young men were sometimes kidnapped from streets of British cities such as Liverpool and Bristol and shipped off to work on plantations. People snatched in this manner were said to have been 'barbadosed', a slang term which tells you how rich and famous Barbados was at that time. These labourers worked for just a few years, after which their contracts ended, or their lives in the tropical climate did, or they escaped.
- In 1640 a group of Barbadian planters visited Dutch plantations in Brazil and were very impressed with the hardiness of the African slaves.
- The English soon became the largest traders of slaves in the world.

Technological factors

- Technology, however, could be considered the most important single factor in determining why Africans were favoured for chattel slavery in the New World.
- Four years after Vasco da Gama reached East Africa he returned with a cannon-filled fleet of ships to take over the port of Kilwa, which was the main transit point for Zimbabwe's gold exports.
- Between 1471 and 1500, Portuguese traders exported about 17 tons of gold from Africa.
- The Europeans' superior weapons would have allowed easy conquest of any African tribe or city if diseases did not stop them sending an army inland.
- The main advantage of European technology was that the Europeans could manufacture goods more cheaply than Africans.
- Africans did have a fairly developed manufacturing capability. They wove their own cloth, and the people in the Sahel region had started making steel in high-temperature furnaces 2,000 years before Europeans discovered the process in the 19th century. Most African households had metal knives, spears, axes and hoes, and African goldsmiths' skills reportedly surpassed the Europeans'.

FAST FACTS

- By the time Europeans reached Africa, their technical advances made both cloth and iron cheaper to produce or trade.
- Glass beads came from Venice, spiced wine and conch shells from the Canary Islands and swords from Spain. African rulers took these goods in exchange for slaves.
- The main item the Europeans traded for the slaves was cloth – and three quarters of the value of trade goods bound for Africa was textiles.
- Most of this cloth was made in England but Indian calicoes were traded as well.
- Non-textile items mainly included raw iron, firearms and cowrie shells.
- Brass goods from Germany, such as pots and basins, were especially popular among African rulers and their wives, and brass bracelets from Bavaria were made specifically to barter for slaves.

Did you know?

The main goods manufactured in Europe in 15th and 16th centuries were:

- textiles – woollen textiles and cloths which were exported within Europe
- wine
- foodstuffs such as butter and cheese
- manufactured items such as cutlery, brass rods, guns, utensils and glassware
- iron and iron products.

The advanced technology of Europe meant that African slaves were worth less to African rulers than European goods, and it also meant that European goods were less valuable to Europeans than African slaves. A slave bought in Africa could be sold for a 200% profit in the Americas. Additionally, African slaves were cheaper to use than English labour on the sugar estates. The wealth brought in by the Atlantic slave trade was so great that, on the coast of West Africa, several fishing villages on the estuary of the Niger almost attained the status of city-states.

Roleplay

Imagine that you are a European merchant. You want to get involved in the trade in enslaved Africans but you have to convince your wife and children that it will be beneficial to the family. Prepare a speech that you will make to them over dinner.

Economic factors

Economics also dictated the need for slaves when the Caribbean islands began growing sugar. This is because sugar cane is a crop which requires many human labourers, so a cheap and plentiful source of slaves or servants had to be found if sugar planters were to make the maximum profit. This was the main advantage of using Africans, since Europeans and Asians were either not plentiful or would have been too expensive to ship from their homelands. The grants started by Charles V allowed the first sugar mill to be built in Puerto Rico in 1523, and by 1530 there were 3,000 slaves on the island and just 327 whites.

Economic principles state that supply increases to meet demand. This was what happened with slaves from Africa. African rulers did not usually sell people from their own tribe, save as a severe punishment, but the different tribal groups were rivals and often at war. So, although enemies were often taken as slaves during tribal wars in Africa, particularly by powerful tribes such as the Dahomey and Ashanti, it appears that after the Europeans started buying slaves there was an increase in the number of wars made by African tribes on one another for the purpose of kidnapping under the guise of taking prisoners. This was not the case everywhere. The kings of Dahomey and Ashanti, when asked in the late 18th century if they waged wars to get slaves, denied this. In Central Africa though, the constant raids by the Lunda people on their neighbours, or the Jagga tribe on theirs, seems to have been exacerbated by the European demand for slaves.

By the time slavery was abolished in the New World in the 19th century, slavery within black Africa had grown by an enormous degree. Between 33% and 50% of the population in the Sudan were slaves, as were 50% of the people in the Sokoto caliphate in northern Nigeria. In Zanzibar the number of slaves increased from 15,000 in 1818 to 100,000 in the 1860s. Slave employment also increased on plantations which produced palm oil, peanuts and cotton for export.

FAST FACTS

- One scholar (Patterson, *Slavery and Social Death*, Harvard University Press, 1990) wrote that, based on the latest historical evidence, of the 1.6 million Africans brought to the New World before the end of the 17th century, as many as 60% may have been the captives of genuine warfare, while slightly less than 33% were kidnapped.
- Patterson also notes that of the estimated 7.4 million transported between 1701 and 1810, the proportions

were approximately reversed – that is, over 70% were kidnapped and under 20% were the victims of genuine wars.

- In the 19th century, a little over 60% of slaves brought to the New World were kidnapped, while a little under 30% were genuine prisoners of war (Patterson, pg 120).
- Another piece of evidence that the slave trade increased slavery in Africa is that slaves had cost less before the Europeans came. The average price per slave in 1601 was £3. Between 1701 and 1732 it was £10, and between 1773 and 1775 it went up to £15 – a five-fold increase since 1601 (Maddison: pg 223).

Trans-Atlantic trade in enslaved Africans

When Europeans arrived in Africa, Africans were growing just five sets of crops. These included barley and wheat in Northern Africa, which had a more temperate climate and more fertile soils than other parts of Africa. Sorghum and pearl millet were cultivated in the Sahel zone, coffee and teff in Ethiopia, bananas and Asian yams in East Africa and African yams and kola nuts in West Africa.

Sorghum a type of cereal which is a major source of grain, native to warm areas of the Old World.

Teff an African cereal, used to make flour, which is mainly grown in Ethiopia.

No one person owned land. Instead, tribes and kin-groups had traditional rights to farm or graze the areas they settled in. Unlike in Europe and Asia, chiefs and rulers did not collect taxes or charge rents for land use. Instead, slaves were the only real form of private property and they were usually obtained by raids or wars on other tribes. This meant that there was a supply of slaves ready to sell when the Europeans first came to Africa.

Chattel slavery a form of slavery in which the enslaved person is considered as property to be bought and sold.

Roleplay

Imagine that you are an African boy or girl who has recently been captured and taken away from your home to work as a slave. Describe how you were captured in your village and how you were taken to the slave ship.

Between 1519 and the late 1860s, 11 to 12 million people were taken from the continent to be sold to European slave traders. The slave trade from Africa to the Arab lands, which had started five centuries earlier, accounted for 14 million more.

FAST FACTS

These are the approximate numbers of enslaved Africans who were transported from West Africa to the Americas.

Region	Total number	Percentage
Brazil	4,000,000	35.4
Spanish Empire	2,500,000	22.1
British West Indies	2,000,000	17.7
French West Indies	1,600,000	14.1
United States of America	500,000	4.4
Dutch West Indies	500,000	4.4
Danish West Indies	280,000	0.2

The Portuguese slave traders, as you have read, came first. French ships started raiding off the African coast in the 1530s, but the first record of a French slave ship is of L'Espérance, which in 1594 took slaves from Gabon to Brazil. The Dutch arrived last, in 1599, but they soon had 20 ships sailing every year to Africa to obtain slaves. Of the Africans they obtained, 80% went to Brazil and the Caribbean, while the rest were sent to Spanish North America and South America. By 1580, slaves made up 50% of all people being transported to the New World; by 1700, they made up 75% and by 1820 the figure was 90%.

The slave trade was well organized. The slave traders often relied on African middle men such as canoe owners to transport the slaves from the coast to the ships.

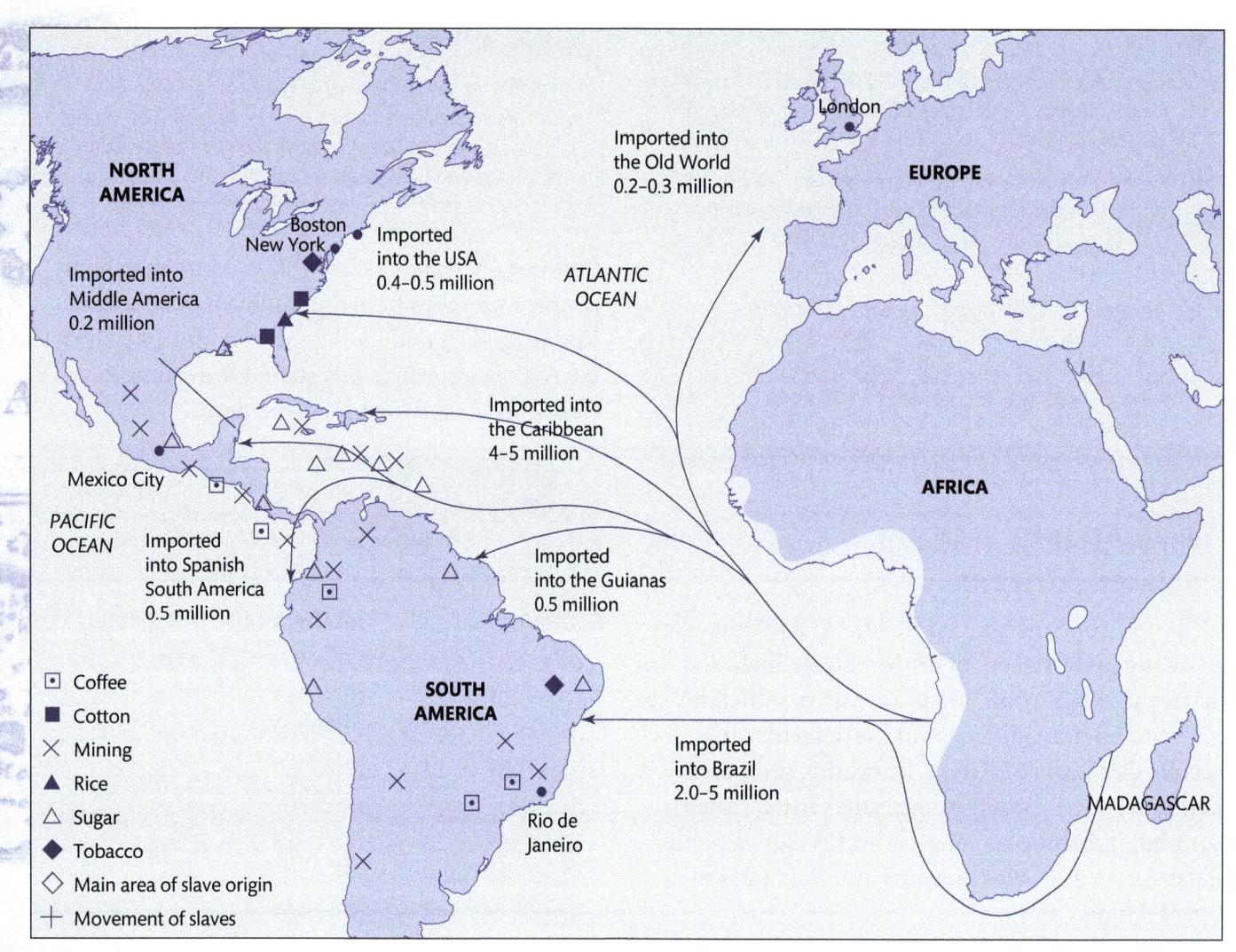

2.4 Trade in enslaved Africans

Table 2.2 Africans transported across the Atlantic

Years	Number per year
1662–80	9,000
1760–89	76,000
1816–30	61,000
1831–50	51,000
1851–65	10,500

Source: Maddison, 2007: pg 223

Activity 2.3

Use Table 2.2 to answer the following questions.

a Why was there such a large increase in the number of enslaved Africans transported across the Atlantic from 1680 to 1760?

b Why do you think the number of enslaved Africans transported across the Atlantic dropped from 51,000 in the period from 1831 to 1850 to 10,500 between 1851 and 1865?

The European slave traders got most of their slaves by buying them from African rulers or merchants. Only a few were obtained by kidnapping. Apart from this, there were many ways a person in Africa became a slave: as a prisoner of war; as a punishment for some crime; or from poverty, when a person was in debt, or when poor parents sold their children. People were even enslaved just because they were considered unusual – such individuals included twins, the mothers of twins, deformed children and girls who had early menstruation.

It is not certain, however, which of the methods of obtaining slaves was most prevalent. In 1721, the

Royal African Company (RAC) held an inquiry on the matter, ordering its agents in Africa to find out whether the slaves they were buying had been enslaved in any other manner than 'being taken prisoners in war time'. This was an issue of concern to Europeans, since enslaving war prisoners was considered more morally acceptable than enslaving people who had been kidnapped specifically to be sold into slavery. However, the RAC also wanted to remain on good terms with the African rulers and buying their kidnapped people might have jeopardized that relationship. The RAC inquiry did not result in any conclusive evidence, though. At a similar inquiry held in Britain in 1789, one slave captain said:

> 'How such a number of slaves are procured is circumstance which I believe no European was ever fully acquainted with. The best information is that great numbers are prisoners taken in war… many are sold for witchcraft and other real or imputed crimes; and are purchased with European goods and salt.'
> Thomas 1997: pg 372

Such testimonies were just opinion though, as the captain noted. However, in the 1850s, a statistical analysis of Africans brought to Sierra Leone, which was then a colony of freed slaves, was carried out to determine how they had become enslaved. These figures showed that 34% were, in fact, war prisoners, but 30% had been kidnapped by other Africans and sold to the Europeans. Another 11% had become slaves after being found guilty of a crime the main crime being adultery. The rest had been sold to pay debts or by relatives. Many of these slaves were obtained at fairs, which had been in existence long before the arrival of the Europeans. In the late 18th century, in Bambarena in Senegambia, the local ruler had set up an entire village where captives were held until they could be sold. In what is now Nigeria, there was an island market at the confluence of the Niger and Benue rivers, where 11,000 slaves were sold every year, some for the Atlantic slave trade, others for the Arab trade.

2.5 Africa: slave canoe, 1849. An embarkation canoe used by West African slave traders to transport slaves from the shore to ocean-going vessels lying off in deeper water. Wood engraving, English, 1849

The trip to the slave forts

From the interior of Africa, the slaves walked hundreds of miles to the coast. They were usually in groups of a hundred, two or three of them bound to one another with irons from the left leg of one person attached to the right leg of another. Another method was to tie 30 or 40 together with a rope, perhaps linking four people together at the neck. Apart from being under guard, the captives were sometimes forced to carry goods, such as water or ivory or hides. They would be made to walk from dawn till early afternoon, when the day became hottest, usually covering about 20 miles. The long journey often took its toll on the captives – many died from malnutrition, exhaustion, exposure to the heat or dysentery.

2.6 Slave port, Badagry, Nigeria

2.7 African captives walking to a slave ship for sale to Europeans

One French slave ship captain wrote:

> '[These people were] severely and barbarously treated by their masters, who… beat them inhumanely, as may be seen by the scabs and wounds on the bodies of many of them when sold to us. They scarcely allow them the least rag to cover their nakedness.'
>
> Thomas, 1997: pg 382

There are slave forts that still stand on the coast of modern-day Ghana, where slaves were brought to be checked by physicians before boarding the waiting ship. The first fort was built by the Portuguese in 1482, although it was first used mainly as a base to attack the Ashanti gold mines. In the fort's main building, the corridor in which the chained slaves walked to the hall was set on the outside wall of the building and was so narrow that people could only walk single-file. This discouraged escape attempts. The holding cell below the fort, where the slaves were imprisoned until it was time to board, had a hole concealed in the roof just outside the door, where a spy who spoke African languages could hide and then inform the slave traders about escape plots.

It was not until the 17th century that the Dutch, British and French started competing with the Portuguese in the slave trade.

2.8 D'Estrees Fort, Goree Island, near modern day Dakar, Senegal, West Africa

2.9 Examples of chains and shackles

2.10 Branding irons

Activity 2.4

Find out more about slave forts using the following as a guideline.

- Find the names of four main forts and the countries in which they can be found.
- Give a description of these forts with the help of photographs.
- Explain the importance of the forts today to the countries in which they are located.

As with the Portuguese and the Spanish, the English Crown oversaw the slave trade. Although English ships had been trading in Africa since the 1530s, they only brought back goods such as gold, ivory and Guinea pepper at first. It was Captain John Hawkins who in 1562 started the English slave trade. Hawkins's father, William, was the first Englishman to sail into the dangerous waters of the Bight of Benin on the western Africa coast, in 1553 and his son presumably learned from him about currents, geography and markets in Africa.

Queen Elizabeth, who approved Hawkins's expedition, told him not to take slaves who did not freely consent to leave their homeland since, she wrote, 'this would be detestable and call down the vengeance of Heaven upon the undertakers' (Thomas, 1997: pg 156). Hawkins sailed with three ships, and in the river Sierra Leone he seized 300 blacks from six Portuguese boats which were transporting them to the Cape Verde Islands. His investors reportedly made a good profit and on his second voyage, in 1564, Queen Elizabeth herself sent a ship with him, named the Jesus of Lübeck. Lübeck, located on the Baltic in Germany, was the world's leading port at the time. On this voyage Hawkins obtained 400 slaves through piracy and barter, and sold them at 60% profit in the island of Margarita off the Venezuelan coast and in Curaçao. When Hawkins received a knighthood in later years, his crest was the image of an African woman.

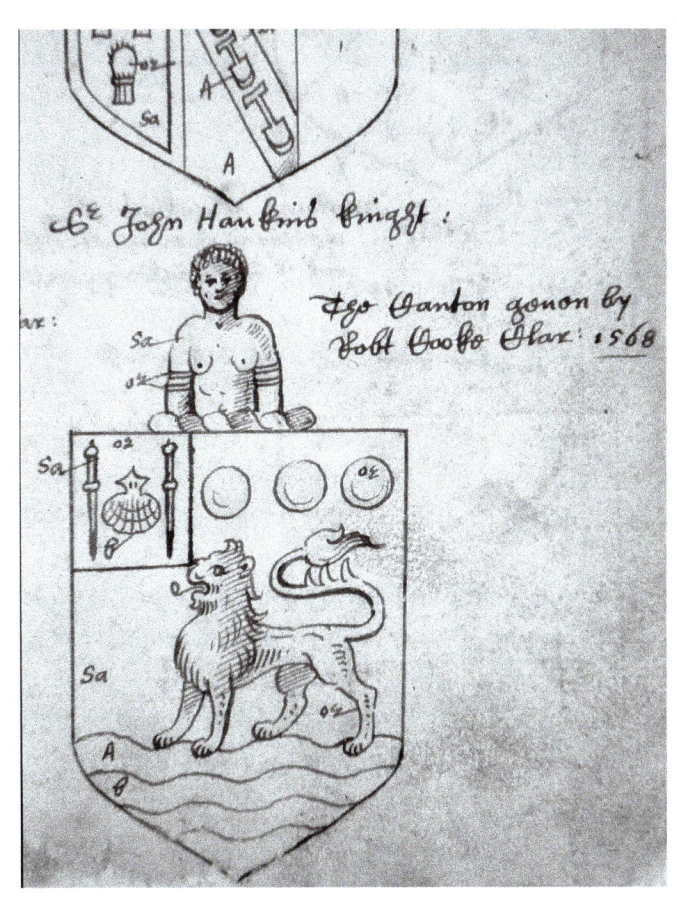

2.11 John Hawkins's coat of arms

> **Roleplay**
> Imagine that you were captured in Africa and taken on board a slave ship. Write a paragraph or two describing the time you spent on board from Africa to the Caribbean.

By the 17th century, the English Crown was attempting to organize the slave trade so it could get as much revenue from it as possible. The main company which handled this business at first was the Royal African Company (RAC). The King, Charles II, gave this company the exclusive right for one thousand years to trade in African slaves.

Joint-stock company a company whose stock is owned jointly by the investors.

FAST FACTS

Joint-stock companies

- The term 'company' was first used about groups of actors who performed in London theatres.
- The first joint-stock company, which was a commercial venture like modern firms, was created in 1555. It was called the Muscovy Company.
- In 1579, the Eastland Company traded in the Baltic.
- The Levant Company, formed in 1581, traded in the eastern Mediterranean which was linked to the valuable routes of Asia.
- In 1588, the Guinea Company for West Africa was founded.
- The most powerful company of all was the East India Company, set up in 1600, which dealt with the Indian sub-continent and the Spice Islands.

Despite this optimism, and despite having eminent investors such as the philosopher John Locke, the RAC only operated from 1672 to 1698. In those 26 years, however, the company shipped 750,000 slaves – almost 29,000 human beings per year. One in six did not survive the trip, and the death rate was even higher among white crew members. In fact, the RAC's records show that 60% of its personnel died in the first year and 80% by the second year, with only one in 10 being discharged alive (Bernstein, 2008: pg 273).

The middle passage the journey from the coast of Africa to the New World.

Although slaves were the main cargo of the middle passage, the shorter hauls also yielded significant profits: indigo was sent from Jamaica to Philadelphia, corn to London, wool from London to Le Havre and French silks to Africa. So trading in human beings was not the only option open to merchants – it was just the most profitable.

In the early 17th century, Dutch ships became essential for trade in the Caribbean. The Dutch had set up slave forts in West Africa and by the mid-17th century they were the main suppliers of enslaved Africans to the Caribbean plantations. The Dutch economy was based on marine trade and the Dutch had established trading posts in St Martin, St Croix and Curaçao. In 1621 the Dutch West India Company was formed to trade directly with non-Dutch colonies in the region. Without Dutch traders, the British, French and Spanish colonists would have found Caribbean life far harder. These traders supplied the settlers and planters with goods and capital, and also bought sugar in the colonies for transport to Europe.

However, the British and French governments soon became concerned over this Dutch dominance which, in their view, was putting wealth from their colonies into Dutch hands. As a result, they passed laws which were meant to ensure that goods were traded exclusively between the colonies and the mother country – that is, British colonies would trade only with Britain and French colonies only with France, and vice-versa. This system was called 'mercantilism'.

In Britain, the mercantile system was started in the 1650s (although it was not actually called this until Adam Smith, the founder of modern economics, coined the term in his 1776 book *The Wealth of Nations*). Navigation Laws were passed in 1650 and 1651, forbidding non-English ships from trading with British colonies. Only British ships, sailing from a port in England, were allowed to carry colonial goods. These laws set off a war between Holland and England in 1652. Another Navigation Act was passed in 1660, which listed the colonial products that could be shipped directly only to England, Ireland or another English colony. These included sugar (until 1739), indigo and tobacco, and in the 18th century rice and molasses were added to the list.

> **What problems did Caribbean planters face in shipping sugar to Europe?**
> - Laws were passed by the British and French governments which were meant to ensure that goods were traded exclusively between the colonies and the mother country – i.e. British colonies would trade only with Britain and French colonies only with France, and vice-versa. This restricted trade with European countries other than Britain and France. (Navigation Laws of 1650 and 1660).
> - High cost of shipping to Europe
> - Competition from sugar which was sold on the world market at a lower cost such as sugar produced in India and Cuba.

This policy actually harmed the British economy, because it forced up freight prices, hence making English manufactured goods less competitive. The tightening of the laws in 1764 also sparked off the American Revolution. The Navigation Laws were repealed in 1849 and 1854.

In France, similar laws were passed in 1661, mainly because the French government wanted to break Dutch dominance over French colonies in the Caribbean. In Guadeloupe and Martinique, for example, 90% of merchant vessels supplying the islands were Dutch. A law, known as 'l'Exclusif' (exclusivity) was passed banning foreigners from owning property in the French colonies. This was aimed specifically at the Dutch, who had extensive investments in sugar mills and warehouses in the French-owned islands. A French West India company was formed, which had exclusive trading rights with all French colonies in the Caribbean. As a result, French shipping expanded from involving four ships in 1662 to just over 200 ships in 1683. However, the policy did not prevent the Dutch from continuing to trade with French colonies.

The middle passage

In the 17th century, with good weather, the trip for Portuguese slavers from Angola to Bahia, in Brazil, took around 35 days. By the 18th century, with larger vessels and better sails, the journey across the South Atlantic usually took no more than a month. For the French and British, the middle passage from West Africa to the Caribbean took between 60 and 70 days.

Slave ships usually carried between 300 and 400 captives per trip. Overcrowding was common. While the men were manacled to the slave deck, the women and children huddled together in a back cabin and slept on top of one another, or were separated from the men by a partition at the main mast.

The slave deck was located between the hold and the main deck. Some ships even had a second tier to hold more slaves. The captives were placed in a space five feet three inches high and four feet four inches wide. They were arranged in a spoon fashion, so it was impossible for them to turn or otherwise change position (called 'tight packing'). Written accounts of conditions aboard these ships note a heat so intense that many of the captives fainted, and a stink so high that it caused nausea and vomiting. Many deaths resulted from malnutrition.

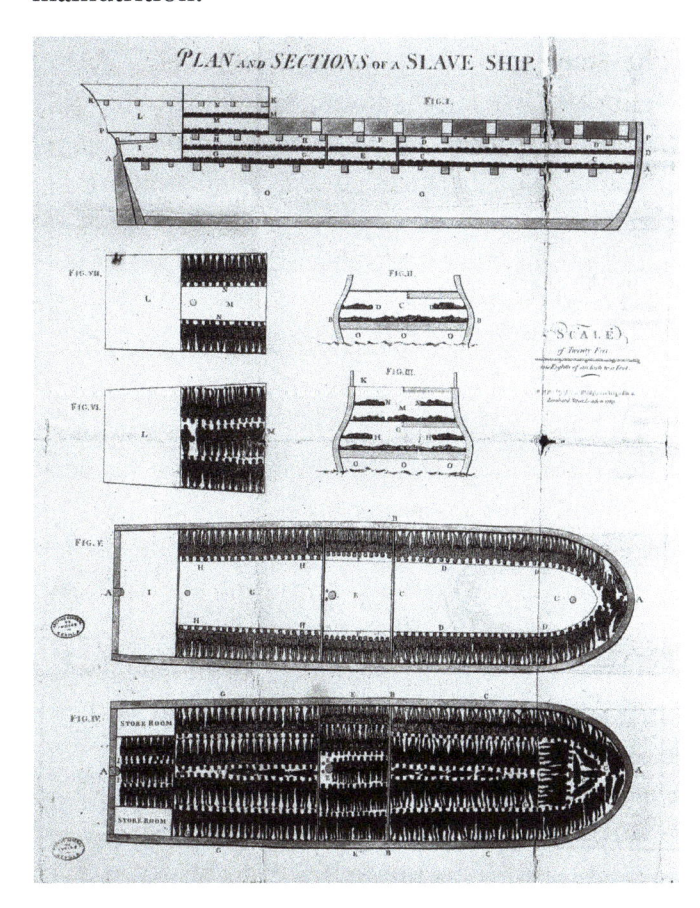

2.12 Plan of a slave ship

The conditions of this journey were so harsh that it is amazing that any of the captives survived at all. An officer from the slave ship Alexander, testifying before the British Parliament, said of the ship's captain:

> 'When employed in stowing the slaves, he made the most of the room and wedged them in. They had not so much room as a man in his coffin, either in length or in breadth. It was impossible for them to turn or shift… he says he cannot conceive of any situation so dreadful and disgusting as that of the slaves when ill of the flux: in the Alexander, the deck was covered with blood and mucus, and resembled a slaughterhouse. The stench and foul air were intolerable.'
> Bernstein, 2008: pg 275

When still in sight of Africa, male slaves were kept chained in pairs, right ankle to the left ankle of the next man. One 17th century report says that the Africans would throw themselves into the sea, or hit their heads against the ship or refuse to eat. They were only allowed on the upper deck after eight days, when no land was in sight. At this point the captives were organized in groups to clean the ship and made to sing while doing so. Heated vinegar in pails was used to scrub decks with brooms, which was then washed down with cold vinegar.

The food varied according to the nationality of the ship. The Portuguese fed the captives cassava, the English and Dutch gave them corn, while the French provided oats. Rice, millet, kidney beans, plantains, yams, coconuts, limes, potatoes and oranges were usually stocked. The crew ate the same food as the captives. The ration per day was: 3½ pounds of yam, 10 ounces of biscuit, 3½ ounces of beans, 2 ounces of flour and a portion of salted beef. The captives were also given a mouthwash of vinegar or lime juice to avoid scurvy.

On French boats a stew of oats was cooked daily in a large copper, with dried turtle meat or dried vegetables added. On English ships beans were boiled with lard or peas and ground Indian corn was boiled until thick, with salt, pepper and palm oil added. The food was given out to 10 slaves at a time, each portion in a small tub, with each slave given a wooden spoon to feed themselves. Meals were eaten on the main deck and forecastle by the male captives. The women remained on the quarterdeck, while the children were put on the poop. Meals were served twice a day, at 10 am and 5 pm.

Activity 2.5 Sketch an outline of a typical slave ship and label the parts mentioned above.

The amount of food was often less than what was needed by the already malnourished Africans. They were also provided with two to three pints of water a day. This would have been enough for normal consumption, but the captives sweated excessively in the heat and many of them also got dysentery which caused dehydration. One third of deaths were, directly and indirectly, caused by diarrhoea. Violence also accounted for some deaths, since there was about one insurrection for every eight to 10 journeys. The mortality rates on board slave ships was between 3% and 30% and the usual ratio was probably around nine out of every hundred people in the 18th century (Thomas, 1997: pg 419).

Arrival in the Caribbean

When the enslaved Africans arrived in the Caribbean colony, they were comparatively well treated – at least for a few days. They were fed and allowed to relax, all for the purpose of ensuring that they were in the best condition to be sold in the slave market. In St Domingue, they were often given liquor to make them cheerful. In Martinique, they would bathe in the sea and rub their bodies with palm oil. In Jamaica, the sick slaves were bathed in water with supposedly curative herbs (what is called a 'bush bath'), given two meals a day and rum to drink.

The captured Africans were sold either by 'scramble' or by auction. In a scramble, a signal would be given, such as drum beat, and the buyers would rush among the slaves, choosing the ones they wanted and having them dragged away at once.

This caused much anguish among the slaves, who would be separated from their friends and family. An auction was conducted in the usual manner, with the slaves being brought up on a platform and the buyers bidding for one or several at a time. The planter rarely paid the full price at once though. Instead, he would buy on credit, perhaps paying a quarter of the price in cash or goods, with the rest to be paid off within a year to 18 months.

Those slaves who were not sold, either because of illness or deformities or some other reason, were simply left in the ports, often to die.

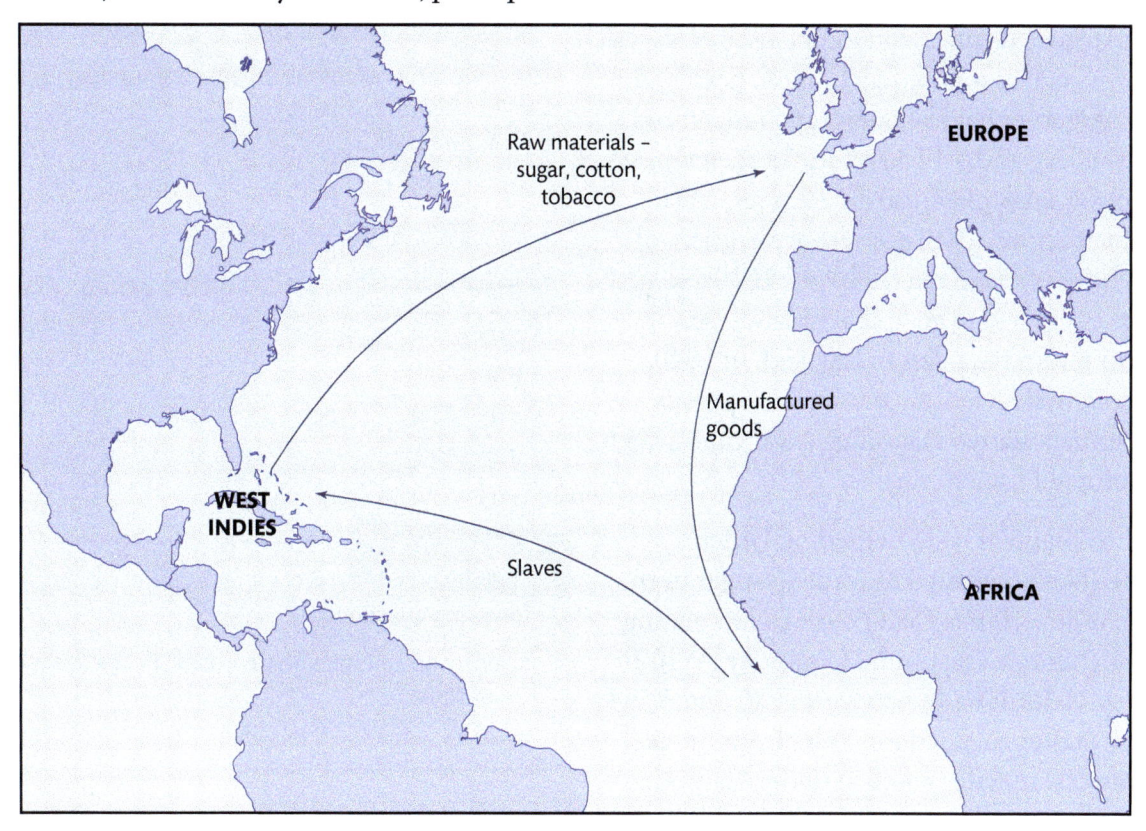

2.13 The middle passage

Activity 2.6

Olaudah Equiano is the author of *The Interesting Narrative of the Life of O. Equiano or G. Vasa, the African... written by himself*. The book became very popular during the British Anti-Slavery movement in Britain. There have been many claims that Equiano was actually born in the USA. Whatever the case, his accounts of 'life under slavery' is very descriptive and can give us a more visual idea of the enslaved experience. Read the following account and the answer the questions that follow.

'I was soon put down under the decks, and there I received such a salutation in my nostrils as I had never experienced in my life: so that, with the loathsomeness of the stench, and crying together, I became so sick and low that I was not able to eat, nor had I the least desire to taste anything. I now wished for the last friend, death, to relieve me; but soon, to my grief, two of the white men offered me eatables; and, on my refusing to eat, one of them held me fast by the hands, and laid me across I think the windlass, and tied my feet, while the other flogged me severely. I have never experienced anything of this kind before; and although, not being used to the water, I naturally feared that element the first time I saw it, yet nevertheless, could I have got over the nettings, I would have jumped over the side, but I could not; and besides, the crew used to watch us very closely who were not chained down to the decks, lest we should leap into the water: and I have seen some of these poor African prisoners most severely cut for attempting to do so, and hourly whipped for not eating. This indeed was often the case with myself.'

- Give two reasons why Equiano was unable to eat.
- Why do you think he was unable to 'jump over the side'?
- State three ways in which the enslaved Africans were controlled on board the ship.
- Equiano was 11 years old at this time. Would the experience of enslavement be worse for an adult or a child?

The plantation economy – sugar

In 1623, the British claimed the small Caribbean island of St Christopher (now St Kitts). This was the English Crown's first West Indian property. In 1627, the Earl of Carlisle won a patent to Barbados from the Crown and distributed the land to 764 settlers. These grants ranged from 30 to 1,000 acres. The first immigrant farmers planted food for themselves, as well as cash crops such as tobacco and cotton. Each of the new landholders got paid labourers and indentured servants from England, who in return for their service were promised small plots, usually 10 acres, when their contracts ended. With an average estate size of 200 acres, however, land ran out by the 1630s, so new immigrants either had to go to other islands, stay in Barbados or return penniless to England. In 1640, however, colonists once again became prosperous when the farmers started cultivating sugar cane, which had been brought from Suriname.

The English planters were helped by Dutch entrepreneurs who wanted to trade in sugar even though their government had passed a law stating that only the Dutch West India Company (WIC) could do so. Additionally, between 1645 and 1654, Portuguese settlers evicted the WIC from Brazil. Jewish growers, unwilling to live under Catholic rulers since they had been oppressed by the Catholic Church in the past, came with their technical expertise in sugar cultivation to the Caribbean. Their ejection from Brazil also reduced the amount of sugar in Europe, so Barbados had a waiting market for its new crop. Development of the sugar industry in Barbados was rapid, and, by 1660, Barbados had more settlers than Virginia or Massachusetts in the USA. In fact, the population density in Barbados was 400 inhabitants per square mile, which was four times the population density of England. Between 1663 and 1775, consumption of sugar in England rose by 20 times. Nearly all this sugar was supplied by plantations in the Americas. As more people in Europe began using sugar, the price went down but demand was so great that profits remained high. Sugar was thus the ideal product in having high demand and an affordable price. Table 2.3 gives calculations of what sugar cost in modern US dollars and shows how the price went down over two centuries.

FAST FACTS

The features of the plantation economy were:

- large-scale cultivation
- monoculture (production of one crop)
- that it was export oriented – the produce was meant for European markets
- that it was labour intensive.

Table 2.3 A history of sugar prices

Period	US$ per kg
1350–1400	$24
1400–1450	$16
1450–1500	$12
1500–1550	$6

Activity 2.7

Work with a partner to answer the following questions.

a Why do you think there was a change in the price of sugar?

b What impact did this change have on the colonies?

Population density the number of people living per unit, for example per square mile, in an area.

Barbados was soon the largest sugar producer in the Caribbean, supplying two thirds of England's consumption. English farmers owned their own land or paid rent, hired their own labour and kept their profits. This gave them more incentive to produce than their larger competitors in Brazil and the Greater Antilles, where overseers and managers ran the estates or in which small farmers sent their cane to the landowner's mill and got only a fraction of the sugar to sell.

By the 1640s, however, many of the first settlers in Barbados had made enough money to retire as wealthy aristocrats to England, often selling their plantations to the younger sons of England's land-owning aristocracy who, although poor since they had

2.14 Sugar production in a sugar factory in the West Indies, circa 1760

little or no inheritance, could obtain credit because of their family connections. By 1680, Barbados was no longer profitable due to falling sugar prices, soils exhausted by over-cultivation, and because its tropical forests had been cleared to make space for the sugar plantations. Many of the planters went to North America, where they started new plantations and a new slave society (Bernstein, 2008: pg 268).

The organization of a typical sugar plantation

Each building was located in a specific area, according to its purpose. Each plantation functioned as both a farm and a factory as the crop was grown and produced within the plantation. The buildings and labour force were organized in a specific manner, planned to maximize profits as far as possible.

The 'great house' was the main residence of the planter and his family. It was normally two stories high. The first floor comprised wooden living quarters, elaborately furnished. There was usually a large central hall with smaller dining, sitting and banquet rooms. Most of the great houses had large verandahs all along one side of the house. The bottom floor was often used as a storm shelter, a stronghold in case of revolts, and a storage shed.

The house was usually made of roughly cut stones and wood. It was located on a hill so that the residents would have a clear view of the plantation in case of revolts, for example.

The mill was the building where the sugar cane was crushed and the juice extracted. There were three types of mill in the Caribbean.

- Water mills were found mostly in Cuba, British Guiana, Jamaica and the Windward Islands. These were the most efficient mills but not always reliable.

- Windmills were found mostly in Barbados and the Leeward Island. While these were the cheapest mills, they were less popular because they depended on the prevalence of wind – otherwise they had to be turned using animal power.

2.15 Layout of a typical West Indian sugar plantation showing the main areas of activity:
(A) the main house on the hill, (B) the fields, (C) the mill, (D) the boiling houses, (E) the slaves' huts

2.16 A sugar plantation in the West Indies, probably the French colony of St Domingue (Haiti), depicting the planter's house at top right (1), the slaves' quarters at bottom right (2), the cane field in the centre (3) and the sugar mill at bottom left (4). Colour French engraving, 18th century

- Animal mills – both water and windmills could also be turned with animal power (mainly from cattle). These were the most reliable types of mill and so the most common.

The boiling and curing houses were situated near to the mill. They were normally made from roughly cut stones to withstand heat and regular use. The furnaces were located here and the cane juice was boiled to produce sugar crystals.

The distillery or still house was where the molasses was taken. Rum was produced there.

The hospital was meant to cater to the needs of the Europeans on the plantation. It was normally a one-room small shack, poorly stacked with medicine.

The barracks were where the enslaved population was housed on the plantations. These were long, poorly constructed cabin-like structures where the enslaved were packed into tightly enclosed spaces. For the most part, the slaves only slept here. The barracks were located close to the cane fields and the mills so that time would not be wasted moving slaves from one location to the other.

In addition to the buildings, each plantation had spaces allocated as 'provision grounds'. The slaves were allowed to grow their own food here, working the ground in whatever free time they were given and on Sundays. This was meant to decrease the cost of feeding the enslaved population – if slaves produced their own food it would cost the planters less than if they had to import food from abroad.

Each plantation had a woodland area which provided fuel for the great house as well as the mills, curing house and distillery; pasture land for the animals which were used to drive the mills or as a food source; and large tracts of sugar-cane fields.

Categories of enslaved Africans

1 **Skilled slaves** included, for example, masons, carpenters, wheelwrights, factory workers (boilers, distillers or potters).
2 **Non-praedial slaves or house slaves** comprised butlers, cooks, washer-women, coachmen, seamstresses and waiting maids, for example.
3 **Praedial slaves or field slaves** – this group was divided into three gangs.
    - **The first or great gang** included the strongest men and women who did all the heavy work, for example digging drains or cutting the cane.
- **The second gang** did the same work as the first gang but was made up of older slaves and pregnant women. Their work was lighter and they worked more slowly than the first gang.
- **The third gang** was also referred to as the hogmeat gang. It comprised children between the ages of four and 10. They were mainly responsible for feeding the smaller animals, weeding and collecting firewood.

Sugar is a relatively simple crop to grow. Once the soil is fertile and irrigated, planting cane is just a matter of digging shallow holes with hoes to put the stalks in. In about 15 months, the canes would be ready for harvesting and processing. This was the heaviest part of the work. Once cut, the canes were carried to the mill to where the juice was ground out of them. The sugar-cane juice was then boiled, skimmed and cooled. This process separated the brown crystals of sugar from the thick gooey molasses. This sugar was then exported to Europe to be refined; although, in time, some planters set up their own refining operations. The crushed stalks were used as fuel. A year later, a second harvest could be reaped from the stumps of the old canes. This yielded less sugar, but the process could be repeated three or four times before the field was exhausted (Thomas, 1997: pg 135–6).

However, despite its simplicity to cultivate, sugar is also a back-breaking crop to harvest and process. It wasn't grown in British North America, which used slave labour mainly for tobacco and cotton. Unlike those crops, sugar meant an early death for the enslaved Africans. In the grinding season, the factories ran around the clock, because cane juice goes sour unless it is crushed and boiled within 24 hours of being cut. The field slaves harvested

The manufacture of sugar

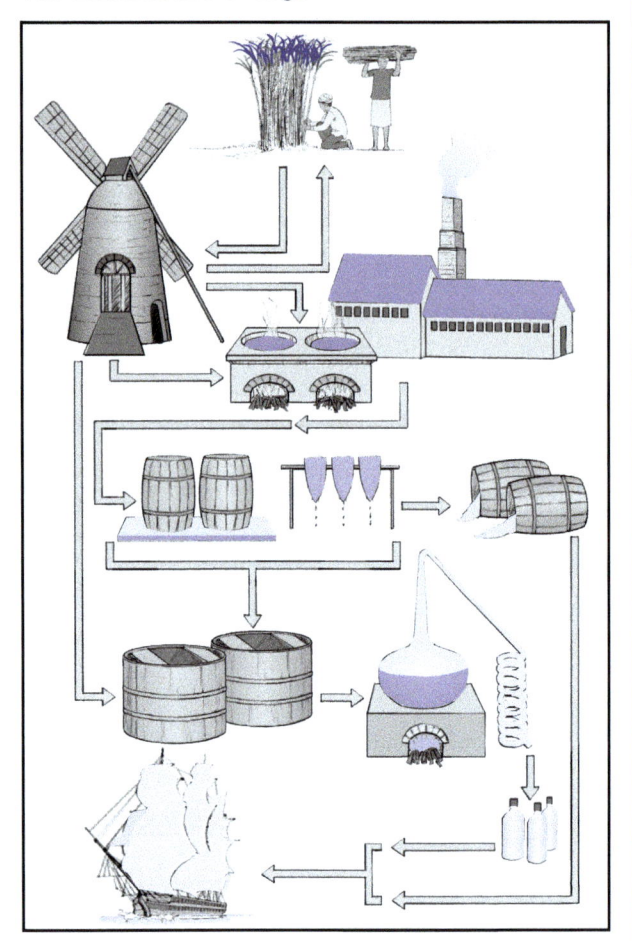

2.17 Steps in the process of manufacturing sugar

The sugar cane is harvested and transported by the slaves to the mills.

The juice is extracted through a process of crushing in the mill. The cane is crushed by huge rollers. The enslaved Africans feed the cane into the rollers by hand.

The juice is transported by wooden troughs from the mills to the storage cisterns in the boiling houses. Some is also sent to the fermentation vats.

The juice is crystallized in the boiling houses with the use of furnaces with copper kettles. The sugar crystals are collected in hogsheads. Some of the crystals are passed through sugar moulds to produce muscovado sugar.

The main by-product of sugar, molasses, is collected and sent to the fermentation vats where it is distilled with cane juice to produce rum.

Both the muscovado sugar and the rum are packed into hogsheads and transported to the port. From here it is shipped to Europe.

the cane which immediately went into the mills, followed by the boiler rooms, which were indeed boiling hot. As a result, overwork, malnutrition and disease killed so many slaves that new ones had to be brought in constantly just to keep the workforce at the same numbers.

A witness before the British House of Commons in 1790, which held an inquiry into the conditions of slaves in the West Indies, testified:

> 'All I ever understood was that purchasing slaves was much the cheapest method of keeping up their numbers; for the mother of a bred slave was taken from the field labour for three years, which labour was of more value than the cost of a prime slave or new Negro.'
> Thomas, 1997: pg 134

Rum

2.18 Hogsheads at a rum distillery in Martinique

Hogshead a wooden barrel.

Apart from sugar itself, rum was the most important product made from sugar cane, and Caribbean rum brands are still among the best-known liquor brands in the world today.

Rum is a distilled liquor which includes both the light-bodied rums, which were made mainly in Cuba and Puerto Rico, and heavier rums made in Jamaica, Guyana and Trinidad. Rum was invented in the Caribbean around the middle of the 17th century. The liquor so produced was called 'kill-devil' or 'rumbullion', but by 1667 was simply referred to as 'rum'. It was a key product of the middle passage: African slaves were traded for molasses, then the molasses was made into rum in New England and then the rum was traded to Africa for more slaves. British sailors received regular rations of rum from the 18th century until 1970.

Most rums are made from molasses. Some countries import molasses for use in rum production. All liquors are made by fermentation. The sugar required for fermentation is already present in the molasses, and rum retains more of the original raw-material taste than most other liquors. The flavour of specific rums is determined by the type of yeast employed for fermentation, the distillation method, ageing conditions and blending.

The first rums were heavy, dark and full bodied and had a strong molasses flavour. These rums are still produced in Jamaica, Barbados and Guyana. Such rums are usually made from molasses enriched with the skimmings, or dunder, remaining in the boilers used for sugar production. This liquid attracts yeast spores from the air and ferments naturally. The rum is distilled twice in pot stills, producing a distillate of clear colour that becomes golden hue as the distillate absorbs substances from the oak of the wooden puncheons used for storage during the ageing period. Caramel added after ageing deepens the colour. The Jamaican rums are always blended and are aged for at least five to seven years before being sold. They are usually marketed with an alcohol content of 43–49% by volume. New England rum, which has been made in the USA from Caribbean molasses since the 17th century, has strong flavour and high alcohol content.

The production of dry, light-bodied rums began in the late 19th century. This type of rum, produced mainly in Puerto Rico and the Virgin Islands, uses cultured yeast in fermentation, and distillation is done in modern stills. The rums are usually blended and are aged from one to four years. These 'white rums' are pale in colour and mild in flavour, while 'gold rums' have a more amber colour and a more pronounced flavour, because of the longer ageing process and the addition of caramel.

Apart from its use in alcoholic drinks, rum is frequently used as a flavouring in dessert sauces and other dishes. It is also used to flavour tobacco.

Activity 2.8

Describe, with the aid of a diagram or flowchart, how sugar and rum were produced.

FAST FACTS

- In the French island of St Domingue (now Haiti), for example, the slave population in 1763 was 206,539. Between 1764 and 1774, a further 102,474 slaves were brought to the island. That totals just over 300,000 people, but in 1776, because of the death rate, the slave population was around 290,000.
- Barbados had an even higher death rate for slaves: in 1764, there were just under 71,000 slaves on the island. Over the next 19 years, more than 40,000 slaves were imported. Yet in 1783, when a natural population should have been over 100,000 people, Barbados had a mere 62,000 slaves.
- Old age was, however, the main single cause of death for enslaved Africans, followed by lung disease, yaws and skin ulcers, heart and lymphatic diseases and dysentery.
- Africans born in the Caribbean had a better diet than native Africans. We know this because the former were taller than the latter, indicating better nutrition for mother and child. The slaves were fed about a half-pound of dried beef or saltfish daily and a pint of corn meal or rice. The slaves supplemented this diet with provisions and vegetables they grew themselves (yam, taro root, plantains and bananas).
- Nonetheless, enslaved Africans were often not fed enough for the hard labour they had to do. They only got 20 grams of fat from their diet, whereas the average requirement is 80–125 grams.
- Ironically, their most healthy period was during the harvest, when they were allowed to drink sugar-cane juice from the copper. This juice was rich in iron and B vitamins, which the Africans did not get in their diet for the rest of the year (Kiple and Kiple, 1980: pg 201).

The non-sugar environment

We have established that sugar became the major West Indian crop after others had been tried first. The non-sugar environment comprised mahogany, logwood, tobacco, cotton, cocoa and coffee.

Tobacco

Tobacco and cotton were the first crops which were grown on a commercial scale in the islands. The Europeans first encountered tobacco when they met the Aztecs and Incas, and pipe smoking soon became popular in Europe. Tobacco did not require much land and could be grown by the landowner and his family, with just a few additional labourers if needed. However, when tobacco became a plantation crop in the US colonies, the competition undermined the industry in the West Indies.

Cotton was already one of the most valuable imports in Europe. Most of the cloth came from India. Cotton cloth was as expensive as silk, so growing cotton in the West Indies made financial sense, even though picking the bolls and weaving the threads on a loom was long, exacting and arduous work. However, even before cotton became cheaper after the invention of the spinning jenny and other machines during the Industrial Revolution, sugar cane was the more valuable crop.

Timber

Timber was another major resource that sparked European interest in the New World. Between 1750 and 1850, the population had doubled, by which time much of the continent's forests had been cut down. France, for example, lost 70% of its forest by 1700 and Denmark lost about 80% between 1500 and 1800. Most of this wood was used for heating, building construction and for making ships. The discovery and use of coal helped meet heating needs, but wood was still needed for ship building in particular, especially in a sea-going nation such as England. British colonists thus favoured heavily forested colonies which had high-quality timber, and by the time of the American Revolution in 1776, one of every three British merchant ships was built in North America (Beattie, 2009: pg 88-9).

The economic law of diminishing returns soon set in though – that is, every new ship had less value than it would have previously because there were already enough ships for trade and war. This made supplying timber less profitable. On the other hand, there were more wealthy people in Britain and other European countries, so there was a higher demand for finished goods, such as furniture. Mahogany and other woods used for making furniture, doors and craft items thus became more valuable.

Logwood was the first major timber export from the Caribbean and was produced mainly in Belize. It was very valuable for its dye, which was used by wool manufacturers. Spanish ships carrying logwood were often attacked by British pirates, who stole the cargo and re-sold it. However, the buccaneers soon decided that cutting the logwood trees themselves was an easier and safer way to turn a profit. These new producers caused a glut on the market (meaning that there was more logwood to be sold than there were buyers for it). This resulted in prices falling in the 1760s and so mahogany replaced logwood as Belize's main wood export.

Since mahogany wood was harder to produce than logwood, the economy of Belize (renamed the British Honduras after Britain colonized it in 1798) changed drastically. Logwood was a small tree which required only a few men to cut it. Mahogany, which was a thick tree, needed both machinery and more men to make production economical. Inevitably, this meant an increase in enslaved Africans. Slavery had started in Belize in 1724, but there were relatively few enslaved Africans until the 1770s, after which the number of Africans expanded to more than three quarters of the entire population of about 5,000 people. Mahogany production created new jobs, for example as huntsmen, axe men and cattlemen, and many of these jobs were done by skilled slaves. The huntsmen went into the forest to find mahogany trees, the axe men did the chopping and trimming of the trees, and the cattlemen took care of the animals used to transport the logs. These enslaved men, their masters and overseers had to cover long distances to find the trees, which did not grow in clumps like the logwood but were located singly and often far apart. The difference in the relationship between slave and master here should be pointed out. Logging was a seasonal activity, so the journeys took place only for part of the year.

Coffee

Coffee was a valuable crop in many of the islands until sugar cane became dominant. It first came to the Caribbean in 1714, when a Dutch plant was brought by the French from Paris. Coffee was grown in Trinidad, the Windward Islands, Dominica, Martinique, Cuba, Jamaica and Haiti. It continued to be extensively grown in these last two islands even after sugar cane took over most of the fertile lands and it never completely vanished from most of the other islands. Haiti was the leading coffee producer, but with revolution in 1791 most of the island's 2,500 coffee plantations were damaged and there were fewer workers, so production declined to almost zero. This actually led to increased production in other islands, such as Cuba and Jamaica, since coffee producers left Haiti for these territories. Since coffee was grown on higher land, it was possible for coffee and sugar cane to co-exist. Planters only abandoned coffee because production of sugar cane was so much more profitable.

Cocoa

As mentioned in Chapter 1, cocoa originated with the Maya. The Aztec recipe for xocoatl (chocolate drink) was brought to Europe by the Spanish conqueror Henan Cortés in 1528, after his 1519 expedition to the Aztec empire. However, the Spanish nobles did not like the drink until eventually they started adding sugar to it. Cocoa consumption then increased in the courts of Spain, hence leading to the creation of cocoa plantations in Spanish Caribbean islands such as the Dominican Republic, Haiti and Trinidad. These ventures were at first unsuccessful, and it was the Spanish Capucin friars in Ecuador who supplied Spain with cocoa from 1635. In the late 17th century, France introduced the cacao bean to its Caribbean territories, starting in 1660 in St Lucia and Martinique. Cocoa then came to the Dominica Republic (1665), Brazil (1677), the Guianas (1684) and Grenada (1714). The Dutch had began planting cocoa even earlier, in 1620 in Curaçao and the British were growing it in Jamaica by 1670. The most successful cocoa plantations were in Trinidad, which began growing cocoa trees in the mid-18th century after a better variety of bean, called forastero, replaced the criollo type, which had been wiped out either by disease or a hurricane in 1727. Cocoa production on that island collapsed in the early 20th century, first because of a drop in prices after the First World War and then because of witches' broom disease in 1928. The industry never recovered.

During the 18th century, Europe got most of its cocoa supplies from Spanish colonies in South America, mainly Venezuela. In the early 19th century, wars between these colonies and Spain reduced the supply of cocoa, which resulted in increased prices. Remember, high demand and limited supply always makes goods more expensive. This led to increased production in the Caribbean, particularly in Trinidad. After 1870, when chocolate confectionary was invented and chocolate drinks became very popular in the USA, the demand for cocoa rose.

Cotton

Cotton travelled between the Old World and the New World long before humans. Scientists have recently analysed cotton's DNA and found that the cotton plant has four complete sets of chromosomes, unlike most plants and animals, which have just two. Many varieties of cotton have one pair of chromosomes from the Asian continent and one pair from the Americas. Using 'molecular clocks', scientists have calculated that this hybridization between Old World and New World strains of cotton happened about 10 million years ago. For the past few million years, different species of cotton have grown in widely separated places, such as eastern and southern Africa, Egypt, India, Peru, Australia and Arabia. The cotton seed was able to spread itself so widely because it can survive in salt water for several years and it can float.

Activity 2.9 Find out more about molecular clocks. Present your findings to the class.

Calico a plain white or unbleached cotton cloth.

Cotton might be described as the most important plant ever domesticated by human beings, because it was the production of cotton cloth which drove the Industrial Revolution in England, and the Industrial Revolution marked the beginning of the modern world. It was also this demand which led to the planting of cotton in the Caribbean. In 1765, cotton factories in England made half a million pounds of cloth every year. By 1775, this production figure rose to two million pounds of cloth a year and by 1784 it was 14 million pounds. Cotton was grown in Barbados, Haiti, the Leeward Islands, St Lucia, St Vincent, Grenada, British Guiana, the Bahamas, Trinidad and Martinique. However, despite the high demand for cotton in England, most planters still preferred to plant the more profitable sugar cane. Only in Haiti and Trinidad was cotton a significant crop. The former island had 800 cotton plantations when the French Revolution began in 1789, and in Trinidad in 1788 cotton accounted for 70% of the exports from just over 100 cotton plantations. Slave labour made cotton production profitable, although the Caribbean planters could not compete with the US planters, from whom Britain got most of its cotton for weaving into cloth. Disease also wiped out the cotton industry in the Caribbean, with the boll weevil, red bug and chenille attacking plants in the late 18th century. By the 19th century, cotton was hardly produced on any island.

Activity 2.10
Draw a sketch map of the Americas. On this map indicate the location of various economic activities in each territory facilitated by slave labour such as sugar, tobacco and so on. Use a key to organize your map.

The plantation society

New slaves were usually handed over to a trusted older slave to be instructed in how to behave on the plantation. Discipline was enforced with whip and gun by the overseers, who were usually white but could also be mixed-race (that is, they had one

FAST FACTS
- On arrival in the New World the first thing a newly enslaved African lost was his or her name.
- Changing enslaved people's names was an act intended to remove their former identity and to let them know that they were now the property of the planter, who could do with them as he wished.
- Slaves were given classical names such as Phoebe or Cyrus, or insulting nicknames such as Carefree, Villain or Strumpet.
- In Jamaica, African names were used or adapted as English names (Patterson, 1990: pg 57).

black and one white parent). As slave generations passed, colour was the main signifier of status on the plantation and in the wider society. Those with lighter skin and straight hair had higher status.

Social stratification the process whereby groups in a society are divided by criteria such as wealth, race, complexion or religion.

The population of the Caribbean islands was divided into three main groups: at the top were the whites, in the middle were the mixed-race people and freed Africans, and at the bottom were the enslaved Africans. However, there were also status divisions within each of these groups. Among the whites, for example, status was determined largely by occupation. First were the large planters, attorneys and managers of large estates. Then there were merchants and professionals, such as doctors and lawyers; followed by overseers, bookkeepers, skilled craftsmen and shopkeepers. Lowest on this tier were poor whites and missionaries.

Social pyramid a ranking of the different groups in a society according to status, wealth and so on.

Status among non-whites was determined by a combination of complexion, legal status and occupation. At the top of this sector were the free mixed-race people and freed Africans who owned property. The next level was filled by farmers, then craftsmen, followed by paid labourers. Among the slaves, the highest of the low were the artisans, then the domestic slaves. The field slaves had no status at all, save perhaps personal status within the group that would have been determined by purely personal traits: charisma, physical appearance and intelligence. No matter what personal attributes any individual had though, it was the society which determined his or her status, since status is essentially a matter of power.

Thus, only whites could hold political office in the legislative assembly and the councils. Since they had superior weaponry and an organized militia, whites could pass and enforce laws to control the free mixed-race and Africans, whether economically by limiting ownership of property or inheritance or by imposing higher taxes, or socially by harsher legal sanctions. Striking a white person, for example, could be punished by imprisonment, whipping or even by chopping off arms and legs. Free mixed-race people and Africans were also banned from holding any political office and could not even participate in elections to the assemblies or councils. Where they were allowed to carry weapons, it was only as members of a militia supervised by white officers. When missionaries are included, whites also controlled the church and its financial and social resources.

The enslaved Africans had no real rights. While all the European Crowns had passed codes which were supposed to regulate the treatment of slaves, enforcement was rare or non-existent. The planter had the power of life and death, and all punishments in between, over his slaves (see Chapter 3).

The typical day of the field slaves was filled with unremitting toil. They planted and reaped all day in blazing sun or pelting rain, while the few house slaves had lighter work washing, cooking and sweeping in the master's great house. The artisans made carts and barrels or constructed and repaired buildings. In a sense, this last group was the most privileged – or the least underprivileged – in that a skilled artisan was often in demand among different estates (with the master sometimes hiring out his labour and less likely to punish him since an unwilling skilled slave was harder to coerce into doing good work). He also had marketable skills when slavery was abolished, unlike most of the domestic and field slaves.

This system naturally shaped the personal relationships of the population, enslaved and free, black and white. It would probably be a false picture to see the daily life in the islands as one where white masters constantly threatened and whipped sullen or hopeless blacks. Instead, it was mostly a functional society, with goods being produced and shipped to seaside ports, people interacting with conversation and banter, and the wealthy enjoying their luxuries. Life in the colonies, in other words, was not so different from the similarly harsh life in other parts of the world in that era.

As systems change, so do people's relationships. Where the plantation economy was dominant, demand for slaves was high and males were in the majority among both masters and slaves, so slave unions and households tended to be very unstable. However, when external supplies curtailed or cut off, as happened when the slave trade was banned by England in 1807, it became profitable for masters to have their slaves reproduce, and marriage and strong families were encouraged in the British and French Caribbean in the late 18th and early 19th centuries.

Even the slave system evolved, as shown by the fact that towards the end of the 18th century in Jamaica many slaves took surnames, often those of respected whites in the area, and also changed their first name, a ritual that usually occurred during baptism and which may have fostered the spread of Christianity in the island.

Various groups in the plantation society

The whites

- They were either born in Europe or in the colonies (those born in the colonies were called Creoles) of European origin.
- They were normally employed in the army or were governors, navy officers, plantation owners, bookkeepers, overseers or skilled workers.
- They were the only group with political power and they had complete liberty to do as they pleased as no restrictions were placed on them.
- They were usually outnumbered by the African population and as such were always fearful of revolts by the enslaved Africans.
- They considered themselves superior in every manner to the other groups in the society.
- They attempted to control and suppress the other groups in a variety of ways.

The free blacks or free coloureds

- They were not slaves but at the same time they did not have the complete freedom of the whites. They were restricted from holding positions in the legislature, for example.
- Some were wealthy, educated and were also slave owners but this hardly gave them any favourable position in the society.
- They aspired to equality with the whites in the society but were always seen as inferior in the eyes of the whites.
- They considered themselves superior to the enslaved Africans.

The enslaved Africans

- They were the lowest group in the plantation society.
- They were separated from the whites both by colour and by law.
- They were separated from the free blacks by law only.
- They were considered inferior to everyone else in the West Indian society and were treated as inhumane objects.
- They did not have any political power, personal liberty or legal rights.
- They were considered the property of the other two groups and, as such, they could be bought and sold as inanimate objects.
- They could not practise their cultural artforms or engage in any social activities as a group. In fact, they were not allowed to hold gatherings without the permission of their masters.

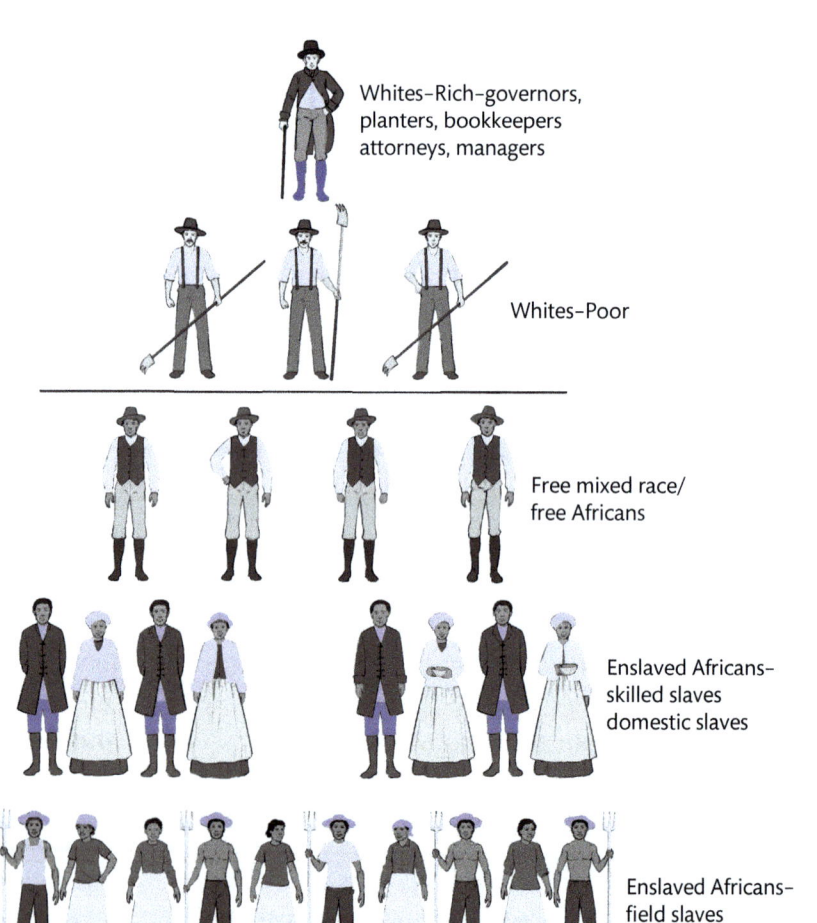

Whites-Rich-governors, planters, bookkeepers attorneys, managers

Whites-Poor

Free mixed race/ free Africans

Enslaved Africans- skilled slaves domestic slaves

Enslaved Africans- field slaves

2.19 Social levels in the plantation society

African cultural forms in the Caribbean up to 1838

2.20 Calinda – stick fighting

Calinda stick fighting; also the name for an early form of calypso, usually sung at stick fights.

To what extent did enslaved Africans retain the cultures of the tribes they came from? This is a difficult question to answer because cultural traits:

- can be the same in different societies which have never had any contact with one another
- may be adapted to new circumstances in ways which, even though drawn from ancestral culture, may appear different
- practised by one group in a new society may not be the result of retention, but of creation.

For example, it has been argued that calypso and 'mas' in carnival are retained cultural traits which are based on song and masks traditional in certain African societies. However, satirical and bawdy songs are also an English tradition and the 'masque' (from which comes the word 'masquerade') is a French tradition. How do we know which tradition – Yoruba, English or French – the enslaved Africans drew on in adapting to life on the plantation? Moreover, the planters made it a practice never to have many slaves from one particular tribe on their plantations, knowing that the cultural and language differences would make rebellion more difficult. Indeed, it was partly because the planters in St Domingue ignored this rule that the Haitian Revolution was possible (see Chapter 3).

Syncretism the process by which different religions take beliefs and rituals from one another, to create a different religion with traits from each.

One way to resolve these problems is to examine how many slaves were brought from Africa and how many were born in the New World. By 1808, for example, nearly all North American slaves were native-born. This would imply that within one generation ancestral cultural traits would be diluted or disappear. In Jamaica, the proportion of native Africans dropped from 50% in 1792 to just 10% in 1838. Even so, since reproduction rates were very low in the Caribbean, African cultural traits should have been retained to a greater degree than in North America. Indeed, Yoruba flourished in Cuba well into 20th century, while the persistence of African-Caribbean religions – Santeria in Cuba, Vodun in Haiti, Cumina and Myal in Jamaica and Orisa in Trinidad – implies that syncretism, at least, was a strong cultural force. Religion is linked to leadership in all non-modern societies, and it is influential in several 21st century countries as well. Some African cultural practices which were retained in this regard included rituals involving ancestral spirits, taking an oath on the family name and sealing an oath with blood. Many of these practices were intended to solidify group bonds between Africans on the plantations. One interesting mutation of a traditional African belief was that the spirit of a dead person returned to the ancestors: to this was added the belief that the person's spirit returned to Africa.

Dance forms and musical genres also appear to retain some elements of African traditions. Evening dances were a notable practice among the enslaved Africans, and the movements, which were also linked to ancestor worship, were distinctly of African origin. In Antigua and the Bahamas, the jukanoo dance is of African origin, as is the kumina dance in Jamaica. However, the musical forms which are identified with people of African descent in the Americas – jazz, rhythm and blues, reggae and calypso – are essentially New World creations, though musicologists identify African elements in these genres.

> **Activity 2.11** The African presence is visible in society today. Conduct some research on African cultural forms in your country. Use the following as a guide.
> - Name two dances with African origins.
> - Describe one religious practice which has its origins in Africa.
> - Give two African proverbs or examples of folklore which came from Africa.

We can also examine linguistic features of Caribbean dialects to see if they have any traits in common with West African languages. As far back as 1889, the Trinidadian scholar J. J. Thomas argued that Creole was 'a dialect framed by Africans from a European tongue'.

2.21 Shango religious ritual in modern-day Trinidad

Certain words in Caribbean dialects seem to be translated directly from African tongues: 'big-eye' for 'greedy', for instance, is the same in Ibo and Twi. Then there are what are called 'loan translations' from West African languages: phrases such as 'sweet mouth' (to flatter), 'eye water' (tears), or 'door mouth' (entrance to building). Repetition is also a feature of Yoruba and many Caribbean dialects have this trait – 'big big' for 'huge'; 'fluky fluky' for 'very fussy'; and 'poto poto' for 'very slimy'.

However, 17th century English has also left its mark on Caribbean Anglophone dialect: 'aks' for 'ask' comes from the original pronunciation of 'ax' in Old English; so too 'cripsy' for 'crispy' (Bragg, 2003: pg 272). Linguists also believe that Creole languages represent a biological ability in the human species to re-create language when individuals are deprived of their mother tongue, so this must be kept in mind when looking to language to discover cultural retention (Bickerton, 1990: pg 171).

> ### JOHN JACOB THOMAS
> (c. 1840–89)
>
> John Jacob Thomas was born sometime around 1840 and was of African descent. Although he did not experience slavery, since he was born after emancipation, his parents and most of the adults he knew had been enslaved.
>
> In 1858, Thomas enrolled as a paying student in the Woodbrook Normal School to train as a student teacher and in early 1859 he was awarded one of just six teaching places which had a government allowance of between £20 and £40 a year. In 1860, Thomas was put in charge of the Ward School, where he worked for five years. In 1867, after taking a civil service examination and coming first, he was appointed Third Locker Clerk in the Receiver-General's Office. By 1869, he was a Clerk of the Peace and a year later he was Secretary to the Board of Education.
>
> This was an extraordinary achievement for a person of African descent at that time. In 1873, after writing a paper entitled 'On some peculiarities of the Creole language', Thomas was elected a member of the Philological Society of Britain, which was the pre-eminent organization in the field of linguistics in the world.
>
> Thomas died in 1889, at the early age of 49, from tuberculosis.

REVISION QUESTIONS

1 Read the passage below then answer the questions that follow.

   Caribbean sugar reached shops in Britain after various stages of production, beginning with the preparation of the land for the cultivation of sugar cane. The cane was later taken to the factory where the sugar was manufactured. Planters faced many problems in shipping the sugar to Europe and selling it there.

   a Describe the various stages of production involved in the cultivation of sugar cane and the manufacture of sugar. *(12 marks)*
   b Describe the steps which planters took to market their sugar. *(9 marks)*
   c What problems did Caribbean planters face in shipping sugar to Europe? *(4 marks)*
   (Total = 25 marks)
   CXC Past Papers, General Proficiency, May/June 2000

2 Read the passage below then answer the question that follows.

   The sugar plantation was a social, political and economic organization in which planters exercised control over the enslaved people. Roles were allocated to individuals and groups according to their place in society. Slave society was sharply divided and there were strict rules which governed the relations among the social groups.

   Describe the social organization of British Caribbean society during the days of enslavement. Illustrate your answer with the aid of a pyramid (Δ), showing the positions of the various social groups. **(25 marks)**
   CXC Past Papers, General Proficiency, May/June 2002

3 Examine the ways in which enslaved Africans were controlled and discuss the success of these methods. **(25 marks)**

4 Examine the African cultural forms which were transported to the West Indies and the ways in which the colonizers attempted to suppress these. How successful were the colonizers in their attempts? **(25 marks)**

References and recommended reading

- Beattie, A. *False Economy: A surprising economic history of the world*, London, Viking Press, 2009
- Bernstein, W. *A Splendid Exchange: How Trade Has Shaped the World from Prehistory to the Present*, Atlantic Books, 2008
- Bickerton, D. *Language and Species*, Chicago, University of Chicago Press, 1990
- Bragg, M. *The Adventure of English: The biography of a language*, London, Hodder & Stoughton, 2003
- Curtin, P. *The Atlantic Slave Trade – A census*, Madison: University of Wisconsin Press, 1965
- Diamond, J. *Guns, Germs and Steel*, London: Vintage, 2005
- Goveia, E. *The West Indian Slave Laws of the Eighteenth Century*, Kingston: Jamaica Publishing House Ltd, 2001
- Halcrow, E.M. *Canes and Chains*, Oxford: Heinemann CXC History Series, 1982
- Kiple, K. and Kiple, V. 'Slave nutrition and disease' *Journal of Interdisciplinary History*, Vol II no. 2, 1980
- Klein, M. *Breaking the Chains: Slavery Bondage and Emancipation in modern Africa and Asia*, Madison: University of Wisconsin Press, 1993
- Maddison, A. *Contours of the World Economy*, Oxford: Oxford University Press, 2007
- Patterson, O. *Slavery and Social Death*, Harvard University Press, 1990
- Sheridan, R. *Sugar and Slavery*, Kingston: Canoe Press, 1994
- Thomas, H. *The Slave Trade – The history of the Atlantic slave trade 1440–1870*, London: Phoenix, 1997
- Vansina, J. *How Societies are Born*, Virginia: University of Virginia Press, 2005

3 Resistance and revolt

This chapter will answer the following questions.
- How were enslaved Africans controlled in the British, French and Spanish Caribbean?
- Why and how did enslaved men and women resist slavery?
- Why were there major slave revolts in the Caribbean and what were the consequences of these?
- Why was there a revolution in Haiti?
- What was the impact of the Haitian Revolution on Haiti and the wider Caribbean?

History is about events, but history is also about people. Events tell you *what* happened, but to understand *why* these events happened, you have to understand human beings. What makes people act the way they do? Why do they make certain choices and not others? What do human beings want? Only by answering such questions can we truly understand the events of history.

In this chapter, we look at resistance and revolt by the enslaved Africans. We will try to understand why they rose up against their masters and, just as importantly, why they did not. Although it might seem that the planters, who had weapons and were organized, had total control over the enslaved people, the situation was not so simple. You can glean some idea of the complex master–slave relationship from the extracts in the three letters on this page. In the example from 1518, when slavery was being established, the judge is dismissive of the slaves and punishes them brutally. Just 24 years later, however, the archdeacon paints a picture of slaves who are carrying on their own economic activities under the masters' noses, and four years after that an official is saying that the masters need to control their tone with the slaves.

There may be some exaggeration in this last letter, perhaps because the officials were trying to get the Crown to send more soldiers and other resources. Yet the fact remains that the planters were in constant fear of the slaves rising up against them.

1518, Judge Alonso Zuaso to Cardinal Ximenes

'It is idle to fear that the Blacks may rebel: there are widows living calmly on the Portuguese islands with as many as 800 slaves: everything depends on how they are governed. I found that on the arrival of some Spanish-speaking Blacks others fled to the hills. I whipped some, cut off the ears of others, and there were no further complaints.'

1542, Archdeacon Alvaro de Castro to the Council of the Indies

'The Blacks are already doing business and trading among themselves to an extent involving great value and cunning and, as a result, big and notable robberies are being committed on all the farms in the country... if the Blacks wish to rebel outright, one hundred of them would be sufficient to conquer the island, and twenty thousand Spaniards would not suffice to bring them to subjection. The island is large and well-wooded, and they are war-like and expert at hiding in the forests.'

1546, Audiencia of Hispaniola to Charles V

'On account of the habits of Blacks to rise up in revolt, the settlers dare not give their slaves an order except in the gentlest manner.'

Revolt uprising, rebellion.

Reflecting this fear, there were laws which allowed whites (and some mixed-race people) to carry arms, while every island had a militia. In some islands, such as Jamaica, Cuba and Haiti, some of the very large plantations had their own mercenary soldiers in enough numbers to keep the large workforce of enslaved Africans under control, if they decided to rebel, until government reinforcements could arrive. Apart from these militias, there were garrisons of regular army troops, a small 'police' force, and individuals who hunted escaped slaves. It should be noted that free mixed and black people often served as part of the island's security force. In the latter part of the 17th century and the early part of the 18th, there were troops stationed in Antigua and Barbados. This may be why the enslaved Africans on these islands did not revolt as often as in the others, where the government forces were not as ready to quell rebellions. Cuba is a good example of what happened when troops were not present, since there were several uprisings in that island in the late 18th century, when Spanish troops who had been stationed there were sent to Santo Domingo, Florida and Louisiana.

Most enslaved Africans were located on the plantations, but their presence in the towns also worried the white population on the various islands. Enslaved Africans in towns were the equivalent of 'house slaves' on the plantations. They were often domestic workers, skilled craftsmen, fishermen, sailors, even soldiers. As such, they were more independent than their brethren on the plantations and, indeed, their white masters often complained how rude their slaves were. One strategy used to keep these enslaved Africans obedient was the threat to send them to work on the plantations, since the town slaves knew they had a relatively privileged life. Even so, there were special laws intended to control these enslaved Africans. In the Dutch colonies, for example, no slave was allowed to be out on the streets, or to play music, or to buy alcohol after 9 pm. In Jamaica and Barbados, the towns had their own guards, whose main duty was to police the enslaved.

As you can see from Table 3.1, the Europeans were so outnumbered that, if the slaves did rebel in an organized fashion, there was no way that they could be stopped. Remember that the deadliest weapons in this time were rifles which could only fire one shot and then had to be re-loaded. In 1696 in Jamaica, for example, there were already six Africans to one European. By 1778, the ratio was 11 to one.

Table 3.1 Slave population

Territory	Years	Slaves (%)
St John (St Croix)	1728	85
	1739	87
	1787	92
Jamaica	1658	24
	1664	57
	1730	91
	1758	89
	1775	89
Antigua	1678	48
	1720	84
	1756	90
	1775	94
Guadeloupe	1700	62
	1788	84
Martinique	1664	54
	1696	65
	1727	77
	1751	83
Nevis	1678	52
	1756	89
Suriname	1790	91
Montserrat	1678	27
	1775	80
Barbados	1643	24
	1768	80

However, this raises another puzzle. If it was so easy to break the chains of slavery, why didn't all the slaves rise up and do so?

The account below is from an observer in 1657, a sugar planter named Richard Ligon, about this situation. Ligon identified three main reasons why the enslaved Africans did not revolt more frequently: they had no access to weapons; they were psychologically cowed; and because they were from different ethnic groups, they could not communicate with one another well enough to become organized for a revolt.

> **An account by a sugar planter, Richard Ligon**
>
> 'It has been accounted a strange thing that the Negroes being more than double the number of Christians that are here, and they are accounted a bloody people, would have the power or advantage and commit some horrid massacre upon the Christians, thereby to enfranchise themselves, and become masters of the island. But there are three reasons that take away this wonder: the one is, that they are not suffered to touch or handle any weapons: the other, that they are held in such awe and slavery, as they are fearful to appear in any daring act; besides, there is a third reason which stops all designs of that kind, and that is they were fetched from several parts of Africa who can speak several languages, and by that means one of them understands not the other.'

When there were many more Africans than Europeans on any particular colony, the authorities were apt to make alliances with the mixed and free black groups in order to strengthen themselves against the numerically superior enslaved Africans. In 18th century Jamaica, for example, where slaves made up nearly 90% of the population, mixed groups were granted property and other rights by the white authorities. In Barbados, where the proportion was 80%, free mixed people were also allowed to own property. In 1816, there was a rebellion which was quelled with the help of the mixed group who fought in the militia against the enslaved Africans. For this effort, the mixed group was granted further rights, such as being able to testify in court matters.

Table 3.2 Slave revolts

Year	Island
1733	St John
1734	Jamaica
1736	Antigua
1737	Guadeloupe
1746	Jamaica
1752	Guadeloupe
1746	Jamaica
1752	Martinique
1760	Jamaica
1761	Nevis
1763	Suriname
1765	Jamaica
1769	Jamaica
1772	Suriname
1776	Jamaica, Montserrat
1791	Hispaniola

> **FAST FACTS**
>
> - On average, there was one uprising every three years, which means that planters had more to worry about from the annual hurricanes.
> - Most of the islands only had one revolt while some, such as Barbados, had none – Barbados had several plots to revolt but only one rebellion in a specific parish in 1816 actually got underway.
> - With one exception, none of these revolts lasted, in that the slaves never succeeded in taking over the island.
> - For the whole time the slave system existed, this only happened in one country, St Dominigue (now Haiti), and we will examine the reasons for that success in the last section of this chapter.

Caribbean slave laws

When you read about the slave laws in the British, Spanish and French territories, you should keep in mind that what the laws say is not always what was actually done. This was so, both for laws which protected slaves, and for laws which oppressed them. Laws reflect the wishes of those in authority, but enforcing laws, or getting them followed, is a different matter altogether.

In the case of the British colonies, for example, the laws were passed by elected people, who lived on the islands, and approved by Crown officials. In the case of the Spanish and the French though, it was the rulers in Europe who drafted the laws with the expectation that their subjects in the Caribbean would obey them. The Spanish code was based on an existing document written in 1265 called the 'Siete Partidas' (Seven-part Code), and which, even though first created to deal with Jews and Moors living in Spain, was applied to the New World slave system. The different British colonies had their own slave laws; the main one was the Barbados Slave Code of 1661 which was written to regulate the indentured servants. The French, however, drew up a 'Code Noir' in 1685 which was supposed to deal with issues that had arisen as Frenchmen colonized the West Indies and set up sugar plantations. For this reason, the Siete Partidas was often concerned with preserving the Catholic religion and preventing inter-marriage. The English regulations were mostly concerned with preventing slaves from owning property or engaging in commercial activities. Clause 19 of the 1661 Barbados Slave Code said that:

> 'Diverse Negroes are and long since have been runaway into woods and other fastness of the Island do continually much mischief… hiding themselves, sometimes in one place and sometimes in another, so that with much difficulty they are to be found, unless by some sudden surprise.'

The law authorized armed patrols to capture such runaways 'either alive or dead' and offered 500 pounds of sugar for enslaved Africans who had been missing for six months, and twice that for those who had escaped for more than a year. Richard Ligon, a planter and slave owner, in his book written about Barbados in 1657, noted that the runaways:

> 'harbour themselves in woods and caves, living upon pillage for many months together. These caves are very frequent, some small, others extremely large and capacious. The runaway Negroes often shelter themselves in these coverts, for a long time, and in the night range abroad the countery, and steale pigs, plantins, potatoes, and pullin, and bring it there; and feast all day, upon what they stole the night before; and the nights being dark, and their bodies black, they scape undiscern'd.'

Activity 3.1
Form three groups. Imagine that each is a group of planters from English, French and Spanish colonies respectively. Each group needs to point out to the other groups the advantages of using their slave codes and show how they are the best codes to use to control the enslaved Africans.

Escaped slaves worried the planters because they undermined the plantation system and also attacked the planters and their property. They reduced a slave owner's workforce, could not be easily found, lived off food they stole from white lands and could incite or encourage other slaves to run away. The planters were fearful that runaway slaves were conspiring with one another 'for raising mutinyes or rebellion'.

In response to an attempted uprising in 1676, the Barbados legislature passed an act which extended the 1661 law. The new Act specified the punishments for particular crimes. It also dealt with issues such as slave assaults on whites and the theft and destruction of white property, and it limited the involvement of slaves in the skilled trades. The planters were concerned about internal movement of enslaved Africans, which was more common among the skilled artisans and facilitated contact among people from different plantations. The Act regulated the number of slaves hired out, noting that because of their movements 'from plantation to plantation' they 'have more opportunity of contriving mischief and rebellion than the Negroes employed only in their master's plantations.' The Act also tried to 'restrain the wanderings and meetings of Negroes at all times, especially on Saturday nights, Sundays, or other holy days,' and ordered regular searches of slaves' houses for runaways, 'clubs, wooden swords, or other mischievous weapons,' stolen goods, and 'drums, horns, shells, or other loud instruments which may call [them] together to give sign or notice to one another of their wicked designs and purposes.' Slave owners were also fined if they permitted slaves 'to beat drums, blow shells, or use any other loud instrument,' and they had to pay an even heavier fee if they permitted 'any public meeting or feasting of strange Negroes in their plantations'.

The Code Noir directly addressed issues of punishment for slaves and masters' responsibilities.

The enslaved Africans were not allowed to own property, especially when it came to owning and selling sugar cane. Any African who attacked a white person would be executed. Africans were not allowed to gather in groups, not even for social occasions such as marriage or worship.

The Code allowed slaves to complain to the authorities if their owners mistreated them. The masters were supposed to baptize the African slaves, teach them the Catholic faith and not break up families. The masters were also supposed to allow slaves to buy their freedom. The Code specified how much food and clothing was to be provided to the enslaved workers and it banned torture (although whipping was allowed).

However, you should keep in mind that, given the length of time it took to send messages between the Caribbean and Europe, disagreements would take a very long time to settle. This is why the Crowns had officials in the colonies and why these officials had soldiers to enforce the Crowns' will. Even then, such enforcement depended on the officials being loyal, proactive in enforcing the law and unwilling to take bribes from the colonists. That combination was more the exception than the rule.

You might also ask why the rulers in Europe found it necessary to draw up slave codes at all, rather than just letting the colonists handle their business. The two main reasons were that Crowns wanted to ensure that:

- they got revenues from the vast sugar wealth coming from the colonies
- the colonists did not end up fighting one another over the spoils of this wealth.

So, what were the main provisions of the various slave codes? The historian Isaac Dookhan distilled the clauses of the Code Noir, the Siete Partidas and the Barbados Code and divided them into two sections. One set of provisions was for the protection of the slaves and the other for protection of the planters. Dookhan categorized these as 'disability clauses' and 'beneficent clauses'. Under the first, these were some of the main points.

- Slaves could not carry weapons, unless hunting for their masters.
- Slaves owned by different masters could not gather at any time for any purpose.
- Slaves could not sell sugar cane, provisions, firewood and a host of other goods.
- Theft of large animals and other valuable property was punishable by death.
- Slaves who ran away once and were then caught would have their ears cut off and be branded; twice, branded again; and, if they ran away three times, they would be executed.
- Slaves could not own property or fill any office.

Then there were the beneficent clauses, which included the following provisions.

- Masters were to give a weekly supply of food to their slaves aged above 10 years: two-and-half pots of flour, two pounds of salt beef and three pounds of fish.
- Each slave was to get two linen suits or four ells of linen every year.
- Slaves should not be tortured or mutilated and, if they were, they would be confiscated and the master prosecuted.
- Families were not to be broken up when slaves were sold.
- Slaves who were old, sick or otherwise weak should be cared for by their master.

3.1 Shackles

Did the planters and other whites abide by these codes? There is some evidence to substantiate claims of abuse – the high death rate cannot just be attributed to overwork. Many uprisings were due to more extreme treatment – especially in times of hardship. However if the planters were breaking the law, whether by treating the slaves well or treating them horrendously, they would hardly have admitted it – and all the records we have from that time were written by the Europeans. Sometimes, though, accounts written by travellers and some legal documents give a insight into the day-to-day workings of the slave societies. We know that some planters granted slaves their freedom after they became too old to work, so the planter would no longer have to feed and clothe them. We also know that some slaves were allowed to trade and to hire themselves out.

The slave laws were intended to deny any rights, and indeed any humanity, to the Africans. The Barbados Code contained a lot of non-legal phrases, asserting that Africans were 'wholly unqualified to be governed by the laws, customs, and practices of the English nation' and describing them as having 'a barbarous, wild and savage nature'. All this was intended to justify enslavement, and is in fact an admission that the slave owners at some level knew that their actions were morally indefensible. When human beings attempt to deny such moral guilt, especially to themselves, they often act even more reprehensibly. For example, English colonists executed any enslaved African suspected of serious offences (particularly planning a rebellion, and certainly attempting one). They also tortured offenders in public, by branding them with hot irons, whipping them and cutting off limbs.

3.2 Punishment using a 'tread wheel'

3.3 The Negro's Complaint, The Torture, 1826, British Library

We know that planters did mutilate and torture slaves, which means that they did ignore the beneficial provisions of the slave codes – in fact, the actions of a sadistic French planter named Le Jeune, who you will read more about in the section on the Haitian Revolution, may have helped spark that revolt. We even have records from an English estate manager named Thomas Thistlewood, who kept a diary which ran to over ten thousand pages and which includes details of the shocking punishments Thistlewood meted out to slaves. Yet the very fact that Thistlewood wrote down these accounts so casually suggests that he considered such brutal acts quite normal. However, the slave owners were partly constrained by the fact that they needed to maintain their 'property' so the enslaved Africans could produce for the owners' plantations.

Even if a white person murdered an enslaved African, the white was never guilty of murder, but of damage to property, for which the usual fine was £15. However, this law was changed in the 1830s, and murdering a slave became an offence that, as with murdering a white person, was punishable by death in the British colonies. This brings us to the various methods used to control the enslaved Africans.

> **Roleplay**
>
> Imagine that you are a sugar planter in the British West Indies. You have 20 enslaved Africans on your plantation. Write a list of three ways in which you will make sure they obey you at all times.

Physical control

Physical punishment is often the first option human beings use when they want to get other human beings to obey them. On the sugar plantation the whip was the main device used to punish slaves. There were several different kinds of whip, but the main one was the bullwhip, which was made of plaited leather and which could be as deadly as a knife or cutlass. A bullwhip, when wielded by an overseer or driver who knew how to use it, could inflict deep cuts because of the speed at which the tip accelerated.

Slaves could be whipped while at work in the fields, if the overseer thought they were not working hard enough or fast enough. For specific infractions, however, the slave was usually tied to a post (or posts) and given a number of lashes.

Other punishments might include putting the slaves in foot irons for some days, or chaining them to heavy blocks of wood, which they had to carry around as they worked in the fields. Apart from the effort of walking with these items, the rubbing of the irons or the collar inflicted additional pain as the skin became raw. The planters also used tin-plate masks which could be locked, to prevent the slaves eating the sugar cane or food cooked for the whites.

Slaves were mutilated, with limbs and ears and even genitals being cut off. Mutilated slaves were, by their very appearance, a warning to other slaves to behave. Psychopathic masters sometimes tortured their slaves to death, burning them alive or burying them up to the head near ants' nests and smearing them with sugar.

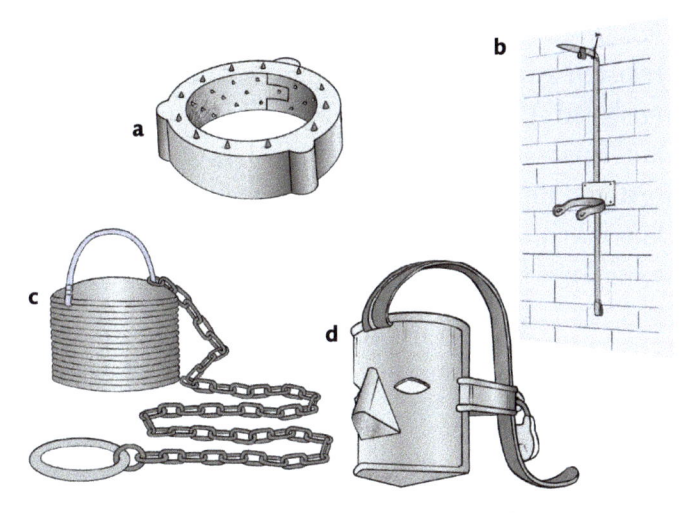

3.5 a Slave collar b bell rack c slave chain d slave mask

Ideological and psychological control

Physical punishment, however, has its limits in a slave system. After all, the planter wanted his slaves fit to work. Punishing the slaves psychologically, so as to get them docile and obedient, was just as important as physical coercion. A French book by Hilliard d'Auberteuil published in the 1750s, that had the official blessing of the French government, asserted:

'Interest and security demand that we overwhelm the black race with such disdain that whoever descends from it until the sixth generation shall be covered with an indelible stain.'

This disdain generally involved portraying the African as less than human, or as a mentally and emotionally undeveloped human being. Psychological abuse of the slave also served as psychological balm for the master, because such abuse made it easier for the master to justify the cruelties and exploitation of other human beings. The stereotype of the enslaved African was labelled Sambo in North America and Quashee in 18th century Jamaica. According to this stereotype, the typical plantation slave was 'docile but irresponsible, loyal but lazy, humble but chronically given to lying and stealing; his behaviour was full of infantile silliness and his talk inflated with childish exaggeration'.

3.4 Enslaved Africans at work on a plantation in Antigua under watch by the overseers or slave drivers

As you will see later in this chapter, however, this stereotype was actually a factor used by the slaves to undermine the masters.

The European planters made sure to reinforce the slaves' inferior status to them at every turn. Apart from the laws which stopped them from getting any financial independence, slaves were not supposed to look at any white person in the eyes, they always had to address white people respectfully and bow their heads when the master or any white person walked by. Ragged clothes were also used as a psychological device to display the blacks' inferior status, with some colonies actually having laws which made it a criminal offence for any slave to wear fine garments.

Yet all this was still not enough for the Europeans to prove to themselves how inferior the Africans were. In 1696, a law was passed in Jamaica saying that no slave was free just because he or she became a Christian. This was partly a matter of language – Europeans had not yet started calling themselves white, but instead usually described themselves as Christian (the implication being that the world was divided into Christians and heathens). However, when some slaves started converting to Christianity, this label had to be changed. A visitor to Barbados in the mid-17th century recorded:

'[I met] a slave who wished to be Christian, but on interceding with the slave's master, I was told that the people of the Island were governed by the Lawes of England, and by those Lawes, we could not make a Christian a slave.'

This position had obviously changed 50 years later, since a law was now deemed necessary to keep black Christians enslaved. The French philosopher Montesquieu, whose ideas were part of the basis for the American constitution, mocked this approach by noting, 'The blacks could not be men for, otherwise, the whites could not be Christians.'

For this and other reasons, the white colonists often resisted attempts by missionaries to teach the enslaved Africans Christianity, even in the French and Spanish colonies where the Crown had ordered this be done. The extract from a 1764 letter written by the Governor of Martinique explains why.

'Religious instruction could give to the blacks here an opening to other knowledge, to a kind of reason. The safety of the whites, fewer in number, surrounded by people on their estates and at their mercy, demands that they be kept in profoundest ignorance.'

When the colonists eventually relented, or were forced to by the authorities in the mother countries, religion was used as a form of control. Quoting passages on slavery from the Bible, the planters and church officials used Christianity to justify slavery. In those colonies where religious conversion and instruction was allowed, the emphasis was on remaining obedient and content with your lot in order to inherit the Kingdom of Heaven after death. Christianity was therefore used to pacify the slaves just as it had been used to justify enslaving them in the early period of slavery.

Within Europe itself, there was much debate on whether slavery was right or wrong. In 1685, the Council of the Indies in Spain issued, after being asked to do so by the King, an opinion that the slave trade was lawful, that the Catholic faith would not be perverted and noting that St Paul in the Bible had ordered slaves to accept their status. In France, a book published in 1675 argued in favour of enslaving Africans on the grounds that Christian merchants thus saved African souls by removing them from a land where idolatry or Islam ruled.

Philosophers also joined in this discussion. The Englishman John Locke, whose ideas helped create modern Western democracy, argued that slavery was justified when it was the outcome of a 'lawful war', but he also wrote that:

'slavery is so vile and miserable an estate of man, and so directly opposite to the generous temper and courage of our nation, that it is hardly to be conceived that an Englishman, much less a gentleman, should plead for it.'

This opinion did not prevent Locke from investing in the Royal African Company (RAC) when it started trading slaves. The Scottish philosopher David Hume wrote in 1754 of Africans that:

'there scarcely ever was a civilised nation of that complexion, not even any individual, eminent either in action or in speculation. No ingenious manufactures among them, no arts, no sciences...'.

Ironically, one of Hume's major contributions to philosophical thought is the idea that, just because two events happen together, it does not mean that one caused the other. Therefore, by his own logic, he should not have concluded that his list was any evidence of African inferiority.

> **FAST FACTS**
> - John Locke (29 August 1632 – 28 October 1704), is widely known as the Father of Liberalism.
> - He was an English philosopher and physician and is regarded as one of the most influential of the Enlightenment thinkers.
> - Locke believed that human nature is characterized by reason and tolerance but that the introduction of monetary currency allowed men to become selfish.
> - Locke said that in a natural state all people were equal and independent, and everyone had a natural right to defend his "Life, health, Liberty, or Possessions". This statement was the inspiration for the phrase in the American Declaration of Independence; "Life, liberty, and the pursuit of happiness".

3.6 Enslaved Africans being baptised in a Moravian church

By contrast, the political philosopher and founder of modern economics Adam Smith wrote in 1759:

> 'There is not a Negro from the coast of Africa who does not… possess a degree of magnanimity, which the soul of his sordid master is too often scarce capable of conceiving.'

The natural philosopher Charles Darwin, co-discoverer of organic evolution, described his countrymen as 'polished savages in England' who did not count blacks as 'their brethren, even in God's eyes'.

It was the French philosophers, such as Rousseau, Diderot and Condorcet, who had the most immediate impact, however. Their arguments on the rights and equality of all human beings contributed to the French Revolution of 1789 and that sparked off the Haitian Revolution two years later.

3.7 A statue of David Hume

3.8 a Adam Smith **b** Charles Darwin

You might find it strange that the Europeans debated this issue so much among themselves. This was partly because slavery itself contradicted some of the fundamental ideas that were bringing about social and political changes in Europe, especially in the late 18th century. Freedom itself was a notion that first arose in Western civilization. In most non-Western languages, no word for 'freedom' even existed before encounters with Europeans. So the Europeans found it necessary to find ideological justifications even for themselves. As we will see in Chapter 4, however, the contradictions of trying to believe in freedom while enslaving another race helped bring about the abolition of slavery.

How were enslaved Africans controlled?

- **Physical punishments** were used. Slaves were chained together; whipped and beaten for minor offences; mutilated, hanged and burnt in public.
- **Legal control** was imposed. Laws were passed in the colonies to prevent enslaved Africans from having rights such as political rights.
- **Social control** was used. Slaves were prevented from mixing with other groups in the society, they could not move around freely and they were unable to gather in groups.
- **Cultural control** meant that they were not allowed to practise their African cultural forms. This was done to strip them of an identity so they would be easier to control.
- **Divide and rule** strategy was used. The enslaved population was divided into different groups and deliberate efforts were make to keep them apart. Some slaves were appointed as headmen and drivers to keep a check on the others.
- **Economic control** was exercised. By their very nature slaves were property and therefore were not supposed to own property of their own. They were also prohibited from certain economic activities.

Socio-cultural control

Culture is the foundation of all human groups. When people share the same religion, play the same games, dress in a similar fashion, eat in the same manner and so on, they bond with one another. The more people bond through culture, the more organized they become as a group. For the white populace in the Caribbean, such organizing by the enslaved Africans would have posed a serious threat, so they did everything in their power to eradicate any cultural activities that the blacks might have brought with them from Africa, or that they might have created in the Caribbean.

It was for this reason that the authorities in the Caribbean passed laws which banned drumming and dancing by the blacks. Some of these laws existed well into the 20th century.

Did you know?

Drumming was used as a form of communication among enslaved Africans. The modern day steelpan evolved out of these practices, even though drumming was officially outlawed by the British in 1883.

The planters also made sure that they did not buy slaves only from one tribe, since this would have made it easier for them to communicate with one another and to plan revolts. Table 3.3 shows how no set of slaves from one region in Africa dominated any Caribbean island, and, bear in mind that even in one region the slaves would have consisted of different tribal groups who were often in conflict. This technique worked well in all the islands except Jamaica, and we will explain why Jamaica was the exception in the section on resistance by slaves.

Activity 3.2

A calypso named 'Shango Song' by Cobra was banned in 1937 because the Shango religion (also called Orisa) was still illegal in Trinidad. The following verse from the calypso recounts a vision the song's protagonist has when possessed.

> Now I am going to tell you just what I see
> The night I had the Shango jumbie
> I saw a man sitting on a bed
> With lighted candles upon his head
> The man was like a grizzly bear
> And Jack Spaniards all in his hair
> And the Oken kneeling down at his feet
> Drinking the goat blood and eating the meat.

Refer to the 'Shango Song' calypso to answer the following questions.

- Who or what is the 'jumbie?'
- Who or what is the 'Oken'?
- What exactly is the author describing?

> **Activity 3.3**
> On a map of modern west Africa identify the areas listed in Table 3.3.

The whites also further divided the slaves by making some of them house slaves and treating them, arguably, better than their fellows in the field. House slaves were also appointed as drivers, with responsibility to maintain discipline among the field slaves. Such techniques helped prevent any attempt by the slaves to become organized. Indeed, when revolts were being planned, the favoured slaves would often warn the master, thus allowing the whites to nip the plan in the bud, usually hanging the leaders immediately. Of all rebellions in the English colonies between 1649 and 1833, nearly half were stopped right at the start because of betrayal or because the slave owners found out about them through other means.

Another important part of socio-cultural control was ensuring that slaves did not gain even minimal economic independence. In 1711, a law was passed which forbade slaves to keep horses or cattle. Another law said that any slaves who sold fish, manufactured articles or sugar, or who hired themselves out would be punished by whipping. As we have noted, however, these laws were often ignored in the colonies, particularly when a planter had a skilled artisan he could hire out to other planters.

Women's situation under slavery

Conditions on the plantations were similar for both men and women, except in cases where the woman was the concubine of a planter or slave owner. Only then might she have received better treatment than other slaves. In the end, however, the experience of slavery was brutal for both sexes.

> **Emasculate** to deprive a man of his male role or function; to make an individual weaker.

In an attempt to control the enslaved Africans, families were separated – husbands and wives were sold separately and children were taken from their mothers. This had serious implications on the social lives of the enslaved Africans. Also, African men were emasculated and many women were raped and sexually abused. It is important to note the following.

- Enslaved women worked alongside men in the fields and were expected to perform similar duties. They were valued more for their ability to work than for their ability to reproduce until the slave trade was abolished.
- Enslaved women were punished just like the enslaved males. They were whipped and beaten for minor offences; chained together; mutilated, hanged and burnt in public.
- Laws were passed in the colonies to prevent enslaved women from having rights, such as political rights.
- Enslaved women were prevented from mixing with other groups in the society; they could not move around freely; they were unable to gather in groups. However, as enslaved women played an important role in cultivating the provision grounds and were some of the main traders at the Sunday markets, they were crucial in the spread of news within the plantation and from one plantation to the next. In this way they acted as communicators and were instrumental in planning revolts by passing information from one group to the next.

Table 3.3 Regional origins of slaves in British Caribbean 1658–1713

African region	Barbados (%)	Jamaica (%)	Antigua (%)	Nevis (%)
Gold Coast	39	36	44	32
Bight of Benin	25	26	13	12
Bight of Biafra	13	11	32	24
West and Central Africa	10	20	4	13

Note: Not all regions have been included, so the percentages do not add up to 100%.

- Enslaved women, like all other enslaved Africans, were disallowed from practising their African cultural forms. However, as mothers, they resisted slavery by teaching their children about indigenous African cultures.
- Rape and sexual assault were a common feature of slavery. Many girls and women were raped from the time of capture.
- Female slaves, especially those who were mothers, may have experienced more psychological trauma than enslaved men.
- Enslaved women sometimes practised forms of contraception, abortion and infanticide to deprive the master of gaining more slaves.

3.9 A slave woman, slavery memorial in Zanzibar, Tanzania

Activity 3.4

Debate the following statement.

The experience of slavery was worse for enslaved women than for enslaved men.

Resistance by enslaved Africans

Non-insurrectionary resistance non-violent or individual actions against enslavement.

Non-insurrectionary resistance

The Jamaican proverb 'Play fool, to catch wise' encapsulates the non-violent means the Africans used to rebel against their enslavement in the Caribbean. While the slaveholder defined the slave as dependent, the slaves tried to ensure that the master's actions were predictable. This was why they played up to the master's opinion of them as child-like or foolish, as a way of deflecting aggression. Yet observers noted that the slaves' interactions with one another were those of individuals who seemed to enjoy life far more than their circumstances would seem to allow. This, then, was a very subtle form of resistance by the enslaved Africans.

Another method was to live up to the master's opinion of the slave as lazy. If it was believed that the slaves were lazy, this gave them a reason to do less work than they actually could, which meant less productivity, which meant harming the master where it most counted – in his profits. Such a strategy had to be finely judged though, as too much slacking off would result in whipping, or worse.

A more direct method of rebellion was poisoning the slave owners – relatively easy to do because the slaves were cooks, maids and cleaners. One well-known case was that of a runaway slave named Macandal in St Domingue (formerly Santo Domingo when owned by the Spanish). Macandal used to sneak on to the plantations and give the house slaves poison to put in the masters' food or drink. He did this for eight years, until he was caught and burned alive.

A third method of rebellion was infanticide – some female slaves killed their babies as soon as they were born, so the master would not get another slave. However, as you would expect, most mothers baulked at infanticide and the number of Creole slaves (slaves born in the islands, not in Africa) continued to grow in all the colonies.

> **Roleplay**
>
> Imagine you are an enslaved African. Your master is a very unsympathetic man who recently punished another slave with 10 strokes, in front of all the other slaves. You cannot put up with these conditions anymore. What do you do and why?

One aspect of slavery which has often been overlooked because of inadequacies of source material is concubinage. Historian Barbara Bush noted that white men 'utilised the alleged physical and moral inferiority of the black women… to establish them firmly in the role of the "other woman". While concubinage may have been European planters' and managers' ways of taking advantage of enslaved women, these women were sometimes able to turn the tables and use this to their advantage. Concubinage became one of the ways in which enslaved women used their bodies to resist their everyday situation. By using sexual relations with the planters they were able to improve their daily conditions to some extent – perhaps through better meals, better accommodation or other tangible forms of reimbursement for their efforts. Some enslaved mothers even sought concubinage for their daughters because of the rewards that could result and because children of such unions might have better opportunities than other children.

In other instances, enslaved women would use their concubine status to attempt to undermine the role of the planter's wife and to increase their own status. European women were therefore generally annoyed about cases of sexual relations between white men and enslaved African women.

'The jealousy of the white Creole ladies is intense. The easy availability of other women reduces their status. They are intended to breed illegitimate heirs and nothing else.'

Enslaved women were obviously willing to grasp whatever opportunities came their way and, while the planters and masters thought they were using the women, it could potentially be seen as the women who were using their bodies to their advantage.

Many times enslaved women could use their femininity to become close to the white planters, gain their trust and gather information. On the other hand, social interactions are complex, and there are examples where women provided warnings to the planters about planned revolts. In one such case in Barbados in 1676, a domestic slave by the name of Fortunna overheard a conversation about a planned revolt and informed her master. The authorities quickly arrested named participants and arraigned them before a court martial. 17 were rapidly found guilty and executed, while six were burned alive and 11 others beheaded and their bodies dragged through the streets at Speightstown and afterwards burned with others who were burned alive. On 24 November 1675, the House of Assembly freed Fortunna as a reward for 'her eminent service to the good of this country in discovering the intended plotted rebellion of the Negroes'.

Resistance by enslaved women

Methods of resistance included:

- prolongation of the weaning period
- poisoning masters (especially by those enslaved women who were cooks)
- infanticide
- cultural resistance – mothers passed on cultural traditions to their children
- acting as communicators (for example at Sunday markets)
- running away and joining Maroon settlements (see the section 'Marronage' in this chapter).
- concubinage

3 Resistance and revolt

> **The impact of resistance by enslaved women on the emancipation process**
>
> - Female slaves played a significant role in cultural resistance, for example through dress.
> - Some enslaved women emerged as leaders in the resistance movement, for example Nanny of the Maroons was a notable military leader.
> - Enslaved women played a significant role in undermining the entire system of slavery by acting as communicators. During the Sunday markets, for example, enslaved women spread information on planned revolts and other uprisings.
>
> *Flagellation of a Female Samboe Slave.*
>
> 3.10 Flagellation of a female slave, 1796, British Library

Insurrectionary resistance violent actions against enslavement carried out by groups.

As the planters were completely focused on profit maximization and were reluctant to feed their slaves properly, enslaved Africans were allowed to grow their own food on secondary land called provision grounds. The food produced on this land contributed towards the daily maintenance of the enslaved. However, the provision grounds also gave the enslaved men and women a sense of independence and created a sense of identity. The slaves gained a respite from the daily routine on the plantations as they were freed from plantation labour for one and a half days a week to work their provision grounds.

Women played a significant role not only as cultivators in the provision grounds, but also entrepreneurs in the Sunday markets where slaves were allowed to trade their produce. As mentioned earlier in this chapter, they acted as an important medium of communication among the enslaved population and were instrumental in spreading messages of revolts. To this extent, they therefore played a significant role in undermining the system of slavery as it existed in the Caribbean.

Culture

Women also acted as a main medium of culture through communication with their children and as the caregivers in the home. They were in many ways responsible for cultural transmission and perpetuation. They used the practice of their indigenous African cultures to show that they were unwilling to conform to what was required of them. Even when they converted to Christianity, they introduced certain aspects of their cultural lifestyles to the various churches. In this way, they played an important role in modifying European culture and propagating their own.

Dress

Enslaved African women used dress as a form of resistance. Their imitation of the styles of the white women was intended to show that they were on equal footing with these women. They also tied

Activity 3.5 Imagine that you are a teacher and you have to tell your students about Nanny of the Maroons. Use the following headlines as a guide for your research and presentation

- Family life
- Resistance activities
- Her contribution as leader

their head ties in particular ways which were symbolic to them alone and in so doing they were able to carry messages. This was especially prevalent in the French islands.

Dance and music

The drum was used to transmit messages to other enslaved people on other plantations. More importantly, dance and music also gave the slaves a sense of identity, helped them to retain solidarity and gave them strength to cope with their daily situation as well as to resist their position as enslaved people.

Insurrectionary resistance

The first slave revolt in the Caribbean area happened before sugar was the main crop, on the Portuguese colony of São Tomé in 1517. The first revolt by enslaved Africans, interestingly, happened in the same island that was to have the only successful revolution 274 years later, in Spanish-governed Hispaniola. The first revolt in a sugar colony happened in 1656, on the French island of Guadeloupe.

Estimates of total rebellions between the mid-17th century and the 1830s number around 70, which is a total average rate of less than one per year. As you can see from Table 3.4, the number of revolts more than doubled during the 18th century, for a variety of reasons. There were more Creole slaves than African ones, which not only made communication easier but also ensured that ancient ethnic rivalries did not stand in the way of getting organized. The slave owners also became harsher in their treatment of the slaves, partly because they had become accustomed to the idea that there was a race of people who, in their minds, they had total power over.

Table 3.4 Revolts by century in the British Caribbean

Century	Total revolts
17th	15
18th	36
19th	23

Odd as it might seem, revolts became more common because the situation of the slaves improved. They knew they had some protection under the law, some of them had learned to read and more had been freed or were allowed more freedom in their daily activities. Revolutions generally do not happen when people are totally subjugated, but when they have tasted a bit of liberty. The drop in revolts in the 19th century is therefore misleading, since the abolition of slavery in the English colonies meant that there was no need for any more revolts.

> **Roleplay**
>
> Imagine that you are an enslaved African who has decided to plan a revolt and entice other slaves to rebel. List three main things you must take into consideration in order to cause maximum damage to the plantations. Remember, if you get caught you will be punished severely.

Major revolts by enslaved Africans in the West Indies

Berbice 1763

When: 23 February 1763 to December 1763

Where: Berbice, Surinam (the largest Dutch colony in the 18th century)

Who

- Kofi (Cuffy) was the main leader.
- Atta and Akara were other leaders.
- The revolt started with about 75 slaves and quickly spread to other plantations.

Why did the revolt happen?

- The revolt arose from slaves' dissatisfaction with everyday conditions – harsh treatment, injustice and severe punishments.
- They knew that the whites were a weakened group (numerically as well as physically because of an epidemic which had struck the colony).

Was it a success?

- The ratio of enslaved Africans to whites was 11:1, so the slaves had an advantage over the white population.

- The whites were weakened due to the epidemic which had caused a high death rate among their group.
- The element of surprise was used – the white population was caught unprepared.
- In March 1763 the rebels were in a position to defeat the whites completely but due to poor strategy on their part (Kofi attempted to come to a compromise with the Governor) they did not attack and the whites were able to strengthen their position.
- About 130 enslaved Africans were captured and put to death by torture and burning. Some were also broken on the wheel. Atta was tortured by having his flesh torn out and then he was burnt at the stake.
- Berbice suffered an economic decline shortly afterwards as plantations were devastated.

Barbados, 1816 (also called the Easter Rebellion)

When: April 1816 (the revolt lasted three days from 14 April 1816)

Where: It started in the St Phillip Parish and spread to the parishes of St John and St George.

Who
- Bussa, an African who was captured in Africa and brought to Barbados was one of the main leaders.
- Other enslaved Africans such as Nanny Griggs, Jackey, Roach and Ranger played a role.
- Washington Francklyn and Cain Davis, who were free coloureds, also played a role.

Why did the revolt happen?
- The group revolted because of the Registration Bill which they thought granted them freedom.

3.11 Statue of Bussa: one of the main leaders of the Easter Rebellion

- Under this Bill the planters had to register all births and deaths in the colonies so as to keep a check on all illegal importation of slaves.
- Britain placed pressure on planters in Barbados to pass the Bill but the planters objected.
- The enslaved Africans misinterpreted the anger of the whites and thought that the whites were refusing to grant them their freedom.

3.12 Photograph showing Le Resouvenir, a plantation in British Guiana (now Guyana). Reverend John Smith's mission is located on the right.

Was it a success?

- The revolt was planned and executed well and initially was successful because of the element of surprise.
- More than 1,000 enslaved Africans were killed in the revolt, while 144 were executed and 123 were deported.

Demerara, 1823

When: 18 August 1823

Where: It started on Plantation Success and spread to other estates on the East Coast of Demerara.

Who

- The leaders were:
  - Quamina, a slave who was a deacon
  - John Wray, a missionary of the Bethel Chapel associated with the London Missionary Society, who taught principles of freedom to the slaves
  - Reverend John Smith, a white clergymen, who was in charge of the Bethel Chapel.

Why did the revolt happen?

- It happened in response to amelioration proposals. The slaves thought that freedom had been granted but the planters were withholding it from them.

Was it a success?

- John Smith was arrested, found guilty and sentenced to hang, but he died in prison.
- There was widespread persecution of ministers, mainly baptists and methodists.
- The slaves attempted to negotiate peacefully but they were not entertained, instead the revolt was suppressed.
- Over 100 slaves were killed in the rebellion, 47 were hanged and many others were flogged and imprisoned.
- Christian slaves played a prominent role in this revolt.
- The rebellion drew the attention of British anti-slavery groups, especially as a white clergyman had been killed.

Jamaica, Christmas Rebellion, 1831

When: 28 December 1831 to 5 January 1832

Where: St James Parish

Who

- The leader was Samuel Sharpe, an educated Creole slave.

3.13 A statue of Samuel Sharpe

Why did the revolt happen?

- Sharpe's aim was that the enslaved Africans would not work on Christmas Day in protest to their inhumane treatment and grievances about their working conditions.
- He wanted the enslaved Africans to stop working as a peaceful protest and unite so that after Christmas they would not work unless paid for their labour. The idea was that withholding their labour would force the planters to start paying wages.

Was it a success?

- The revolt spread to plantations in Trelawney, St Elizabeth and Hanover.
- More than 20,000 enslaved Africans were involved in the rebellion.
- Sharpe's army lacked training and experience and the white forces were able to suppress his rebels.
- Approximately 207 enslaved Africans were shot.
- Sharpe was captured and hanged in public and more than 500 enslaved Africans were tried and executed.
- There was extensive damage to plantations, estimated at £1.25 million.

Table 3.5 Proportion of revolts in selected English colonies

Island	Revolts (%)
Barbados	9
Jamaica	30
Antigua	7
St. Kitts	4
Belize	7
St. Vincent	3
Tobago	7
Trinidad	3

Marronage

Those slaves who ran away and established small settlements in the mountainous areas of Jamaica, British Guiana and Suriname were called the Maroons. The word is derived from 'marronage' which came from the Spanish word 'cimarron', meaning fugitive or runaway.

Two types can be distinguished – 'grand marronage' refers to large groups of people who ran away from plantations and 'petit marronage' describes individuals or small groups who ran away. The grand marronage led to the establishment of Maroon communities while the petit marronage was comprised of people who would sometimes return to the plantations and who can be seen as habitual runaways or people who just tried to get away from their situation temporarily.

> **Roleplay**
>
> Imagine you are a slave. You have heard that four field slaves from your plantation ran away last night to join the Maroons. Explain to your brother three reasons why you are going to join in the plan to run away.

As the Maroon communities increased the slave owners felt more threatened. Successful Maroon communities were established in Jamaica, as seen with the Sambo-Mosquito on the Mosquito Coast, Cudjoe Town (named after leader General Cudjoe) and Nanny Town.

Symbiotic relationship a relationship which is mutually beneficial. That is, each individual or group benefits from the interaction.

TRELAWNEY TOWN, the CHIEF RESIDENCE of the MAROONS.

3.14 View of a Maroon village, early 19th century

Reasons for the success of Maroon communities

- **Geographical topography was used to advantage.** They settled on mountainous regions such as the 'cockpit country' in Jamaica which received its name because of the many cockpits and caves in the area. The Europeans had difficulties in traversing these areas and so the Maroons were able to exist without much harassment by the planters.
- **The Maroons established well-planned communities.** They carefully chose where to settle and when they established their communities they had an organized system of government (they appointed leaders) and engaged in agriculture and trade.
- **They became self-sufficient communities.** They produced enough to feed themselves. They planted a variety of crops which included ground provisions (sweet potatoes and yams), plantains, bananas, tobacco, coffee, beans and some sugar cane in the larger communities.
- **They established symbiotic relations with the indigenous peoples.** They met smaller Taino groups in the mountainous areas and formed several 'agreements' with them. The two groups traded their surplus food. It was a symbiotic relationship in that the Tainos taught the Maroons to survive in the forests and the Maroons returned the favour by introducing the Tainos to new types of crops and methods of farming.
- **Their knowledge and practice of guerilla warfare was valuable.** They frequently used this knowledge defending themselves against European trackers who attempted to find their communities. It also helped when the Maroons raided plantations for supplies.
- **The Maroon leaders were very effective.** Various Maroon leaders helped to maintain well-organized communities through their administrative skills. They also played an important role in creating and maintaining a sense of unity and confidence among community members. They planned successful raids on the plantations and made decisions regarding the community. For example, General Cudjoe signed a treaty with the colonial government to gain its cooperation and to ensure that the Maroon community would survive with little interference from the Europeans.
- **To some extent Maroon communities survived because Europeans grew to fear and even respect them.** This is evident by the treaties which were signed with some Maroons after the First Maroon War (1729–39) and the Second Maroon War (1795–96).

Maroon communities were one of the great contradictions of slavery, proving to the master that Africans were not childlike and docile. They served as a constant reminder to the white community that Africans wanted their freedom and could be self-governing. They also reminded the slaves that there was an alternative to their current situation, and were therefore a source of hope.

First Maroon War (1729–39) After a long period of conflict with the Maroons the British government in Jamaica came to an agreement. This treaty gave the Maroons the right to their independent communities. In return, the Maroons pledged their support to the colonial regime, agreed to help capture runaway slaves and to help in the defence of the colony.

Second Maroon War (1795–96) The Maroons felt they were being mistreated and conflict began again in 1795. Another treaty was signed whereby the Maroons would return all runaway slaves, ask for the King's forgiveness and be relocated to other parts of Jamaica.

Groupwork

In a group of three or four people, discuss why you think the British colonials in Jamaica were interested in signing a peace treaty with the Maroons. If you were a group of British colonials, what would you say to persuade the Maroon leaders to sign a treaty with you?

The Haitian Revolution

In 1788, a coffee planter in St Domingue (soon to be Haiti) murdered four of his slaves and tortured two more. The planter's name was Le Jeune, and his odd justification for these acts was to prevent his slaves being poisoned, because he found too many of them had been dying. The two slaves he tortured were women. He roasted their legs and elbows over a fire. Le Jeune knew it was against the law to torture, so he threatened his slaves with execution if they told anyone what he had done. However, slaves in St Domingue knew their rights and 14 of them laid a complaint to the authorities. A commission was appointed, which actually found the two women still chained where they had been tortured, their elbows and legs rotting from being burned. Both of them eventually died from their injuries.

Le Jeune fled the island before he could be arrested, but he need not have worried. After a hearing and several petitions to the Governor, despite the evidence gathered by the commission which confirmed the slaves' accusations, Le Jeune was acquitted of all charges. The other planters displayed some disagreement in their responses to the case. Some demanded that Le Jeune be freed and the 14 slaves given 50 lashes each for accusing him. The Chamber of Agriculture, however, along with 70 planters, wrote to the Governor saying that Le Jeune should be banished from the colony. When the charges were dropped, the public prosecutor demanded an appeal, but Le Jeune's acquittal was eventually upheld.

This case had two effects. It showed the slaves that they would not get justice from the planters, but it also showed them that action could have consequences – after all, Le Jeune had been forced to leave St Domingue. This combination of frustration and confidence prepared the ground for when the French Revolution, with its watchwords of 'Liberty, Fraternity, Equality' erupted in France just one year later.

Causes of the Haitian Revolution

The Haitian Revolution of 1791 is unique in that the slaves succeeded in overthrowing the planters, taking over the island completely, and remaining in power. Haiti thus became the first black-ruled nation in the Western hemisphere. However, several factors had to come together for this to happen.

The main ones were:

- the collapse of the French monarchy
- the large numbers of African slaves imported into St Domingue in a short period of time
- the existence of a large mixed-race class
- an intelligent and strong-willed leader in Toussaint L'Ouverture
- the extreme conditions in St Domingue.

If one or more of these factors had been missing, the Haitian Revolution might still have happened, but it is less likely to have lasted. Other colonies had some of these factors, but none had all. Many historians have focused on Toussaint as the key to the Revolution's success but this 'Great Man theory' of history is now largely dismissed, since we have come to understand that the social and political conditions must also exist for great leaders to rise.

If any single factor was most crucial, it was probably the instability of the revolutionary government in France, whose members had executed the king and most of the aristocrats and then began murdering one another as plots and counter-plots multiplied. The revolutionary government, sticking to its ideal of equality, also mandated that slavery had to be abolished. The slaves in St Domingue thus had the belief that they had been freed but the planters were opposing their own government. This belief would have emboldened the slaves to revolt against a system which, always unjust, they now believed was also illegal.

The second factor was the huge numbers of Africans in the island. St Domingue was, at this time, the wealthiest colony in the Caribbean. By 1754, it had 599 sugar plantations and over 3,000 indigo plantations. When the Seven Years' War (1756–63) ended, production increased even more as trade resumed. In 1767, St Domingue exported 32 million kilograms of raw sugar and 23 million kilograms of refined sugar, 400,000 kilos of indigo and 800,000 kilos of cotton, along with rum, molasses, cocoa and coffee.

The colonists began importing slaves in ever larger numbers to keep up production and profits. From 1764 to 1771, between 10,000 and 15,000 slaves were brought in every year. By 1786, it was 27,000 and by 1787 more than 40,000 slaves were being brought in annually. By 1789, more than 66% of the 500,000 slaves in St Domingue had been born in Africa. The result was not only an increasing disproportion of numbers between whites and blacks, but also closer unity among the slaves who were brought in tribal batches, which resulted in a more close-knit slave community.

The third factor, the mixed-race class, was also important. First of all, their very existence showed that any gap between white and black was not unbridgeable. As you learned in the section on ideological control, the whites tried to justify slavery by claiming that the blacks were less than human – but then they had increasing numbers of children with them. This is another great contradiction of the slavery period. Ideology cannot withstand biology.

Second, the mulattoes were potential allies for the slaves, even though some of them were planters and slave owners themselves and even though most of them tried to win favour with the whites. In 1790 though, inspired by the revolutionary events and rhetoric from France, they rebelled and demanded full equality with the whites. This rebellion was put down, but then the French government agreed to the demands from the mixed-race group. This resulted in an internal war between the 35,000 mixed-race and the 42,000 whites, with both sides using the 400,000 blacks to fight their battles. It was that fighting which provided the opportunity for the enslaved Africans to take control.

The conditions, therefore, were right for a leader of Toussaint's stature to emerge. In revolutions, leaders have rarely been from the oppressed group. Instead, they are more often relatively privileged people who, for various reasons, take up the cause of the underclass.

> **Roleplay**
>
> Imagine that you are an influential leader in Haiti in 1791. You have the opportunity to address about 50 enslaved Africans on a sugar plantation. Write a short speech which you think would incite them to revolt.

TOUSSAINT L'OUVERTURE
(1743–1803)

Toussaint L'Ouverture, born in St Domingue in 1743, was a domestic slave who became steward of all the livestock on his master's estate – a position usually given to a white man. He had some medical knowledge and was able to read.

He was already 45 years old when he joined the Haitian Revolution, so he had already passed the average lifespan of a slave. The revolt had been going on for one month, and Toussaint, with his combination of experience, intelligence and charisma, soon became its key leader.

He eventually established control of the island, using military and economic tactics to gain power and improve the livelihood of the majority of people. Sadly, he was deported to France where he died in 1803 without living to see an independent Haiti. He is recognised as the father of Haiti and a key leader in the overthrow of slavery in the New World.

3.15 Toussaint L'Ouverture

> **Main leaders of the Haitian Revolution**
>
> Other than Toussaint L'Ouverture, these were the main leaders.
>
> **Boukman Dutty** was a Jamaican-born slave who practised Vodun (Voodoo). He was sold by his British masters to a French plantation whose owner put him to work as a slave driver. He later became a carriage driver and the headman of a plantation. He got his name from his English nickname, Book Man, which he was given because he could read. Early in the revolution he was captured by French troops and beheaded.

Jean Francois (Papillion) was a fugitive from the north, who became a Maroon long before the revolt began. He took the title Grand Admiral of France and General-in-Chief, and had a habit of wearing elaborate costumes covered with stripes, braid and medals. He was one of the main leaders of the black insurrections up to 1795 and fought on behalf of the Spanish loyalists for a short time. He later migrated to Spain where he died.

Jorge Biassou was the son of slaves. He was a lieutenant to Jean Francois and 50 years old when he joined the revolution. He commanded an army of 40,000 slaves and was responsible for the destruction of numerous plantations and the murder of many slave owners. He used to fill his tent with cats, dead men's bones and other objects to inspire superstitious awe in his followers.

Jean-Jacques Dessalines was born into slavery and was already 40 years old when the revolution began. He later became Emperor of Haiti or Governor-General for life. Under this title, he was given power to make laws and to choose his successor. He crowned himself as Emperor Jacques I in an elaborate ceremony.

3.16 Jean-Jacques Dessalines

Factors contributing to the success of the Haitian Revolution

The success of the French Revolution had an impact.

- Free mixed-race and slaves in Haiti wanted equality as was given to the higher classes in France.
- The French Revolution had an ideological influence – 'Liberty, Equality, Fraternity'.

Disunity among free mixed-race and planters gave the enslaved Africans a good opportunity to fight for their own freedom.

- Enslaved Africans were able to use the disunity to gain information from both groups.

Strong leadership played a role in the successful outcome of the Haitian Revolution.

- Leaders emerged who gave proper guidance to the enslaved Africans.
- Some leaders, such as Toussaint L'Ouverture, were good strategists who acted at opportune times.
- Leaders emerged who were trained in guerilla warfare and who then used their knowledge to train an enslaved 'army'.

The Haitian Revolution: timeline

14 July 1789 – The Bastille fort in Paris is taken by revolutionary forces, marking the start of the French Revolution.

September 1789 – A mixed-race delegation asks St Domingue whites for equal rights, and is refused.

April 1790 – The Constituent Assembly in France debates the rights of mixed-race people and decides that every mixed-race person with two free parents should be given the vote. There are 400 such people in St Domingue.

October 1790 – Oge, representing the Friends of the Negroes organization, goes to St Domingue to plead for the cause of mixed-race people as slave owners. He is arrested and executed.

March 1791 – Two regiments of French soldiers sent to help the government keep order throw their support behind the mixed-race group and the Africans, telling them that the National Assembly had declared all men equal and free.

August 1791 – Under Boukman, a Vodun priest, several thousand slaves revolt. Slave gangs murder their masters and set fire to plantations. They take control of the countryside, but not the capital city, Port-au-Prince.

September 1791 – Toussaint L'Ouverture joins the revolutionaries.

19 October 1791 – A concordat is signed between the royalist commandants, the rich whites and the mixed-race group. The terms are: full rights for all mixed-race; two battalions of the National Guard to be recruited from among the mixed-race; the Provincial Assembly (which had assumed official governance of the western part of the colony) to be dissolved; and Oge to be declared a hero. The concordat was to be presented to the National Assembly for ratification.

24 October 1791 – The leaders of the whites and the leaders of the mixed-race group march arm in arm into Port-au-Prince with their troops, celebrating their unity.

21 November 1791 – Voting for ratification of the concordat commences. A member of the mixed-race is hanged by some whites, an incident which sparks off fighting in the streets. Violence spreads, fire breaks out and by the end of the day two thirds of Port-au-Prince is burned to the ground.

29 November 1791 – Three commissioners from the National Assembly arrive in St Domingue to restore order. The revolt has been halted at the western provinces of the island and, having destroyed the land around them, they are starting to starve. The revolutionaries meet with the leader Jean Francois, who agrees to lead his followers back into slavery if 400 leaders in the revolt are given their freedom. The delegates, led by Toussaint L'Ouverture, meet with the National Assembly, but refuse to agree to grant the leaders freedom, even though Toussaint reduces the number from 400 to a mere 60. Toussaint decides to continue the revolt and not stop until every person in St Domingue is free.

4 April 1792 – A decree giving mixed-race people equal rights is passed in France.

April 1792 – The white patriots in Port-au-Prince are under siege from an alliance of royalist commanders, white planters, mixed-race and blacks.

July 1792 – Toussaint has formed an army, starting with a few hundred selected men, training them in camp to be effective soldiers.

18 September 1792 – Three commissioners sent by the National Assembly arrive in St Domingue to suppress the revolt with 6,000 soldiers and 15 ships.

30 September 1792 – The Governor, the commander of the naval station, and the Treasurer write to the commissioners stating that the whites have accepted the 4 April decree.

21 January 1793 – The French king is executed.

June 1793 – The Spanish authorities offer the blacks an alliance against the French government. Jean Francois and Biassou are appointed lieutenants-general of the armies of the King of Spain and Toussaint is made a colonel in command of 600 men.

29 August 1793 – One of the commissioners, Sonthonax, declares slavery abolished. Whites in West Province accept, but Toussaint, Biassou and Jean Francois continue fighting alongside the Spanish. In the southern part of the island the slaves are defeating the whites and the mixed-race group.

9 September 1793 – British forces land in St Domingue to help suppress the slave revolt.

December 1793 – Toussaint's forces take major garrisons, and their soldiers, including white troops, join him.

January 1794 – The British take control of the seaboard of Port-au-Prince, the West Province and most of the south.

May 1794 – Toussaint joins the French.

June 1794 – Toussaint, with 4,000 troops, attacks former allies Jean Francois and Biassou and re-takes the North Province from the Spanish, partially driving back the British, who still remain in control of a key fort and the most fertile districts in St Domingue.

January 1796 – Toussaint is made proconsul of his district.

March 1796 – The mixed-race stage a coup, which is put down by Toussaint.

17 August 1796 – Toussaint is made a general by the French government.

Early 1797 – The British decide to withdraw from St Domingue.

2 May 1797 – Toussaint is confirmed as Commander in Chief and Governor of St Domingue by French ruler Napoleon Bonaparte.

November 1798 – The British sign a treaty with Toussaint and leave the island.

9 October 1801 – Napoleon sends 20,000 troops to St Domingue under the command of General Leclerc to overthrow Toussaint and restore slavery in the colony.

February–March 1802 – Around 5,000 French soldiers are killed and 5,000 hospitalized.

April 1802 – Toussaint sends a letter to Charles Leclerc (Napoleon's brother-in-law), addressed to Napoleon, offering a truce. Conditions are freedom for all blacks in St Domingue, preservation of the ranks and duties of native army officers and Toussaint and his staff to continue functioning until he chooses to retire in any part of the colony.

5 May 1802 – Leclerc sends a letter to the French Minister of Marine, claiming: 'General Toussaint has surrendered here. He left perfectly satisfied with me and ready to carry out all my orders.'

6 May 1802 – Toussaint rides victoriously into the city of Le Cap with his staff and dragoons, accompanied by French General Hardy. Dessalines arrives a few days later to make a formal submission to the French.

6 June 1802 – Leclerc sends a letter to the Minister of Marine requesting 10,000 more men, since 30 to 50 men are dying daily from yellow fever.

7 June 1802 – General Brunet requests a meeting with Toussaint. At the meeting, Toussaint is arrested. The French soldiers later loot his house and burn his plantations. Along with his wife, son and niece, Toussaint is put on a ship waiting in the Le Cap harbour and carried to France.

July 1802 – Blacks begin revolting in the north, then in the south and west regions. Rumours are spreading that the French government is restoring slavery on the colony.

24 August 1802 – Toussaint is imprisoned in the Fort-de-Joux in the Jura Mountains.

26 September 1802 – Leclerc sends a letter to the First Consul, saying, 'San Domingo is lost to France if I have not received on the 16th January 10,000 men who must all come at the same time.'

2 November 1802 – Leclerc dies from yellow fever. Of the total 34,000 French soldiers who had come to St Domingue, around 24,000 are dead and 8,000 are in hospital. General Rochambeau takes over, obtaining an additional 10,000 troops. The French now control only Le Cap and a few towns in the north and west, but Spanish San Domingo is peaceful and the mixed-race in the south are loyal to the French.

15 January 1803 – Rochambeau sends a letter to the Colonial Minister requesting authorization to restore slavery on the colony. His army attacks the mixed-race group, killing hundreds.

March 1803 – The mixed-race are now in revolt against the French, but the Spaniards in the west remain loyal. Rochambeau gets 10,000 more soldiers from France. Over 1,500 hunting dogs are brought to the island and trained to attack the blacks at first scent.

7 April 1803 – Toussaint dies aged 57.

16 November 1803 – Blacks and mixed-race under Dessalines attack Le Cap. Rochambeau decides to evacuate the island.

28 November 1803 – Rochambeau surrenders to the British.

31 December 1803 – A declaration of independence is officially read. The colony is renamed Haiti.

October 1804 – Dessalines declares himself Emperor of Haiti.

January 1805 – All whites in Haiti are massacred on orders from Dessalines.

Impact of the Haitian Revolution on Haiti and the wider Caribbean

The Haitian Revolution led to the complete abolition of slavery in St Domingue.

It brought about the emergence of some influential leaders such as Boukman Dutty, Andre Riguad, Alexandre Petion and Toussaint L'Ouverture.

It severely changed Haiti's economic status.
- The country's infrastructure, such as roads, harbours and bridges, was destroyed.
- Sugar production declined from 163.4 million pounds in 1791 to 20.2 million pounds in 1818.

It led to changes in Haiti's agricultural policies.
- Estates would be returned to individuals and families who formerly owned them.

It led to an exodus of whites from the islands.
- They carried with them their capital, technology and skills in sugar production.

There was an increase in production in some other Caribbean countries.
- For example, the decline in St Domingue's coffee industry provided an opportunity for Cuba and Jamaica to increase their markets for coffee.

- Some planters who left St Domingue migrated to Cuba and Jamaica (that is, were émigrés) and established plantations in these colonies.

It exacerbated poor relations between Africans and free coloureds, and whites in St Domingue.

- Syrians were exiled from the colony as a result of anti-Syrian sentiments from 1903 to 1905.

- This exodus led to a loss of St Domingue's skilled working class.

It promoted the idea of the abolition of slavery in British colonies.

- Some abolitionists used the Haitian Revolution to justify their anti-slavery views.

It served as inspiration to the enslaved population and created fear among the enslavers.

REVISION QUESTIONS

1 Read the passage below, then answer the questions that follow.

Enslaved women were...punished brutally for their resistance activities...but they did not stop their antislavery activities because of these forms of punishment, and were active in various forms of resistance until slavery ended.

a Describe the forms of resistance that were especially used by women in their fight against slavery. *(12 marks)*

b Outline three forms of slave resistance in which both men and woman were involved. *(9 marks)*

c Give two ways in which women were punished for resistance activities during slavery. *(4 marks)*

(Total = 25 marks)

CXC Past Paper, General Proficiency, May/June 2004

2 Read the passage below then answer the questions that follow.

Violent rebellion was the most extreme method adopted by enslaved men and women to resist slavery. However, there were other methods, which were less extreme, but which also challenged the slave system.

a Describe how enslaved men and women used 'less extreme' methods to resist slavery. *(12 marks)*

b Explain why most slave protests and rebellions failed to destroy slavery. *(13 marks)*

(Total = 25 marks)

CXC Past Papers, General Proficiency, May/June 2002

3 What was the impact of the Haitian Revolution on Haiti and the wider Caribbean? *(25 marks)*

4 Critically discuss this statement: 'Enslaved Africans resisted the control imposed over them from the time they were captured, during the middle passage and while on the plantations.' *(25 marks)*

References and recommended reading

- Bryan, P. *The Haitian Revolution and its Effects*, Kingston: Heinemann, 1984
- Craton, M. *Testing the Chains: Resistance to slavery in the British West Indies*, Ithaca: Cornell University Press, 1982
- Edwards, P. *Equiano's Travels*, London: Heinemann Educational Books, 1967
- Eltis, D. *The Rise of African Slavery in the Americas*, Cambridge: Cambridge University Press, 2000
- Hillman, R. and D'Agostino. T. *Understanding the Contemporary Caribbean*, London: Lynne Rienner Publishers, 2009
- James, C.L.R. *The Black Jacobins*, London: Penguin Books, 2001
- Mathurin, L. *The Rebel Woman in the British West Indies During Slavery*, Kingston: African-Caribbean Publications, 1975
- Montejo, E. *The Autobiography of a Runaway Slave*, London: The Bodley Head, 1968
- Thompson, A. *Flight to Freedom: African runaways and Maroons in the Americas*, Kingston: UWI Press, 2006

4 The metropolitan movement towards emancipation

This chapter will answer the following questions.
- Why was the slave trade from Africa to Europe abolished?
- What were the arguments for and against the abolition of slavery?
- How was amelioration different in British, French and Spanish colonies?
- What were the main features of the anti-slavery movement?
- What were the main stipulations of the British Emancipation Act?
- Why was an apprenticeship system introduced in some colonies and what were the problems associated with this system?

When, in the late 18th century, British citizens and leaders began taking action against the slave trade and slavery, it was the first time in human history that any society decided that enslaving other human beings is morally wrong. From the time civilization started with the Sumerians more than 5,000 years ago, slavery had been an established institution. It existed in Egypt, China, Europe, the Indus Valley, South America and Persia. Some of these societies had laws protecting slaves and religious texts which said that masters benefited spiritually from treating their slaves kindly. Some even had debates on what groups of people should or should not be enslaved. Slavery lasted for over five millennia before influential people in any nation even suggested that it should not exist at all.

As you will see, this was not because human nature had suddenly become more conscientious or because the British were inherently more enlightened than other people. Instead, it was because Britain had become so advanced technologically that slavery was no longer needed for its elites to have a high standard of living.

Even so, since slavery had been part of the world for so long, it is not surprising that stopping the slave trade and abolishing slavery should have encountered so many obstacles.

Roleplay

It is January 1838. Imagine that you are an enslaved African and you have heard rumours that the abolition of slavery is near. Explain your future plans to a fellow slave.

Reasons for the abolition of the slave trade

The campaign by the abolitionists

Since slavery was such a well-established practice and central to economic activity in the colonies, it could not have been abolished in one fell swoop.

Instead, those who were working to stop the enslavement of Africans had to proceed in stages. Indeed, the politician who became the best-known leader of the abolition movement, William Wilberforce (see the biography box on page 94), actually rejected in 1814 a suggestion that all enslaved Africans brought illegally into British territories should be freed. 'Our object and our universal language was, and is, to produce by abolition a disposition to breed instead of buying,' he wrote. In other words, at that point the goal was to get the slave trade, not slavery itself, eradicated by persuading planters to obtain more slaves though reproduction, rather than by kidnapping additional slaves from Africa. Even when in 1823 the abolitionists decided to focus on emancipation, their leader in Parliament, Sir Thomas Buxton, urged restraint and patience, saying: 'Nothing rash, nothing rapid, nothing abrupt, nothing bearing any feature of violence.' Slavery, he said, would naturally decline as the abolitionists pursued their public education programme in Britain.

As Britain was the main slave-owning nation by the 18th century and since the main opponents of the slave trade were English, the first step was to get the slave trade abolished in England.

This occurred mainly through the efforts of one man, Granville Sharp, a junior clerk in the Ordinance Office who came from a family of Anglican clergymen.

Sharp first became involved in the slavery issue when he encountered a slave named Jonathan Strong on the streets of London. Strong had been attacked by his master and nearly killed, but Sharp and his brother William, who was a surgeon, saved Strong's life and nursed him back to health, after which Strong got a job with an apothecary. Then his former master saw Strong and hired two slave hunters to capture him and put him aboard a ship bound for Jamaica, to be sold to a new master for £30. Sharp was able to get Strong freed and went to court to get the English law on slavery clarified.

> **Activity 4.1**
>
> We have learned that:
> - William Wilberforce rejected a suggestion that all enslaved Africans brought illegally into British territories should be freed
> - Sir Thomas Buxton did not want to rush abolition and noted that slavery would decline naturally as the abolitionists pursued their public education programme in Britain.
>
> What does this suggest about the abolitionists?
>
> Why do you think they were in favour of abolition but not interested in revolution?

PERSECUTION & SLAVERY.

Friends & Fellow Countrymen,

Think of the present state of things in the West-Indies. Realize the miseries, the wrongs, which are there endured; where hundreds of thousands of your fellow subjects are violently robbed of their dearest rights, and cruelly kept toiling, by terror of the lash, sixteen hours on an average out of every twenty four throughout the year, without domestic comforts, without conjugal rights, and with a constant liability to merciless floggings, at the will of brutal overseers, and scarcely less brutal owners. Look especially at the violated rights of British subjects, and the persecution of christian missionaries, and of all other christians. Several places of worship have been tumultuously pulled down, the negroes are flogged for praying; the missionaries are robbed, shot at, imprisoned, and by notorious perjury tried for their lives. Will you support such a state of things as this? Or are you resolved that it shall cease? *Remember that all the money you pay for Sugar raised by slave labour goes to support slavery, and the evils which that system perpetuates. Renounce slave-grown sugar, and slavery must fall.* Give, then, this practical proof to the government and the slave-holders that you are *in earnest.* Let every one who is the friend of civil and religious liberty, of the slave and of the missionary, (and these will be found to be the best friends to the Planter likewise, who will soon be ruined by the continuance of the present system) come forward and *give a pledge to use no more Sugar raised by slave labour,* since it is stained with his brother's blood. If this resolution were general through the country, (and by means of active associations it might speedily be rendered so,) it would strengthen and quicken all the measures now in operation, and Slavery would receive its *death blow.* There is other slave produce, but nothing that can be compared with Sugar, either in the quantity consumed, or in its ill effects on the comfort and life of the slave; while FREE LABOUR SUGAR can now be obtained both cheap and good, and a little encouragement will render it cheaper and better. You will not hurt the slave by lessening the demand for his labour, but on the contrary you will do him good, by getting more time for him to rest, and to raise his own provisions. And as to hurting the planters, tell them you will leave it off *the moment they set the negroes free.*

Sold by B. WHITE, Broad-Street, Reading, at 6d. per hundred or 1d. per doz

4.1 Abolitionist tract: 'Remarks on the methods of procuring slaves with a short account of their treatment in the West-Indies, etc.' English abolitionist publication, price 3 pennies, printed in London, 1794

4.2 Granville Sharp

Neither Strong's former master nor his next one in Jamaica contested the case. In 1772, Sharp also went to court to free a slave named James Somerset, who had escaped from an American named Charles Stewart living in England. Somerset was recaptured and put on a boat for Jamaica, where he was to be sold, but Sharp was able to free him before the ship sailed. Eventually, after several months of trial, the English court under Judge Mansfield decided that there was no legal definition of slavery in England.

This decision made it illegal to take a slave against his will back to the slave colonies, so a slave could 'walk away' from slavery by refusing to go back and merging with the free black population in England. The Mansfield judgment helped bolster public opinion against slavery. Influential figures such as Dr Samuel Johnson, compiler of the first authoritative English dictionary, became involved. 'It is impossible not to conceive that men in their original state were equal… no man is by nature the property of another [so] the defendant is by nature free,' Dr Johnson wrote in one essay.

In 1775, prompted by Quakers, a commission of the House of Commons was appointed to take evidence of the slave trade. In 1776, after the report was submitted, David Hartley, Member of Parliament for Hull, introduced a debate: 'That the slave trade is contrary to the laws of God and the rights of men'. This indicated a shift in opinion among law makers, although the debate did not lead to any change in legislation. In 1787, the Quakers formed 'The Society for Effecting the Abolition of the Slave Trade'.

This Society set up branches in Britain's large towns, with town leaders organizing meetings and getting petitions signed. This strategy was very successful, with 100 petitions going to Parliament in the same year the Society was formed and 500 petitions in 1792. Numerous pamphlets were also written and distributed throughout England. Producing and distributing pamphlets in the 18th and 19th centuries can be compared with sending e-mails today. Thomas Clarkson wrote an essay entitled 'A Summary View of the Slave Trade and the Probable Consequences of its Abolition', which was printed in pamphlet form and 15,000 copies were distributed. The Reverend James Ramsay, who had lived in the Caribbean for 19 years, published in 1784 an 'Essay on the Treatment and Conversion of the African Slaves in the Sugar Colonies', which was also widely read. Other pamphlets highlighted cases of cruelty by British Caribbean planters which had reached the courts. The poet William Cowper wrote an anti-slavery poem called 'The Negro's Complaint' which was widely read. Several thousand copies were printed on high-quality paper for distribution to upper-class women as a conversation piece, and the words were also set to music.

> Still in thought as free as ever
> What are England's rights, I ask,
> Made from my delight to sever,
> Me to torture, me to task?
> Fleecy locks, and black complexion
> Cannot forfeit Nature's claim;
> Skins may differ, but affection
> Dwells in white and black the same.

Activity 4.2 Read the poem on page 93 and answer the following question.

- What is the main message that the poet is trying to convey to his readers?
- Is there terminology in the poem that would be considered racist today?

You should understand that the abolitionists' campaign was not aimed at a popular audience, in the modern meaning of that term, when campaigns are aimed at reaching a majority of people. Even if that were possible in Britain in the 19th century, such a campaign would have been pointless and ineffective, since the ordinary person did not have much social or political influence. Instead, the abolitionists were trying to persuade the aristocrats, Members of Parliament (MPs), the wealthy and others who held important offices. In 1830, at a meeting of the Society, a motion was put forward to call on the British Parliament to emancipate the slaves at once. This caused conflict between the two factions of the Society, one side wanting a more cautious and gradual approach, the other insisting that what must be done was best done quickly. After heated discussion, the motion was carried.

FAST FACTS

- The Quakers were one of the few Christian groups which actively opposed slavery, perhaps because since the Quakers had formed in the early 17th century they had been persecuted for what were considered unconventional Christian practices.
- The Toleration Act of 1689 gave the Quakers legal protection and ended the worst violence against them in Britain, although they were still disadvantaged as a religious group.
- In Barbados, Quakers were often fined for allowing slaves to worship with them.

WILLIAM WILBERFORCE
(1759–1833)

Wilberforce was born on 24 August 1759 in Hull in Yorkshire, England. He was a politician and philanthropist who from 1787 led the struggle to abolish the slave trade and then to abolish slavery itself in the British colonies.

Wilberforce became a member of the House of Commons in 1780, along with his good friend from university William Pitt the Younger, who was to become Prime Minister. Wilberforce soon began to support parliamentary reform and Roman Catholic political emancipation, and from 1815 he upheld the Corn Laws (tariffs on imported grain) and repressive measures against working-class public demonstrations.

Wilberforce's abolitionism came in part from evangelical Christianity, to which he converted in 1784. In 1787, he helped to found a society for the 'reformation of manners' called the Proclamation Society (to suppress the publication of obscenity) and the Society for Effecting the Abolition of the Slave Trade. He and his associates – Thomas Clarkson, Granville Sharp, Henry Thornton, Charles Grant, Edward James Eliot, Zachary Macaulay and James Stephen – were first called the Saints and afterwards (from 1797) the Clapham Sect, which Wilberforce led. In 1823, he helped to organize, and became a vice president of, the Society for the Mitigation and Gradual Abolition of Slavery Throughout the British

4.3 William Wilberforce

Dominions – more commonly called the Anti-Slavery Society. Turning over the parliamentary leadership of the abolition movement, he retired from the House of Commons in 1825. The Abolition Act was passed one month after his death on 29 July 1833.

> **Fraternity** a feeling of frendship and mutual support.

The French Revolution, which erupted in 1789, had the slogan, 'Liberty, Fraternity, Equality'. This was used by the abolitionists, while the St Domingue Revolution (see Chapter 3) also kept the conditions of enslaved Africans as a topic of conversation and concern.

The abolitionists used the 'population principle' to argue that St Domingue, now called Haiti, was proof of the rightness of freedom. This argument basically rested on the fact that the African population in the slave colonies did not increase except through imports of more enslaved people, whereas in Haiti the population had expanded above its 500,000 total in 1791. In 1823, when Buxton was still arguing for gradual emancipation, he told the British Parliament that Haiti enjoyed 'all the blessings which freedom brings'. In 1830, he specified increased population as the main blessing, noting that, despite wars and emigration and civil violence, Haiti's population had increased from 423,000 in 1804 to 935,000 in 1831. These figures are too precise to be accurate, and Buxton was accused by anti-abolitionists of doubling the true population figure of Haiti. However, it does seem that there was a significant increase in population in those 27 years. Buxton also argued that there was a correlation between the end of sugar production and this population increase in Haiti, saying that it was the back-breaking labour on the sugar plantations which caused the high mortality rates among blacks in the slave colonies. As you will see in Chapter 5, in the section on sugar production, this assertion had some empirical basis. The anti-abolitionists used this same point to shift the debate from population to economics, arguing that the failure of Haiti to produce sugar after the revolution showed that free labour was not productive.

During the Napoleonic war between France and Britain and other European powers (see the section 'The French slave trade' in this chapter), the politician William Wilberforce had kept the abolition issue alive in the British Parliament.

The British government now took decisive action. The Act of 1807 permitted seizure of pirates; and bounties of £60 per male, £30 per female, and £10 per child were to be paid by the Admiralty to naval officers and other beneficiaries for every slave liberated. The signs that indicated a possible slave ship were made clear to the navy. Some of these included a ship being anchored off the African coast with more supplies than could be consumed by a crew of 30; having spare planks in its hold, which could be used to make a slave deck; having hatches with open gratings instead of closed tops; and carrying shackles and handcuffs.

A British West Africa Squadron was established to ensure that no British captain from any port traded slaves along 3,000 miles of the African coast.

4.4 Image widely used in abolitionist and anti-slavery campaigns

At first, this squadron consisted of just two ships, which had 32 and 18 cannons respectively, but by 1811 there were three well-armed ships, with 74 cannons between them. In that year, too, an updated law made slaving a felony punishable by transport to Australia for 14 years.

None of this impressed the other European powers, however. The French and Spanish thought that abolition was just a ploy by the British to strengthen their military control of the sea. The German writer Goethe said:

> 'Everybody knows [the English] declamations against the slave trade; and, while they have palmed off on us all sorts of humane maxims as the foundation of their proceedings, it is at last discovered that their true motive is a practical object… In their extensive domains on the west coast of Africa, they themselves use the blacks, and it is against their interest for the blacks to be carried off.'

In fact, there were actually objections from some of the Gold Coast rulers when they learned that the British government had stopped the slave trade, because enslaved Africans were now the main source of wealth for the West African slave-trading kingdoms of Dahomey, Bonny and Lagos, accounting for three quarters of West Africa's exports in the 18th century. The King of Bonny reportedly told a British captain:

> 'We think this trade must go on. That is the verdict of our oracle and our priests. They say that your country, however great, can never stop a trade ordained by God himself.'

However, the effectiveness of the British measures should not be overestimated. In March 1824, a Bill was passed in Parliament declaring that any British subject trading slaves should be deemed guilty of 'felony, piracy, and robbery, and should suffer death without benefit of clergy and loss of lands, goods, and chattels.' No one was ever prosecuted, though. Also, Britain could only board the ships of enemy nations, which included France and the USA, but the two largest slave shippers at that time were Spain and Portugal. Britain was not at war with either of these countries. Spain, like Britain, was also fighting France, and the British government had just signed a most-favoured nation treaty with Portugal. In this treaty, Portugal agreed with Britain's abolition aims, but Portugal, which had started the Atlantic slave trade, would become the second-to-last European nation to end slavery, in 1869. Also, the seizures of ships carried out by the British made little impact on slave traffic at first: the British boarded just 37 ships in 1825 and 14 in 1826, freeing less than 15,000 people.

Even so, the British were moving faster to abolish slavery than were Spain and France, as we will see in the following sections.

The response from the planters

The British Caribbean sugar planters responded quickly to the campaign by the anti-slavery lobby. They also printed pamphlets and distributed them to MPs, several of whom owned their seats to financial support from the planters or who themselves owned plantations in the Caribbean.

The planters claimed that the slave trade saved African lives, since many of the enslaved were criminals who would have been executed. They also argued that the sugar industry was essential for England's prosperity. They even used the Bible, arguing that the Bible justified slavery and that the African's souls would be saved by conversion to Christianity. Naturally, they did not highlight the fact that they had long been the main opponents to the teaching of Christianity to the enslaved Africans.

The planters also tried to discredit some of the more prominent abolitionists. Wilberforce was too well connected to powerful people to attack, but Reverend James Ramsay was subject to vicious rumours planted by the anti-abolitionists, who circulated stories about his supposed sexual depravity from his time in the Caribbean. The stress was said to have caused Ramsay's premature death in 1789.

4 The metropolitan movement towards emancipation

4.5 The abolition of the slave trade: English anti-slavery cartoon, 1792

Despite this, the Caribbean planters realized that their opponents were winning the battle. As a result, they started buying enslaved Africans at inflated prices. Table 4.1 shows the rise and fall in prices between 1793 and 1820, taking the number 100 as the average price of slaves before 1793. As you can see, prices reached their peak in 1807, then started falling when the ban was in place. It appears that, because of the British and US abolition of the slave trade, the trade became less profitable.

Table 4.1 Rise and fall in the price of slaves 1793–1820

Years	Average price = 100
1793–97	91
1798–1802	122
1803–07	132
1808–14	74
1815–20	40

Roleplay

Slavery has just been abolished in the British West Indies. Imagine that you used to be a skilled slave working in the factory and now you are free. One day you meet a friend who was a field slave on the same plantation with you. Tell him of all the options that you think you now have. Which would you choose and why?

Spanish abolition

The war with France was not going well for Spain. Napoleon's armies had defeated the Spanish soldiers in battle after battle and by 1811 the French controlled most of Spain. On March 26, the Spanish insurrectionists who were battling Napoleon's army passed a new constitution which gave the Spanish colonists more legal powers. This was because the Spanish government needed its colonies in the fight against France.

The Deputy of Tlaxcala New Spain, José Guridi y Alcócer, who was also a priest, used these new powers to present to the Cortes of Cádiz the first formal Spanish project for the abolition of slavery, which he argued was contrary to natural law.

However, the Deputy from Bogotá, though agreeing that the abolition of the slave trade was an 'urgent necessity', said that slavery required more thought and the matter was deferred until a new constitution was written and approved. It seemed, however, that Spanish officials had become sensitive to the evils of slavery. On April 2, Deputy Agustín de Argülles proposed condemnation of slave trade, saying 'Spain ought to be in line with Britain' so it could ally against Napoleon.

These initiatives, although they did not lead to action, had Cuba's planters worried. On July 7, they sent a message to the Cortes asking the government to tread cautiously on abolition of trade 'in order not to lose this important island'. They followed this up a week later with a 92-page memorandum, including the statement: 'The slaves have come and are here, to our misfortune; not by our fault, but by those who first initiated and encouraged this commerce in the name of law and religion.' ('Those' was a reference to las Casas who had argued that the Africans should replace the Amerindians for labour in the mines and plantations).

Still, the calls for the abolition of the Spanish slave trade continued. A respected scholar, Francisco de Arango, argued that Spain should settle its constitution issues and give 20-year moratorium to planters, since Britain and the USA had done so. On 23 November 1812, geographer Isidoro Antillón proposed complete abolition and a few days later he was attacked in the street by three assailants and so badly injured that he died a year later. It is not known if his attackers were, in fact, pro-slavers, but that lobby had certainly begun to use dirty politics, such as planting rumours that Spanish abolitionists were allies of the English.

The pro-slavery lobby was on the wrong side of history, however. In July 1815, in the Treaty of Madrid with Britain, the Spanish government agreed with Britain's position and promised to ban Spanish subjects from supplying foreign countries with slaves. Spain also agreed to complete abolition in eight years. By 1818, the England-Spanish treaty was signed, prohibiting all Spanish subjects from engaging in the slave trade after 30 May 1820. The cut-off date was later extended to October 31. The British government paid the Spanish government £400,000 in compensation. The King of Spain used this money to buy eight warships to go to South America to recapture former colonies. Cuba, however, refused to abide by the treaty.

In 1868, the pro-slavery Spanish monarchy was replaced by a republican government which had many anti-slavery activists in its ranks. This new government intended to eradicate slavery in the Spanish colonies of Cuba and Puerto Rico, and it was assisted by the revolutionaries who were fighting the colonial authorities in those islands. By 1880, the Spanish government started its emancipation plan. Unlike the British and French plans, this was to be carried out in stages. Spain at this time had over 200,000 enslaved people in its colonies. Over the next five years, 90% of these slaves were freed, and all by 1886. Unlike the British, the Spanish gave no compensation to the former slave owners.

Spain was the last major colonial power to free the enslaved Africans, finally doing so in 1886. This delay was actually caused partly by the English and French emancipating their enslaved, because the Spanish government expected that sugar production in the British and French Caribbean would collapse and Spanish colonies would then reap enormous profits from sugar production. In fact, many British businessmen decided to take advantage of the expected profits and started investing in the Spanish colonies, giving sugar producers money to buy modern machinery and to build railways to reduce transportation costs. As you will read in more detail in Chapter 6, Cuba actually increased its number of slaves in the latter half of the 19th century, even supplying slaves to the US and European slave traders who continued to operate despite laws against such trade passed in their own countries. Only the abolition of slavery in the USA after the American Civil War of 1865 undermined slavery in Cuba, since the Cubans were dependent on that market.

The French slave trade

Of all the major Western powers, the French were the most reluctant to abolish the slave trade. In 1791, the French Assembly had condemned the slave trade and slavery, and in 1794 abolished slavery within France. This was because the French Revolution in 1789 was based on the ideals of liberty, brotherhood and equality, and slavery was an embarrassing contradiction to these watchwords. In 1802, however, Napoleon outraged the abolition movement when he allowed the revival of slavery which had been in limbo during the Revolution. Napoleon planned to expand France's overseas territories, and he wanted to start with the recapture of St Domingue. However, 13 years later, in an equally sudden turnaround, Napoleon abolished the French slave trade. He did this in the hope that he would win British approval, since he had been ousted from power in 1814 by an alliance of Britain, Austria, Russia and Prussia.

NAPOLEON BONAPARTE
(1769–1821)

4.6 Napoleon Bonaparte

Summary of key events 1799–1821

- **November 1799** – Napoleon was already France's foremost general and he led a successful coup to take control of the French government.
- **February 1800** – A new constitution, which allowed Napoleon to appoint ministers, generals, civil servants, magistrates and the members of the Council of State, was submitted to and approved by an overwhelming majority.
- **May 1802** – The French people voted in favour in a referendum on the following question: 'Shall Napoleon Bonaparte be consul for life?'
- **May 1803** – England declared war on France, over possession of the island of Malta.
- **December 1804** – At the behest of Napoleon, who needed its naval assistance to match the British fleets, Spain declared war on England.
- **21 October 1805** – At the Battle of Trafalgar, the Franco-Spanish fleet was totally destroyed by the British navy, commanded by Admiral Horatio Nelson, who died in the battle.
- **1809** – Spanish guerrillas, supported by British troops, harassed the French army.
- **1812** – The national Cortes was convened at Cádiz by the Spanish insurrectionaries. A constitution was passed, inspired by the ideas of the French Revolution of 1789 and by British institutions.
- **1814** – In the Treaty of Chaumont of March 1814, Austria, Russia, Prussia and Britain bound themselves together for 20 years, promising to continue the struggle until Napoleon was overthrown.
- **6 April 1814** – Faced with defeat, Napoleon abdicated. He was exiled to the island of Elba.
- **1 March 1815** – With the government experiencing internal conflict, Napoleon landed at Cannes with a detachment of his guard, and took back his rule of France.
- **18 June 1815** – Napoleon was defeated by the armies of the Duke of Wellington at the Battle of Waterloo.
- **22 June 1815** – The French parliament forced Napoleon to abdicate.
- **5 May 1821** – Napoleon died in exile on the island of St Helena, aged 51.

When Napoleon was overthrown neither the French King, Louis XVIII, nor the Foreign Minister, Talleyrand, was concerned about abolition. The British thought that the French's gratitude for British help against Spain would cause them to join the abolition movement, but the French government was too busy dealing with the effects of the war to pay any attention to social causes. However, the British anti-slavery movement sent 800 petitions with 750,000 signatures, calling on the British government to persuade the French monarchy to end the slave trade. At the same time, the French government was receiving petitions from merchants of Nantes and the Chamber of Commerce in Guadeloupe calling for the slave trade to be restored. The British government had more sway, however, and on 30 May 1814 the First Treaty of Paris was signed, with France agreeing to cooperate with Britain to stamp out the slave trade. The British were not happy about the treaty though, because specific terms of agreement were not included, and France's colonies taken during war were given back by the British. The abolitionists were also outraged at the five-year grace period before total abolition.

Caveat a warning of specific provision.

Every step forward in the battle against the slave trade had caveats. In February 1815 Britain, France, Spain, Sweden, Austria, Prussia, Russia and Portugal all signed a declaration saying that since 'the commerce known by the name of the African slave trade is repugnant to the principles of humanity and universal morality', it was a 'duty and necessity' to abolish it as soon as possible. At the same time, the declaration also said that no nation could abolish the trade 'without due regard to the interests, the habits, and even the prejudices' of its peoples.

In November, the Second Treaty of Paris was signed by Britain, France, Austria, Prussia and Russia, who all pledged the 'entire and definite' abolition of the slave trade which was 'so strongly condemned by laws of religion and nature' with no grace period being granted.

French ship owners, who were already prepared to sail to Africa because they thought they had five more years to buy Africans, lobbied to be allowed to carry out these last voyages to re-stock the colonies with slaves ('in the national interest', as they termed it). The French government was divided on the matter (Napoleon's defeat at Waterloo was still two months away). Then the British navy seized three French ships suspected of being slave ships, causing anger in France and hardening opposition to the British. In 1816, 36 ships were allowed to leave France to buy slaves in West Africa, stopping at the Cape Verde islands then sailing to Angola, Madagascar and Zanzibar.

Not until 1817 was further action against the slave trade taken, when the Duke of Richelieu announced that any slave ship found in French colonies would be confiscated and the captain banned permanently from command. It must be noted, though, that this statement did not ban bringing slaves to France itself or transporting them to non-French colonies. So, in fact, the slave trade to Cuba and other countries increased. In March 1818, France finally declared the trade illegal. This still did not completely stop the traffic. It only made slave traders more cautious. The number of slave ships actually doubled, from about 30 ships in 1818 to 60 ships in 1819.

Activity 4.3 Work with a partner and research the following question. Why did the number of slave ships actually double rather than decrease?

Between 1818 and 1831 there were about 500 slaving expeditions from France. These voyages earned an average profit of 180,000 to 200,000 francs, which was more than slave traders made in the 18th century. In 1820, there were reports of 25 to 30 slave ships flying a French flag off the coast of Africa in the first six months alone. However, by 1823 a shift had occurred. There were signs of decline in the number of slave ships and public opinion in France appeared to be also turning against slavery, as indicated by the publication of several acclaimed novels with black heroes. From 1825, the French government finally began backing words with money, with crews in the French navy being given 100 francs for every slave freed. After 1830, a law was passed to make the penalties for slave trading more severe – the traders would be classified as criminals, which meant they could be jailed for two to five years if they were caught in French waters, and 10 to 20 years if apprehended on the high seas. In 1844, an organization of workers in Paris sent a petition to the French government calling for the immediate abolition of slavery. 'French soil cannot support slavery any longer,' they said. These measures seemed to have worked – between 1832 and 1850, just 20 ships sailed from France to Africa to buy slaves.

In those years the French government went further toward emancipation. It removed a tax which any owner who wished to free an enslaved person had to pay, and made it illegal to brand a slave. In 1833, a law was passed giving those of mixed-race the same rights as whites, and every black person who set foot in France was automatically free. Attempts were made by the government to encourage education and marriage among the enslaved Africans. A new law also required planters to record all punishments meted out to slaves, with magistrates given the responsibility to inspect plantations in order to report abuse of slaves. In 1840, the French government showed it intended to emancipate all slaves when it set up a Commission of Enquiry into slavery, which had a mandate to recommend measures to achieve this goal. The commission submitted its report in 1843, outlining two strategies. The first recommended full emancipation after 10 years along with compensation for the slave owners. The second recommended emancipation in stages, starting with children, then skilled slaves, then domestic slaves and then field slaves.

The main personality in the French abolitionist movement was named Victor Schoelcher. Like Clarkson and Wilberforce, he was a forceful speaker and a prolific writer of pamphlets. He had first-hand knowledge of slave colonies, having travelled throughout the French Caribbean, as well as to Cuba and the USA. Having successfully brought the slavery question into the consciousness of French citizens, Schoelcher in 1847 presented the legislature with 16 points against slavery. These were some of the points.

- Property of man in man is a crime.
- The vices of slavery can only be destroyed by abolishing slavery itself.
- All notions of justice and humanity are lost in a slave society.
- There is an annual excess of births over deaths in a slave population.
- The honour of France is compromised by tinkering with a dying institution.
- It is more costly to maintain slavery than to abolish it.
- By virtue of the solidarity which binds all members of a nation, each of us is partly responsible for the crimes engendered by slavery.

Not all of Schoelcher's points were completely factual. For example, he claimed that British emancipation had had 'satisfactory moral and material results' and that the slave owners had accepted emancipation as the right course. However, he was interested in effective propaganda rather than making a purely intellectual argument. In 1848, there was a revolution in France and the government was overthrown. Schoelcher was appointed Under Secretary of State in the Navy with authority over all French Caribbean colonies. He now had the power to carry out his ideas. He was made president of a commission with responsibility for drafting emancipation legislation. His eventual report insisted that slavery was no longer practical from an economic viewpoint and that emancipation was morally correct as well as best for the colonies.

The French Emancipation Act was eventually passed in 1848, granting full freedom to all enslaved Africans.

An extract from Schoelcher's report on emancipation states:

'The Republic rejects distinctions in the human family. It does not believe that a people glorifying in freedom can pass over in silence a whole class of men kept outside the pale of the common rights of humanity. It has taken its principles seriously. It is making reparation to these unfortunate people for the crimes which it committed against their ancestors and the land of their birth by giving them France as their fatherland and all the rights of French citizens as their heritage, thereby bearing witness that it excludes no one from its immortal motto: Liberty, Fraternity, Equality.'

Timeline

- 1787 – The USA said it would end its slave trade in 1807.
- 1788 – A Bill was passed in the British Parliament limiting the number of slaves who could be carried on a ship.
- 1789 – The French Revolution was fought.
- 1791 – Denmark set a deadline of 1802 for the abolition of its slave trade.
- 1793 – Britain was at war with France. This meant that the British government, as well as the public, stopped paying attention to abolition.
- 1804 – In Britain the Abolition Bill was passed in the House of Commons but rejected in the House of Lords.
- 1806 – The British Prime Minister, Charles James Fox, moved a resolution in Parliament for the total abolition of the slave trade.
- 1807 (March 25) – the British Abolition Bill was given royal assent and it was to be effective from 1 May 1807.
- 1807 (April 30) – The last legal slave trader sailed from a British port. In the preceeding years, between 1801 and 1807, over 266,000 enslaved Africans were transported by British ships from the continent to the Caribbean.

Activity 4.4 Construct a table showing the similarities and differences in the process of abolition of the slave trade in the British, French and Spanish colonies.

Amelioration the act of making something better.

Amelioration proposals

British amelioration

The abolitionists had also begun implementing the second phase of their plan. Amelioration, as the word implies, was an attempt to improve the conditions of the enslaved Africans, as the abolitionists worked towards freeing them completely.

At first, the planters strongly resisted all such attempts, based on the concept that if you give someone an inch, that person will take a yard.

In 1816, Jamaica had already passed the Consolidated Slave Law. This mandated that slaves should have Sunday off work, as well as one other day every fortnight to do their own planting. They were to have at least 26 days off work every year, and not made to mill cane between 7 pm on Saturday and 5 am on Monday. Their work day was also to be no longer than 5 am to 7 pm, with 30 minutes for breakfast and a two-hour lunch break. This, however, still meant a 12-hour work day, six days a week. How strictly the new law was enforced is not certain.

In 1823, the British abolitionists formed a new organization, called the Society for the Gradual Abolition of Slavery. Their plan was to campaign for an immediate improvement in the conditions of enslaved Africans and then to get slavery completely abolished. By now experienced from their campaign against the slave trade, the abolitionists were able to set up over 200 branches of the new society in a year. By then, Parliament had received 750 petitions calling for the abolition of slavery, so the MPs knew that a significant number of votes depended on what position they took on the slavery question.

The British Caribbean planters soon realized that public opinion was not on their side, and that they might also lose the support of MPs if and when anti-slavery legislation came to Parliament. So they changed strategy and decided to propose amelioration to Parliament themselves. Their representatives in London sent their policy suggestions to the Colonial Secretary, who accepted them and forwarded a despatch to the legislative assemblies of the self-governing colonies. In Crown Colonies, where as the title suggests the Crown ruled more directly through its appointed governor and a council of nominated members loyal to the British government, the policy was simply implemented by an order.

These were some of the proposals made.

- No slave women should be whipped.
- A male slave who was to be whipped should be given one day's notice before the punishment was administered.
- All floggings which exceeded three strokes were to be recorded by estate officials and the records submitted every three months to a magistrate.
- Slave families were not to be split up by traders selling family members to different owners.
- Slaves could not be sold to pay off debts.
- Planters were no longer to frustrate or prevent the missionaries or other clergy from preaching to the slaves, so the Africans could be converted to Christianity.
- Slaves should have a legal right to give evidence in court, once sponsored by a member of the clergy.

Many of these same proposals had been made before by the British government at the end of the 18th century, but the planters had ignored them even when they became law. Now, although the amelioration proposals had been made by wealthy absentee planters living in England, the planter assemblies in Jamaica, Barbados, Dominica and St Vincent resisted the policy. They agreed to put into law just some of the proposals. They refused outright to let any enslaved person testify in court and they made the teaching of Christianity to slaves subject to so many regulations that it would have been virtually impossible for any missionary to do so. For example, the Jamaican assembly forbid any missionary from collecting a fee from the enslaved Africans for religious instruction, on the basis that, 'Under pretence of offerings and contributions, large sums of money have been extorted by designing men professing to be leaders of religion.' No services were allowed between sunset and sunrise, even though the slaves worked for most of the daylight hours. Enslaved Africans who were discovered preaching without their owners' permission could be flogged.

However, these regulations were rejected by the British government. The Colonial Secretary, in a strongly worded despatch to the Governor of Jamaica, said:

'I cannot too distinctly impress upon you that it is the settled purpose of His Majesty's Government to sanction no colonial law which needlessly infringes on the religious liberty of any class of His Majesty's subjects.'

The planters, however, defiantly re-enacted the law and set up a committee to investigate the activities of missionaries. Members of this committee harassed various missionary groups and then wrote a report in which they accused missionaries of causing unrest in the colony and tricking people into giving them money. This report was sent to the British government, which ignored it. The report caused a backlash, however, because it started a rumour among the enslaved Africans that they had been freed by the British government but the planters were hiding the document. When a slave revolt erupted in Jamaica after 25 December 1831, the planters, apparently believing their own propaganda, arrested several missionaries and put them on trial. They also destroyed several of their church buildings.

Yet the missionaries, far from causing the uprising, had actually tried to stop it. One preacher, William Knibb, tried to prevent his congregation of slaves from joining the rebellion, telling them that there was no truth to the rumour that they had been freed by the King of England.

This violence against missionaries in Jamaica and other colonies further lowered public opinion in England against the Caribbean planters and their representatives. This was because the Non-Conformist churches, who sent out most of these missionaries to the colonies, also had a significant membership in England. The British congregations made contributions to the missionaries' work in the Caribbean and saw the preaching of Christianity to the Africans as a divine obligation which they should support. People who had not been moved by the issue of slavery were now outraged at the treatment of the missionaries. It was ironic that amelioration had been proposed by absentee owners representing the West Indies in London, and the planters in the colonies scuttled the proposals.

In 1831, the Society for the Gradual Abolition of Slavery stepped up its anti-slavery campaign. It had already won over public opinion, but this did not necessarily mean that Parliament would pass a law abolishing slavery. The Society realized that what was needed were new MPs who would be prepared to support such legislation. In England, thanks in large part to the Industrial Revolution, a new class of powerful men had been created. Previously, landowners were the wealthiest individuals and made up the ruling class. Part of their power lay in the law which allowed only property owners to vote. Some MPs had even gained their positions in Parliament through what were called 'rotten boroughs'. These were areas where few people lived, but where a property owner had the right to appoint an MP. Several wealthy planters had returned to live in England, purchased such boroughs and appointed an MP or become one themselves, in order to safeguard their interests in respect to sugar and other trade laws.

Now, though, there were people who had become just as rich and influential as the landowners through manufacturing and trade. These individuals opposed the landowners, not least because they wanted a different set of laws which would help their businesses. The planters, for example, wanted their MPs to pass laws which gave British colonies preferred access to the British market, whereas the businessmen wanted to be free to trade with other countries, since this meant cheaper goods to buy and sell and more profits for them. The 1830 election in Britain brought in a majority of members who were prepared to vote against slavery. MPs for 85 of the 'rotten boroughs' were removed and replaced by seats in the industrial towns, such as Manchester, Sheffield and Leeds. The vote was also given to townsmen who paid at least £10 in rent annually. This meant that factory owners and merchants could now vote, and since these people had supported the abolition of slavery, MPs had to pay attention to their wishes.

The Society pressed its advantage, hiring six lecturers, as well as a panel of effective speakers, to go around the country giving talks on why slavery should be abolished. In the 1832 election, the Society persuaded many of the candidates to support abolition. The first Reform Act was passed in that year. The planters had now effectively lost political power. They had not adhered to the amelioration proposals made by their own colleagues in London. They could not lobby the new MPs in Parliament, who represented industrialists. The public was against them on the issue of slavery, and even economically, since sugar from the British colonies was more expensive than sugar from Cuba, Brazil or Mauritius. In the spring of 1833, the Society repeated its petition campaign, getting over 1.3 million signatures, while the number of its local branches increased to 1,300. A Bill to abolish slavery was brought to Parliament in May 1833.

> **Activity 4.5** Imagine you are members of the British Parliament. Divide the class into two groups and debate the issue of slavery in Parliament.

The debate over the Bill lasted over three months, with the session becoming one of the longest in the British Parliament's history. The Bill had four connected principles.

1. All slaves were to be freed at the same time.
2. Most of the former slaves were to become 'apprentices' who would have to work for their former masters for a fixed number of hours per day for a specified number of years.
3. The slave owners were to be paid a monetary sum as compensation for the loss of their slaves.
4. The money for this payment was to come from raising the duties on sugar from the colonies.

Interestingly, even the MPs who argued against the motion did not bring up the issue of race. This was in stark contrast to the same debate in 1823, when the Prime Minister George Canning had described black people as 'being with the form and strength of a man but with the intellect only of a child.' Both the pro-and anti-abolitionists agreed that blacks and whites had the same motivations and attributes. In debates among legislators in the USA, African's backwardness and their 'savage nature' was usually raised by pro-slavery speakers. In Britain, by contrast, race was dismissed even in the public debate outside Parliament. The Tory *Morning Herald* newspaper, for example, argued against 'the supposed racial inferiority of the negro', while the *Westminster Review* described ideas of racial superiority and inferiority as 'absurd arguments'. Also, while the Colonial Office's plans for the freed blacks might have been oppressive, as you will read in Chapter 5, their rationale didn't invoke any stereotypes of race. Where race entered the debate, it was in terms of characteristics. The Tory leader Robert Peel, for instance, spoke of 'the distinction of colour', hastening to add that he was not referring to 'any inferiority of black to white' but was noting a factor that would create problems 'in amalgamating the slave population with the free, which did not exist either in any country of Europe or in any country of the East where slavery was extinguished.'

The Emancipation Act was passed in Parliament in August 1833.

> **Activity 4.6** In the above paragraph it was noted that even the MPs who argued against the Bill to abolish slavery did not bring up the issue of race. Does this mean that British society was no longer racist? Give reasons for your answer.

French amelioration

> **Manumission** the freeing of a slave by a master, either freely or in return for payment by the enslaved person.

Unlike the British movement, the amelioration measures in the French colonies were driven less by public opinion and more by political concerns. There were slave rebellions in Martinique in 1822, 1824 and 1833 and, given what had occurred in St Domingue, the French government decided to try a policy of amelioration. The tax on manumissions was repealed in 1832, and the procedures were also simplified, making it easier for blacks to buy their freedom. In 1833, the French government passed a law making it compulsory to register slaves and, perhaps remembering the St Domingue planter Le Jeune, banned any mutilation and branding.

In 1834, which was the same year that the British introduced their apprenticeship proposal, a French abolition group formed, the 'Société française pour l'abolition de l'esclavage'. This marked a turning point in public opinion and in 1836 slavery was outlawed in France (though not in the colonies). By 1840, the Société was able to get legislation introduced in the French Assembly to abolish slavery. The law was not passed, but eight years later the French Emancipation Act was finally proclaimed.

The planters had unintentionally helped bring this about because, by displaying their lack of humane feelings toward the enslaved Africans, they made it apparent that only full abolition could improve the lot of black people in the Caribbean.

> **Activity 4.7** List three main differences between the British and French abolition processes.

Social, economic and political factors leading to abolition

When change happens in a society, there are usually many reasons for it. Slavery was abolished because people wanted it (social factors), because there were now better ways to make money (economic factors) and because the leaders in society gained more power by stopping slavery (political factors). Very often, all these factors are interconnected. The economic reasons influence the social values, the social movements shape the political arguments and the politicians are motivated by economic reasons.

Social factors

In the previous section, on the abolition of the slave trade, you learned about the condemnation of slavery by the Quakers and by individuals who argued by word and deed that slavery was immoral. The abolition movement had many influential people leading it, such as the politician William Pitt the Younger, the writer Edmund Burke and the poet Samuel Taylor Coleridge. By spreading their message through speeches, writing pamphlets and books, and persuading powerful people that their cause was just, the abolitionists succeeded in creating widespread opposition to slavery. The philanthropist Josiah Wedgwood produced thousands of anti-slavery badges with a black figure and a motto saying, 'Am I not a man and a brother?'

In the city of Manchester 11,000 people signed a petition calling for an end to the slave trade. So politicians had to take action for, if they had not, they might have become very unpopular and lost their positions. All this represented a change in values among British citizens, or at least those who were literate and therefore more influential in the society. Why was Britain the first European country to engage in this debate for change?

> **Feudalism** a system which existed in medieval Europe. Under this system, the nobles held land from the Crown in exchange for military service. The peasants would live on and work the land. They would give a share of their produce to the nobles in exchange for protection.

One significant factor was that, historically, England had been the first nation in Europe to abolish feudalism, which was a system whereby landowners had nearly total rights over the peasants who occupied the land. The lord allowed the peasant to occupy his land in return for tribute, which may have been in the form of produce or coin, or for military service when the lord went to war. This was essentially a slave system, so its end in the 14th century meant that Englishmen were more open to arguments about freedom than other Europeans, where feudalism continued as late as the 19th century in some countries. Another factor related to England's progressive values was that the nation had formed its own Church, when Henry VIII created the

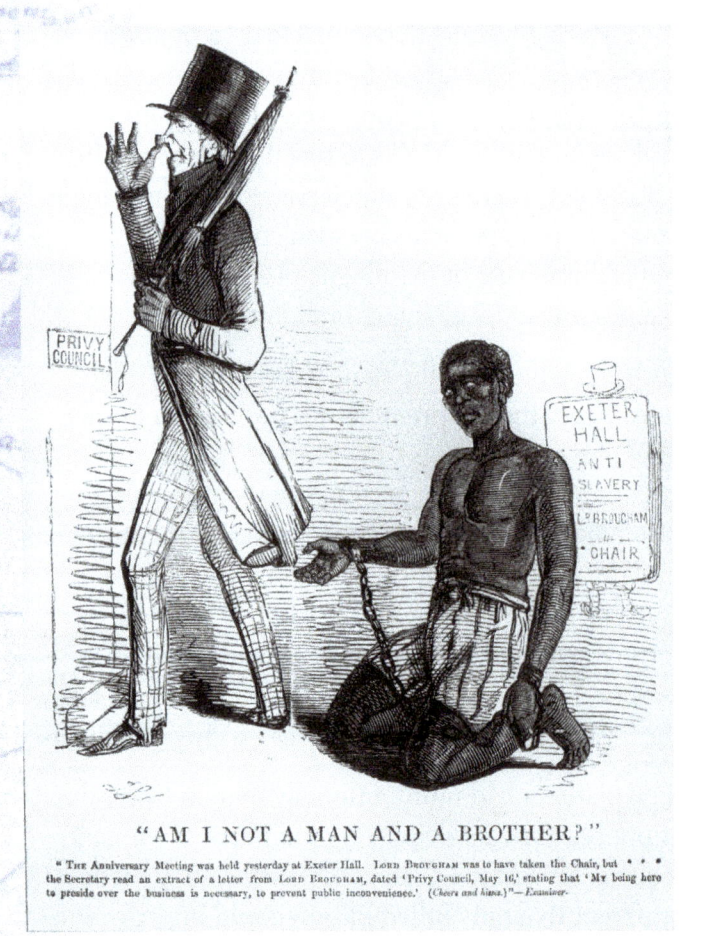

4.7 Anti-slavery badge produced by Josiah Wedgwood

Anglican Church in order to break away from the Roman Catholic Church when the Pope refused to continue giving him marriage annulments. With the rise of other Non-Conformist Christian churches, it has been argued that the English were more open to ideas which opposed the status quo.

> **Activity 4.8** Find out more about the feudal system which existed in Europe. How was it similar to, or different from, chattel slavery in the Caribbean?

Political factors

Politicians, both then and now, need money to win elections. Even before the 19th century, as you have read earlier in this chapter, many wealthy sugar planters had retired to England and purchased posts in Parliament by buying up 'rotten boroughs' (a borough was a town which sent representatives to Parliament) at sums ranging from £3,000 to £4,000. At the same time, popularity alone does not guarantee political power. Under the British system of government, this let planters become, or influence, MPs in the House of Commons. In one day in 1661, King Charles II made 13 plantation owners from Barbados into baronets, which gave them political influence in Britain. As MPs, the planters or their representatives were able to vote against laws which threatened their profits, such as allowing import of sugar from non-British colonies or the abolition of slavery. In fact, it was partly because the British government needed the votes of MPs who were controlled by West Indian slave owners that abolition did not happen sooner.

However, the Industrial Revolution had also made factory owners and merchants rich, and so their influence on politicians was growing. Additionally, the West Indian planters were opposed by another group which also made profits from sugar. The East India Company (EIC) was producing sugar in India with hired, not slave, labour by 1792. The company began a propaganda war against the West Indian sugar producers, distributing sugar bowls which had written on their sides 'East India sugar not made by slaves', and spreading the claim that a West Indian slave's life cost 450 pounds of sugar. 'A family that uses 5 pounds of sugar a week will kill a slave every 21 months,' said the company in its pamphlets. You should not assume, however, that the people who owned and ran the EIC were humanitarians. Three of the most powerful opponents of abolition were actually board members of the EIC. Their sugar cost 140 shillings per hundredweight whereas West Indian sugar which cost 70 to 80 shillings per hundredweight, so the EIC needed to give consumers a moral reason to buy its much more expensive product. The company's tactic was to make British citizens feel guilty about using West Indies sugar in their tea. It seems that the EIC was successful, since the amount of sugar produced in East India and sold in England increased 28 times between 1791 and 1833.

> **Did you know?**
>
> Up to 1971 British currency comprised **pounds (£), shillings (s)** and **pence (d)**. The smallest unit of currency was a **penny**, the plural of which was **pence** (or **pennies**). There were 12 pence in a shilling and 20 shillings in a pound. The pound came in the form of a paper bill, called a **note**, or a gold coin, called a **sovereign**.
>
> Since 1971, the monetary system of Britain has been based on the decimal system. The basic unit of British currency is the **pound**, which is divided into **one hundred pence**. Its full name is **pounds sterling**. The term **pound** originates from the value of one pound Tower weight of high purity silver known as **sterling silver**. Sterling silver is an alloy of silver containing 92.5% pure silver and 7.5% other metals, usually copper.

International politics – in this case, rivalry between European nations – also played a part in bringing about the abolition of slavery. When Britain stopped their slave trade in 1807, they then became concerned about stopping the trade by other nations. This was partly because the British Caribbean was no longer getting new enslaved Africans to labour on its plantations, while the colonies of the other European powers continued to do so. A memorandum written in

1818 by the abolitionist James Stephen warned that:

> 'Reconquest of Haiti would mean restoration of the slave trade. It is politic to consider if the people of England are thus to lose their commerce, their money, and their benevolent hopes, by the moral apostasy of France and her breach of solemn engagements, they may not add to it the loss of their temper; and whether, at some point, at some not far distant crisis, the peace of Europe may not be broken on the slave coast.'

Stephen was arguing that, if Britain's prosperity was harmed because it had abolished the slave trade while other nations had not, this might lead to war. It may well have been this concern, along with its commitment to humanitarian principles, which led to the British government offering £3 million to France in return for a promise to end the slave trade.

Ironically, it was this situation that led to the British planters themselves calling for an end to the slave trade. When the West India Interest (a group of sugar planters who had become wealthy from their Caribbean holdings and returned to live in England) met in London in 1830 over this question, they called on the government:

> 'to adopt more decisive measures than any that have hitherto been employed, to stop the foreign slave trade, on the effectual suppression of which the prosperity of the British West Indian colonies, and the consequent success of the measures of amelioration now in progress in them, ultimately depend.'

Note that the planters were actually claiming that ending the slave trade was essential if the situation of the enslaved Africans on their plantations was to improve. The planters also attempted to distinguish between sugar grown by slaves and that grown by free labourers, arguing that if the slaves were emancipated in the British colonies then the sugar produced by the former slaves should be given protected status in the British market.

Economic factors

This brings us to the economic argument for abolition. The price difference between Indian sugar and Caribbean sugar suggests that Adam Smith was wrong when he argued that 'the work done by freemen comes cheaper in the end than that performed by slaves'. This may be true for manufactured items, but for raw sugar it seems that slave labour was more efficient than paid labour. ('Efficient' here means only that the costs of production were less.) Even if the enslaved Africans were unwilling to work, the threats of whipping and other punishments ensured that they did work quite hard, since overwork was one of the reasons for the high death rates cited by the EIC.

The first historian to argue that slavery in the New World was abolished because it was no longer profitable was Eric Williams, in his book *Capitalism and Slavery*, written in 1944. Williams was also the first Prime Minister of Trinidad and Tobago (see Chapter 8). Williams wrote that slave traders often made between 20% and 30% profits on their sugar cargoes. By 1800, profits were declining, dropping from £18 per hundredweight in 1803 to zero in 1807. Plantations also began to close, with 65 being abandoned in Jamaica between 1799 and 1807, and another 32 sold because of debts.

By the end of the 18th century, the West Indies provided between 8% and 10% of England's total income. However, England also had to spend money to earn these profits, with costs such as maintaining 19 warships and between three and seven regiments of soldiers in the Caribbean. West Indian sugar was also more expensive than sugar produced from other areas, so the British government was actually losing money by only allowing West Indian sugar to be sold in England. This, plus the costs of maintaining military strength in the Caribbean, actually cost more than the 8–10% profit that came back to the British government.

On the other hand, a broader look at the figures show that overall profits from Britain's colonial territories were still high the first part of the 19th century. From 1824 to 1826, these profits totalled almost £16 million, whereas from 1784 to 1786 profits were just £5.6 million.

However, this was also the period when the Industrial Revolution was accelerating in Britain.

> **FAST FACTS**
>
> **Synopsis of the Industrial Revolution**
>
> - The Industrial Revolution can be dated from the second half of the 18th century. It was the most important event in the modern world, because it laid the foundation for technological progress.
> - Textiles were the driving force of the Industrial Revolution, with the invention of machines such as the flying shuttle in 1733, the spinning jenny in 1769, the cotton gin in 1793 and the self-acting mule in 1830, as well as many other innovations. Before these devices were invented, it took 18 hours of one worker's time to change a pound of cotton into cloth; by the 1830s, this task took just 1½ hours of a worker's time.
> - The technological progress brought by the Industrial Revolution resulted in a higher standard of living for people in Britain than in other European countries.

If the New World had not been supplying raw materials for the Industrial Revolution, the economic transformation in Britain might not have happened so rapidly, hence creating a new class of entrepreneurs who were able to oppose the sugar plantation owners. It was not coincidental that the majority of supporters in the anti-slavery battle were located in Britain's main industrial centres: Manchester, Birmingham and Sheffield. Table 4.2 shows that Britain was more advanced than France and Spain in the early 19th century, because the former had more people living in cities than the latter.

> **Gross domestic product (GDP)** a basic measure of a country's or region's economic performance based on the market value of all goods and services made there in a year.

Table 4.2 Economic status of the main European powers in the 19th century

Country	Year	Urban	Agriculture	1820 GDP (1990 international $)
Britain	1834	29%	35%	$36 million
France	1848	13%	59%	$35 million
Spain	1867	20%	64%	$12 million

> **Activity 4.9** Look at Table 4.2 and answer the following questions:
>
> a Which country had the highest GDP in the 19th century?
> b Which country had the lowest GDP in the 19th century?
> c Which country was more dependent on agriculture?
> d Which country was the least dependent on agriculture?

The industrialists wanted their workers to have cheap food, including stimulants such as tea, coffee and sugar, so they would have energy to work long hours in the factory. While sugar had originally been a luxury for the rich, consumption increased five-fold during the 19th century and the British wanted their sweet tooth satisfied for the cheapest possible price. Removing the preferential treatment for sugar bought exclusively from the British colonies would lower prices.

Shipping companies also joined the side of the anti-abolitionists. This was a turnaround on their part, since slavery made great profits for ship builders and shipping companies during the slave trade. They were losing money because the sugar planters' products had a protected market in Britain. Laws prevented shipping companies from transporting goods from other European nations. In 1833, the Brazilian Association of Liverpool (Liverpool had been the main centre for slave traders in Britain in the 18th century) argued that more than £2 million was lost to the British economy due to these protectionist policies, as foreign ships and foreign companies got profits from cargo, freight charges, sales commissions and so on. Liverpool's economy was still based on slavery, except now it centred on cotton produced by enslaved Africans in the USA, rather than sugar produced in the Caribbean.

Sugar refiners were another important business group supporting abolition. Again, their main motive was not moral, but financial. In both Britain and France, refiners wanted raw sugar at the lowest possible price for processing. You will read more about sugar refining in Chapter 5. As the law only allowed refiners to buy from their governments' respective colonies, neither the French nor the British sugar refiners could get enough of the raw product at the lowest price to supply their customers at the best profit. As with the shipping interests, this too was a change in position, since the refiners had supported protectionism when it had meant higher profits for them.

The voices of these various business groups helped bring about the abolition of slavery by Britain.

French economic factors

In France, the economic factors which led to abolition were somewhat different. We have shown how the Industrial Revolution in Britain was an important part of the emancipation of enslaved Africans. This process started in Britain in the latter half of the 18th century. In France, however, the Industrial Revolution did not take off until the middle of the 19th century. There were several reasons for this. One reason was the French Revolution in 1789, which disrupted the scientific, intellectual and political institutions. Another reason, perhaps more significant, was that France's iron industry was not as advanced as Britain's economically or technologically. Britain had more coal reserves than France, and so had cheaper energy, which allowed Britain to produce more manufactured goods at lower costs. The iron smelting technology that allowed France to catch up with Britain was not invented until furnace designs were improved by 1850, and even then those designs were invented in Britain.

> **Beet** a plant widely cultivated as a source of food for humans and livestock, and for processing into sugar. Some varieties are grown for their leaves and some for their large nutritious root.

Another relevant economic factor in France was the development of beet sugar. By 1813, France had set up 334 factories producing 4,000 tons of beet sugar a year. By 1826, France had 1,900 factories producing 24,000 tons of sugar a year. By 1835, French beet sugar producers could meet the entire demand for sugar in that nation and produce extra sugar for export. This meant that cane sugar produced in the colonies was now less profitable in general, and could not even be sold in France, except under a protected market, which made it more expensive for the French to buy. From the 1830s, too, sugar production in the French Caribbean started to go down. Between 1836 and 1848, sugar production in Martinique dropped by more than half (from 25 million kgs per year to 12 million kgs). In Guadeloupe, it went down by nearly two thirds (from 35 million kgs to 12 million kgs).

This inevitably resulted in political conflict between beet sugar producers and cane sugar producers. Both sides asked the French government for tax concessions. Spokesmen for the beet sugar manufacturers asked why the domestic market of 33 million French people should be put behind a colonial market of 113,000 consumers and 286,000 slaves. Even so, the French government eventually decided that it was more important to protect its colonies than French beet sugar producers, and in 1839 imposed a tax on them which added a cost of 10 francs for every 100 kgs of sugar. However, the production process for beet sugar was so much more technologically advanced than sugar cane production that even with this tax the beet sugar producers were still able to undersell their colonial competitors. Sugar prices fell so low because of too much sugar on the market that several sugar plantations in Martinique and Guadeloupe collapsed.

The Emancipation Act

Once the British government had decided to free the enslaved Africans, its members wanted to ensure that the colonies' business would not be disrupted by this social revolution. So, the main concerns of the Emancipation Act, as stated in its very title, were to:

- ensure that the former slaves had the protection of the law
- ensure that there would be a transition period between slavery and full freedom
- placate the planters whose business would be disrupted by these changes.

These points were justified in the opening clause of the Act which stated that it was 'just and expedient' that the persons who were now enslaved should be freed, but that a 'reasonable compensation' should be given to slave owners for their being deprived of the 'services' of the freed persons and that a 'necessary time' for adjustment to the new laws would be given. Since the language of the Act is in the old formal English of that time, we have included an explanation in boxes.

> **Activity 4.10** Read the Emancipation proclamation and answer the following questions:
>
> a Which clauses favoured the slaves and which clauses favoured the planters?
>
> b How much compensation would the planter recieve? Is this a fair amount? Give two reasons for your answer.

An Act for the Abolition of Slavery throughout the *British Colonies*; for promoting the Industry of the manumitted Slaves; and for compensating the Persons hitherto entitled to the Services of such Slaves.

I WHEREAS divers Persons are holden in Slavery within divers of His Majesty's Colonies, and it is just and expedient that all such Persons should be manumitted and set free, and that a reasonable Compensation should be made to the Persons hitherto entitled to the Services of such Slaves for the Loss which they will incur by being deprived of their Right to such Services.

> This means that various ('divers') people have been held ('holden') as slaves, and it is fair and practical than these people be set free. The owners of these slaves will be paid in compensation for losing the services of their slaves.

In order to afford the necessary Time for such Adaptation of the said Laws, a short Interval should elapse before such Manumission should take effect.

> Before the new law against slavery takes full effect, there will be a short period for adjustment.

II During the Continuance of the Apprenticeship of any such apprenticed Labourer such Person or Persons shall be entitled to the Services of such apprenticed Labourer as would for the Time being have been entitled to his or her Services as a Slave if this Act had not been made.

> There will be an apprenticeship period during which the former owners will still have the now free people to work for them, in the same way as if slavery was still in force.

IV All such apprenticed Labourers should, for the Purposes herein-after mentioned, be divided into Three distinct Classes, the First of such Classes consisting of praedial apprenticed Labourers attached to the Soil, and comprising all Persons who in their State of Slavery were usually employed in Agriculture, or in the Manufacture of Colonial Produce or otherwise, upon Lands belonging to their Owners; the Second of such Classes consisting of praedial apprenticed Labourers not attached to the Soil, and comprising all Persons who in their State of Slavery were usually employed in Agriculture, or in the Manufacture of Colonial Produce or otherwise, upon Lands not belonging to their Owners; and the Third of such Classes consisting of non praedial apprenticed Labourers and comprising all apprenticed Labourers not included within either of the Two preceding Classes.

> The former slaves will be divided into three groups: (1) field workers; (2) artisans and those who worked on plots of land other than the sugar plantation producing goods for their masters; (3) domestic workers and others.

IX No praedial apprenticed Labourer who may in Manner aforesaid become attached to the Soil shall be subject or liable to perform any Labour in the Service of his or her Employer or Employers except upon or in or about the Works and Business of the Plantations or Estates.

> The ex-slaves cannot be forced to do labour outside the plantation.

XI During the Continuance of any such Apprenticeship as aforesaid the Person or Persons for the Time being entitled to the Services of every such apprenticed Labourer shall be and is and are hereby required to supply him or her with such Food, Clothing, Lodging, Medicine, Medical Attendance, and such other Maintenance and

Allowances as by any Law now in force in the Colony to which such apprenticed Labourer may belong an Owner is required to supply to and for any Slave being of the same Age and Sex as such apprenticed Labourer shall be; and in Cases in which the Food of any such praedial apprenticed Labourer shall be supplied, not by the Delivery to him or her of Provisions, but by the Cultivation by such praedial apprenticed Labourer of Ground set apart for the Growth of Provisions, the Person or Persons entitled to his or her Services shall and is or are hereby required to provide such praedial apprenticed Labourer with Ground adequate, both in Quantity and Quality, for his or her Support, and within a reasonable distance of his or her usual Place of Abode, and to allow to such praedial apprenticed Labourer, from and out of the annual Time during which he or she may be required to labour, after the Rate of forty-five Hours *per* Week as aforesaid, in the Service of such his or her Employer or Employers, such a Portion of Time as shall be adequate for the proper Cultivation of such Ground, and for the raising and securing the Crops thereon grown.

> For the period of apprenticeship, the former masters shall continue to supply the former slaves with food, clothing, shelter and medicine. If food is not supplied, the former slave owner has to provide the former enslaved people with enough land for them to grow their own food. This land must be located close to their living quarters and they must also be given enough time out of their duties to cultivate their crops.

XVII That it shall not be lawful for any such Governor, Council, and Assembly, or other Colonial Legislature, or for His Majesty in Council, by any such Act, Ordinance, or Order in Council, to authorize any Person or Persons entitled to the Services of any such apprenticed Labourer, or any other Person or Persons other than such Justices of the Peace holding such Special Commissions as aforesaid, to punish any such apprenticed Labourer for any Offence by him or her committed or alleged to have been committed by the whipping, beating, or Imprisonment of his or her Person.

> Only Justices of the Peace have authority to punish former slaves. The Governor and legislative bodies cannot punish former slaves.

XXI That neither under the Provisions of this Act, nor under the Obligations imposed by this Act, or to be imposed by any Act of any General Assembly, Ordnance, or Order in Council, shall any apprenticed Labourer be compelled or compellable to labour on *Sundays*, except in Works of Necessity or in Domestic Services, or in the Protection of Property, or in tending of Cattle, nor shall any apprenticed Labourer be liable to be hindered or prevented from attending anywhere on *Sundays* for Religious Worship, at his or her free Will or Pleasure, but shall be at full Liberty so to do without any Let, Denial, or Interruption whatsoever.

> Sunday shall be a rest day, and no apprenticed worker can be forced to work on that day by any law.

XXIV And whereas, towards compensating the Persons at present entitled to the Services of the Slaves to be manumitted and set free by virtue of this Act for the Loss of such Services, His Majesty's most dutiful and loyal Subjects the Commons of *Great Britain* and *Ireland* in Parliament assembled have resolved to give and grant to His Majesty the Sum of Twenty Millions Pounds Sterling.

> Compensation to the former slave owners will be £20 million.

XLV And be it further enacted, That the said Commissioners shall proceed to apportion the said Sum into Nineteen different Shares, which shall be respectively assigned to the several *British* Colonies or Possessions herein-after mentioned: (that is to say,) the *Bermuda Islands*, the *Bahama Islands*, *Jamaica*, *Honduras*, the *Virgin Islands*, *Antigua*, *Montserrat*, *Nevis*, *Saint Christopher's*, *Dominica*, *Barbadoes*, *Grenada*, *Saint Vincent's*, *Tobago*, *Saint Lucia*, *Trinadad*, *British Guinea*, the *Cape of Good Hope*, and *Mauritius*.

> The £20 million will be divided between the 19 colonies listed.

LXI And whereas in some of the Colonies aforesaid a certain Statute, made in the Thirteenth and Fourteenth Years of King *Charles* the Second, intituled *An Act for preventing the Mischiefs and Dangers that may arise by certain Persons called Quakers and others refusing to take lawful Oaths*;

and a certain other Statute made in the Seventeenth Year of King *Charles* the Second, intituled *An Act for restraining Nonconformists from inhabiting in Corporations*; and a certain other Statute, made in the Twenty-second Year of King *Charles* the Second, intituled *An Act to prevent and suppress seditious Conventicles*; and a certain other Statute, made in the First and Second Year of King *William* and Queen *Mary*, intituled *An Act for exempting Their Majesties Protestant Subjects dissenting from the Church of England from the Penalties of certain Laws*;.. a certain Statute made in the Fifty-second Year of His late Majesty King *George* the Third, intituled *An Act to repeal certain Acts and amend other Acts relating to Religious Worship and Assemblies, and Persons teaching or preaching therein*, shall be and is hereby declared to be in force as fully and effectually as is such Colonies had been expressly named and enumerated for that Purpose in such last-recited Statute.

All laws banning Quakers and other Non-Conformist religious groups are repealed.

It has been argued that the Emancipation Act was unfair in that it gave monetary compensation to the planters, but none to the enslaved Africans for their years of unpaid labour. This is undoubtedly true, but at the same time the fact of freedom alone was so gigantic a step that making payments to the former slaves was politically unrealistic. It may be worth noting that, of the 66 clauses of the Emancipation Act, 20 are concerned with laws to protect the former slaves while just 16 deal with compensation to the plantation owners. Clause XVII, for example, made it illegal for anyone except a Justice of the Peace to punish any apprenticed labourer 'by the whipping, beating, or imprisonment of his or her person' – a clause which shows how well the British government knew the habits of the former slave owners. Clauses XXI and LXI were intended to ensure that the planters did not prevent the former slaves from receiving religious instruction, as had been the case during slavery.

4.8 This illustration of emancipation was included in a 19th century English history book.

> **Groupwork**
>
> Get into groups of three or four people and imagine you are a group of planters in the British West Indies. Discuss your main concerns about the proposed abolition of slavery.

It is cruel irony that is was the masters and not the slaves who were awarded compensation. The Act provided £20 million in compensation to the plantation owners. However, other historians put the value of British Caribbean property at £130 million. In either case, £20 million was a huge sum, since this was 40% of the government's annual revenue. The implementation of the Act was to encounter problems because of one aspect: the six-year apprenticeship period.

Stipendiary magistrate a government official responsible for overseeing the apprenticeship system.

Apprentice a beginner, a learner.

The apprenticeship system

Aims of apprenticeship

The aims were to:

- prepare the ex-slaves for final freedom
- give them time to learn 'habits of industry'
- allow time for legal changes – to facilitate the change from slave codes to new laws
- provide sufficient time for the establishment of colonial banking institutions to meet the needs of a free society
- give the planters time to introduce new equipment, technology and labour management.

Structure of apprenticeship

- Non-field slaves were to be apprentices for a period of four years and field slaves for a period of six years.
- All children under the age of six years were freed.
- Destitute mothers could indenture their free children on estates until they reached age 21.
- Stipendiary magistrates were appointed by the Crown to protect the freed Africans against overwork, maltreatment and abuse. These stipendiary magistrates were paid by the Crown.
- All apprentices were to work 40½ hours per week.
- Food allowances would continue as during slavery.
- The apprentices had the option of performing extra labour or purchasing their freedom.

Supervision of apprenticeship

- 100 stipendiary magistrates were appointed in the Crown colonies. These magistrates had greater powers than the governors in some respects.
- In the colonies which had representative legislatures, the British government allowed each colony to pass its own Emancipation Act, although the Crown had to approve it.

Note: The apprenticeship system did not apply in Antigua, where the government opted for complete emancipation.

> **Roleplay**
>
> As an enslaved African in a British West Indian colony, you have heard that emancipation is imminent and you have been waiting impatiently for that day. However, now you are being told that you have to become an apprentice before you are given final freedom. Express your feelings in some dramatic manner (in a poem, monologue, song or dance).

Problems with the apprenticeship system

The title of the Emancipation Act said that the apprenticeship system was intended to 'promote the industry' of the freed Africans. There is evidence of the racist stereotyping of the day here as the implication is that the Africans would otherwise spend their new-found freedom lazing about 'eating watermelons'. It was also intended to ensure that the planters themselves did not suddenly have to work hard, since Clause II stated that they were entitled to the ex-slaves' 'services as a slave as if this Act had not been made'.

It was almost inevitable that there were going to be issues and problems, although the true horrors of the apprenticeship system could not have been anticipated. As soon as the Emancipation Act was proclaimed, rumours started among the blacks that the British government had ended slavery but the planters were pretending that blacks had to continue working as slaves for another six years. Even when they were assured that this was not the case by whites they trusted (in particular, the stipendiary magistrates), they were quite naturally resentful that they had to take orders from their former masters.

In St Kitts, many of the freed Africans refused to go back to their plantations, and the militia were called out to drive them back. In Guyana, there were protests against the Apprenticeship clause, with the people demanding immediate and full freedom. Similar action in Jamaica resulted in military action, with the ringleaders tried and sentenced to be whipped in public.

Praedial relating to land.

The planters, in their turn, often tried to break or bend the new laws, particularly in Jamaica. One contemporary report notes the following abuses.

- Enslaved Africans were reclassified by the planters from non-praedial to praedial, so they would be forced to work in the fields, and do so for six years instead of four.
- There was no proper registration of the slaves, so the stipendiary magistrates who were appointed to oversee and enforce the new system did not have proper records to base their decisions on.
- Women and children were overworked.
- Work hours were extended beyond the 40½ stipulated in the Act to 45 and even 50 hours.
- The work day was extended from 9 to 11 hours.
- Food, clothing and other requirements specified in Clause XI of the Act were withheld.

The planters abused the process even though a complaint against them might have prevented them getting their part of the £20 million compensation. The only stipulation which they appeared to follow was in respect to not obstructing religious instruction, since by 1840 most of the former slaves had converted to Christianity and were regular church goers.

Another underhand strategy used by the planters was making a high valuation of apprenticed labourers who wanted to buy full freedom immediately. In one case of a Jamaican woman named Sally, her former master wanted her to pay £41 for her freedom, although she would probably have been bought for less than £20 during slavery. The apprenticed labourers had their own strategies for getting the price lowered. For example, they would pretend to be ill, or claim to be much older than they really were. Of course, most of the ex-slaves did not have enough money to buy their freedom. Still, in Jamaica nearly 1,500 of them did so, as did about 900 in Barbados. This shows how determined people were to overcome any obstacle in order to truly gain independence.

The British government also passed laws intended to keep the population controlled. Vagrancy laws were passed which were intended to keep the ex-slaves from 'lazing' as well as restrict their movements off the plantations. For example, Jamaica passed a Vagrancy Act in 1833, one year before emancipation, which allowed the arrest of any individuals who threatened to run away from the plantation (whether or not they actually did so). In Dominica, a similar act allowed the arrest of any black people who made too much noise in the towns. Other vagrancy acts were passed in Barbados, Antigua and Guyana. The penalties for such transgressions could be 60 lashes or six months in jail. The police were given additional powers, and military forces were put in place in several colonies. Many histories have argued that the treatment of black people in the Caribbean actually deteriorated under the apprenticeship system. Planters in the large part still saw black people as chattel property and wanted to squeeze the last amount of labour from them. The magistrate's records indicate people were charged with the pettiest of offences.

The stipendiary magistrates

These magistrates were appointed by the British government to protect the rights of the formerly enslaved Africans and to settle disputes between employers and labourers. Some of them did their best, although many others sided with the planters in continuing to oppress the newly freed populace. In either case, there were simply not enough stipendiary magistrates to oversee the colonies properly. There were 150 in all, and 60 of them were based in Jamaica. Their contracts were for two years only, so if they did not do their job to the government's satisfaction they could be dismissed long before the apprenticeship system was supposed to end. They were paid a relatively low salary of £300 a year (later increased to £450), which meant they were easily bribed. Also, many died from diseases. Despite all this, several of the magistrates seemed to have won the respect of the freed blacks, who saw them as the only trustworthy white men in the colonies.

Failure of the apprenticeship system

The system was ended prematurely mainly because the planters continued to try and oppress their former slaves and the free blacks refused to allow this. The British government itself was never satisfied with how the apprenticeship system functioned and thought that the best way to stave off any potentially violent conflict, as well as getting the colonies economically functional, was officially to grant full freedom once and for all.

There were still activist groups in Britain, the members of which had agitated for abolition, and who now opposed apprenticeship. By 1837, these groups had succeeded in mobilizing public opinion against the system, building on the anti-planter sentiment which had helped bring about emancipation in the first place. Within the colonies, too, brave protest action by the freed blacks, ranging from refusal to work, to vandalism, to demonstrations also helped undermine the apprenticeship system, convincing the authorities that it was unworkable. A House of Commons committee appointed to examine the system found that the freed blacks continued to be treated like slaves under the system in Jamaica, Grenada, Guyana and St Lucia, where they were overworked and flogged, and that stipendiary magistrates in Barbados were deeply corrupt, taking bribes to decide matters in favour of the planters.

Several petitions were sent to Parliament by the Society for the Gradual Abolition of Slavery and other groups, calling for the apprenticeship system to be reformed. The planters did not support this, in fact preferring that the system be ended completely, since any reforms would hardly have been to their advantage. Many of the planters had already begun looking for other sources of labour, since they knew that getting their ex-slaves to work on the plantations might be an impossible task.

The British government was at first hesitant to give full freedom since, despite the peaceful transition to emancipation, its members still feared uprisings by the freed blacks. However, since the non-praedial workers were to be freed in 1838, there was also a risk that the field workers, who were supposed to be apprenticed for a further two years, might riot. The planters still wanted the system to run its full course, with those in Jamaica and Belize even demanding further compensation for the premature termination. However, other planters wanted the system ended mainly because they wanted to be free of the expense of providing food, shelter and medical care to the apprentices. In fact, the colonies actually ended up passing their own emancipation acts to end the system early, starting with Jamaica, after which the British government followed suit.

For these and other reasons, the apprenticeship system was stopped in 1838, two years before it was supposed to end.

REVISION QUESTIONS

1 Read the passage below then answer the questions that follow.

Organized protests against the slave trade and against Caribbean slavery began in England in 1787, and later in France. Owing partly to the work of some outstanding leaders, slavery was abolished in the British Caribbean in 1834 and in the French Caribbean in 1848. There were many similarities between the British and the French anti-slavery movements.

   a Outline the main achievements of the British anti-slavery movement up to 1834. *(15 marks)*
   b What were the main similarities between the British and French anti-slavery movements? *(10 marks)*

(Total = 25 marks)
CXC Past Paper, General Proficiency, May/June 2000

2 Read the passage below and answer the questions that follow.

During the days of slavery, two Englishmen in the Caribbean, Reverend Joseph, a Christian missionary, and John, a sugar planter, had the following conversation:
Reverent Joseph: 'John, I hate slavery. It should be abolished because of religious and humanitarian reasons.'
John: 'Sir, I do not agree with you. Slavery should be allowed to continue. If it is abolished, I will be ruined economically, as well as the island and England.'

   a Explain the religious and humanitarian reasons that made many Christian missionaries in the Caribbean support the abolition of slavery. *(15 marks)*
   b Outline the economic arguments used by many British Caribbean planters to defend slavery. *(10 marks)*

(Total = 25 marks)
CXC Past Paper, General Proficiency, May/June 2002

3 Critically discuss this statement: 'Slavery was abolished due to the work of the humanitarians in Britain.'
(25 marks)

4 Why was the apprenticeship system ended prematurely in the British West Indies? *(25 marks)*

References and recommended reading

- Blackburn, R. *The Overthrow of Colonial Slavery 1776–1848*, London: Verso, 1988
- Findlay, R and O'Rourke, K. H. *Power and Plenty: Trade, war, and the world economy in the second millennium*, Princeton University Press: Princeton, NJ, 2009
- Green, W. *British Slave Emancipation: The sugar colonies and the great experiment 1830–1865*, London: Clarendon Press, 1994
- Maddison, Findlay, R and O'Rourke, K. H. *Power and Plenty: Trade, war, and the world economy in the second millennium*, Princeton University Press: Princeton, NJ, 2009
- Smith, R. T. 'Social stratification, cultural pluralism and integration in West Indian societies' in S. Lewis and T. G. Mathews (eds) *Caribbean Integration: Papers on social, political and economic integration*, Rio Pedras, Puerto Rico: Institute of Caribbean Studies, University of Puerto Rico, 1967, pg 226-58
- Williams, E. *Capitalism and Slavery*, London: Deutsch, 1972

5 Adjustments to emancipation 1838–76

This chapter will answer the following questions.
- What were the main problems affecting the sugar industry in the post-emancipation period up to 1876?
- What measures were implemented to deal with these problems?
- What impact did immigration have on the colonies?
- What factors promoted and hindered the emergence of free villages?
- How did peasants contribute to Caribbean economy and society?
- Why was Crown Colony government adopted in the English Caribbean in the 19th century?

Emancipation did not mean an easy life for the Africans in the Caribbean. They could no longer be punished at will by their former masters, but they were still on the bottom rung of the social ladder. They could not vote and they had few or no rights to own property so they could not hold public office. Also, they now had to find ways to get their own food, clothing, shelter and tools.

As you learned in Chapter 4, the enslaved Africans were freed partly because sugar was no longer as profitable as it used to be. However, because sugar was no longer so profitable, the planters were not willing to pay high wages to their former slaves, while the latter wanted to work for a sum that they considered fair.

The compromises reached were sometimes, but not always, determined by the availability of land – in the larger colonies, such as Trinidad, British Guiana and Jamaica, the Africans could find land to grow their own crops, whereas this was more difficult in small islands such as Barbados and St Kitts. At the same time, the larger islands had bigger populations of Africans who needed to earn wages in order to buy necessities, so the supply of labour was sometimes greater than the demand for it.

We will look at this issue in more detail later in this chapter, but first we must examine the state of the sugar industry after 1838.

Problems affecting the sugar industry 1838–54

Although it cannot be said to have on exact start, the decline of the Caribbean sugar industry might be dated from 1747, when in Germany the chemist Andreas Maggraf (1709–82) showed that sugar in the root of the beet is the same as the sugar obtained from cane.

It would take another half-century for beet sugar production to start on a commercial scale, because it was still cheaper to make sugar from cane in the Caribbean using slave labour, so beet sugar only began to compete seriously with cane sugar after 1870. Even so, by 1813, Napoleon's war against other European countries caused blockades between France and its colonies, so France had set up 334 factories producing 4,000 tons of beet sugar a year. These factories were closed when the war ended, since cheaper cane sugar once again became available, but they started production again in 1816 after France lost the profitable colony of Mauritius. By 1826, France had 1900 factories producing 24,000 tons of sugar a year.

By 1833, beet sugar production had become so efficient that 400 factories made nearly twice the amount – 40,000 tons every year. A half-century later, the world would be producing more beet than cane sugar.

The policies of the British government after emancipation actually helped undermine the sugar industry in its colonies. As a general rule, the 'Mother Country' did not want its colonies making manufactured goods to compete with products from England. This policy was called 'mercantilism' – the idea that a country's prosperity depended on getting cheap raw materials from colonies, making manufactured goods from these materials then selling the goods within national borders, back to the colonies, and to other countries.

> **Mercantilism explained**
>
> Mercantilism was based on the belief that a country's prosperity depended on how much gold and silver it had stocked up. Its supporters argued that a country should export as many goods as possible and import very few. Ideally, they said, a nation should import only raw materials (such as cotton or iron) and export finished manufactured products (such as clothes or pitchforks), since this would provide employment for its citizens. Imports of manufactured goods from other countries were limited by imposing high taxes (or duties) on goods coming from foreign nations. This is called protectionism.
>
> The Navigation Act of 1651 stated that goods being carried from England to the colonies or vice versa had to be transported in English or colonial ships and was intended to stop the Dutch from trading with British colonies. The second Navigation Act of 1660 made it illegal for other countries to export goods such as sugar, tobacco and cotton to England or the British colonies. The 1663 Staple Act said that goods from other European countries first had to be shipped to England before they could be sent to the colonies and then only in British ships. The Plantation Duties Act of 1673 imposed duties on certain goods, which had to be paid before the commodities were even shipped from one colony to the next.
>
> Political philosophers such as Adam Smith and David Hume opposed mercantilism, arguing that a country's prosperity did not depend on precious metals, but on land, labour and capital. These critics of mercantilism said that free trade would make a nation wealthier than protectionism. Protectionism may have made sense in a time when nations were very likely to go to war. However, history eventually proved Adam Smith right – for example, Spain, which obtained tons of silver by being the first European nation in South America, never became more prosperous than trading nations such as Holland and Britain.

This policy even included refined sugar. So even though the West Indian plantations were technically capable of making refined sugar, instead of just exporting brown sugar to England to be processed into white sugar, the British government charged higher duties on refined sugar coming from its colonies.

> **Problems affecting the West Indian sugar industry in the post-emancipation period**
>
> Increasing cost of production
> - There was mismanagement of estates by managers who were in charge because of absentee ownership.
> - Labourers had to be paid wages now that slavery was abolished.
>
> Increasing debts
> - Planters had borrowed extensively from British merchants and were unable to repay their loans because of low profits.
> - Many continued to borrow in an attempt to revive their plantations.
> - However, banks and merchant houses were more sceptical about giving loans to West Indian planters. The Bank of British Guiana and the Planters' Bank of Jamaica did not want to use estates as security for loans anymore and the Colonial Bank of the West Indies did not make any substantial loans to planters.
>
> Shortage of a regular, relatively cheap supply of labour
> - After emancipation there was an exodus of ex-slaves from the plantations in the colonies with higher populations.
> - Those who left the plantations established themselves as peasant cultivators; they planted small-scale market crops and provisions and they kept livestock. Skilled Africans moved to the towns where they were employed as blacksmiths and carpenters, for example.

- Africans often supplemented their incomes by working part time on the plantations but the planters found their labour unsatisfactory – the planters wanted cheap, full-time labourers as they had been accustomed to during slavery.

Decline in markets for West Indian sugar

- Preferential duties on West Indian sugar were removed under the Sugar Duties Equalization Act, 1846.
- Duties were equalized on British West Indian, British East Indian and foreign colonial sugar entering the British market, which meant that West Indian planters now had more competition for markets for their sugar.
- The principle of economies of scale refers to the cost advantages of expansion. The British West Indies could no longer compete against much larger suppliers.

Since the late 17th century, the British government had imposed tariffs on sugar coming from outside British territories, so that the colonies were able to sell their sugar to Britain at a cheaper price (although this made sugar more expensive for British consumers). In 1846 though, the British government started lowering this tariff and by 1854 a single duty rate was applied to all sugar of a given quality entering Britain. This meant that sugar from the British Caribbean colonies had to compete with the cheaper sugar being produced in Cuba and Brazil and other parts of the world. At the same time, the 'Mother Country' still tried to give some protection to its Caribbean colonies, by having a tariff which charged higher duties on refined sugar and lower duties on partially refined and muscovado sugar. This helped the West Indian planters, since they produced mostly muscovado, which was the low-quality sugar produced by the basic process of evaporating the juice of sugar cane and draining off the molasses. However, the advantage of lower duties was not enough to offset these planters' production costs, which were higher than those of other sugar producers.

The planters, faced with all these challenges, tried to make their production of sugar more efficient, often using the new technologies of the Industrial Revolution. For example, some of them used a vacuum pan, a device which let more of the cane syrup turn into crystals to produce a higher proportion of sugar. When the first vacuum pan sugar arrived in England in 1833 though, the government decided that its high quality made it liable to a tax of £8/8 shillings per hundredweight. This was reduced by 1845 to 16 shillings, compared with 14 shillings for other classes of sugar, but the duties still prevented the vacuum pan from becoming widely used in the West Indies. By contrast, in Java, the vacuum pan was used in all sugar factories by 1865.

Measures adopted to try to deal with the problems in the West Indian sugar economy

Alternative labour sources
- Indian indentured labourers were used. This will be discussed in more detail later in this chapter.

Mechanization of production
- Steam mills replaced animal mills.
- New equipment was installed, such as vacuum pans and the centrifuge.

Introduction of new varieties of cane
- Attempts were made to improve the varieties of cane so that cane had higher sugar content.

New techniques
- New techniques developed on the fields included use of:
  - the plough and harrow
  - different types of fertilizers
  - irrigation schemes
  - proper drainage systems.

Amalgamation of estates
- Smaller estates were joined together to form larger ones. This allowed for more efficient use of factory equipment and generally better management of estates. It also meant that labour was more readily available and estates could share marketing facilities.
- More land was available for cultivation so therefore the most fertile areas were cultivated.
- A large estate was more likely to get loans which could then by divided and given to individual planters.

West Indian planters attempted to establish newer markets

- Some planters turned to the USA to export their sugar. As the USA is relatively close to the West Indies, transport costs were lower and prices were better than when supplying sugar to Britain, for example.

Technical advice

- Many colonial governments employed skilled engineers to give advice to planters, for example on new types of manufacturing techniques which could save cost.
- Departments of agriculture were established by some governments. These gave advice to sugar cane farmers and offered technical assistance and financial advice on increasing production. These government departments also conducted research on new types of crops.

Note: The above measures were adopted in different degrees according to the size and wealth of the colony and what individual planters could afford.

Despite all the measures mentioned, production of sugar in the British colonies declined in the years just before and after emancipation. From 1831 to 1838, there was an overall decline of 20%, and by 1842 this decline had reached 40%.

Table 5.1 Sugar production in selected colonies 1831–42

Colony	Percentage change
Barbados	−11
Nevis	−48
Jamaica	−52

This fall in production was due to several factors, including:

- the trade policies of the British government
- competition from Spanish and French sugar producers
- a glut on the sugar market
- shortage of labour.

As you will see in the next section, however, this last factor did not always apply.

Roleplay

Imagine that you are a sugar planter in one of the larger West Indian islands in the 1840s.

Say whether you are a rich or a poor planter. Make a speech in which you:

- list three problems you are presently experiencing.
- give five methods you are considering adopting to solve your problems and give one reason for each.

Attitudes to labour after 1838

After emancipation in the British colonies, the whites and the blacks had different concerns. For example, white planters wanted to ensure that they had labour for their sugar plantations, while the former slaves wanted to get a good wage for any work they did. These goals were not always compatible.

A memo written in 1832 by a member of the House of Lords who had helped bring about emancipation revealed the main worry of the British government.

> 'The great problem to be solved in drawing up any plan for the emancipation of slaves in our colonies, is to devise some mode of inducing them, when relieved of the fear of the driver and his whip, to undergo the regular and continuous labour which is indispensable to carrying on the production of sugar… it is to the imposition of a considerable tax upon land that I chiefly look for the means of enabling the planter to continue his business when emancipation shall have taken place.'

This meant that the government and the planters would try to stop the emancipated Africans from acquiring land by making it too expensive for them to buy. The typical attitude is also summed up in the following passage from an essay written by the British historian Thomas Carlyle (1795–1881) who, even by the more narrow-minded standards of those times, can be described as a bigot.

Carlyle wrote in 1849 that the emancipated Africans, who no longer needed to work because they could eat the free-growing watermelons (which he mistakenly called pumpkins), would ruin the West Indian sugar industry. He wrote:

> '... with beautiful muzzles up to the ears in pumpkins... cheap as grass in those rich climates, while the sugar-crops rot round them uncut, because labour cannot be hired'.

He went on to recommend that:

> 'If quashee will not honestly aid in bringing out those sugars, cinnamons, and nobler products of the West India islands, for the benefit of all mankind, then I say neither will the powers permit quashee to continue growing pumpkins there for his own lazy benefit...'

This, then, was the attitude of many whites. What was the attitude of the blacks, though, towards labour after emancipation? The former slaves did not leave their own written accounts, but some whites did examine the post-emancipation conditions in the colonies. The abolitionists Joseph Sturge and Thomas Harvey went to Jamaica, where they conducted interviews and wrote an account of what they found. The reports of the stipendiary magistrates also had useful information about employment of the blacks.

Groupwork

Get into groups of four or five students. Imagine you are slaves and slavery is about to be abolished. You have two choices — you can either remain on the plantations and work for the planters or leave the plantations and become independent peasants. In your groups discuss the advantages and disadvantages of each option and make a final decision about what you will do.

One contemporary letter talks about the situation in Montego Bay where there were 'thousands in the islands out of employ', asserting that 'in the interior and on many of the pens there is an immense population who would willingly locate on estates.' Montego Bay, you should note, was in the large island of Jamaica, where there was plenty of land and where, as you learned in Chapter 3, there existed free black communities long before emancipation (the Maroon communities).

Factors encouraging ex-slaves to leave the plantations

These included:

- psychological desire for personal liberty and land ownership
- insecurity of tenure on the estates
- high rent on estate houses
- low wages
- familiarity with agriculture
- availability of land for cultivation in some colonies.

Activity 5.1

Which factor do you think was the most important in determining whether emancipated Africans left the plantation?

FAST FACTS

- Alternative forms of employment were also available to those who left the plantations:
  - for women – sewing, handicraft, peddling, shop keeping
  - for men – local small trading, peddling, shop keeping.

Children could attend schools since educational facilities were available more than previously, through the missionary schools.

- The exodus from the plantation was greatest in Jamaica, Trinidad and British Guiana where large areas of unoccupied land were available.
- Peasant holdings normally comprised:
  - marginal, uncleared and unsurveyed land
  - land that was usually located far from the markets where goods were sold.
- Peasant holdings were normally a half acre to 2 acres.
- The land was usually used for:
  - growing provisions, fruits and vegetables
  - rearing livestock such as cattle, sheep, goats, pigs and poultry.
- Peasants normally practised subsistence agriculture where sufficient crops were grown to feed the family.
- Some peasants supplemented their income by working part time on the estates for wages.

> **Activity 5.2**
>
> Find out more about peasants today in any one Caribbean country. Use the following headings to guide you in your research.
>
> a   Types of crops grown
> b   Size of landholdings
> c   Social life
> d   Contribution to the country's economy

In British Guiana, where there was also a lot of land available, the governor announced that six former slaves had bought an abandoned sugar estate for £2,000, 150 labourers bought a cotton plantation for £11,000 and other labourers bought another for £16,000. This was in 1839, just one year after emancipation.

> **Factors encouraging the emergence of a West Indian peasantry**
>
> **Availability of land in larger colonies such as Trinidad, Jamaica and British Guiana**
> - Ex-slaves pooled their money to purchase plots of land.
> - Missionaries bought large tracts of land and divided it into smaller plots and sold it to the ex-slaves at a lower price. This also acted as an incentive to ex-slaves to convert to Christianity and to become members of the Christian churches.
> - Many ex-slaves squatted on Crown Land where available.
> - Some estates were abandoned and the land sold at a low cost to the ex-slaves.
>
> **Experience as 'small-scale farmers' during enslavement**
> - Enslaved Africans were allowed to cultivate provision grounds and this experience may have helped convince them to move away from the plantations.
> - Some had sold their produce in the Sunday markets and were able to save small sums of money which helped to buy land when they became free.
>
> **Work of missionaries**
> - Missionary groups assisted in the acquisition of land.
> - They helped in the growth of the free village movement.
> - In Jamaica, Baptist ministers assisted by bargaining with landowners to get land at a lower cost.

However, one governor would condemn this entrepreneurship, claiming it had.

> 'not been so much the sign of superior intelligence or manly independence, as of… a love of uncivilised ease; the freeholders beings, I am inclined to think, as a body far less industrious than the older and steadier Negroes who… have remained on the plantations.'

On the other hand, Lord John Russell, the Secretary of State for the Colonies, noted in an 1840 dispatch:

> 'None of the most inveterate opponents of our recent measures of emancipation allege that the Negroes have turned robbers, or plunderers, or bloodthirsty insurgents. What appears from their statement is, that they have become shop-keepers, and petty traders, and hucksters, and small freeholders.'

Additionally, up to 1842, reports from stipendiary magistrates in British Guiana and from official committees in Jamaica (both colonies, as you have read, with land available for squatting or purchase) show that the majority of ex-slaves had, in fact, remained on the plantations to work. They were not satisfied with the arrangements, however, complaining to a magistrate that: 'We are told we must pay for our provision ground, doctor fees, finding ourselves with all necessary, etc. What will be remaining for us in case of sickness?'

Africans had received food, plots of land, shelter and medical care for free during slavery and so reasonably considered these should be part of their compensation now that they were freed. The planters, on the other hand, tried to charge rents on both accommodation and gardens so they could pay their former slaves less. It seems that it was often resentment at this tactic, rather than memory of the traumas of enslavement, which led to flight from the estates.

The evidence suggests that the freed Africans were not lazy, as their racist former masters claimed, nor did the sugar industry collapse because they were unwilling to work.

Much depended on the circumstances in each particular island. In Barbados, for example, the labourers complained of a shortage of work, while in Trinidad the labourers were said to control the level of wages. Table 5.2 shows the different arrangements for payment in different islands. For a reminder of shillings and pence refer to page 112.

Table 5.2 Wage rates in the 1840s

Colony	Daily wages (shillings 's', pence 'd')
Trinidad	2s
British Guiana	2s
Jamaica	1s 8d (with cottage and land)
St Lucia	1s 5d (with cottage and land)
St Kitts	1s
Barbados	9d (with cottage and land)
Antigua	9d (with cottage, land, medical care)
Nevis	A share of the estate's produce

By 1842, sugar output had returned to pre-emancipation levels in islands such as Antigua, St Kitts, Barbados, Trinidad and British Guiana. Nonetheless, the planters still felt they would make more profits if they could pay lower wages, so they lobbied the British government to bring in immigrants so that they would not have to depend solely on their former slaves for labour.

Factors hindering the development of a West Indian peasantry

- There were problems with the acquisition of land due to high rents, lack of Crown Land and planters' reluctance to sell land.
- Planters charged high rents on land and the peasants could not afford these.
- Planters used legislation, such as the Squatters' Act and the Tenancy Act, to make it difficult for peasants to acquire land.

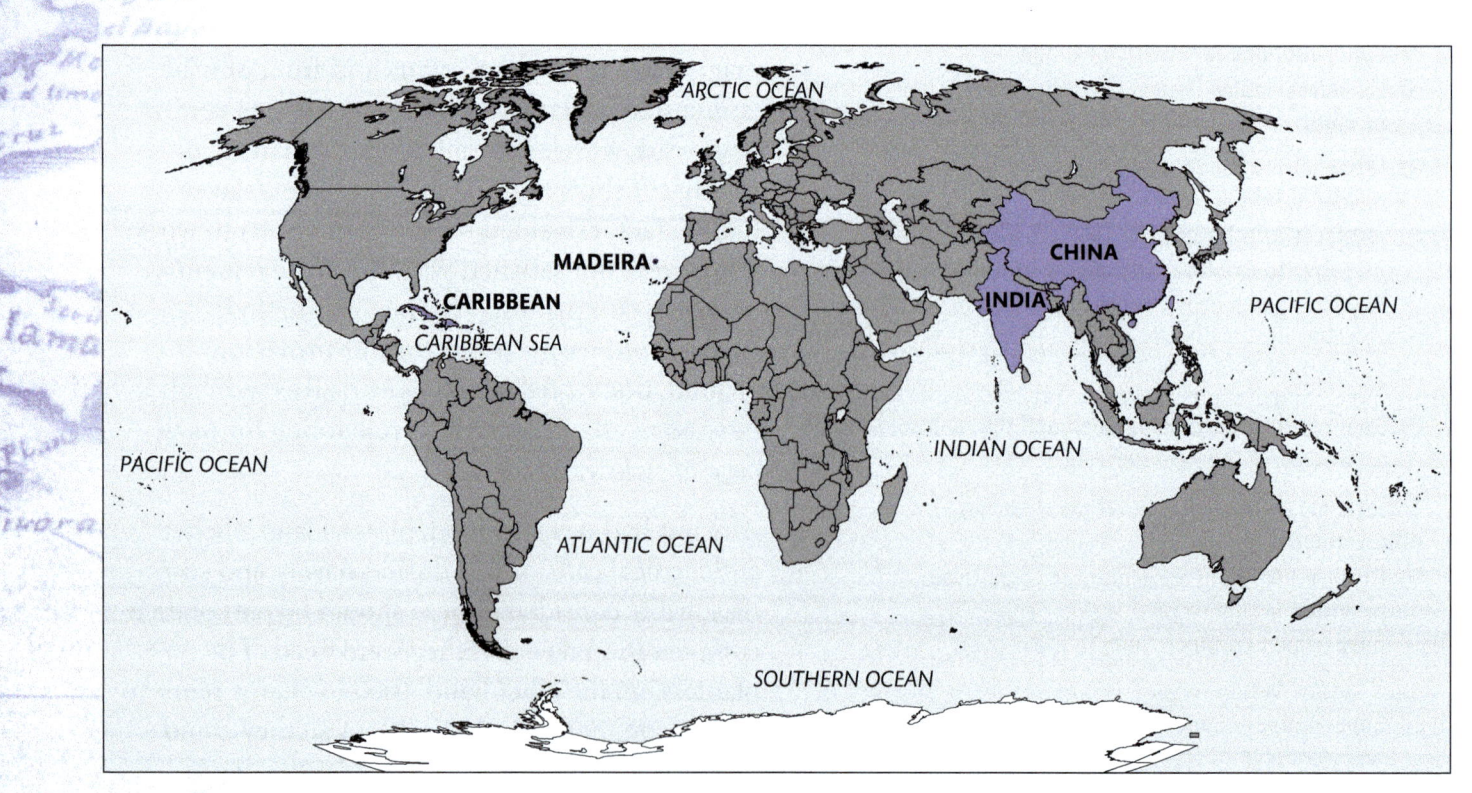

5.1 Countries used as sources of new plantation labour

Migration schemes as a solution to the labour problem

Indenture legal contract reflecting a debt or purchase.

China and India were the first places that Europeans checked for replacement labour after slavery ended. The planters had already tried using other Europeans before the slave trade from Africa became a full-fledged industry and already knew that this strategy would not work, if only because they would have to pay high wages to white labourers. This was exactly what they wanted to avoid. China and India seemed ideal sources of labour. Both were poor countries with large populations, which meant that there were many people who would see even the hard labour on the sugar plantations as an opportunity for a better life.

China in the 19th century had a population of over 350 million. In 1842 it had been forced to open its ports to foreign traders after the opium wars. England, France and the USA established consulates in China two years later. As with Africa before emancipation, these powerful nations saw China as a new source of cheap, plentiful labour. India had a population of about 250 million and was already occupied by Britain which, by contrast, had a population of just 31 million.

The first shipment of labourers left India just before the apprenticeship period drew to a close, in 1838. Of the 414 Indians who came, 18 died on board the ship and another 98 died within five years of landing in the colony. 238 Indians later returned to the subcontinent and just 60 decided to stay in the Caribbean. Emigration from India was suspended until 1844 because of this high mortality rate, while the authorities examined the conditions of recruitment and shipping.

Between 1845 and 1847, Jamaica received 4,551 Indians and 507 Chinese. By 1854 though, just over 1,800 of these immigrants had died or disappeared. It is likely that many of them were killed by a cholera epidemic which swept through Jamaica in 1850. Between 1838 and 1917, Jamaica received 21,500 Indians, St Lucia received 1,550, St Vincent 1,820 and Grenada 2,570. The largest numbers went to Trinidad (145,000) and British Guiana (238,000).

5.2 A group of newly arrived Indian indentured labourers at the depot on Nelson Island

Some people in Jamaica were against this importation of immigrants. An 1847 letter in a Jamaican newspapers said that the presence of the Indian labourers:

> 'tends to demoralise our peasantry without benefiting any party. If we must import human beings, let them be Africans who have already demonstrated to the West Indian planters that they are more capable than any other race to carry out the object required, namely, good and cheap cultivation of the soil.'

Some churches also opposed Indian immigration, worrying about the effects such 'pagans' might have on their African Christian converts. In Santo Domingo, the mulattos staged public protests against the immigration of Africans. The Anti-Slavery Society in England also opposed Indian immigration, saying it would reverse the social and moral gains made by abolition.

The planters, however, saw immigration as the key solution to their financial problems, and it was their voices the British government listened to. The Crown had four main aims in supporting immigration, which were to:

- restore and even expand the sugar economy
- create a steady supply of labourers

- ensure that the ruling class in the colonies maintained control over the labour force
- keep wages low by having immigrant labour compete for wages with the freed populace.

The planters' goals were clear: they wanted to have labourers in sufficient numbers who would work cheaply. Only in islands such as the Leewards, Barbados and Belize was there opposition to immigration schemes from the ruling whites, and this was only because the labour supply in these territories was adequate. Even this situation soon changed, however, as the freed blacks refused to work for low wages and became more independent, so that by the late 19th century planters in small islands like Antigua, St Kitts and Nevis were also calling for immigrant labour.

By the end of the 19th century, the West Indies had received over 300,000 Indian labourers to join the 700,000 descendants of Africans in the British Caribbean at the end of slavery. Some Chinese and Portuguese labourers were also brought in, but in small numbers.

5.4 Example of an Emigrant pass, 1883

Immigration from Europe and Africa

European immigration

In order to obtain labour, several colonies brought in Europeans and Africans to work as paid labourers. Between 1835 and 1838, small groups of whites were brought from Germany, England, Ireland, Scotland and Malta to the British colonies. About 200 immigrants came from France to Martinique between 1848 and 1859. Suriname in 1860 received 348 Dutch farmers. The largest number of white labourers came from Spain to Cuba: about 8,000 between 1882 and 1885.

Generally, these attempts to gain labour were failures. Governor Fiéron of Guadeloupe described the European labourers as 'weakly, overworked, beaten up' individuals who succumbed easily to diseases. There was also a social obstacle, since many white labourers refused to work alongside the blacks, as doing so meant that their status was no better than that of the ex-slaves.

Martinique paid 100,000 francs to bring in just 500 French and Portuguese immigrants between

5.3 A photograph of Indian children brought to the Caribbean

1848 and 1859. Since their labour value could not justify this outlay, it seems that other motives were at work – most likely, the desire of the colonial governments to increase the numbers of whites now that the numerically superior blacks were freed. Nor did the profile of the white people matter: in 1852, French prisoners were brought to French Guiana as labourers. Cuba had the largest influx of white immigrants, with several thousands being brought from Spain, the Canary Islands and the USA between 1834 and 1839. In the Dutch colony of Suriname, there was a failed attempt to bring in white farmers in 1860. Of the 348 people who came, many died from diseases and the rest left the farms for the town or returned to Europe.

The Portuguese labourers did not come directly from Portugal, but from the island of Madeira, which was a port of call on the trade routes between Europe and the New World. They were brought to several colonies, but most went to British Guiana.

Between 1835 and 1850, about 17,000 Portuguese were brought in and, between 1851 and 1881, another 13,000. The authorities in British Guiana were especially anxious to get Portuguese labourers, in part because they had a reputation as good workers but also because they were white. Since whites, although still ruling the colony, were a small minority compared to the former slaves and the Amerindians, the planters wanted to bring in more whites to increase their numbers. One governor wrote, 'It is of immense importance to the future prosperity of the Colony that a large industrious body of whites should be established.'

However, the scheme had a rocky start. In 1841, the number of immigrants brought in was 4,321, but 282 died en route. For this reason, the British government stopped paying for Portuguese immigration for five years while the causes of this high mortality rate were investigated. However, the labourers continued to be brought in by private buyers. Official immigration started again in 1846, but the death rate actually doubled to 12%.

Also, even more Portuguese labourers died after they started working in the colony. Madeira was a poor island and many of the labourers came already weak from famine. In the tropical climate, they then succumbed to diseases such as yellow fever and to the heat.

Those who survived, though, eventually became quite prosperous in the colony. This was partly because, as whites, they were given privileges that the non-white indentured labourers were not. For example, the Portuguese did not have to pay a monthly tax for initial expenses and were not tied to three-term contracts with no commutation option. When the Portuguese started opening their own stores, they were given credit by white merchants who did not extend the same privilege to blacks. As early as 1842, one historian records, there were 139 new shops in Georgetown, of which 42 were owned by Portuguese. By the 1850s, the Portuguese controlled the retail trade in the colony. This is an example of social engineering: here immigration was used deliberately to design a society of the racial composition desired by the planters. The presence of the Portuguese was designed to keep the Africans at the bottom of the social pyramid.

> **Commutation** giving up one's right to return to one's homeland in return for a grant of land or money.

The financial success of the Portuguese, and the perception that they had been given unfair advantages, created resentment among the African labourers in British Guiana. Anti-Portuguese riots occurred in 1848, 1856 and 1889, supposedly because of the high profits charged by Portuguese shop owners.

Other colonies received Portuguese immigrants much later and in fewer numbers. In 1882, 1,000 went to Trinidad, 2,500 to Antigua, 2,100 to St Vincent and 2,100 to St Kitts-Nevis and some went to some of the other colonies.

African immigration

Since Africans had already proven their worth as workers during slavery, the planters naturally wanted to continue using them as cheap labour. They wanted new Africans though, partly because they did not wish to pay higher wages to their former slaves, who often expected to get shelter and food as part of their compensation.

These attempts to bring in African labourers began even before emancipation, when the abolition of the slave trade reduced the supply of enslaved Africans. Between 1811 and 1860, 6,000 West Africans were brought to the Bahamas. In 1838, about 500 Africans came to Grenada as indentured labourers. The French colonies, in total, brought in about 17,000 Africans. Up to 1859, Guadeloupe received 6,000, Martinique 10,000 and French Guiana 1,500. This trade stopped in 1871.

There were also attempts to get Africans from the USA and Canada. Although few African-Americans wanted to come to Jamaica, mainly because the wages there were not attractive, some did go to Trinidad, where the pay was higher. The first group of 216 arrived in Trinidad in 1839 and another 1,307 came in 1847. They found the work on the plantations too hard, however, and by 1848 records show only 148 of the original 1,523 immigrants remained. Most seem to have found other work as artisans or by taking other non-agricultural jobs. Some Africans from Canada did go to Jamaica, but they soon returned to Canada because the conditions in Jamaica were worse.

These attempts to use African indentured labour usually failed, mainly because the African-Caribbean and the Indian indentured labourers were cheaper.

Immigration from China and Madeira

Chinese immigration

Although there had been attempts to bring in Chinese labourers before, it was only in 1852 that large-scale Chinese immigration from the Portuguese colony of Macao began. Most of these individuals were convicts and prisoners of war, and this, plus the fact that no Chinese women were brought to the colonies, caused many problems such as violence, runaways and inadequate work output. So, in 1860, British Guiana sent an agent to Canton to recruit Chinese families. However, the agent often gave a false picture to the Chinese people about the kind of work they would be doing and most of the people who came to the colony were small farmers and market gardeners, not plantation labourers. When they found out that they had been deceived, many of them refused to work.

It was also more expensive to bring Chinese labourer, since it cost £25 to import one Chinese worker from Canton compared with £15 for an Indian from Calcutta. Nonetheless, between 1852 and 1893 approximately 20,000 Chinese came to the West Indies. Around 12,000 went to British Guiana, 5,000 to Jamaica and 2,500 to Trinidad.

In the Caribbean as a whole, however, the largest number of Chinese went to Cuba. Cuba abolished the slave trade in 1845, although slavery itself was not abolished until 1886. In 1847, 600 Chinese labourers were brought to Cuba. The Chinese were contracted to work for eight years for 12 hours a day. Apart from their wages, the owner of their contract was obliged to feed them and provide two changes of clothing a year. Like the enslaved Africans, the Chinese labourers could be whipped for disobedience. They also cost only a little more: eight years' labour cost 720 pesos (at 4 pesos a month in wages) compared with the 600 pesos the Cuban planters had paid for an enslaved African.

Between 1848 and 1874, Cuba imported 124,813 Chinese labourers. The mortality rate for any particular year ranged from a low of 2.2% to a high of 19%. This was only a slight improvement over the mortality rate for enslaved Africans and, indeed, the Chinese were transported on the ships in similar conditions. Of the total number who came to Cuba, 12% died at sea.

> **Anglophone Caribbean** the islands of the Caribbean where English is the main language.

> **Francophone Caribbean** the islands of the Caribbean where French is the main language, such as Martinique and Guadeloupe.

Despite this large migration of Chinese to Cuba, most Caribbean people of Chinese descent are now found in the Anglophone Caribbean countries, such as Trinidad and Tobago, Jamaica and Guyana.

Indian immigration and settlement

The Indian immigrants proved to be the most successful in terms of providing labour for the sugar plantations.

Indian immigration became fully fledged after 1845, when it became clear that the other immigrants were not meeting the requirements of the planters or the British government. Apart from the fact that they were hard-working and accustomed to agricultural labour, the Indians were also used to migration and it was relatively easy to transfer them from one British-occupied territory to another.

Additionally, there were many people willing to leave India, where there had been famines, high taxes and loss of land, and where poverty was generally worsening under the 'Raj', as the British authorities in India were called. Certain aspects of Indian society, such as the caste system and the difficulty widows had in remarrying, also made many people willing to emigrate.

> **Caste system** a social order where people's status is determined by their birth into an assigned category and which they therefore can never change.

Activity 5.3 Find out more about the Indian caste system. Draw a diagram to explain the different groups according to this system.

Between 1845 and 1870, Trinidad received 38,413 Indian labourers. Another 67,100 went to British Guiana. Although mortality on the ships transporting them was not as high as with the Portuguese and Chinese, many Indians died while waiting for transport from the emigration depots in India. There was an average death rate of 11% in the 1870s. In Trinidad and British Guiana high mortality also became a matter of concern to the colonial authorities. The death rate among the indentured labourers in Trinidad was 12% in 1865. Investigations determined that, as with the Portuguese, malnutrition was a key cause. A law was passed stating that the planters had to provide daily rations for the first year of indentureship to all immigrants and the mortality rate fell to 2%. In British Guiana, the death rate was approximately 30% in the 1870s, dropping to under 20% only by the end of the 19th century.

Recruitment of Indian indentured labourers for British colonies

Indian labourers were recruited in the villages and districts of India as well as in crowded cities where large numbers of unemployed Indians could be found looking for jobs. Listed below are the steps which normally occurred before a recruiter was sent out to find Indians who were willing to sign contracts as indentured labourers.

- The planters in the colonies would normally tell the governor and his officials in each colony how many labourers they needed for the year.
- The governor would inform the Colonial Office in London (the office that was in charge of all Britain's colonies) of the total number of labourers needed and how much it would cost to import them.
- Those in the office in London would then send word to the government of India, telling officials how many labourers were needed.
- The government of India appointed one agent to oversee the emigration scheme in India. He was known as the Emigration Agent in Calcutta. He would give out licenses to recruiters for a specific number of labourers. For example, one recruiter might get a license to obtain 20 Indian labourers. The recruiters would hire sub-recruiters or sub-agents who would go out to the rural areas to look for labourers. They often told the labourers positive stories of indentureship to convince them to register for the system. For example, the sub-recruiters and recruiters would normally tell the Indians that they would not have to do any hard work, they would get free housing, food and clothes and they could return to India whenever they wanted.
- Once the sub-agents found enough labourers who wanted to sign contracts, they would take them to the depot in Calcutta.

- When there were enough labourers to fill a ship, they would board at Calcutta (and sometimes at the port in Madras) and from here they left for the Caribbean.

> **Activity 5.4** On an outline map of India, locate the following areas from where emigrants left for the Caribbean: Calcutta, Madras, Bombay, Lucknow, Bengal, Bihar.

Schooner a sailing ship with two or more masts.

Shipping

Shipping indentured labourers to the Caribbean was a money-making activity. In 1875, the James Nourse Shipping Company was awarded the contract to transport Indian labourers to the Caribbean in 1875. The ships used were usually schooners with three masts, weighing about 500 tons. The journey lasted an average of 20 weeks for a sailing ship and 13 weeks for a steamer. The Nourse shipping line was paid £11 12s 6d per adult. The following can be noted regarding shipping Indian indentured labourers to the Caribbean.

- All ships were required to have some kind of hospital with a medical doctor on board and enough medical supplies to cover the length of the journey. All emigrants were supposed to be given constant medical care.
- The recommended number of emigrants was restricted to 350 in any one vessel so as to prevent overcrowding. However, almost all the ships that left India had more than this number on board.
- As the number of passengers was often very high and overcrowding frequently occurred, diseases were always common on board the ships. The most common diseases were motion sickness, different types of fever, measles, meningitis and mumps.

> **Activity 5.5** Draw up a table to show the similarities and differences between African slavery and the Indian indentureship system. Why do you think we know more details regarding the Indian system?

Contract stipulations

While the contracts varied according to colonies, the main stipulations were as follows.

- Each labourer would be 'engaged in the cultivation of the soil or the manufacture of produce on any plantation, every day except Sundays and authorized holidays'.
- The labourer was required to work for nine hours in each working day and was attached to the specific plantation for five years from the date that person was sent to a plantation.
- At the end of the five years the labourers were to be given a certificate of exemption from labour and permitted to return to India at their own cost.
- However, the labourer had to work for another five years on any plantation before he or she could be given a free or partially paid return passage to India.
- The Indians received about 25 cents for a day's labour; this amount varied, although it never fell below 20 cents per task (a particular amount of work that was supposed to be done).
- The planters were supposed to provide some form of medical care and maintenance free of charge for labourers during sickness.
- The labourers would be given housing (normally the barracks where the enslaved Africans had lived previously).
- They were supposed to be given a stipulated amount of food but the cost of this was deducted from their wages. A child under the age of 10 was to receive one third of the ration free of cost.

It must be noted that the stipulated hours were often increased by the planters during crop time, and the Indians were also forbidden to leave the estates without a pass. If they did so, they could be arrested and jailed. In 1861, 17% of newly arrived labourers in Trinidad had been charged for running away, which they had done mainly because they had not expected the work to be so difficult. This problem was reduced by 1865 though, with just 3% of arrivals breaking their contracts.

Another problem was caused by the fact that many more Indian men than women were brought to the West Indies – about one woman to every three men. Jealousy and infidelity led to several murders in the Indian communities. In a five-year period, 14 of 19 Indians murdered in British Guiana were women, as were all seven Indians murdered in Trinidad.

When their contracts ended, many of the indentured labourers chose to stay in the Caribbean. Between 1845 and 1917, only about 25% of the labourers decided to return to India – about 125,000 out of a total of 500,000 who had come to the region.

> **Roleplay**
>
> Imagine that you are living in China, India or Madeira in 1850. You have heard of the opportunities to migrate to the West Indies as indentured labour. Write one paragraph in which you try to convince your friend to migrate with you.

> **Activity 5.6**
>
> Construct a table showing the countries from which immigrants came, the numbers that came and the Caribbean colonies they went to.

Effects of immigration on the sugar industry

It is difficult to say whether immigration really saved the sugar industry. Sugar production up to 1842 declined in most of the British colonies (see Table 5.1 on page 121 for figures for three colonies). Table 5.3 shows that by the 1850s production had increased in Barbados, which did not have immigrants because there were enough labourers there who were willing to or who had to work. However, in Jamaica, which immigrants did go to, exports dropped.

Table 5.3 Sugar exports before (1820s) and after emancipation (1850s)

Colony	Slave production	Paid labour production
Barbados	32,800,000 lbs	78,000,000 lbs
Antigua	20,580,000 lbs	26,174,000 lbs
St Kitts	12,000,000 lbs	10,000,000 lbs
Nevis	5,000,000 lbs	4,4000,000 lbs
Jamaica	90,000 (hogsheads)	28,000 (hogsheads)

Table 5.4 compares sugar exports 10 years before emancipation and 40 years after starting to use immigrant labour. It lists the same islands as Table 5.3, plus Trinidad and British Guiana.

Table 5.4 Sugar exports (in tons)

Colony	1828	1882
Barbados	16,942	48,325
Antigua	8,848	12,670
St. Kitts/Nevis	6,060	16,664
Jamaica	72,198	32,638
Trinidad	13,285	55,327
British Guiana	40,115	124,102

Immigration may have helped increase sugar production, except in Jamaica, where it declined. This can be explained as Jamaica did not invest as heavily in immigration. In Barbados, production rose three-fold, even though the island received no immigrant labour.

> **Activity 5.7**
>
> 'Indian immigration saved the plantation economy.' How true is this statement with reference to either Trinidad or British Guiana?

At best, then, all we can say is that immigrant labour may have helped some colonies and made no difference in others. For the West Indies as a whole, sugar exports in this period increased from 202,396 tons to 315,136 tons, but this may have been due to factors other than immigration. You should also bear in mind that profits would not have increased in tandem with increased exports, because sugar after emancipation was sold at lower prices.

Effects of immigrant groups on society

If it is difficult to measure the economic impact of immigrants, it is even harder to determine what social impact they had in the various islands they settled in. Indians were numerically the largest group of immigrants, but they settled in significant numbers only in two colonies – British Guiana (now Guyana) and Trinidad (now the Republic of Trinidad and Tobago). In other islands, Indians were so few that they were either absorbed into the wider society, kept so much to themselves that they had no social impact, or migrated to the two colonies which already had large Indian settlements.

Two other immigrant groups who were brought as labourers in small numbers were the Chinese and the Portuguese. These groups often started retail businesses or became merchants.

Plural society a society where several ethnic groups co-exist.

Still, no matter how large or small the different immigrant groups, their presence changed the Caribbean islands into what are sometimes called 'plural societies' or 'multi-ethnic societies'. In other words, there are people in the Caribbean who are citizens of the same country, but who belong to different racial groups, different ancestral cultures, different religions or all of these.

The plural society was first defined by an anthropologist named J.S. Furnivall, who studied Dutch colonies in East Asia. He wrote:

> 'There is a plural society, with different sections of the community living side by side, but separately, within the same political unit. Even in the economic sphere, there is a division along racial lines.'

Contribution of free peasants to Caribbean society

Every country in the world has had peasants and many still do. The *Oxford English Dictionary* defines a peasant as 'a poor smallholder or agricultural labourer of low social status'. In the Caribbean, the term 'free peasants' is used to distinguish between those people who cultivated land when they were still enslaved or who were never enslaved and the blacks who became landholders after emancipation. So, except in Haiti, a peasant class only arose after 1838 in the British Caribbean and later still in the other Spanish and French colonies.

Agrarian society a society based on agriculture.

In the British colonies this new group was formed fairly quickly. By 1859, just over 10 years after they were freed, there were 50,000 small proprietors in Jamaica and by 1880 the colony records show that there were 36,756 landholdings, each under five acres. Between 1844 and 1859 in Barbados, the number of small farmers increased from 1,110 to 3,537, proving wrong the stipendiary magistrate who in 1842 wrote:

> 'as the land is principally divided into plantations, the proprietors are not likely to sell off small plots… and there being no public lands available, it is plain that freeholders to any extent cannot be established in this country'.

Within 10 years after emancipation in Trinidad, there were 7,000 smallholders. By 1861 this figure had increased to 11,000.

In Haiti, which had 8,000 plantations before the 1791 revolution, more than 46,000 people in the independent nation became small landowners, while the other two thirds of the population either squatted or worked for wages. Most of the Haitian freeholders were subsistence farmers, but some produced coffee and other crops to sell in the markets in Port-au-Prince and other urban centres.

In Guadeloupe, although there is little data on landowners, the number of market gardens gives an indication of the growing peasant class, since these gardens increased from 1,128 in 1847 to 3,467 by 1859.

In the Dutch colonies, where emancipation occurred in 1863, many planters simply abandoned their estates. In Suriname, where there was a lot of land, the freed Africans migrated to the main urban centre, Paramaribo. In small islands, such as Aruba, the Dutch government sold land to the blacks, which helped to create a large peasant class.

The zeal with which the emancipated Africans approached land ownership demonstrated, first, their understanding of the value of land in an agrarian society and, second, it showed their desire for economic and social independence.

The first contribution made to Caribbean society was economic. They produced more crops for sale and use, such as honey, ginger, bananas and arrowroot. Other products were spices, logwood, cotton, cocoa, coffee and rum. Trade also increased because the ex-slaves now had to buy their own food, clothing and equipment. By 1850 in Jamaica, goods produced by the peasants made up 10% of the colony's exports. By 1890, the peasant class produced 39% of Jamaica's exports, especially ground provisions.

The simple fact that the blacks were able to become landowners was important in itself. It showed that they could overcome the obstacles set against them by both the planters and the British government. For example, squatting was legally forbidden after 1838 and the British government even passed a law which prevented planters from selling land to the blacks for less than £1 per acre or selling less than a certain amount of land (such as 40 acres) so that the blacks could not own large plots of land. The planters themselves were often reluctant to sell land to the former slaves.

Yet, as you have read, the blacks were still able to purchase land and sometimes even estates, both individually and by pooling their resources. Still, in certain colonies, these obstacles prevented the rise of an independent peasantry. One such colony was Belize, where cultivable land was far from the markets where produce could be sold and where the timber industry, particularly in mahogany exports, provided employment for the ex-slaves. Smaller islands, such as St Kitts and Antigua, also had fewer free peasants, because of the limited availability of land to buy or to squat on.

The rise of the peasant class also had some negative effects as time went on. These effects, which included poverty and lack of educational progress, became pronounced in the 20th century as economies changed after the Second World War, as the colonies became independent in the 1960s and as the populations in the islands became less rural and more urban in the 1970s. We will examine these effects in more detail in Chapter 8.

Impact of free villages

No matter how many blacks became small landowners, they could not resist the oppressive system unless they cooperated as a group. This is why the formation of free villages was so important. For the first time, the Africans who had been bought and brought to the Caribbean could interact with one another as free people. Living in a village helped create a sense of community.

> **Free village movement** after slavery was abolished in the British West Indies, some ex-slaves moved out of the plantations in some colonies and settled in 'free villages'.

It is also important to note that by 1840 most of the black people of the West Indies were following one or another Christian faith and many of them were attending churches. Proximity is not enough to make individuals into a community. Shared beliefs and values are also essential and since most of the emancipated Africans had been unable to practise, or had never known, African religions, Christianity became an important binding force. The church was also the main institution through which the blacks could make political protests (against unfair laws, or to obtain government services) or to learn to read and write.

Some free villages had been established long before emancipation, by runaway slaves, in the Guiyana hinterland and the mountains of Jamaica. The planters had argued that, after emancipation, the former slaves would join these villages or flee to the remote areas and set up new villages. This did not happen. In fact, on a plantation near New Amsterdam in Berbice, the newly emancipated slaves gave a full dress party and invited the governor and the military commander, serving the finest wines and foods available in the colony.

The formation of free villages happened quite rapidly. In Jamaica, the first free village, called Sligoville, was set up by a Baptist Minister just one year after emancipation, in 1835. when emancipation was declared, about 100 families went there. In 1838, another village named Sturge Town, built on land purchased by the Anglican Church, was started on the north coast of Jamaica. A church and school were built and 70 families came. By 1842, there were over 200 free villages on the island, with about 20,000 inhabitants. These villagers occupied about 100,000 acres which had cost the ex-slaves about £70,000 to purchase.

British Guiana also had free villages soon after emancipation. By 1848, about 10,000 people owned and occupied their own cottages. By 1858 in Antigua, there were 67 villages with 5,187 houses and 15,644 inhabitants. By 1857 in St Vincent, there were over 8,000 people living in their own houses and in Grenada over 10,000. Many of the villages were named after anti-slavery activists: Wilberforce, Clarkson, Sturge and Sligo.

Reasons for Crown Colony government in the 19th century

Old Representative System a system of government which consisted of a governor, an assembly (elected Lower House), and a council (nominated Upper House). Under this system, the governor had power and no authority, and the assembly had authority but no power.

Crown Colony a system of government prevalent in the British West Indies until the colonies became independent in the 20th century.

Government in the West Indies was a copy of the British system of Parliament. Each island had a governor (who was equivalent to the English monarch), a council that was appointed (equivalent to the House of Lords), and an elected assembly (equivalent to the House of Commons).

A short explanation of the British Parliament

Medieval kings were expected to pay for all their expenses from their own revenues. When extra revenue was required (usually to wage a war) the king would request help from his barons. These were the precursors to the House of Lords (so called because they were aristocrats). In the 13th century, however, several kings and barons were unable to raise the required revenues, so they also summoned representatives of the counties, cities and towns to get their agreement to extra taxes. These persons were the precursors to the House of Commons (named this because its members were commoners).

The term 'parliament', which originally meant a meeting for 'parley' or discussion, was first used in 1236, and the first convening of Parliament is dated in 1295. By the middle of the 14th century, Parliament was officially divided into two Houses: the House of Lords, which was made up of persons summoned by the king (mostly barons, bishops, and abbots); and the House of Commons, which was made up of elected representatives (of counties, cities, and boroughs).

The British government could just have given the governor and his nominated council total powers, but they needed to have the cooperation of the wealthy planters in the islands, who paid taxes and were influential within the colonies. Candidates could only go up for elections based on land ownership, so planters were favoured over even well-off merchants. This meant that the assembly would sometimes favour policies that the British government opposed.

In this system, called the Old Representative System, the governor passed all laws, but the assembly often had control of the colony's annual budget (or what were called money bills). Every year, there was a vote which allocated money for the governing of the island and the governor needed the assembly's support or else the government would not be able to buy supplies or pay salaries.

In Jamaica, the assembly even controlled how this money was to be spent. The British government was defeated by the Jamaican assembly in 1678, when the government tried to pass laws which would have taken away the assembly's powers.

In Grenada, when the British government imposed a 4.5% export duty without the consent of the local legislature, the law was defeated in the English court.

After emancipation, the disagreements between the 'Mother Country' and its colonies became more acute, partly because the British government was more concerned about the former slaves than the colonists. More plantation owners had returned to England, leaving their estates to be managed by attorneys and overseers who, according to one historian, 'paid little attention to agricultural efficiency or to humanitarian or social considerations'. Of course, the planters had never had social considerations either, but mismanagement was a factor in the plantations making less profits. This led to more government employees being retrenched because there was not enough money to pay them.

This happened twice in 1853 in British Guiana and Jamaica, and after the second time the British government decided that the colonial system would have to be changed to use the financial resources of the islands more efficiently. Sir Henry Barkly was sent by the British government to Jamaica with an offer to wipe out most of the debt if the assembly and the council passed legislation to give the governor more powers. After several months, this was done.

The structure of the assembly remained the same, but private members could no longer propose money bills. Instead, there was now an executive committee, consisting of one council member and a maximum of three assembly members, who were the liaison between the governor and the law-making bodies. This committee presented the annual estimates for the budget. The council was enlarged and given the power to introduce legislation which did not have to do with money bills.

This new system started 1854 in Jamaica and Tobago and in 1859 in St Kitts, Antigua, Nevis and St Vincent. By 1875, all these islands, plus Dominica and Grenada, had a 'unicameral legislature' – that is, a government made up of just the governor and a council with a majority of nominated members. There was no elected assembly. A government system with two law-making bodies, such as a council and an assembly, is called a 'bicameral legislature'. Most of the independent Caribbean countries have a bicameral legislature, with two chambers called the House of Representatives and the Senate. In Trinidad and St Lucia, the council was made up entirely of nominated members. Only Barbados and the Bahamas kept the old colonial system.

This Crown Colony system was the prevailing form of government until the 20th century. This is one historian's explanation of it:

> 'It was a system by which the imperial government could hold the white oligarchy in check and give some consideration to the needs of overwhelming majority of Negroes and East Indians – a sort of non-elective virtual representation through the governor and the Colonial Office.'

The system was often criticized by the colonists, who said that the nominated members of Legislative Council were only there for show, since the governor could do whatever he wanted. In Jamaica the colonists also argued that this system was too expensive and that too many government positions were held by Englishmen instead of Jamaicans.

The emancipated Africans seemed to support the new system. In Jamaica, they had been able to put their money in the government savings bank, buy land and build cottages. One comment that represented the black view was: 'We are a law-abiding people, being fully conscious that without the protection of Government our fellow colonists would not permit us to enjoy the breath we breathe.'

REVISION QUESTIONS

1 Read the passage below and answer the questions that follow.

The fear was widespread that, after full emancipation, the sugar industry would be ruined. The planters, therefore, adopted new measures to save the sugar industry. Immigration was one such measure.

   a Give four reasons why the planters feared that the sugar industry would be ruined after emancipation.
(10 marks)
   b Explain two steps in the development of Indian immigration to the Caribbean between 1838 and 1876. *(5 marks)*
   c Discuss four ways in which immigration affected the Caribbean economy and society. *(10 marks)*

(Total = 25 marks)
CXC Past Papers, General Proficiency, May/June 2003

2 a Explain the major problems faced by sugar planters in the first 10 years after emancipation in the British Caribbean. *(15 marks)*
   b Explain why the sugar industry in Guyana and Trinidad recovered and expanded by 1876. *(10 marks)*

(Total = 25 marks)
CXC Past Papers, General Proficiency, May/June 2002

3 Examine the socio-economic impact of Indian immigration on any one named West Indian colony. *(25 marks)*

4 'Missionaries played a substantial role in the emergence of free villages.' Critically assess this statement. *(25 marks)*

Recommended reading

- Green, W. *British Slave Emancipation: The sugar colonies and the great experiment 1830–1865,* London: Clarendon Press, 1994
- Hamilton-Willie, D. *Adjustments to Emancipation 1838–1876,* Kingston: Ian Randle Publishers, 2007
- Laurence, K. O. *A Question of Labour: Indentured immigration into Trinidad and British Guiana 1875–1917,* Kingston: Ian Randle Publishers, 1994

6 The Caribbean economy 1875–1985

This chapter will answer the following questions.
- Why was there a crisis in the sugar industry in the British Caribbean?
- What measures were undertaken to resolve this crisis?
- Why was there a growth in the Cuban sugar industry in the 19th century?
- Why was there a growth (and survival) of alternative agricultural enterprises in the British Caribbean up to 1935?
- What is the importance of tourism to the Caribbean?
- What factors led to the establishment and growth of extractive industries in the Caribbean up to 1985?
- What were the effects of industrialization on the English-speaking Caribbean?

The book you are reading is the product of economic processes, which involve the production of raw materials (for example wood), manufacturing (inks, different types of paper), technology (computerized typesetting, the printing press and bindery), labour (typesetters, press operators, book sellers and so on) and ideas (academics, writers, editors, for example).

An economy, therefore, consists of the people, ideas, institutions and devices which produce goods and services that people need and want. Different economies produce different sorts of goods, because countries and regions have different resources (materials and skills) or the same resources in varying quantities. So this book, for example, might have been made in the Caribbean, Europe, the Americas or Asia. The paper may have been made in India, perhaps using wood from trees in Brazil, the pages may have been printed and bound on a press manufactured by a US company, with ink made in China, and it is produced by a British publisher, to record information generated by Caribbean as well as other scholars.

The only thing new about such economic activity is its scope. Since prehistoric times, human beings have traded with one another to obtain different sorts of goods or services. Some countries and peoples produce goods of higher value, others of lower value. This is often because various countries have different histories, and history influences how resources are used.

In this chapter, we will be looking at the kinds of goods produced in the Caribbean. We will look at the kinds of resources the area has, and how our history has determined how people use or misuse these resources.

The Caribbean economy

All the territories in the Caribbean share important facets of history, and that history has shaped the economy of the region as a whole. The two most important economic factors are plantation slavery and the indentureship system that came after emancipation. Another commonality is dependence on natural resources (also called 'commodities') to earn foreign exchange. Commodities range from minerals such as oil, bauxite and gold to agricultural products such as sugar, coffee and cotton. The important point is that such products are exported with little or no processing and they are used to produce manufactured goods, for example when cotton is made into clothes. Processing and manufacturing both add value to commodities, and advanced economies are based on such 'added value', whereas backward economies depend mainly on raw products.

As you have read in previous chapters, Caribbean economies developed with almost total dependence on one crop – in most cases, sugar. Once the enslaved Africans were freed and the sugar industry all but collapsed, the Caribbean economies began to diversify. This diversification was still based mainly on agriculture. Crops that had been cultivated when the Caribbean was first colonized in the 15th century began to be planted again in the 19th century. These crops included cocoa, coffee, citrus fruit and bananas. In the 20th century, further diversification occurred with the investment and exploitation of minerals in those territories which possessed them. Bauxite was mined in Jamaica, Guyana and Suriname, while oil was drilled in Trinidad. Tourism also became an important part of the economies of many of the smaller islands, which promoted the 'sun, sea and sand' image to attract tourists from the USA and Europe seeking to escape the winter.

An important factor that affects the economies of most Caribbean territories is the size of the area. Nearly all Caribbean territories are islands and have limited land space. Guyana and Suriname, which are considered Caribbean although located on the South American continent, have limited populations. When a country has a small land space, there will only be a few resources which can be used for economic activity. When a country has a small population, its internal market is limited in terms of goods which can be sold. For these two basic reasons, Caribbean economies are very dependent on exports. Moreover, only a few products are exported by each territory.

There are five main factors which affect the Caribbean economy. These are:

- one main crop — sugar — which was produced primarily as a raw material rather than processed when the Caribbean was colonized
- foreign ownership and decision making
- a production system based on preferences in developed nations
- competition between islands for markets
- lack of regional integration.

Impact of the five factors which affect the Caribbean economy

How do the five factors in our list hinder the development of the Caribbean? Some explanations are given below, but it is also possible that these same factors could help the region's economic development.

Factor 1 Relying on one crop, whether it is sugar or something else, means that changes in prices for that one product determine how prosperous or poor the country is. Also, lack of processing (for example processing brown sugar into white, or bananas into flavouring) means that less value is added to the product, which means lower profits for the producer. However, it is also the case that specializing in a particular product, then trading that product for other goods, might be the most effective policy, since the producer becomes highly skilled in making that product. In economics, this is known as 'comparative advantage'.

Factor 2 Foreign ownership can mean that decisions are made in the interests of foreigners rather than the people who work in the sector, or that decisions will not be as well informed as those made by local people, and local markets and entrepreneurs have fewer opportunities to develop. On the other hand, foreigners may have more experience or expertise in the industry.

Factor 3 If production is decided by what people in the USA or Europe want, then local resources are used less, so innovation is stymied. Then again, if a Caribbean production system is geared toward metropolitan wants, this could create more profitable industries within the region.

Factor 4 Competition between the islands reduces the profits for each island – for example, each island tries to get tourists for itself, which costs more in advertising than if the region advertised as one destination. Yet it is also a basic principle of economics that competition helps ensure that market forces work for the good of the consumer.

Factor 5 Regional integration would create a larger internal market and allow specialization for each island – that is, each island could produce specific goods, with the profits shared between a unified regional group. However, no economists, technocrats, policy makers or politicians have yet worked out how to reduce the costs of communications between the islands, how to create a Caribbean currency, how to set up a Caribbean central bank or solved the other economic challenges to regional integration. This could also be attributed to a lack of political will or desire by the majority of people for a common currency etc.

Food is the main sector in which production is mostly for internal use. Food production ranges from supplying vegetables, to locally produced chicken, pork, fish and beef. In 1881, there were approximately 400,000 people engaged in agriculture in the British Caribbean. By 1911, this figure had increased to almost half a million, but by 1946 the number had dropped back to under 400,000. By the mid-20th century, less than half the labour force was engaged in agriculture in all save the smaller islands.

Table 6.1 Percentage of labour force by sector, 1945

Colony	Agriculture (%)	Manufacturing (%)
Barbados	28	20
Guyana	40	15
Jamaica	44	12
St Kitts	51	9
Trinidad	25	18

Apart from agriculture, mineral extraction and light manufacturing, there are three other sectors which have become significant in the Caribbean economy.

- Offshore financial services – mainly involving banking services. Such services are called 'offshore' because the accounts are not subject to the normal rules and regulations of the country offering the services, which means that people from other countries can bypass their countries' rules and regulations. Offshore banking services are used mainly by individuals who, and companies which, do not wish to deposit or transfer cash within their own jurisdictions. This may be for tax reasons, but offshore financial services have also been known to be used by drug traffickers, for example, to launder the money from their illegal trade. The main Caribbean territories providing offshore financial services are Antigua and Barbuda, the Bahamas, Barbados, the Cayman Islands, the Netherland Antilles, and St Vincent and the Grenadines.
- Information processing. This involves inputting data provided by organizations, usually from more developed countries, which find it cheaper to use labour from the Caribbean. This has expanded and become particularly economically viable with the development of computers and the Internet. In 1993, information processing provided employment for about 5,000 people, but within two years over 7,500 people were employed in the sector.
- Export processing zones or EPZs. These are specific areas in a country where normal laws related to trade and other business regulations are not applied. Several Caribbean countries, such as Jamaica and the Dominican Republic, have passed laws creating EPZs in order to attract foreign investment and create jobs. Companies set up within these zones because they can get cheaper labour and pay lower taxes than in other locations. Clothing and textile companies are the main companies which use EPZs, as well as light manufacturers.

In terms of their economies, the Caribbean territories are divided into four categories: large islands, small islands, mainland states (those countries which are considered Caribbean although located in the South American continent) and dependent states. The fourth category, dependent states, refers to those territories which are still politically linked to the metropolitan nations which colonized them, and which therefore receive economic benefits from them. The categories are listed in Table 6.2, and Table 6.3 shows the income levels in these four categories.

Table 6.2 Economic categories of Caribbean territories

Category	Territories
Large island states	Cuba, the Dominican Republic, Haiti, Jamaica
Small island states	Antigua and Barbuda, the Bahamas, Barbados, Dominica, Grenada, St Lucia, St Kitts and Nevis, Trinidad and Tobago
Mainland states	Belize, Guyana, Suriname
Dependent states	Aruba, Netherland Antilles, Anguilla, Montserrat, British Virgin Islands, Caymans, Turks and Caicos, French Guiana, Guadeloupe, Martinique, Puerto Rico, United States Virgin Islands

Source: Adapted from Pantin and Attz, 2009

Table 6.3 lists 27 countries, 14 of which chose to become independent in the 1960s. Of those, eight have lower-middle to low incomes, five have upper-middle incomes, and only one, the Bahamas, has a high income. On the other hand, of the 13 countries which have remained formally linked to the metropolitan nations, four have high incomes, five have high to upper-middle incomes and four have upper-middle incomes. Of course, measuring the benefits of independence needs to look beyond purely economic categorization.

Table 6.3 Income and political status of Caribbean territories, 1999

Sovereign status	Countries	Income category
British dependency	Anguilla, Bermuda, British Virgin Islands, Montserrat, Turks and Caicos	High* to upper middle
Territory of the USA, France, Netherlands	United States Virgin Islands, French Guiana, Aruba, Netherland Antilles	High
Territory of the USA, France	Puerto Rico, Guadeloupe, Martinique, St Martin	Upper middle
Independent	Bahamas	High
Independent	Antigua and Barbuda, Barbados, St Kitts and Nevis, St Lucia, Trinidad and Tobago	Upper middle
Independent	St Vincent and Grenadines, Jamaica, Grenada, Belize, Cuba, Suriname, Guyana, Haiti	Lower middle to low

*1999 per capita income in excess of US$9,266.

> **GDP** Grass domestic product refers to the value of all goods and services produced within a country in a given period.

In four major Anglophone Caribbean countries (Barbados; Guyana, formerly British Guiana; Jamaica; and Trinidad and Tobago) trade increased significantly between 1955 and 1983. Exports in 1955 totalled US$352 million; by 1983, this figure had grown to US$3,602 million. The value of imports also grew more than ten-fold, from US$425 in 1955 to US$5,235 in 1983. You should note that, in both periods, the region was importing more than it was exporting. However, when a country imports goods, it must pay the country the goods are coming from. That is why, for most countries, either imports equal exports or a country exports more than it imports. How could the Caribbean be buying more than it was selling? It could be that various countries were going into debt (they were living beyond their means) or that many people in the Caribbean were receiving remittances (including foreign currency, such as US dollars or UK pounds sterling) sent by their relatives living in these countries. In 2007, Jamaica, for example, received US$2 billion from Jamaicans living abroad, mainly in the USA (60%) and the United Kingdom (25%). This was a significant 13% of Jamaica's GDP. Guyana received US$278 million, Barbados US$140 million, and Trinidad and Tobago US$92 million. Remittances are therefore a significant economic activity linking the Caribbean and the more developed countries.

Up to the 1980s, unemployment was a major problem in all the Anglophone islands, and it remains so today. In recent decades, in Jamaica unemployment averaged between 20% and 30% of the workforce; in Barbados, and Trinidad and Tobago, it was 17–18%; and in the smaller islands more than 20% of the workforce usually did not have a job. In more developed countries, the unemployment rate is usually below 10%.

Several factors explain the different economic performance in different Caribbean countries. Perhaps the most important is size. The second factor is tourism, which is dealt with in more detail later in this chapter. A third factor is government policy in respect to the economy: the exchange rate, levels of duties and tariffs, tax breaks and so on. All these factors have an impact on four major economic challenges of the region. These challenges are:

- unemployment
- volatile world markets for Caribbean products
- foreign debt
- natural disasters.

Unemployment obviously means not having a job at all, but having a job where the pay cannot meet living needs or having a job only occasionally (known as underemployment) are also employment problems. Unemployment and underemployment are especially high among young people in the region. This factor is related to crime, which further undermines the economy, especially in the territories where tourism is a main income source, since tourists are less likely to visit places where they do not feel safe. Unemployment is also related to the fact that most Caribbean economies are not properly diversified, so there are fewer job opportunities available. This also leads to many qualified people leaving the region to settle in developed nations. This 'brain drain', as it is called, reduces economic development because there are fewer skilled persons in the region.

It is also important to examine the challenge of volatile world markets affecting Caribbean products. Whether the product is oil, bauxite or bananas, demand on the world market often determines whether Caribbean economies will be prosperous or poor. In Trinidad and Tobago the economy depends mostly on oil and natural gas. Trinidad and Tobago has experienced two 'boom and bust' cycles, in the 1970s and between 2003 and 2005. When manufactured goods are in high demand in the developed countries, aluminium, which is made from the raw material of bauxite, is in high demand. Agricultural products are less subject to such cycles, but are nonetheless affected by trade negotiations in the developed countries.

> **CARICOM** The Caribbean community is an organization of 15 Caribbean nations.

The third challenge in the list, foreign debt, affects countries which have borrowed heavily in the past in order to build infrastructure or fund education and health initiatives. Jamaica and Guyana have had to use a significant part of their foreign exchange earnings every year to pay off these debts. CARICOM countries also use up foreign exchange to import services, relating to commissions, royalties, patents and advertising, as well as managerial, professional and technical services. See more information on CARICOM in Chapter 8. Foreign exchange issues also affect relations between Caribbean countries, because when there is a shortage of US dollars, Caribbean governments often raise protectionist barriers. This happened in the early 1980s in CARICOM. Another policy measure used by governments is currency devaluation – that is, lowering the value of their local currency in relation to the US dollar (or some other currency such as pounds sterling). Jamaica, Guyana, and Trinidad and Tobago all adopted this strategy in the 1980s. The first two of these countries had to go to the International Monetary Fund for a loan and currency devaluation was part of the agreement. Trinidad and Tobago devalued its currency voluntarily in an attempt to deal with foreign exchange problems following the bust of the 1970s oil boom.

The final challenge in the list, natural disasters, can mean economic collapse for countries dependent on tourism or the destruction of crops, which may be wiped out by hurricanes and flooding. In 1995, hurricanes Luis and Marilyn caused severe damage to hotels in Antigua and Barbuda. In 1998, hurricanes George and Mitch reduced Jamaica's tourist earnings. In 2004, Hurricane Ivan virtually flattened Grenada, with 90% of the country's hotels and tourist apartments destroyed. The island has rebuilt its infrastructure through international loans and charitable donations.

Year	Country	% GDP lost
1988	Jamaica	65%
1989	Montserrat	200%
1994	St Lucia	18%
1995	Antigua	65%
2004	Caymans	183%
	Grenada	212%

Table 6.4 Economic effects of hurricanes on selected Caribbean countries

Problems of the sugar industry 1875–1985

> **Free trade** people in different countries can exchange goods and services with each other without interference from government or other authorities. The opposition of free trade is 'protectionism'. The main measures governments use to put up trade barriers are tariffs, quotas and subsidies.

The discovery that sugar could be obtained from beet was made in 1747. However, it was not until a century later that beet sugar production started to compete with cane sugar production. From 1850, beet sugar started to improve its crop yields (that is, give more sugar per beet), the manufacturing process became more efficient and beet producers marketed their sugar better than the cane producers. By 1880, beet producers were making half of the world's sugar and by 1890 they were making 59% of it.

However, beet producers also benefited from European governments' policies. Since beet was grown in European countries, the governments subsidized the costs of production and also put up tariffs which made cane sugar very expensive to import into their countries – a policy called 'protectionism'. This meant that beet sugar was competing with cane sugar on unfair terms.

> **Tariff** a tax on imports, which makes imported goods more expensive to sell than locally produced ones, even if the foreign goods are produced more cheaply.

For example, in the 1880s, sugar made in France was selling for 15% less than it cost to produce. These policies resulted in a decline in the prices for cane sugar. Between 1870 and 1880, world sugar production rose by 44% but prices held steady at 20 shillings per hundredweight (cwt). In 1884, thanks to beet sugar flooding the British market, the price fell to 13 shillings. Yet British Caribbean sugar cost on average about 16 shillings per cwt to produce, so there was no way for the planters to make a profit.

Additionally, improved production methods and better packing (in bags instead of barrels) meant that more sugar could be stored for longer. Sugar sellers were therefore able to demand lower prices from sugar producers, because they did not have to sell the sugar as quickly. By 1897, the price of sugar was below 10 shillings per cwt.

This crisis led to the setting up of a Royal Commission, which recommended ending the system of subsidizing beet sugar exports. This was partially achieved by the Brussels Convention in 1902, but this did not help the British Caribbean sugar producers very much. The planters begged the British government to restore protective tariffs, but the government was following free trade principles and British consumers wanted cheap sugar.

> **Quota** a law which allows only a certain quantity of foreign goods to enter a country. This often makes it unprofitable for foreign producers to sell to another country.

> **Subsidies** money given by government to a particular industry, allowing that industry to sell at lower prices than foreign competitors, since the industry's production costs are artificially lowered.

As a result, the planters turned to the US market, and this strategy was more successful. By 1900, more than 65% of British Caribbean sugar was going to the USA. However, this market was profitable only for a limited time, since the British sugar plantations were unable to compete with the larger, more modern Cuban ones.

> **Roleplay**
> Imagine that you are a planter living in the British Caribbean territory in 1890. Write a letter to the governor, outlining the problems you are experiencing with your plantation. Suggest actions you think will help to remedy your problems.

So by the end of the 19th century, British Caribbean sugar producers had three main problems. They were:

- falling sugar prices
- competition from beet sugar
- backward technology.

The planters used several strategies to overcome these challenges, which you will read about in the next section. Other problems persisted into the 20th century though. A major issue was employment. Since the Caribbean colonies had mainly produced sugar, a large proportion of the population was employed in the industry both before and after the abolition of slavery. However, as the industry declined, many people had to find other ways to make a living. After the First World War (1914–18), there was a boom in sugar prices. Sugar was selling at US$100 per tonne, but then prices collapsed in 1921 and 1922. Afterwards, there was the economic collapse of the 1930s and sugar prices dropped to just US $20 a tonne. The prices of most other primary products also dropped and this badly affected the Caribbean which produced mostly primary, rather than manufactured or processed, products. In 1920, the sugar industry employed one person per 1½ acres, but by 1950 it employed 1 person for every 2 acres. 'It is impossible for a man to get a decent standard of living from two acres of land from any staple crop in any part of the world,' wrote the Caribbean's most famous economist, W. Arthur Lewis.

The Brussels Convention of 1902 was only the first of efforts to regularize the sugar industry, with similar negotiations taking place up to the 1980s. In 1931 and in 1937, International Sugar Agreements were signed, aiming to keep a balance between the global demand for sugar and supply from sugar producers. The idea was to use quotas and stock controls to regulate production, and to control consumption by getting sugar importers to agree to bring in the smallest amounts needed for domestic use in their countries. When the Second World War started in 1939, however, these efforts all came to naught.

During this war, Britain bought all the British Caribbean's sugar at an agreed price. When the war ended, sugar refiners in Britain lobbied the government to ensure that they would continue to get the raw material they needed from the Caribbean. The British government in 1948 agreed to provide quotas and price guarantees to the suppliers, as had been done under the previous Sugar Agreements. In 1951, the Commonwealth Sugar Agreement was signed, under which Britain agreed to import 1.7 million tons of sugar annually. The Caribbean colonies provided 70–80% of this quota at an agreed price. However, when Britain joined the European Economic Community (EEC) in 1974, the Agreement was changed to the Sugar Protocol.

This Protocol was an agreement between the EEC and the former colonies, which were now called the African-Caribbean-Pacific group (ACP). The agreement was a government-to-government legal document which specified the amount of sugar and at what prices the ACP countries would supply to the EEC. This price was £147 per ton, and when the Protocol was signed the world price of sugar was two-and-a-half times higher. At the time, the EEC was the world's largest importer of sugar. By the 1990s it was still the largest importer but now also the largest exporter. The protected sugar brought into Europe under the Protocol was exported from the EEC's domestic supply, which included beet sugar. This dumping resulted in lower sugar prices. However, these same lower world prices meant that CARICOM countries benefited in the long run from the preferential arrangement – by one calculation, to the tune of US$1.4 billion between 1975 and 1992.

Activity 6.1

Find out more about the First World War. Which countries were involved in the war? How did the war affect the Caribbean?

W. ARTHUR LEWIS
(1915–91)

6.1 W. Arthur Lewis

William Arthur Lewis was born in St Lucia in 1915. His parents were school teachers who had emigrated to St Lucia from Antigua. As a child, he was always ahead of his classmates in school and at the age of 14 he graduated from high school. As he was too young to take the examination for a government scholarship, he started work as a clerk in a government's office. Three years later, at the age of 17, he won the scholarship and attended the London School of Economics (LSE). He graduated in 1937 with first class honours in economics. He was immediately offered a scholarship to continue at LSE and he pursued a doctorate in industrial economics.

He graduated with a PhD in 1940 and was employed as a lecturer at LSE from 1938 to 1947. The following are some of the distinguished posts he held:

- Professor of Economics at the University of Manchester, 1947–58
- Principal of the University College of the West Indies, 1959–62
- First Vice Chancellor of UWI, 1962–63
- UN Economic Adviser to the Prime Minister of Ghana, 1957–63
- First President of the Caribbean Development Bank, 1970–73
- Professor at Princeton University, 1963–83.

In 1979, he was awarded the Nobel Prize in economics and was the first person of non-European descent to receive it. He wrote four books on development economics, as well as many important essays. Lewis died in 1991 in Barbados.

In 1938, daily wages for unskilled sugar workers in the British Caribbean colonies ranged between 28 cents in St Vincent to a high of 60 cents in Jamaica. In Cuba, the minimum daily wage was 80 cents for an unskilled worker.

However, this did not mean that the Cuban sugar workers were better off than those in the British islands. Generally speaking, poorer people spend a higher proportion of their income on food than richer people. In Barbados, a labourer was paid about 30 cents a day and had to spend 7 cents on food, which was 23% of his wages. In Cuba, food cost about 47 cents a day, and the Cuban worker had to spend nearly 59% of his wages on food. The Cuban, by this measure, was actually poorer than the Barbadian labourer.

The Great Depression (1929 to about 1939)

6.2 Homeless family: a destitute farmer with his family seated beside railroad tracks after travelling by freight train to the Yakima Valley, Toppenish, Washington State. Photograph by Dorothea Lange, August 1939

In 1929, the US economy started having serious problems. Production fell by 30%, unemployment rose to 17% and about half of the country's 25,000 banks had to close down.

As the US economy was so large, with trading links to other nations, countries around the world also began to experience economic problems, with businesses and banks collapsing and many people losing their jobs. This situation lasted until 1939, when the Second World War started. It was the longest economic downturn ever experienced in the industrialized countries of the Western World.

The Great Depression was mainly characterized by:

- the stock market crash
- closure of banks and other businesses
- high unemployment
- a rise in poverty
- uneven distribution of wealth which led to a small group of very wealthy people and a large percentage of very poor people
- a rise in the number of hunger marches
- an increase in the numbers of suicide.

The amount of land planting sugar also declined as the crop became less profitable, which meant that fewer people were employed as sugar workers.

Table 6.5 Percentage of land under sugar cultivation, 1958

Country	Acreage (%)
Barbados	69
Guyana	28
Jamaica	23
St Lucia	8
Trinidad	28

Sugar production stopped in Antigua, St Lucia, St Vincent and Grenada in the early 1970s. Between 1950 and 1980, production dropped by 33% in Barbados, 45% in Trinidad and Tobago, and 33% in Jamaica. In Guyana (formerly British Guiana), production went up by 25% compared with that of 1950, but the sugar industry there had dropped by half during the 1960s.

Sugar and its by-products (rum and molasses) earned less in export dollars between the 1950s and 1980s. As you will see in the sections in this chapter on industrialization and alternative agriculture, this percentage drop was partly because the territories were earning money from other products.

Table 6.6 Sugar by-products as a percentage of exports

Country	1957 (%)	1984 (%)
Barbados	92	12
Guyana	56	36
Jamaica	51*	27*
St Lucia	32	0
Trinidad and Tobago	8	1.5

*This does not include alumina and bauxite products

Solving the problems

If you are making bracelets for $5 and selling them for $3, you will soon have no money to make bracelets. In economic terms, if your costs of production are more than the profits from your sales, you go out of business. The solution, obviously, is to sell your bracelets for more than $5, but this might not be possible if someone else is selling bracelets for less. This was the basic problem facing British Caribbean sugar producers, so the first thing they did was try to reduce the cost of making sugar.

Several factors made this possible in the larger colonies, such as British Guiana, Trinidad and Jamaica, but not always in the smaller islands. These factors included:

- improved cane species which resulted in higher yields per acre
- lower wages for workers
- better tools
- use of fertilizers
- better irrigation systems
- a differently organized plantation
- investment in new mills and machinery.

This last factor was particularly important. Old machines which were entirely operated by manual labour were replaced by new advanced machines which required skilled operators and efficient technical supervision. The new mills ran on steam power, rather than on human or animal power, and had a larger capacity. In 1860, the old-style sugar mills ground cane from about 400 to 500 hectares of land. By 1890, the new mills could grind canes from 1,200 to 1,500 hectares, and they also extracted twice the amount of sugar. Also important was the use of the vacuum pan, referred to in Chapter 5. In 1891 in Trinidad, 43% of sugar exported was made by vacuum pan, and by 1896 this was up to 53%.

All these factors meant that small plantations could no longer be profitable. For one thing, they could not afford the new equipment and, even if they had installed new mills, they could not produce enough sugar cane to make the mills cost-effective. As a result, small plantations were sometimes combined into one large plantation, mostly in the large colonies such as British Guiana and Trinidad. Also, rather than each plantation having its own factory, some colonies set up one central factory which purchased sugar cane from the various plantations. Between 1884 and 1894, the central factory built by the Colonial Company in Trinidad reduced production costs by half. By 1897, British Guiana planters had reduced their production costs to

9 shillings per cwt, as had planters in Barbados, while in Trinidad and Jamaica the production cost was 7 shillings per cwt.

> **FAST FACTS**
>
> The Lomé Convention was a trade agreement between the European Union (EU) and the Caribbean nations (as well as African and Pacific countries) signed in Lomé, Togo, in 1975. It was established to promote the economic and socio-cultural development of these areas. The Convention gave duty-free access to most Caribbean products, without requiring the Caribbean countries to give the same access to goods from EU countries.

Many of these upgrades were financed on credit from British-based merchant houses, which meant that the British Caribbean sugar industry became mostly owned by firms and individuals in the 'Mother Country'. Barbados was one of the few exceptions. Here the colonial government put money into the sugar industry, passing the Agricultural Aids Act 1887 which was based on loans from private individuals guaranteed by the government. However, most of the merchant houses preferred to invest in the larger colonies, such as Trinidad and Guiana, which had more fertile soil and which allowed several small plantations to be combined into a large one. Between 1870 and 1900, the sugar industry was controlled by a small group of refiners and bankers who created a cartel that fixed prices.

In the last years of the 19th century, these investors started using modern techniques such as sampling to predict world sugar production, instituted new management practices, created better statistics and took advantage of better communications through the telegraph and the telephone. For example, they learned London's closing prices before the New York Stock Exchange opened, due to the five-hour time difference, and so they knew when to buy and sell sugar stocks so as to make a profit, depending on whether share prices were going up or down.

The Caribbean sugar industry in the 20th century survived. The availability of labour was possible because international policies such as the Lomé Agreement let Caribbean sugar be sold at preferred rates in European countries, and provided funding to sustain the sugar industry. In Trinidad, the government also subsidized the sugar industry after 1975, when the British owners of the largest sugar and agricultural products firm, Caroni Ltd, decided to close the company and it became a state-owned company.

Activity 6.2

- On a map of the world, locate Lome.
- Make a list of all the members from the European Union.
- Make a list of all the members from the African, Caribbean and Pacific countries.

Only in one Caribbean island did sugar production thrive for several decades. This country was Cuba. The main reasons for its successful sugar production are given in the next section.

The growth of the Cuban sugar industry

Even as the British Caribbean colonies struggled to revive a declining industry, the sugar planters in Cuba were adapting to the challenges so effectively that Cuban sugar production itself became a challenge to the British islands. From 1829, Cuba became the world's largest producer of sugar.

The Cubans were successful for four main reasons.

- They had already begun to modernize their factories.
- They had more land for their plantations.
- They were able to obtain financing.
- They did not abolish slavery.

Whereas the British sugar colonies often tried to diversify their agricultural production to meet the sugar crisis, the Cubans went the other way and made their economy even more dependent on sugar cane. By 1855, sugar and its by-products accounted for 84% of Cuba's exports. Land that had been used for growing coffee, tobacco and cotton was planted with sugar cane instead. In 1846, there were 1,670 coffee farms in Cuba. By 1862, there were just 782 and by the late 1870s fewer than 200 farms were still running.

In 1860, Cuba had 1,318 mills producing some 515,000 metric tons of sugar a year. By 1895, the island had just 250 mills, but these were so much more efficient that they produced 1.5 million tonnes annually. Also, quantity was not the only advantage. The sugar produced in the modern factories was also of higher quality. Before modernization, the quality of the sugar depended on the ripeness of the cane, the purity of the juice, the intensity of the fire that heated the boilers and the skill of the overseer in coordinating the various stages of production. The new process, by contrast, was scientifically standardized and run by technically trained professionals.

In addition, rather than two or three different kinds of sugar, between 14 and 21 types were now made, differentiated by colour and texture. So by one main measuring system, the lowest quality, grade 1, was the brown mass called muscovado, while the highest, grade 21, was powdered white sugar. There was also a purity measure, called pol, and most of the exports from Cuba to its main market, the USA, were categorized as pol 95%. This meant the sugar would not spoil and, since the sellers could store it for longer, they did not have to worry about less profit due to spoilage. The sugar importers thus made the producers lower their prices, since the importers were buying larger quantities of sugar in any single purchase.

Even packing became more advanced. Previously, sugar had been transported in wooden boxes or hogsheads. After modernization, nearly all sugar was packed in bags. This reduced transport and storage costs, because boxes and barrels were heavier and took up more space than bags. Also, in 1871, the tonnage carried by steam ships finally surpassed that of sailing ships. This meant a more reliable supply for merchants and consumers,

6.3 Sugar mill and refinery in Miranda, Cuba

since steam ships did not depend on good winds and a steamer could carry five times the cargo of a sailing ship. Freight rates between Europe and the USA fell 25% between 1860 and 1880, and 63% between Europe and the Asian colonies (India, Java, Mauritius and the Philippines). Before this, the Caribbean colonies had lower freight rates, since they were closer to the main markets. Now, with the drop in costs, they lost that advantage.

> **Roleplay**
>
> Imagine that you are manager of sales in an advertising agency. Your agency has been hired by a Cuban planter who is interested in increasing sales of his product. In a speech to the planter, describe three ways in which you will promote his sugar.

All this helped Cuba. It must be emphasized, though, that the modernization process applied only to the sugar cane factories, not to the cane fields. The methods of cultivation and harvesting did not change, so productivity per agricultural worker stayed the same. However, the productivity of factory workers rose, since the new machines let them do their work more quickly and efficiently. This, in turn, meant that the supply of canes from the fields had to be increased, so more workers had to be used. Chinese indentured workers, as you read in Chapter 5, were imported in the 1850s, and the Cuban planters also tried to get slaves from Africa, Puerto Rico and Brazil. The slave trade had been declared illegal in the 1817 treaty between England and Spain, but it was not until the 1860s that the British, with the assistance of a new US policy, actually stopped the supply of enslaved Africans to Cuba. Enslaved Africans, either owned or rented by the planters, indentured Chinese, convicts, and wage workers of all races worked side by side on the Cuban estates.

> **Abolition of slavery in Cuba**
>
> 1868 – During the Ten Years' War (1868–78), which was started by small-scale Cuban planters who wanted independence from Spain, enslaved Africans were declared free. The planters did this to get the slaves to fight for them.
>
> 1870 – In response, the Spanish government adopted the Moret Law, which stated that all children born after 1868, and all slaves over 60 years of age, were free.
>
> 1878 – The peace treaty ending the Ten Years' War freed all slaves who had fought with the planters or with the Spanish soldiers.
>
> 1879 – Slaves in Cuba's eastern province refused to work unless also given their freedom. The planters promised freedom in four years' time and wages until then.
>
> 1880 – The Spanish government declared an end to slavery and implemented an apprenticeship system to last until 1888.
>
> 1886 – Due to protests from abolitionists and refusal of both slaves and planters to follow the regulations, apprenticeship ended two years prematurely.

These new Cuban plantations were very different from the traditional ones. Due to the huge investments, the owners needed new sources of income. They had built railways to transport the canes to the central factories and these trains also carried other cargo, as well as passengers.

> **FAST FACTS**
>
> The first railway in Latin America was built in Cuba in 1837 and was used for carrying sugar and molasses from the mills to the ports.

The foundry did not only make tools for the labourers, but also park benches and man-hole covers to sell to the government. Some plantations even had their own general stores, hotels, barber shop and butcher's shop, which were patronized mainly by the plantation workers.

> **FAST FACTS**
>
> The Santa Lucia mill in Gabara had five general stores, seven groceries, a shoe shop, a distillery, three barber shops, one school, one confectionary shop, two eating places, three blacksmiths, three clothing stores, two tailor shops and one leather goods store.

The owners benefited from this financially. They often ended up having to pay workers only 10% of the wages, since the rest had been docked in advance for goods bought by their employees. Also, those purchases were made using sugar tokens issued by the owners, who refused to take the official paper currency issued by the Bank of Spain, and the tokens were more than 10% off the face value of that currency — that is, a sugar token dollar would buy 90 cents' worth of goods instead of a dollar's worth.

These new owners were not the Cubans who had once controlled the industry. As large investments were needed for modernization, the old class of Cuban planters was replaced by financial entrepreneurs from the USA and Spain, and by 1865 only 17% of owners were from the old plantation families. However, unlike the situation in the British colonies, there were few absentee owners. Cuban and Spanish capital financed 93% of the sugar mills.

Cuba depended on the US market to sustain its sugar production. In the 1860s, Cuba supplied 60% of the USA's sugar imports, with the rest supplied mainly by Puerto Rico and Brazil. The Cuban sugar industry thrived, even after slavery was finally abolished in 1886. Sugar production was interrupted only by two Cuban wars against Spain: the Ten Years' Wars (1868–78) and the War of Independence (1895–98).

The first war actually helped the sugar industry, since many of the old mills were destroyed while the new ones were not. The war also provided opportunities for Spanish and some Cuban merchants to make huge profits from transporting military supplies and this, along with sugar prices that were increased by the war, provided more financing for modernization.

In the War of Independence, the Spanish government sent 400,000 soldiers to stop the rebels, or one soldier to every three Cubans. This response was mainly because Spanish business interests had invested heavily in Cuba, and it was their money which controlled the sugar industry in the island.

As the industry grew in the 20th century, more labour was required. Tens of thousands of contract

...ed onto a cart on a Cuban sugar plantation. c. 1904

labourers, mostly from Haiti and Jamaica, arrived. Plantation (known as hacienda) owners built villages for their labourers in order to keep them close to the fields, and out of the big towns and cities. Nevertheless, many workers migrated to the cities looking for work. With the industrialization of the late 19th century bringing railways, the processing and transportation of sugar in Cuba was done in ever-larger numbers.

As we have seen, one-crop economies are sensitive to world market prices, the price of sugar rose during the First World War and US companies secured control of over half the sugar industry in Cuba. Wealth became concentrated among these US shareholders and the Cuban elite.

New agricultural enterprises

The 1897 West India Royal Commission, which was appointed to analyse the sugar crisis in the British Caribbean, recommended agricultural diversification as the key to saving the economy. The commissioners wrote:

> 'No reform affords so good a prospect for the permanent welfare in the future of the West Indies as the settlement of the labouring population on the land as small peasant proprietors… so long as they remain dependent on sugar, their position can never be sound or secure… Where sugar can be completely, or very largely, replaced by other industries, the Colonies in question will be in a much sounder position, both politically and economically, when they have ceased to depend wholly, or to a very great extent, upon the continued prosperity of a single industry.'

In Jamaica and in Trinidad (the latter united with Tobago in 1889), the colonial authorities pursued agricultural diversification as their main strategy for saving the economies of the islands. New crops such as bananas, cocoa, coffee and pimento were cultivated in various colonies. Pest-control measures were expanded, and low-interest loans were given to farmers so they could improve the infrastructure on their land, through irrigation, roads and better equipment. These measures were somewhat successful in Jamaica. The larger sugar estates were still making profits, but the number of plantation workers dropped from 30,000 in 1860 to 20,000 in 1910. Instead, the number of peasant farmers increased, especially the number growing bananas for export. After 1884, Jamaica had ceased to be a major exporter of sugar, turning instead to rum, bananas and citrus fruit. By 1896, sugar was no longer a mainstay of the Jamaican economy, contributing just 18% of the value of the island's exports.

> **Activity 6.3**
> Discuss as a class why you think it took so long for the British West Indies to diversify economically.

By 1910 though, there was still very little diversification in the British Caribbean. Arrowroot became a staple in St Vincent, and bananas were grown in Jamaica and Belize. However, these were all islands which had downgraded or abandoned sugar cane. In islands where sugar cane was still a major crop, the owners of the plantations opposed agricultural diversification. This was because if the workers became 'sound and secure' or 'small proprietors who owned their own land', this would reduce the planters' supply of cheap labour and land for planting sugar.

The situation had not changed 20 years later, when a similar body, the Olivier Sugar Commission of 1930, also noted:

> 'It is impossible to expect any sound permanent development of such cultivation unless steps are taken to enable the small cultivators to obtain and posses their land in freehold.'

For the smaller islands, bananas replaced sugar as the main cash crop. In Dominica, St Lucia, St Vincent and Grenada banana production increased from 21 tons per annum in 1958 to between 100 and 150 tons in the 1960s and continued to hold steady in the 1980s. In the 1990s, bananas contributed 5%

St Vincent's GDP and 18% of Dominica's, while employing one in every three members of the islands' labour force. Nearly all of the Windward Islands bananas are sold to the United Kingdom.

In the larger islands, such as Jamaica, coffee cultivation and livestock rearing became important industries. Although production dropped after emancipation, it started to pick back up in the 20th century, largely because small farmers started planting coffee. Blue Mountain coffee is now a brand recognized by coffee drinkers around the world. Jamaica also entered the banana industry in a significant way, with many former sugar estates becoming banana plantations. By 1914, bananas made up just over half of Jamaica's export earnings. The industry was controlled by a US company, the United Fruit Company, up to 1930. The island's sugar industry also began to recover to become a significant exporter once again in the early 20th century.

As for livestock, the rearing of cattle had always taken place, but the industry grew in the late 19th century, with Jamaica even starting to export cattle to Cuba. New breeds, such as the Jamaica Hope and Jamaica Red, were established by cross-breeding with Indian cattle.

Another important crop was rice, which was cultivated mainly in Guyana and Trinidad. After indentureship ended on 1 January 1920, the Indian labourers dominated the field – or, more precisely, the lagoons where rice was grown. Most of the rice grown in Trinidad was for local consumption, but by 1922 Guyana was exporting rice to other Caribbean countries, as well as Britain and Canada.

Cocoa was another crop that once earned significant profits, especially in Trinidad, where the genetic variety made the island's cocoa popular with chocolate manufacturers around the world. By 1900, cocoa was Trinidad's most valuable export

6.5 Banana carriers, Jamaica, c. 1905

6.6 Gathering bananas, Jamaica, c.1900

crop, and by 1920 it accounted for 43% of Trinidad's non-petroleum exports, earning over £1.5 million. Cocoa prices were especially high during the two world wars. In 1928 though, the cocoa trees were hit by witchbroom disease. The government provided farmers with financial assistance and new seedlings, although it was mainly the larger cocoa farmers who benefited from this. The industry never totally recovered.

A major non-sugar and processed product was bitters, created by the Siegert family who had started their business in 1824 in Angostura in Venezuela but who came to Trinidad in 1875. Their brand, Angostura Bitters, is famous worldwide as an ingredient in mixed drinks and cocktails.

The Caribbean countries were also often at a disadvantage when it came to selling crops in the international market. For example, Britain had been the major buyer of limes, but artificial citric acid was developed and the British importers also started buying from producers in the Mediterranean to reduce transport costs.

Similarly, Caribbean fruit had to compete in Europe with larger suppliers from South America, South Africa and the Middle East. Grenada, known as 'The Spice Isle', had to compete with products from India and Zanzibar, while cotton producers found sales dropping as artificial materials such as polyester became more widely used to make clothes.

In the 1980s, nearly all the CARICOM governments tried to introduce agricultural diversification programmes. The goal was to increase the number of different crops beyond the standard bananas, coffee, sugar, rice and citrus fruit. Growing more tropical fruit for export was a key focus. Mangoes, avocados (zaboca), pineapple, paw-paw (papaya), sour-sop and passion fruit were considered the most potentially profitable. Some of the Windward Islands did increase production of tubers and fruit. Dominica is the leading exporter of plantain in the region, earning an average of US$1 million every year from the crop. St Vincent and the Grenadines is the main exporter of root crops. However, most of these programmes failed to achieve significant changes.

> **Roleplay**
>
> It is 1900. Imagine that you are the President of St James Planters' Association. At your regular monthly meeting, present five arguments to your fellow planters on why they should introduce new crops on plantations.

Tourism

Tourism in the Caribbean began at the end of the 19th century, and most visitors came for health reasons. Given what you have read in earlier chapters of this book about the diseases and the hardships of the tropical climate, this is ironic. But one hundred years ago, as now, tourists from Europe and North America came to the Caribbean to escape their cold winters. A 1905 tourist brochure from a British tour company promoted Jamaica for its "warm, healthy climate... recommended by the medical faculty." Shipping lines advertised trips under such slogans as "Winter in the West Indies".

The colonial history of the region largely determined where the visitors from various metropolitan countries came to within the Caribbean. Thus, British tourists went mostly to Barbados and Jamaica; French tourists went to Martinique; and Dutch ones to Curaçao. At that time, North Americans went mainly to the Bahamas and Cuba, because these islands were nearest to the Florida coast. Nearly all these tourists were wealthy, since commercial air travel would only become affordable to ordinary people in the 1960s. Even so, the early tourist industry was profitable enough for hotels to be built even in the 19th century. The Royal Victorian Hotel in the Bahamas was opened in 1861; the Crane Beach hotel in Barbados started operations in 1887; and in Jamaica the Mandeville, the Titchfield and the Myrtle Bank hotels were built in the 1880s. Between 1890 and 1969, 106 hotels were opened in Jamaica. Cuba was a favoured destination for American tourists, so that by 1915 there were 72 hotels on the island, with more than one-third of them located in the capital city, Havana. By the 1950s, tourism was Cuba's second largest earner of foreign exchange, after sugar, with over 300 000 visitors coming to the island every year. In Jamaica and the Bahamas in the 1940s, after the Second World War, foreign investors were wooed to develop the tourist industry in the islands. Between 1949 and 1961 in the Bahamas, hotels and casinos were built and tourist arrivals increased from 30 000 to 365 000 a year. In 1958 in Jamaica, over £2 million was spent to build new hotels, but even in the decade before that the number of rooms in the island had increased five-fold.

Tourism started overtaking sugar as a major source of income in the 1960s, when the long-haul jet aeroplane made air travel between the metropolitan cities and the region quick, easy, and affordable. This allowed the development of a new tourist market catering to less wealthy visitors, even as the luxury market also continued for the multi-millionaires. Because of this new mass market, metropolitan-based hotel chains and tour operators began looking at the region as a potential source of new profits. Some the world's richest people even purchased some small islands – the Rockefellers bought part of St John's in the US Virgin Islands. In 1967, the Organisation for Economic Cooperation and Development (OECD) reported that tourism in the Caribbean was "a promising new resource for economic development". Tourists have now become more valuable than sugar-cane in the old sugar-based economies such as Barbados, the Dominican Republic, Jamaica, and Trinidad and Tobago. Islands such as the Dominican Republic, Antigua, Barbados, Grenada, St Kitts-Nevis and the Bahamas now earn more from tourism than from all other sectors.

Many of the Caribbean countries, especially the smaller islands, depend on tourism to generate revenue, earn foreign exchange and provide employment for their citizens. Tourism does not only involve visitors from other countries coming to stay in hotels or guest houses. It includes cruise ship visits, yachting, cultural activities (such as music concerts and dance performances), nature sites (such as wildlife sanctuaries, hiking trails and coral reef tours), and sports (for example international cricket competitions and golf tournaments). Visitors to the Caribbean are mainly the stay-over visitors or tourists who spend a day or more in a particular destination, as well as cruise-ship passengers who usually stay for less than a day since their tour includes several destinations.

The other main category of tourists are people on yachts, who may stay in one place for weeks. The business of chartering yachts for pleasure started in the 1960s and was operated mainly by private individuals who owned just one boat. In the 1980s, the industry became a multi-million dollar business as companies began operating charter and fishing services for tourists. Despite this, most Caribbean governments did not create the infrastructure needed to facilitate the industry. Charter companies are still mostly foreign-owned. The Caribbean's warm weather and its proximity to the USA have made it the leading destination in the world for cruise ships and yachts. Nearly 10 million tourists, or almost half the total who visit the Caribbean per year, come to the region by this route. Additional draws for this segment of the tourist market are the Antigua Sail Week at the end of April and the St Maarten Heineken Regatta in the first week of March.

As the 'sun, sea and sand' approach has become less effective in attracting visitors, Caribbean governments and tour companies have begun to promote 'niche tourism' – that is, advertising to tourists who have special travel interests. Such niche markets are catered to by community tourism (tours of villages, showing how ordinary Caribbean people live), heritage (tours of historical sites and buildings) and eco-tourism (nature tours). Hoteliers are also trying to get a greater share of the conference and business tourism market. Another approach has been to target the high-end tourism market. Such people expect the best services and products, and pay a lot for them. The advantage of such a clientele is that, even when there is an economic downturn in their countries, as in the mid-1980s and in 2008, they continue to travel and buy luxury goods, whereas the average person from the USA or Europe may either take no vacation or, since transportation costs are a major expense of a total tourism package from Europe and the USA to the Caribbean, they may choose a cheaper destination, perhaps within their own country.

The money earned from tourism benefits several sectors. Tourist dollars go first to those people directly involved in the industry, such as hotel owners or the workers employed there. People selling craft items, or local foods at tourist sites, along with tour companies and guides, also benefit economically. Tourism also helps to bolster other economic activities, such as construction (not only hotels, but general infrastructure such as roads must be provided for visitors' convenience), communications (tourists are less likely to visit an island which does not have fast and reliable Internet service or cell-phone roaming), transportation and even manufacturing. Some countries get as much as 50% of their GDP from tourism as an industry. These islands include Anguilla, Antigua and Barbuda, Grenada and St Lucia. The amount of money spent directly by tourists (not including multiplier effects as this money travels through the economy) contributes 17% of Jamaica's GDP, 13% of the GDP of Barbados and just 2% of the GDP of Trinidad and Tobago.

For the region as a whole, the per capita expenditure per visitor is US$3,197. In other words, this is the amount of money every Caribbean person would get if the money spent by tourists were to be divided equally. Per capita value in the sector ranged from more than US$ 13,000 in the Cayman Islands to just US$7 in Haiti. The Bahamas has a per capita visitor expenditure of US$5,000, St Lucia US$1,713 and Jamaica US$433.

However, not all this money actually stays in the region, because of a lot of it goes back to travel agencies, hotel chains and other businesses which are based in the USA and Europe. Caribbean governments encourage foreign and local investors to build hotels and other facilities by giving them tax concessions and tax holidays for a number of years, including duty-free imports of some items and materials.

Tourism has become even more important in the 21st century, with the number of visitors to the region increasing from 16 million per year in the 1990s to nearly 22 million now. Two out of every hundred tourists worldwide come to the Caribbean. This is a very good share of the tourist market, considering how small the region is. With such a large increase in visitors over the past decade, accommodation for tourists has also increased. In 1995, the region had just 122,000 establishments for tourists to stay in. By 2000, there were 900,000 such places, ranging from hotels to guest houses, to apartments, to homes offering bed and breakfast.

In 1985, tourists spent about US$6 billion every year in the region; in 1995, the total spent went up to US$14 billion; and by 2000, tourists were spending almost US$20 billion. Most of these visitors are from the USA and Europe, although in recent times tourists from Japan and China have begun to increase. The USA is the main source of visitors for the region, accounting for over half of the total number of tourist arrivals. This is followed by Europe, with one in every four tourists coming from that continent. Intra-Caribbean tourism, which means residents from one island visiting another, represents 6% of the total. For a map of the CARICOM countries (see Chapter 8 page 201), the US market represents 38% of all visitors, followed by internal Caribbean travel at 28%, then Europe at 23%.

The total quality of the tourism product determines what destination travellers choose. Tourists want high-quality services delivered in an efficient and timely manner. They also want a wider variety of attractions and services, and this is why the 'sun, sea and sand' strategy in the Caribbean has been working less effectively. Instead, entertainment events such as Carnival in Trinidad and Tobago, Reggae Sunsplash in Jamaica and the St Lucia Jazz Festival have become important draws for visitors to the region. However, the tourist market has not expanded significantly in the region as a whole.

Industrialization

By the early 20th century, agriculture was not providing enough money or jobs for the growing population in the Caribbean. Since land is limited, it can only produce so many crops, which can only be sold for so much money. While technology had increased the amount of yields per acre, land use had peaked in Barbados and the Leeward Islands by the late 19th century and in Jamaica and Trinidad by 1917. This was mainly because the former islands had been settled earlier than the latter.

As a result, people started to think about developing the manufacturing, mining and oil industries in the region. It was considered more productive to use the land to build factories, as well as hotels, than to plant crops. By 1879, Trinidad had begun to produce soap, coconut oil and asphalt. In the 1950s, most of the British Caribbean colonies were implementing policies to develop the manufacturing sector.

However, there were several barriers to industrialization, including:

- scarce capital resources
- lack of fuel
- limited knowledge of industry
- few workers with technical skills
- few entrepreneurs.

This meant that the countries in the region had to depend on foreign investors who would provide the money to start various industries, bring in personnel to do more specialized tasks and also train Caribbean workers in these jobs. However, the governments in the region had to give these investors incentives to set up factories in the islands. Some of these incentives were:

- tax breaks
- protection from foreign competition
- tax exemption on raw materials, capital and equipment.

At the time, there was a list of industries which were considered the best investments. These included garment making (making shirts, stockings, gloves and hats), leather goods (shoes and belts), jewellery and items such as umbrellas, cardboard boxes, toys and pens. Few of these industries were ever started, however, and fewer still became profitable. By contrast, some industries which had been considered unfavourable in the 1930s and 1940s were doing fairly well by the 1960s. These included production of fertilizers, milk, margarine, cement, china, beer, cattle food, soap and paint; grain milling; and petroleum refining.

Countries such as Jamaica and Trinidad and Tobago, tripled their manufacturing output between the 1950s and the early 1960s. This was partly because these countries, along with Guyana, had natural resources: oil in Trinidad and Tobago, and bauxite in Jamaica and Guyana. Jamaica, and Trinidad and Tobago, also developed what were called 'screwdriver industries': industries based on automobiles, radios, televisions, aluminium, steel, rubber and plastics. They were called screwdriver industries because, in many of these factories, the workers only put together parts to make the finished product. This was profitable for the foreign investor, because Caribbean workers were paid less than their counterparts in the metropolitan countries.

By 1967, petroleum and its by-products were a major export from Trinidad and Tobago, as were bauxite and alumina from Jamaica and Guyana. After the 1970s, industrial activities centred around consumer goods, such as food, beverages, cigarettes, garments, bricks and furniture. Table 6.4 shows the increase in the manufacturing sector in various countries over a 21-year period.

Table 6.7 Manufacturing sector as a percentage of GDP

Country	1963 (%)	1984 (%)
Barbados	9	13
Guyana	6	13
Jamaica	15	19
St Lucia	5	9
Trinidad and Tobago	13	7*

*The decline in Trinidad and Tobago was due to the drop in oil prices after the oil boom (1973–79).

The manufacturing sector faced several problems, however, which stymied its development. The products had high costs and were often poor in quality. For these reasons, most firms were only able to sell them within their countries or within the region. Manufacturers therefore ended up using more foreign exchange than they earned. In this way, the sector weakened rather than strengthened the region's economy.

Additionally, each government adopted an industrialization policy on an individual country basis, rather than in cooperation with the other islands, which put the entire sector at a disadvantage in negotiating with foreign investors and in ensuring that each island specialized only in the particular products it was good at producing.

Perhaps most negatively of all, none of the Caribbean governments changed their education systems to equip their citizens for an industrialized economy. The focus in the 1960s and 1970s remained on increasing the number of schools and school places rather than changing the curricula. Trinidad and Tobago did introduce technical subjects, such as auto mechanics, electrical skills and plumbing, in the 1970s in the state-run schools, but these programmes were intended to cater to the less academically able and did not create a cadre of technically competent people at the level required for an advanced manufacturing economy. Generally, the Caribbean's education system did not help produce scientifically or entrepreneurially minded individuals. Some of the traits needed – analytical thinking, risk taking and questioning of accepted practices – were indeed usually discouraged in the region's schools. This is to some extent a hold-over from history, when the colonial and church-run education system was intended to produce only people who had practical skills useful for the metropolitan economy, but not to the extent where they might achieve economic self-reliance or gain the knowledge to question authority.

> **Groupwork**
>
> Get into groups of three or four people. Each group should choose one of the following topics and conduct research on it:
> 1. bauxite in Jamaica
> 2. petroleum in Trinidad
> 3. nutmeg in Grenada
> 4. rice in Guyana
> 5. fishing in Barbados.
>
> Make a presentation to the class outlining your research, or present the research in the form of a poster or project.

Effects of industrialization

In 1928, sugar planters told the Olivier Sugar Commission that the field workers refused to work, and never showed up on Mondays because they drank too much bad rum over the weekend — a problem, said the planters, which could be solved by good rum. The sugar planters, who were trying to get financial support from the British government, said:

> 'It is necessary to maintain a constant supply of cheap labour… therefore, no labourer must be too highly paid or given too much employment.'

The commissioners were not fooled, however, noting in their report that there was no problem getting workers in the sugar factories, oilfields or bauxite mines. They said:

> 'The field work is conducted upon a fallacious industrial theory that it is better dealt with laxly and without pressure on the lowest subsistence wages, whereas in the factory the economy of full and continuous work is obvious and dominates practice.'

This implies that industrialization may have had a good social effect, since workers were more likely to be fairly treated and prosper than under a sugar-based economy. An industrial economy is one which is based on the production of minerals, manufacturing and processing. The simplest industrial activity is mining. This involves the extraction of mineral resources, such as bauxite or gold, as well as drilling for crude oil and natural gas. Processing is the next stage, where raw materials are refined in some way. You have read about this process in respect to sugar cane, where refining involved making brown sugar into white, or molasses into rum. Processing in respect to minerals would involve making bauxite into alumina, or oil into petroleum. Manufacturing is the highest stage of industrialization. As you have read, England became the world's most powerful nation mainly by processing cotton into cloth and cloth into clothes. More importantly, the English developed machines which did these things, and that technological knowledge let them invent other machines. Manufacturing can therefore involve minerals, food products or machinery.

Why did the Caribbean need to industrialize after being an agricultural economy for so long? In 1950, W. Arthur Lewis identified overpopulation as the main reason. An economy based on agriculture simply could not support the needs of the Caribbean population. These needs included not just food, but jobs, transport, health, education and other requirements of the modern world. Lewis argued that in Europe one square mile of cultivable land was needed to support just over 50 average families at a subsistence level of living (that is, to provide the basics of food, clothing and shelter, with no extra resources left to sell or buy).

Lewis pointed out that in the Caribbean islands, less than half the land was usually suitable for cultivation. Jamaica, for example, could only support a population density of 60 people per square mile at subsistence level, whereas the actual population density in 1950, when Lewis was writing, was 294 people per square mile. Even in the smaller islands, the population density per square mile was similarly high: 257 in the Leeward Islands, 282 in Trinidad and Tobago, 306 in the Windward Islands and a whopping 1,159 in Barbados. Even though mechanization, advancements in cultivation techniques and, most recently, genetic engineering increased the yields per acre, these factors also meant that fewer workers were needed in agriculture. Therefore, other sources of production and revenue generation had to be found, and industrialization was a key sector.

However, the fact that these ideas began to be discussed in the 1950s was not coincidental, since it was shortages caused by the Second World War which made a light manufacturing sector in the Caribbean viable. Europe's economy had been devastated by the war, and in the interim there was an economic vacuum that other countries, which had not seen their infrastructure destroyed and their population decimated, could step in to fill.

In all industrial economies, three factors are crucial: markets, resources (commodities or human resources) and economic policy. In respect to markets, size was a crucial problem in the Caribbean – there were not enough people to provide a viable internal market. In 1950, Lewis estimated that there was a need for 413,000 extra jobs in the British Caribbean territories. This region would also be the market to buy the goods produced by these workers. However, because of the poverty in the Caribbean, many of these people would not buy manufactured goods, since most of their money would be spent on food and accommodation. If, therefore, the Caribbean was to create and support a viable manufacturing sector, two conditions were necessary: a better standard of living for the population (consumers); and export of manufactured goods outside the region, since the domestic market was too small to provide the level of consumption needed to make manufacturing profitable.

Which industries were chosen depended on these three main factors.

- Relatively small capital per worker was needed.
- There should be low energy consumption.
- Industry should not be concentrated in one place.

Let's explain these three factors. The first means that an industry which needed a lot of investment in, say, machinery, would not be suitable. The second factor means that, because fuel is expensive, industries which did not use much energy would be more likely to succeed; and the final factor means that an industry which had many manufacturing locations (like biscuit making) would have more flexibility in setting up.

> **Industrialization by invitation** formulated by Nobel Laureate W. Arthur Lewis (1915–1991). This is where foreign investors are invited to set up companies in countries through various incentives such as tax breaks.

Lewis recommended that Caribbean governments woo foreign capital and capitalists to set up businesses in the region, a strategy which became known as 'industrialization by invitation'. However, partly for historical reasons, most Caribbean politicians and many ordinary Caribbean people distrusted such investors. Instead, most Caribbean governments decided to pursue nationalization, where the state took over private businesses. The main objective in the 1950s was to create jobs, and several Caribbean countries adopted a half-way approach to industrialization, whereby the emphasis was on the assembly of goods which had in the past been imported whole and the final foreign-made products were subject to high duties which made them affordable only to a wealthy minority.

For example, in Trinidad and Tobago in the 1970s, car assembly plants were created where workers put together imported parts, usually from Japan, to create a product that was sold on the local market. Cars manufactured by this method were usually of lower quality than those made in Japan and they cost more. The rationale was that Trinidad and Tobago would eventually achieve its own car-making capabilities. This never happened and, although some employment was provided through these plants, the capital intensive nature of such firms meant that few jobs were created relative to the size of the investment made. Lewis had warned against this, writing:

> 'At their present low standard of living, the number of persons for whom West Indians can provide employment in manufactures by their own purchases is extremely small. This applies not only to the extra incomes generated by extra employment, but also to the employment already generated by the incomes of those

already employed. This is usually overlooked by people who believe that a great deal of employment could be provided by substituting home manufacture for imports.'

The approach taken by Caribbean governments meant that such industries were often supported by the state through tax dollars, and benefited mostly those who were already well-off. Another effect of this 'import substitution' policy was that financial and human resources went into activities that had protectionist barriers and were therefore safe, rather than businesses which were economically viable and truly entrepreneurial. There was also little coordination between the territories, leading to duplication and waste of regional resources. The high costs of production and the often low quality of manufactured goods meant that sales of them had been largely confined to the regional market. The sector between the 1950s and 1980s generally used more foreign exchange (to buy the materials and sometimes services needed for manufacturing) than it earned.

In addition, this preoccupation with industrialization resulted in the sidelining of agriculture for nearly three decades, despite sporadic attempts at diversification of crops. Lewis had also sounded a warning about this, writing:

'The creation of new industries is an essential part of a programme for agricultural improvement. This is not generally realised. There are still people who discuss industrialisation as if it were an alternative to agricultural improvement… Exactly the opposite is true.'

Table 6.8 Percentage contribution of manufacturing to GDP 1963–1984

Country	Manufacturing
Barbados	8.9–13.3
Guyana	5.8–13
Jamaica	15.4–18.9
St Lucia	5.3–9.6
St Vincent	4.1–9.5
Trinidad and Tobago	13.1–7.5

Source: Ramsaran, 1989

Table 6.8 shows the growth in manufacturing in selected Caribbean countries. There was an increase in all countries except Trinidad and Tobago, where the manufacturing sector went into a slump due to the energy bust in the 1980s. Manufacturing in the region has concentrated on consumer goods. These include simple manufactures such as food and beverages, cigarettes, bricks and furniture, as well as assembly operations on products ranging from motor vehicles to small appliances such as toasters and electrical fans.

At the time governments in the Caribbean were trying to create a manufacturing sector while discouraging foreign investors, several East Asian nations, which in the 1950s were economically on par with, or even below the Caribbean, followed the Lewis strategy. A half-century later, Singapore is among the most developed nations in the world, as are Taiwan, South Korea and Malaysia. While other factors, such as size, were important in contributing to East Asian economic success, the open-door and export-oriented policy proved more effective in creating wealth than the protectionist policy adopted by many Caribbean countries.

In 1950, with regard to barriers to industrialization, Lewis said:

'West Indian nationalist politicians… speak frequently as if manufacturing in the West Indies offered a large profitable market which greedy foreign capitalists are anxious to exploit. They discuss industrialisation in terms of the close restrictions which they would like to impose on such capitalists, and they oppose monopoly rights, tax holidays, and other incentives… The facts are exactly opposite to what they suppose. The West Indies does not offer a large market. There are very few manufacturers who wish to go there. Having regard to the highly developed industrial centres which exist in many parts of the world, offering every convenience, and to the many governments which are now trying to attract industry, it would be surprising if any

> large number of manufacturers were willing to go to the West Indies without being offered substantial concessions.'

Manufacturing was only one facet of the attempt to industrialize. Even before this, mineral processing was the main type of industrial activity in the region. As you have learned by now, the Caribbean has mainly been a producer of raw materials. The region has only two major mineral resources: oil and bauxite, the first mainly located in Trinidad, the latter in Jamaica and Guyana.

Crude oil and natural gas

Oil and natural gas are located mainly in Trinidad. The island had begun to industrialize during the late 19th century. The island's petroleum industry started developing in the early 20th century. The Merrimac Company drilled the country's first exploratory oil well to a depth of 61 metres in 1857. This well was dry, however. The first well that found oil was drilled in 1866 by an US engineer named Captain Walter Darwent. Despite this early exploratory success, the commercial exploitation of the country's crude oil reserves did not start until 1908.

The oil companies were all foreign-owned. From 1905 to 1920, the number of employees in the sector grew from just a handful to over 4,000. Trinidad Leaseholds was the largest company, employing about 1,500 people. It had oilfields in three main areas in the southern part of the island. There were eight other fairly large companies and several smaller ones.

For the next 60 years, the emphasis was on the production of crude oil. In 1963, a commission was established by the government with the following terms of reference.

1. To examine the present situation and future prospects of the oil industry of Trinidad and Tobago in the context of the economics of the world oil industry.
2. To recommend a legal framework for the oil industry of Trinidad and Tobago which would stimulate the operations of foreign investors while safeguarding the interests of the nation.
3. To make recommendations designed to ensure the greatest possible stability compatible with growth in the industry, including the level of employment.

The recommendations of this report led to major changes in the legislation that governed petroleum activities in the country and broadened the mandate of the Ministry of Petroleum and Mines which had only been established in 1963. Other significant events included the government's purchase of British Petroleum's assets in 1969, the establishment of The Trinidad and Tobago National Petroleum Marketing Company in 1972 and the formation of the National Gas Company in 1975.

In late 1973, world oil prices increased four-fold. In this decade, when many of the world's economies entered a deep recession because of this rise, Trinidad and Tobago's economy experienced annual growth of 9.6% from 1974 to 1979. However, because the government spent most of this money, inflation also rose four-fold, thus reducing any real buying power.

Emphasis was placed on crude oil production, while natural gas was ignored even though gas had been used as an energy source before crude oil. In the earlier part of the 20th century, the industrial use of natural gas was limited to the oil field or refinery operations of the petroleum sector. In the 1950s, however, this changed. This process started in 1953 when the electricity company began using natural gas for the generation of electricity at its Penal power station. In the late 1960s, significant reserves of natural gas were discovered during exploration activities off the east coast of Trinidad.

Bauxite

The mining and processing of bauxite in Jamaica started in the mid-20th century, although the mineral had been discovered several years before. During the Second World War, there was a demand for bauxite to make aluminium. Guyana was already producing bauxite and its reserves had a higher alumina content – six tons of Jamaican bauxite were needed to make one ton of aluminium, compared with four tons of Guyanese bauxite.

Initially, its lower-quality bauxite made processing economically unfeasible for Jamaica. However, as the processing methods became more technologically advanced, the advantages of Jamaica's bauxite offset the lower alumina content. These advantages were as follows.

- Jamaica had large reserves.
- The rock was near the surface so excavation was easy.
- Freight costs to the USA were low.

When the Second World War ended, Canadian and US companies set up bauxite processing plants, using the latest technology. In the 1940s, with developing industries and increased exports, the port cities became commercial centres and more Jamaicans left the countryside in search of jobs in the urban centres. In the 1960s, tourism started to play a bigger role in the economy, and both bauxite and agricultural exports grew.

The amount of bauxite mined rose from 400,000 tons in 1952 to over 12 million tons in 1972. Jamaica is now the third largest bauxite producer in the world. Mining is carried out by open-pit methods, which means that no miners work underground. The topsoil is cleared from a few acres and the underlying bauxite is removed with huge mechanical shovels. A 50-acre plot can yield over 5 million tons of bauxite. Some of the mining companies export the raw material to alumina factories in the USA. Other companies extract the alumina on sites in Jamaica.

Jamaica also has small deposits of other useful minerals, such as marble and silica, and ores of copper, lead, zinc, manganese and iron. Silica sand found near the Black River is made into glass bottles. Bat guano, found in caves in limestone areas, is used locally as fertilizer as it is rich in phosphates. Mining accounts for 9% of the GDP and employs about 6,000 people. From 1993 to 1997, manufacturing produced $2 billion in exports, mostly to the USA. The industry accounts for 13% of GDP, employs 9.4% of the workforce and has become a significant part of the Jamaican economy.

Guyana also mines bauxite, which is one of its major exports. The first published report of bauxite, by Sir John Harrison, appeared in the Official Gazette of 16 June 1910. In 1914, the Demerara Bauxite Company Limited (Demba), owned by Aluminum Company of America (Alcoa), secured leases around the Mackenzie area where bauxite deposits had been found. Mining started in 1917. The industry was controlled by foreign companies until the early part of the 1970s, when the government nationalized them.

Guyana achieved political independence in 1966, but the economy was still controlled by foreign-owned companies. Two particularly important firms were the British companies Booker McConnell and Jessel Securities, which owned the country's largest sugar estates. In the early 1970s, Booker McConnell accounted for almost one third of Guyana's GDP, producing 85% of Guyana's sugar, employing 13% of the workforce and earning more than 30% of the country's foreign exchange.

Two other foreign companies controlled the mining sector: the Demerara Bauxite Company (Demba), a subsidiary of the Aluminum Company of Canada (Alcan), which bought the company from its American owners in 1929; and the Reynolds Bauxite Company, a subsidiary of the Reynolds Metals Company in the USA. These companies, in their turn, accounted for almost half of the nation's foreign exchange earnings.

Nationalization the transfer of industries or commerce from private to state ownership or control.

The Forbes Burnham government, which took office in 1964, saw continued foreign domination of the economy as an obstacle to progress. In 1970 Burnham proclaimed Guyana as the world's first 'cooperative republic'. During the 1970s, Guyana nationalized the major companies operating in the country. Demba became a state-owned corporation in 1971, as did the Reynolds Bauxite Company in

1974. Jessel Securities was also nationalized in 1975. In 1976 the government nationalized the huge Booker McConnell company. By the late 1970s, the government controlled over 80% of the country's firms, including companies involved in retail and distribution. This nationalization was to have a negative impact on the Guyanese economy.

Bauxite production, which had dropped from 3 million tons per year in the 1960s to 2 million tons in 1971, fell to 1.3 million tons by 1988. Similarly, sugar production declined from 330,000 tons in 1976 to about 245,000 tons in the mid-1980s, and had declined to 168,000 tons by 1988. Rice production never again reached its 1977 peak of 210,000 tons. By 1988, national output of rice was almost 40% lower than in 1977.

Despite this emphasis on natural resources, the Caribbean region has been able to industrialize at the secondary level (processing) and even at the tertiary level (manufacturing) to some extent. In the Caribbean between 1960 and 1980, exports of goods and services per capita rose from US$350 to US$3,259. However, this is the mean average for the Anglophone Caribbean, and the increase is mostly due to a small number of successful countries.

Industrialization has also had good effects on employment for women. When the agricultural sector began declining in the early 20th century, many women had to stay at home because most of the available jobs went to men. Between 1911 and 1943 in Jamaica, for example, the number of employed women dropped from 78% of the female population to just 50%. Between 1891 and 1946 in the Leeward Islands, the ratio dropped from 73% to 48%. This was not because women did not want to work. In Jamaica in the 1940s, 98% of females aged between 15 and 24 wanted a job but had been unable to find one. In the same period when the number of employed women declined from three quarters to just half the total number of women, 137,000 new jobs were created outside the agricultural sector. These were mainly in domestic services (32,000), trade (25,000), construction (21,000) and manufacturing (12,000). Women mainly went into the first two areas.

However, manufacturing firms, especially those involved in the garment industry, provided jobs for women. Industrialization in general has also broadened the number of occupations pursued by Caribbean people, since manufacturing and processing activities require more machine operators, laboratory technicians, mechanics and so on.

> **Effects of industrialization on women**
> - There was an increase in the employment of women. Many factories preferred to employ women because they could be paid less.
> - Women migrated from rural to urban areas.
> - In cases where both parents were employed, children were left unsupervised. Previously, women were the caretakers of the homes.
> - Women's social organizations were established. Many of these were charitable institutions which provided support to women who had migrated to the cities.

Industrialization also increased the number of people living in cities and towns as compared to villages in the countryside. This is known as urbanization. Urbanization occurs because individuals move to the urban areas seeking better jobs and opportunities. While urbanization has both good and bad effects, in the Caribbean it has often led to an increase in violent crime. Also, as the population in the cities and towns grows, more amenities, for example water and electricity supplies, have to be built and this often means that the rural areas receive less attention in this respect.

> **Roleplay**
> Imagine that you are a journalist in a British Caribbean country in 1950. Do some research on the effects of industrialization on women and write a news article on this topic. Make sure you include both positive and negative effects. Interviews may also help you to gather information.

REVISION QUESTIONS

1. Examine the problems sugar planters faced in the post-emancipation period and discuss the methods which were implemented to alleviate these conditions.
(25 marks)

2. For a specific Caribbean country, chose any one alternative to agriculture (tourism, bauxite or oil). State how this industry developed over time and what its contribution was to the country.
(25 marks)

3.
   a. Give two reasons why British West Indian governments started searching for alternative sources of income by the end of the 1800s. *(5 marks)*
   b. For any one named Caribbean territory, state three measures which were implemented to establish these alternative sources of income. *(10 marks)*
   c. How successful were each of the measures you have given in part b? *(10 marks)*
   (Total = 25 marks)

References and recommended reading

- Baptiste, F. A. *The Exploitation of Caribbean Bauxite and Petroleum 1914–1945*, Kingston: University of the West Indies, 1986
- Hillman, R. S. and D'Agostino, T. J. *Understanding the Contemporary Caribbean.* Lynne Rienner Publishers: London, 2009
- Polly Patullo, *Last Resorts*. Ian Randle Publishers, Kingston, 1996
- Pantin, D. and Attzs, M. *The Economics of the Caribbean*, Ian Randle: Jamaica, 2005
- Ramsaran, R. F. *The Commonwealth Caribbean in the World Economy*. Macmillan Publishers Ltd, London, 1989
- Shepherd V. and Beckles, H. *Freedoms Won: Caribbean emancipations, ethnicities and nationhood,* Cambridge: Cambridge University Press, 2006
- Ward, J. R. *Poverty and Progress in the Caribbean,* 1800–1960, London, Macmillan, 1985
- Wint, A. G. *Competitiveness in Small Developing Economies*. UWI Press, Mona, Jamaica, 2003

7 The USA in the Caribbean 1776–1985

This chapter will answer the following questions.
- Why was the USA interested in the Caribbean from 1776 to 1870?
- Why and how was the USA involved in Cuba (1898), Puerto Rico (1898), Panama (1903), Haiti (1915), the Dominican Republic (1916) and Grenada (1893) and what was the impact of the USA's involvement in these territories, up to 1985?
- Why was there a revolution in Cuba in 1959?
- What was the impact of the Cuban Revolution on the Caribbean between 1959 and 1985?
- What was the impact of the USA's involvement in the English-speaking Caribbean from 1939 to 1985?

The USA remains the most powerful, and influential, nation in the world. It has the largest economy, the strongest military force and the most popular cultural products (films, music and books). As such, whatever the USA does, or does not do, affects many other countries. As the Caribbean is geographically close to the USA, the islands have always been a consideration in the policies of the US government. In the 18th and 19th centuries, this consideration was mostly economic, having to do with trade – because during those times the Caribbean was one of the most valuable regions in the world.

After independence in 1776, the USA had two main objectives in respect to other countries. First, it wanted to prevent European countries from interfering in the Americas; second, it wanted to expand across the North American continent. The first aim was stated in the Monroe Doctrine (see page 166). The second aim started with the purchase of Louisiana in 1803, then the acceptance of Texas as a state of the union when that area declared its independence from Mexico in 1836. The USA then went to war with Mexico from 1846 to 1848 in order to acquire more territory. In return for a payment of US$15 million, the Americans obtained the land which now makes up the states of Arizona, California, Colorado, Nevada, New Mexico and Utah. Hawaii was annexed to the USA as a territory in 1898.

The USA – brief timeline

1607 – English colonists form a settlement in Jamestown.

1776 – Congress announces the Declaration of Independence, removing the USA from British authority.

1780 – Britain recognizes US independence in the Treaty of Paris.

1787 – The US Constitution is passed and the Bill of Rights ratified.

1789 – The first elections are held, with George Washington elected first president of the USA.

1860–1865 – The American Civil War is fought between northern and southern states over the issue of slavery.

> 'A new consciousness seems to have come upon us – the consciousness of strength, and with it a new appetite, the yearning to show our strength… The taste of Empire is in the mouth of the people as the taste of blood in the jungle. It means an imperial policy.'
> *The Washington Post*, 1898

It was after this year that the USA became the main power in the Caribbean, replacing Britain and France, and Spain, which the USA had declared war on in 1898 over the Spanish government's failure to control rebellion in Cuba. The quote from the *Washington Post* newspaper reflects the new perspective on conquest in the USA. Britain had its own problems, fighting a war in South Africa (the Boer War) and being worried about the increasing power of Germany, and so was amenable to another nation managing Caribbean matters. Germany, in fact, was the only other powerful nation which briefly challenged the USA in the region. Although Germany did not have any Caribbean and South American colonies, it did have significant business interests in Venezuela. When, in 1901, Venezuela failed to pay back loans to German businesses, Germany sent warships to the region to block Venezuelan harbours until the debts were paid. Germany's leader, Kaiser Wilhelm II, held that Germany should have control of Latin America and Cuba should be made into a European state. Italian and French warships also became active in the Caribbean for similar reasons, and this caused the USA to warn the European countries about interfering with US interests in the region. It also led to US President Theodore Roosevelt declaring that the USA would police the Caribbean to safeguard the region.

US involvement in Haiti was caused not only by historical trade ties, but because the US did not want the Germans to take control of the strategically important deep-water harbour at Môle St Nicolas. US military forces became even more active in the Caribbean after Roosevelt's declaration. They invaded Cuba and the Dominican Republic, entering Cuba twice more in 1906 and 1917. The US scored a 'triple-20': during the first 20 years of the 20th century, the USA launched 20 military invasions of countries in the Caribbean and Central America.

During the Second World War (1939–1945), US dominance in the region was sealed. German submarines were a threat to Caribbean shipping which Britain, occupied by battle in Europe and Africa, could not properly defend. The USA stepped into this breach.

> 'No picture of our future is complete which does not contemplate and comprehend the United States as the dominant power in the Caribbean Sea.'
> Statement by US Assistant Secretary of State Francis Loomis, 1904

Communism a political and economic system, based on *The Communist Manifesto* written by Karl Marx and Frederic Engels, under which the state owns all property and directs all or most economic activities. Each person works and is paid according to abilities and needs.

In the 20th century, especially after 1950, US considerations were political rather than economic, having to do with opposing the Union of Soviet Socialist Republics (the USSR or Soviet Union) and communism. This was because the position of the Caribbean islands, in 'America's backyard', made these countries, along with Central America, strategically important to the USA, in case a war broke out between the USA and the USSR.

In the 1970s, the USA, led by President Jimmy Carter, took a more diplomatic approach to Caribbean and Latin American issues. The Carter administration transferred control of the Panama Canal from the USA to the government of Panama, and prevented military rule in the Dominican Republic after the 1978 election. Carter was replaced by Ronald Reagan in 1981, however, and this new president sought to increase the USA's military power and its presence in the region and in Latin America.

During Reagan's first term as US president, newly elected Caribbean leaders sought closer ties with the USA. These leaders included Edward Seaga in Jamaica, Tom Adams in Barbados, Eugenia Charles in Dominica (not to be confused with the Dominican Republic) and Herbert Blaize in Grenada. These leaders' platforms were based on the need for foreign investment and aid from the USA. A plan from the USA, called the Caribbean Basin Initiative, was supposed to strengthen economic ties between the USA and the region. However, this plan did not compensate for the recession of the 1980s, which saw rising inflation, less employment and growing debt in most Caribbean territories.

Activity 7.1
Find out more about the Caribbean Basin Initiative. Has it benefited the region?

In the 21st century, following the break-up of the USSR and with globalization, the Caribbean is no longer as economically or politically significant to the USA. However, the trade in illegal narcotics, as well as concerns about terrorism taking hold in the region, makes Caribbean security an ongoing concern for the US government.

FAST FACTS
Between 1898 and 1934, there were about 30 separate military interventions by the USA in nine Caribbean countries.

By understanding the role of the USA, therefore, you can better understand the history of our region. First, we will look at some of the events in the 19th century involving US–Caribbean trade. Then we will look at the 20th century and US actions in specific countries such as Haiti, Cuba, Puerto Rico, the Dominican Republic, Grenada and Panama. Finally, we will examine the impact of the USA on Caribbean politics, its economy and culture.

The Monroe Doctrine

7.1 The Monroe Doctrine, 1823: 'The Birth of the Monroe Doctrine.' Left to right: John Quincy Adams, William Harris Crawford, William Wirt, President James Monroe, John C. Calhoun, Daniel D. Tompkins and John McLean

- The **Monroe Doctrine**, proclaimed on 2 December 1823, outlined how the USA would deal with other countries in the Americas (South and Central America and the Caribbean).
- It was named after President James Monroe (1758–1831), the fifth president of the USA, who occupied office from 1817 to 1825.
- The Monroe Doctrine had four basic points:
  - The USA would not interfere in the internal affairs of, or the wars between, European powers.
  - The USA recognizes and would not interfere with existing colonies and dependencies in the Western hemisphere.
  - The Western hemisphere was closed to future colonization.
  - Any attempt by a European power to oppress or control any nation in the Western hemisphere would be viewed as a hostile act against the USA.
- In 1904, President Theodore Roosevelt added the 'Roosevelt Corollary' to the Monroe Doctrine, which stated that in cases of flagrant and chronic wrongdoing by a Latin American nation, the USA could intervene in the internal affairs of that nation.

Roosevelt said:

'Chronic wrong-doing, or an impotence which results in a general loosening of the ties of civilised society, may in America, as elsewhere, ultimately require intervention by some civilised nation, and in the Western hemisphere the adherence of the United States to the Monroe Doctrine may force the United States, however reluctantly, in flagrant cases of wrong-doing or impotence, to the exercise of an international police power.'

> **The Union of Soviet Socialist Republics (USSR)**
> - The USSR had its origin in 1917, when the October Revolution was carried out by the Bolshevik socialists, who took over the government of Russia.
> - The core of the party was small industry workers, who were represented by groups called 'soviets' (workers' and soldiers' councils).
> - The USSR started in 1922 with four republics and by the time it broke up in 1991 there were 35 republics, all controlled by Russia.
> - The USSR was by area the world's largest country, covering some 224 million square kilometres, which was two and a half times the size of the USA.

The USA and the British Caribbean in the 18th century

In the 18th century, America was a major market for sugar and rum from the Caribbean. In return, the Americans supplied the islands with the lumber needed to make barrels for shipping the sugar, as well as food supplies such as flour, corn, herrings, pork, beef and other supplies. These supplies were used mostly to feed the enslaved Africans on the plantations. So when the War of American Independence started in 1775, it caused many problems for the British Caribbean colonies. These problems continued even after the war ended in 1783, because the British government, stung at its defeat by the Americans, imposed trade restrictions between its Caribbean colonies and the USA. On 2 July 1783, the British authorities issued an Order-in-Council, based on the Navigation Act principle, which excluded the USA from colonial markets. Supplies for the Caribbean colonies were now to come from Canada and Ireland. The Caribbean governors, as well as the planters, argued that supplies from these two sources would not be sufficient. This turned out to be the case.

A major effect of the British policies was an increase in the prices of essential supplies. Generally, prices for plantation supplies tripled and quadrupled after 1776. Herrings, for example, were a principle source of protein for the enslaved Africans and their price rose from 45 shillings per barrel in 1791 to 65 shillings in 1793. Corn, another staple for the slaves, went up from 7 shillings per bushel in 1790 to between 10 and 14 shillings in 1792, while flour went up from 37 shillings to £6.

On top of this, the supplies coming from Canada and Ireland were not enough to feed the population or to sustain the agricultural industry. As a result, the colonists used various means to get around the legal restrictions placed on them by the 'Mother Country'. Some islands registered US ships as British, but most just allowed the Americans to enter their ports. Another method was to buy US supplies from French islands. This practice was so common that ports in Martinique and St Domingue became transit points for US supplies to the British Caribbean colonies.

As this was undermining the British monopoly of their colonies' commercial activity, the British Parliament passed a law in April 1787 banning the imports of flour, bread, wheat, rice and lumber from all foreign Caribbean colonies, except in cases of dire need. However, deciding what was 'dire need' was left up to the governors, who exploited this loophole to the fullest and, from 1782 to 1807, often used this power to allow US imports.

The Americans took sugar in exchange for lumber and provisions. This was one factor which let sugar prices remain higher than the British government wanted. As long as the colonies were selling to markets outside the 'Mother Country', imports to Britain were reduced, causing prices to stay the same or rise. Remember the law of economics: the 'iron law of supply and demand' – goods which are scarce but in demand go up in price.

However, because of complaints from Irish, British and Canadian merchants in the early 19th century, the British government took even more drastic action to cut trade between the USA and its colonies. Lord Camden's directive on 5 September 1804 removed governors' authority to open ports. The Assembly of Jamaica objected to Governor Nugent's proclamation of the order on 21 November, which sparked off similar defiance in other islands. At this point, the British government did not want to offend the USA, mainly because the nation was already a major market for British manufactured products. So the British diplomats assured the USA that governors still had the authority to open the ports in cases of dire need.

> **Roleplay**
>
> It is 1790. Imagine that you are the President of the USA. You have to write a speech to Congress dealing with the following questions.
>
> - Why are you interested in developing trading relations in the Caribbean?
> - What two things will you do to maintain good terms with the colonial powers who control the Caribbean?

Nonetheless, the British government's restrictive policy harmed its own colonies, which experienced significant hardship after 1776 and for the first decade of the 19th century. By the 20th century, specifically after the First World War, Britain had given in to US policy, promising not to acquire any more territory in the Americas, with British Prime Minister Arthur Balfour (1848–1930) agreeing with the Monroe Doctrine. The USA also warned other European powers against interfering in the Caribbean. Apart from the Roosevelt Corollary, during the 20th century the USA tried different strategies to maintain stability in Caribbean countries. These included 'dollar diplomacy' and the 'good neighbour policy'.

> **Dollar diplomacy** giving aid and soft loans to Caribbean countries in order to foster good relations and get their leaders to accede to US policies.

> **Good neighbour policy** a policy of non-intervention and non-interference. It repealed the Platt Amendment (see more on this in the section on Cuba) and was geared towards creating more positive, friendly relationships with the countries of Latin America and the Caribbean.

In the next section, we will look at US involvement in five Caribbean countries and one South American one. You will learn about the security issues, political instability in the various countries, interference by other foreign powers and ideological conflicts.

> **US intervention policy**
>
> During the 18th century the two main priorities were to:
>
> - prevent European involvement in the Americas
> - expand territory across North America.
>
> During the 19th and 20th centuries the priority was to control the Caribbean basin, including Central America.

Cuba

> **FAST FACTS**
>
> - Cuba is officially called the Republic of Cuba (in Spanish, República de Cuba).
> - The country consists of one large island and numerous smaller islands, islets and cays.
> - It is 145 km south of the tip of the US state of Florida.
> - Cuba has a land area of 110,861 square km, which makes it the largest country in the Caribbean. The capital is Havana.

From the early 19th century, some Americans wanted to acquire the island of Cuba. In 1823, the US Secretary of State, John Quincy Adams, said that if Cuba was taken from Spain it would naturally join the North American union, since Cuba could not support itself. By the late 19th century, the USA had become a major trading partner with Cuba. The Americans became involved in the second war of Cuban independence (1895–98), which you read about in Chapter 6. Spain had not only refused to let the Cubans govern themselves, but had also increased taxes on the island. This sparked off the war between the Cubans and the Spanish. The Americans were drawn in when there was an explosion aboard one of their ships, the USS Maine, which was anchored in Havana harbour, and they decided to fight against Spain. That the explosion was probably an accident, caused by a fire in the coal bunker, was irrelevant.

The Spanish army was driven out of Cuba and Cuban independence was granted by the Treaty of Paris on 10 December 1898. As it turned out, however, the Cubans had only exchanged one colonial master for another. The USA continued

7.2 Cuba

to occupy Cuba, on the basis that their presence was needed to maintain order and to restore the country's infrastructure which had been damaged in the war. And, in fact, the Americans did build a number of schools, roads and bridges. They transformed Havana into a more modern city and deepened its harbour. They also provided food for the Cubans and took action to eradicate yellow fever. All this was done with the intention to incorporate Cuba into the US economic, cultural and educational systems, but in a way that would exclude Afro-Cubans from government. The US government passed a law in 1901, called the Platt Amendment, that allowed the USA to establish a naval base at Guantánamo Bay at an annual rent of US$5,000, and gave the USA the right to intervene in Cuba to preserve 'a stable government adequately protecting life, property, and individual liberty'.

One year later, Cuba was declared a republic and held its first presidential election. The administration that began on 20 May 1902 under Cuba's first elected president, Tomás Estrada Palma, was immediately opposed by many Cubans because he was seen as a US puppet. There were elections again in 1905 and 1906, but the process was a shambles. The Cubans rebelled, and the USA once again occupied the island on 29 September 1906. President Estrada Palma resigned after negotiations between the rebels and the US government failed. The USA installed a provisional government of Cuban civilians under the Cuban flag and constitution, but it was run by an American. A law commission was set up to revise the procedures for elections and on 28 January 1909 the USA handed over the government to the leader of the Liberal party, José Miguel Gómez, who had run against Palma. Meanwhile, Cuba's economy grew steadily, as sugar prices kept rising until the 1920s.

The Gómez administration, which stayed in office for just four years, was a failure. Its officials were incompetent and corrupt, spent too much money and did not attend to the needs and concerns of citizens – especially Afro-Cubans. One consequence of this was that a group of Afro-Cubans set up an association to lobby for better jobs and more political patronage and to oppose a ban of political associations based on colour and race. In 1912, there were mass demonstrations in Oriente, which were quelled by government troops, with hundreds of Afro-Cubans killed.

Nearly all the Cuban administrations afterwards were run by corrupt leaders. The most significant one was Fulgencio Batista, who controlled the government through figureheads from 1934 to 1939 and then was himself elected from 1940 to 1944 and again from 1952 to 1959. Batista, who overthrew the elected governor in 1933 with US support, kept himself in power by subverting the political process, using the country's military to get support through threats and even by assassinating his opponents.

This kind of politics was facilitated by the US involvement in Cuba. For the first half of the 20th century, the island's revenues continued to be based mainly on sugar, but a tourist industry based on gambling and prostitution also flourished. When the US government outlawed alcohol between 1919 and 1933, through a policy called Prohibition, Havana became an even more popular destination for Americans. This was the start of the tourist industry in Cuba. This situation contributed to anti-US sentiments among Cubans.

Social conditions in Cuba were relatively good, compared with those in other Latin American countries. The literacy rate was 76%, Cuba ranked first in Latin America in television sets per person, life expectancy in the 1950s was about the same as that in the USA, and Cuba actually had more doctors per person than developed countries such as Britain and France. However, the flourishing economy of the period from the 1920s to the 1950s was also a very lopsided one, with most of the wealth going to only a few individuals. Only four out of every 100 Cubans could afford to eat meat regularly. In the rural areas 75% of the dwellings were huts made from palm trees, with only 50% having toilets, 15% having inside running water and less than 10% having electricity. One third of the workforce was poor, and depended on seasonal employment on the sugar estates to earn money. Most of the businesses and industries were controlled by foreigners, who owned about three-quarters of the island's arable land, nearly all the essential services and just under half of the sugar production. Even though Cuba had a per capita income of US$353, which was among the highest in Latin America in the 1950s, there was still widespread unemployment in the island.

In the late 1950s, the USA withdrew its support of Batista, because his repression had become embarrassing to the administration. This facilitated the overthrown of the Batista regime in a coup that began in late 1958, led by a young lawyer named Fidel Castro, with Batista fleeing from the island on December 31, 1958. Castro had been exiled for subversive activities and had been leading a guerrilla war against the Cuban government for several years. At first, the USA backed Castro. Castro, along with Che Guevera, was seen as a romantic rebel, especially among university students.

FIDEL CASTRO
(1926–)

7.3 Fidel Castro Ruz (b. 13 August 1926, near Birán, Cuba). Cuban revolutionary leader and head of state, photographed in 1960

Castro was a political leader of Cuba (from 1959) who transformed his country into the first communist state in the Western hemisphere. He became a symbol of communist revolution in Latin America. He held the title of Premier until 1976, when he became President of the Council of State and the Council of Ministers.

Castro attended Roman Catholic boarding schools in Santiago de Cuba, Oriente province, and then the Catholic high school Belén in Havana, where he proved an outstanding athlete. He entered the School of Law of the University of Havana in 1945 and graduated in five years. After his graduation in 1950, Castro began to practise law and became a member of the reformist Cuban People's Party, the members of which were called Ortodoxos.

He became their candidate for a seat in the House of Representatives (from a Havana district) in the elections scheduled for June 1952. In March of that year, however, the former Cuban President, General Fulgencio Batista, overthrew the government of President Carlos Prío Socarrás and cancelled the elections.

> After legal means failed to dislodge Batista's new dictatorship, Castro began to organize a rebel force for the task in 1953. On 26 July 1953, he led about 160 men in an attack on the Moncada military barracks in Santiago de Cuba in hopes of sparking a popular uprising. Most of the men were killed and Castro himself was arrested.
>
> After a trial in which he conducted an impassioned defence, he was sentenced by the government to 15 years' imprisonment. He and his brother Raúl were released in a political amnesty in 1955 and they went to Mexico to continue their campaign against the Batista regime. There Castro organized Cuban exiles into a revolutionary group called the 26th of July Movement.
>
> On 2 December 1956, Castro and an armed expedition of 81 men landed on the coast of Oriente province, Cuba, from the yacht Granma. All of them were killed or captured except Castro, Raúl, Ernesto (Che) Guevara and nine others, who retreated into the Sierra Maestra of south-western Oriente province to wage guerrilla warfare against the Batista forces.
>
> With the help of growing numbers of revolutionary volunteers throughout the island, Castro's forces won a string of victories over the Batista government's demoralized and poorly led armed forces. Castro's propaganda efforts proved particularly effective, and as internal political support waned and military defeats multiplied, Batista fled the country early on 1 January 1959. Castro's force of 800 guerrillas had defeated the Cuban government's 30,000-strong professional army.

Castro's original goals in overthrowing Batista are not clear. He had networked with many different groups in creating the revolution, from middle-class professionals to the churches to labour unions to communists to capitalists, which is why the USA at first did not see him as a threat but as a likely ally.

However, Castro soon began interfering with US business interests on the island, as well as criticizing those Cubans who had supported the USA during the Batista regime. This rhetoric found favour among ordinary Cubans, who united behind Castro. He appealed to Cuba's historical memory, which included traditions of guerrilla warfare, racial and social justice, and the struggle for nationhood.

Anti-US sentiments were an important key for arousing Cuban nationalist sentiments, since it is part of human psychology that group loyalty is strongest when there is an enemy to fight or hate. Castro's communism, therefore, was only a secondary instrument for his primary goals of nationalism, of making his revolution last, and of establishing personal control of Cuban society.

Activity 7.2

Imagine that you are Fidel Castro. Prepare a speech to be read to a group of students explaining why Cubans need to get rid of US interest and work with the USSR instead.

Although he did not at first declare himself a communist, Castro soon established diplomatic and trade links with the USSR, abolishing capitalism, and nationalizing all the foreign-owned enterprises. This was when US public opinion (excluding the views of left-wing radicals in US universities) turned against him. It was thus Cuba which brought the Cold War to the Caribbean, making the region the stage where the 30-year rivalry between the USA and the USSR was played out in the Western hemisphere.

> **Capitalism** an economic and political system in which a country's trade and industry are controlled by private owners for profit, rather than by the state.

> **Socialism** a political and economic theory which notes that the means of production, distribution and exchange should be owned or regulated by the community as a whole.

Castro built on Cuba's social infrastructure, investing in health care, education and biotechnology. He also made Cuban society more militarized than it had been before. He saw 'exporting the revolution' as a way to keep himself secure within Cuba. Cuba trained and financed thousands of revolutionaries in other Latin American countries. This did not endear him to the leaders of these nations, although they often voiced anti-US sentiments, too.

Activity 7.3

The photographs of a controversial historical figure can be used by opponents and proponents to promote their message. Find a selection of contemporary photographs of Castro from the years 1959–70. Study the image he cultivates and write up a series of captions to describe the man and his politics.

7.4 Castro cutting cane, 1960.

FAST FACTS

The Agrarian Reform Law, which was passed on 17 May 1959, gave land in Cuba to the people who cultivated it and banned ownership of any parcel of land over 995 acres by either an individual or a company.

Cuba was the first communist nation in the Western hemisphere. This disturbed the US government, which had approved of Castro's 'humanistic' revolution, as he called it, until he instituted the Agrarian Reform Law and established official ties with the USSR. US sugar companies stood to lose over a million and a half acres of land because of the Agrarian Reform Law. The purpose of this law was to undermine US and other foreign ownership, eliminate renting and tenancy of land, and create a cadre of small and medium-sized farmers who cultivated a variety of crops.

The Americans were concerned that the USSR now had a possible military launching pad right in the USA's backyard. They were also worried that the Cuban Revolution might spread communism to other Caribbean countries. The US government made many attempts to undermine, overthrow and even assassinate Castro. Within two months of Castro taking power, the US National Security Council began plotting ways 'to bring another government to power in Cuba'. Castro used anti-US sentiments to consolidate his support among the Cuban people.

In January 1961, the US government broke off diplomatic relations with Cuba. The response of the USSR had not reassured the US government about Cuba, since the Soviet Premier Nikita Khrushchev, a coal-miner's son who became the head of the Communist Party in 1953, issued a public warning to the USA that any military action against Cuba would result in retaliation from the USSR. Khrushchev claimed that the USSR wanted only to defend Cuba's experiment with communism. Naturally, these responses also worried the world in general, and the Caribbean in particular, since the USA and USSR were the two major nuclear powers. The USA responded first by placing a trade embargo on Cuba, meaning that no US companies or citizens were allowed to sell goods to Cuba or buy products from there. As a result, Cuban cigars, considered among the world's best by smokers, became the main item illegally brought into the USA. In that year, the US spy department named the Central Intelligence Agency (CIA) supported an operation by 1,500 exiled Cubans, known as the Bay of Pigs invasion. This was repelled by the Cuban army. The US government at first denied any involvement in this operation, but was widely disbelieved, with even its allies in Europe criticizing the USA. On Cuba's side, Castro now strengthened his country's ties with the USSR, and by the end of 1961 had declared himself a fully fledged communist. In October 1962 the world almost came to nuclear war after the Americans discovered, through satellite photographs, that the Soviet government was building missile launch sites in Cuba. These nuclear missiles could have reached any chosen target in the USA and thus doubled the number of US cities and military bases which could be destroyed by the Soviets. This strategic increase was tempting to the Soviets, because the US military arsenal was far superior to that of the USSR – the USA had six inter-continental ballistic missiles (ICBMs) to every one Soviet ICBM. These US missiles could carry a nuclear bomb from the USA to the USSR. The USA also had three times as many long-range bomber aircraft than the USSR. Each nuclear missile was so powerful that just one could have destroyed a city or, for that matter, an entire Caribbean island.

US President John F. Kennedy, who was elected in 1961 and who would be assassinated in 1963 while on an official motorcade, by a Castro sympathizer, announced that the US navy would stop any ship delivering missiles to Cuba. US nuclear submarines and ships gathered in Florida, prepared to attack Cuba. Kennedy also went on television and issued an ultimatum to the USSR to withdraw all missiles and ships already in Cuba. A war was narrowly averted through negotiations between President John F. Kennedy and Soviet Premier Nikita Khrushchev. Both men were aware of the price of war: Kennedy had spoke of 200 million people dead, Khrushchev of 500 million. Castro, for his part, had written a letter to Khrushchev on 27 September 1962, calling on the Soviet leader to launch a nuclear attack if the USA invaded Cuba 'however harsh and terrible the solution would be'. Khrushchev and Kennedy's agreement, after weeks of tension, led to the removal of the missile sites by Khrushchev and a guarantee from Kennedy that the USA would not invade Cuba. Castro played no part in this agreement and was reportedly angry at the outcome, cursing and smashing a mirror when he heard about it.

Although at first it was not known whether Cuba made the offer for the missile site, documents released within the past two decades suggest that it was the USSR which initiated the plan. However, the Soviets did not think that a nuclear war was worth the price of getting dominance in the Caribbean. They were also able to persuade Kennedy to agree to the removal of 15 Jupiter missiles in Turkey, which had the range to reach Russia.

The Cuban Missile Crisis helped prevent the Cold War between the world's two super-powers from becoming a nuclear conflict, with a 'hotline' between US and USSR leaders, as well as other measures, being installed after the incident. The hotline was a direct telephone communication between the US president and the Soviet premier, a suggestion made by economist Thomas Schelling who was an adviser to the US government.

The USA also continued to aid the Caribbean economically, in order to prevent the Cuban revolution spreading.

> **The Cold War** rivalry between the US and the USSR after the Second World War until 1990, in which the two super-powers opposed each other politically and economically, but not militarily except by supplying weapons and finance to leaders and countries whose support they wanted.

Activity 7.4 Find out more about the Cold War. Who were the allies of the USA and of the USSR? What were the main issues and when did the Cold War end?

Cuba's economy continued to be subsidized by the USSR, to the tune of about US$4 billion a year, until that union disintegrated into its satellite states in the early 1990s. With the island's economy contracted by 33%, Castro allowed some economic reforms, such as foreign investment in the tourist industry, allowing the US dollar to be used as legal tender so that Cubans abroad could send money to their relatives in the island and letting state enterprises control their trade and finances. These reforms did not last, and Cuba remained a communist regime, with an inefficient economy and denial of human rights such as freedom of speech and elections between contesting political parties. Repression also occurred, with people opposed to the Castro regime, or calling for a capitalist system, being tortured and jailed.

After 1959, however, Cuban communism was a key factor in US policy towards another Caribbean island: Puerto Rico.

> **Groupwork**
>
> 'Be it resolved that the USA's involvement in the Caribbean was beneficial only to the USA.'
>
> In a group, debate the above topic with reference to either Cuba or Puerto Rico.

Puerto Rico

FAST FACTS

- Officially the Commonwealth of Puerto Rico (in Spanish, Estado Libre Asociado de Puerto Rico) the country is a self-governing island commonwealth in the Caribbean, associated with the USA.
- It covers an area of 9,104 square km and occupies a central position among the islands in the northern Caribbean.
- The capital is San Juan. Two islands off the east coast, Vieques and Culebra, are also part of the nation.
- Puerto Rico is located about 1,600 km south east of Florida.

Puerto Rico was a colony of Spain from 1500 to 1898 and then the island effectively became a US colony. In 1898, the US military occupied the island during the war between Cuba and Spain and the USA. Puerto Rico was still an agricultural economy, its main exports being coffee, sugar and tobacco. The island was occupied by the Americans in the same year as Cuba, but it was turned over to US forces two months earlier, on 18 October, and a US military governor was installed to run the country. It was ceded to the USA by the Treaty of Paris, which was signed on 10 December 1898. As with Cuba, the Americans set about maintaining order and modernizing the country's infrastructure, constructing highways, drainage, improving the water supply and sanitation, and setting up a public education system. The military government ended its rule on 1 May 1900.

In that year, the US Congress passed the Foraker Act, which legalized the occupation of Puerto Rico by appointing US officials as the island's government. The US dollar became the official currency in Puerto Rico and all US laws applied to the island. One advantage Puerto Ricans got from the arrangement was that their income was not taxed by the USA. To this day, Puerto Rico is not an independent country. Although, since 1917 it has had a local legislature, and since 1948 its governors have been elected by the populace, the country is really governed by the USA. Puerto Rico has a delegate in the US House of Representatives, but Puerto Ricans cannot vote in US elections.

As a result of the Foraker Act, Puerto Rico's economy became geared to the USA, with the main exports being sugar and other agricultural products, with some light manufactures. However, all the main industries in Puerto Rico were owned and run by US corporations. In the earlier part of the 20th century, the US government opposed attempts by Puerto Rico to become an independent country. In 1922, for example, the Puerto Rican Nationalist Party, which opposed the country's continued subjection to the USA, was repressed by both the US and the colonial government. Another political organization, the Liberal Party, also favoured independence, but pushed for gradual reform. It should be noted that several referendums have been conducted asking Puerto Ricans if they favour independence and the majority of citizens have voted against the motion.

This was demonstrated in 1938, when a breakaway faction of the Liberal Party, called the Popular Democratic Party (PDP) abandoned pro-independence and won the 1940 election. The PDP sought to maintain the island's 'association' status as a commonwealth or as an improved commonwealth, or to set up a free sovereign-association status or Free Associated Republic. With this platform, the PDP won a plurality vote in referendums on the island's status and remained in power until 1968.

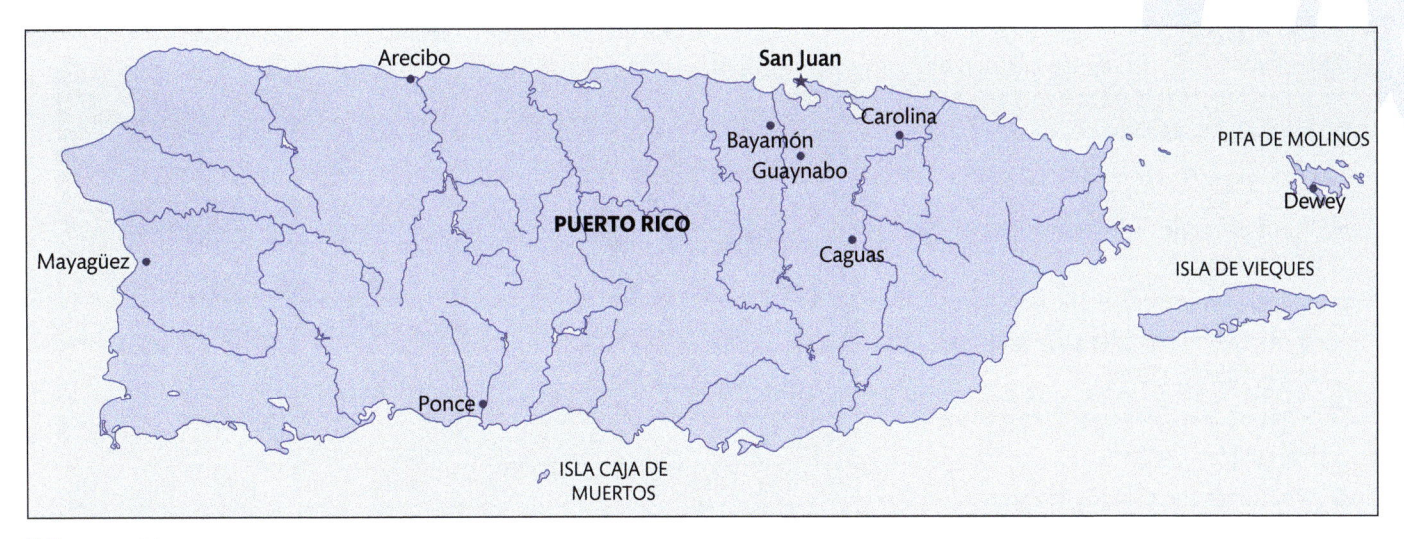

7.5 Puerto Rico

During the Second World War (1939–45) Puerto Rico tried to industrialize by creating state-owned corporations that used local materials and sold to Puerto Ricans. This experiment ended after the war, with the government's five companies being sold to private owners. Based on its relationship with the USA, the Puerto Rican government tried a new strategy, called Operation Bootstrap (in Spanish, Operación Manos a la Obra), which was intended to attract US companies to manufacture goods for export to the USA. This is known as 'industrialization by invitation' and was the brainchild of Caribbean economist Sir W. Arthur Lewis, as you read in Chapter 6.

This policy had three phases. In the first phase, factories were built and operated by the government. In the second phase, which started in 1946, a government agency called the Industrial Development Corporation constructed factory buildings and leased them to private manufacturers. In the third stage, the government got out of any involvement in building factories and concentrated on aid and incentives to attract private sector investors to set up manufacturing plants in Puerto Rico. The policy was largely successful in industrializing the island. In 1947, 20% of the country's GDP came from agriculture and 22% from manufacturing. In 1980, just 3% of GDP was from the agricultural sector and 37% from manufacturing.

> **Gross national product (GNP)** the value of all the goods and services produced in an economy, plus the value of the goods and services imported, minus the goods and services exported.

After the Cuban Revolution, Puerto Rico became more important to the USA, because the US government wanted to showcase the island as a capitalist alternative to the communist system so the Caribbean would not have a 'second Cuba'. This also resulted in communists and socialists being repressed in Puerto Rico, as well as pro-independence groups. One measure of the economic success of Puerto Rico is the gross national product (GNP) which in 1950 was US$342 and which, just 30 years later, had increased ten-fold to US$3,475.

Two important measures instituted in 1976 by the US government were the revamping of section 936 of the US tax code and the extension to Puerto Ricans of the US food stamp programme. The first measure reduced taxes on profits which remained in Puerto Rico. This helped develop the manufacturing sector, especially in pharmaceuticals and machinery.

The US food stamp programme added to the personal income of Puerto Ricans by reducing the amount of money they spent on food. Half of Puerto Rican families took advantage of the food stamp programme, although 69% qualified. In the 1980s, a cap was put on the value of food stamps given out, and now just 40% of families use it,

Activity 7.5

Study the cartoon on the other side of this page and answer the following questions.

- Who does 'Uncle Sam' refer to?
- What are your first impressions of the cartoon?
- Imagine that you are Uncle Sam. Write two things that you might say to the four 'children'.
- What do you think the 'children' are thinking?
- What does the cartoon tell you about Uncle Sam's relationship with the 'children'?

7.6 Imperialism: 'School Begins'. Uncle Sam lecturing four children labelled Philippines, Hawaii, Puerto Rico and Cuba in front of children with books labelled with US states. In the background a Native American holds a book upside down, a Chinese boy stands in the doorway and an African American washes the window. American cartoon, c. 1899

Activity 7.6

'Brain drain' has been common in many Caribbean countries. Find out if your country has ever experienced a brain drain. When did this happen and what impact did it have on your country?

Did you know?

In 2010 there were approximately 2 million Puerto Ricans living in the USA, as well as 1.6 million Cubans and 1.2 million Dominicans.

although 48% of Puerto Rican families are below the poverty line by US standards. However, you should bear in mind that the US standard of poverty is higher than that of developing countries, as shown by the fact that three out of four poor Americans own a car and over 80% have air-conditioned homes.

Most Puerto Ricans see their country as benefiting from the privileged relationship with the USA. Migration to the USA is easy, but it is mostly Puerto Ricans with higher education and professional qualifications who go there. In the 1930s, 48,000 Puerto Ricans migrated to the USA (3% of the total population); in the 1950s, it was 151,000 (9% of the population); and in the 1960s the total number of migrants was 430,000 (18% of the population). This 'brain drain' may have negative effects on Puerto Rico's development.

The Dominican Republic

FAST FACTS

- The Dominican Republic (República Dominicana) occupies the eastern two thirds of Hispaniola, while Haiti occupies the western third of the island.
- Hispaniola lies between the islands of Cuba to the west and Puerto Rico to the east and is situated about 1,080 km southeast of Florida and 515 km north of Colombia and Venezuela.
- The northern shores of the Dominican Republic face the Atlantic Ocean, while the southern shore is bordered by the Caribbean Sea.
- Between the eastern tip of the island and Puerto Rico runs a channel called the Mona Passage.
- The Dominican Republic has an area of 48,443 square km.

7.7 The Dominican Republic

US involvement in the Dominican Republic started in 1865, when the country's dictator leader, President Buenaventura Báez, asked Ulysses S. Grant, then commander of the Union armies during the American Civil War, to make the country a protectorate. In 1861, the previous president had restored the country to its colonial status under Spain, in order to have Spanish protection against attacks from Haiti. Spain withdrew its troops in 1865. Grant agreed to Báez's request, partly because of the Dominican Republic's strategic position on major sea routes leading from both Europe and the USA to the Panama Canal, but the US Senate did not approve the treaty.

Save for a period of prosperity and political stability from 1882 to 1899 under the presidency of the Ulises Heureaux, the Dominican Republic was economically unstable and ruled by dictators. Heureaux was assassinated in 1899 and the USA, now concerned even more with Caribbean matters after it had occupied Cuba and Puerto Rico, also became involved in Dominican affairs. The USA was already the major market for the republic's products, as well as the main supplier of its imports. US firms had also started to invest more in the country. In 1905, when European creditors began making threats over unpaid Dominican debts, the USA took over the administration of the Dominican customs department. In 1916, when the Dominican government collapsed because of internal conflicts, the USA took over governance of the entire country.

Constabulary an armed police force organized as a military unit.

As with Cuba and Puerto Rico, the Americans built roads, schools, communications and sanitation facilities and other projects during the time they occupied the Dominican Republic (1916–24). Another legacy, however, was a modern military constabulary, trained by the US Marine Corps, which future Dominican dictators would use to hold on to power.

In 1924, in elections overseen by US officials, Horacio Vásquez was elected President. He was incompetent and corrupt, and the Great Depression of 1929 to 1930 undermined the Dominican economy. In 1930, there was an uprising against Vásquez. He was ousted from power, and Rafael Trujillo, who controlled the military, took over the country. Trujillo ruled from 1930 to 1961 by holding rigged elections. Although a ruthless dictator, he maintained internal stability, liquidated the national debt and modernized the country. Under his rule, the amount spent by government on the Dominican people rose from US$5.44 per person in 1930 to US$47 per person in 1960, while exports rose from US$10 per head to US$57 per head. However, he also stole and wasted public funds, and in 1937 murdered thousand of Haitians who had fled their country. Despite being a corrupt dictator, Trujillo had the support of the US government, because the USA viewed the Dominican Republic as the country most likely to become a second Cuba.

Democracy a system of government by the whole population or all the eligible members of a state. The government is elected by the people.

When Trujillo was assassinated in 1961, the US government was worried that his successor, Juan Bosch, was backed by communists. Bosch was overthrown by a military coup and fighting broke out between the rebels and Bosch's supporters. In response, US President Lyndon Johnson sent about 23,000 marines to the Dominican Republic, supposedly to protect US civilians. Bosch's faction was defeated because of US help for the rebels, and an anti-communist lawyer named Joaquin Balaguer was installed as president in an election in which only selected persons were allowed to vote. Balaguer stayed in power with five more rigged elections, was succeeded by other dictators, and the Dominican Republic did not become a democracy until the 1990s.

Haiti

> **FAST FACTS**
>
> - Haiti is officially the Republic of Haiti (Haitian Creole: Repiblik Dayti; French: Republique D'Haïti).
> - It is the only independent French-speaking republic in the Americas, occupying the western third of the island of Hispaniola and several nearby small islands.
> - It is situated about 970 km south east of Florida in the Atlantic Ocean and has a total land area of 27,400 square km.
> - The country comprises two peninsulas separated by the Gulf of Gonaïves. Haiti is bordered on the north by the Atlantic Ocean, on the east by the Dominican Republic, and on the south and west by the Caribbean Sea.
> - The capital is Port-au-Prince.

From the time Haiti became the Western hemisphere's first country ruled by Africans, the USA established trading links. This relationship continued to varying degrees throughout the 19th century and, by the 1890s, the Americans increased their efforts to get commercial and military footholds in Haiti. In 1905, the USA took Haiti's custom department into receivership, as they had with the Dominican Republic. Before the First World War (1914–18), US business interests were firmly established in Haiti. By 1915, the US had taken military control of Haiti, an occupation that was to last until 1934. The US government justified this action on the grounds of humanitarian intervention and under the Monroe Doctrine (see page 166).

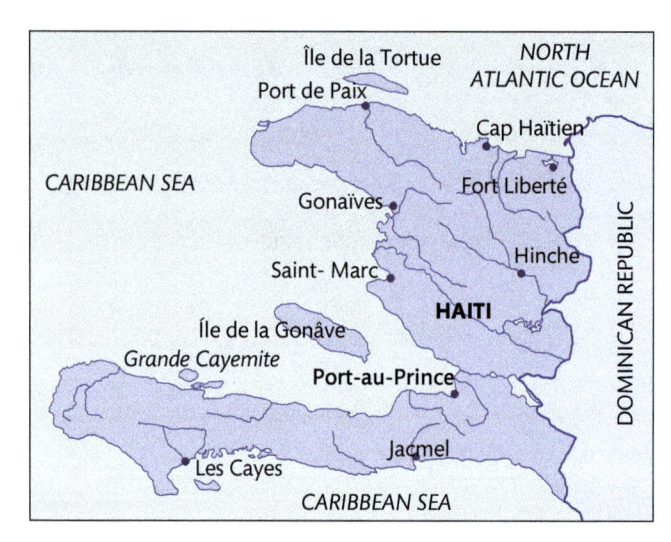

7.8 Haiti

This may have been the case, but protecting US business interests and establishing a base to protect the Panama Canal were also key US concerns. Haiti signed a treaty with the USA establishing US financial and political domination. In 1918, in an election supervised by the US Marine Corps, a new constitution was introduced that permitted foreigners to own land in Haiti.

The US officials running Haiti favoured the mixed-race group. This made many black Haitians resent the US occupation, since they believed they were being deliberately excluded from public office. There were also daily conflicts between the US marines and Haitians. When the Marine Corps invoked a law from as far back as the regime of Henri Christophe to force Haitians into road gangs, there was a revolt. This was soon suppressed. Although the Americans also built up the country's infrastructure, as they had in the other Caribbean countries they occupied, the Haitians felt that not enough was done, especially given the treatment they received at the hands of the marines. A 1921 report from the US Senate found:

> 'a failure of the Departments in Washington to appreciate the importance of selecting for service in Haiti, whether in civil or military capacities, men who were sympathetic to the Haitians and able to maintain cordial personal and official relations with them'.

In October 1930 a national assembly was elected and in August 1934 the US president, Franklin D. Roosevelt, withdrew the Marines. However, the US government continued to direct economic policies in Haiti until 1947. Ten years later, Francis 'Papa Doc' Duvalier was elected President. It took him just seven years to set up a personal military force, called the Tontons Macoutes, and declare himself 'president for life'. He followed in the worst tradition of oppression and corruption until he died in 1971, and was succeeded by his son, Jean-Claude 'Baby Doc' Duvalier. In 1986, street riots forced the junior Duvalier to flee the country, which was then taken over by the army. In 1987, a new constitution was introduced and, in December 1990, Haiti's first free presidential elections were held.

> 'I would dedicate this nation to the policy of the good neighbour — the neighbour who resolutely respects himself and, because he does so, respects the rights of others.'
>
> US President Franklin D. Roosevelt, in his inaugural address on the good neighbour policy, 4 March 1933

Grenada

FAST FACTS

- Sometimes referred to as the Isle of Spice, Grenada is the most southerly of the Windward Islands, situated about 160 km north of the coast of Venezuela in the eastern Caribbean Sea.
- Grenada covers a total land area of 345 square km, including the dependency of the southern Grenadines to the north-northeast.
- The capital is St. George's.

On 25 October 1983, the USA invaded Grenada. The aim was supposedly to rescue Americans on the island after a military coup overthrew the government. In fact, the US government had been keeping a close eye on Grenada since 1979, when a socialist group led by Maurice Bishop had taken over the government in a bloodless coup. In the 1983 coup, however, Bishop himself was killed by his former comrades.

Before the 1979 coup Grenada had been ruled for 16 years by Eric Gairy, with a brief interlude between 1962 and 1967 when he was out of office. Gairy was a trade unionist who headed the Grenada United Labour Party. Grenada became independent in 1974, seven years after Gairy became premier. In that time, Gairy had become controversial and lost popularity because of his violent tactics against his opponents and poor economic management, as well as his unconventional ideas. He once petitioned the United Nations to set up an observatory in Grenada to search for spacecraft from other planets. He set up a paramilitary group called the Green Beasts and a secret police force, The Mongoose Gang, which intimidated, beat up and even murdered his opponents.

By the 1970s, nearly half of the adult population was out of work.

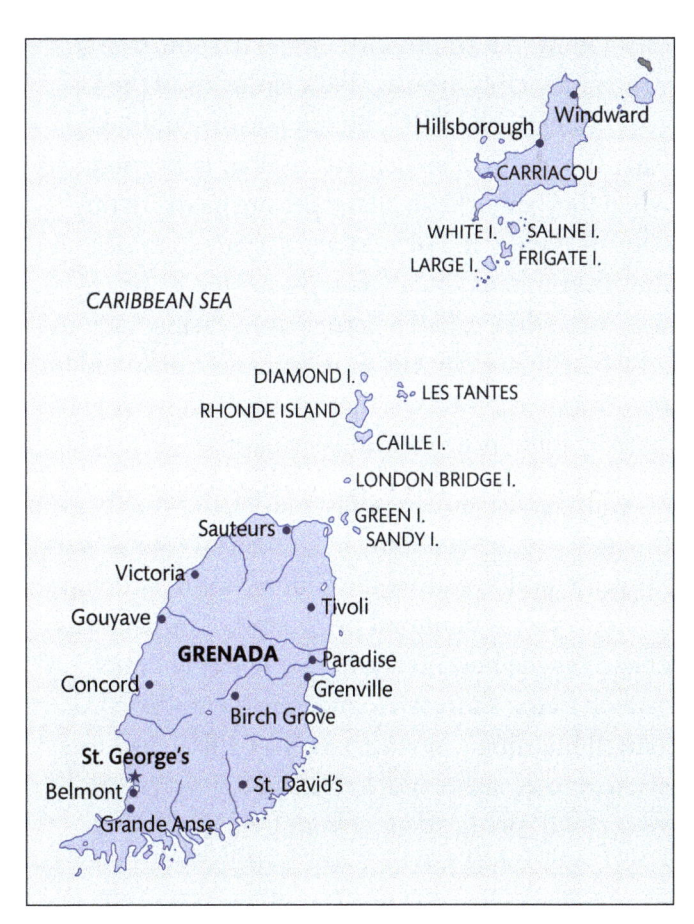

7.9 Grenada

A coalition of political parties called the New Jewel Movement (NJM), headed by Bishop, contested the 1976 election and, while they did not win, they got enough support to become the opposition in parliament. The 1979 coup was executed when Gairy was out of the country. It was the first time an elected leader in the British Caribbean had been removed by a coup.

Bishop and the NJM, which now formed the People's Revolutionary Government (PRG), had many problems to tackle. Apart from the widespread unemployment, infrastructure (roads, water and electricity supply) had become run down, while the institutions of the state, from the civil service to the judiciary, had become corrupt or weak. The PRG blamed this conditions not only on Gairy's misrule, but also on colonialism and the continued ownership of key sectors of the economy by foreign companies. Politically, Bishop and his colleagues were also opposed to the British model of parliament, while economically they rejected capitalism. The PRG thus followed a communist model to some extent, which inevitably aroused the suspicions of the US government. The PRG did not reassure onlookers (save those who also believed in their leftist politics) when they shut down all the private media in the country, saying the owners were trying to undermine the government. The PRG replaced the British model with what they called a participatory democracy, in which ordinary citizens were regularly consulted on policy issues. However, these consultations did not actually influence government policy.

As with the usual communist model, the state became the driver of the economy in Grenada. Projects were implemented to restore the country's infrastructure and improve agricultural production. Tourism was chosen as the best means to generate economic growth in the short term, and to this end the NJM started building a new airport. The PRG's policies seemed to be successful between 1979 and 1982, when GDP per head grew from US$1,710 to US$1,826, while inflation was reduced from 20% to 8%. However, most of this growth came from government-funded construction, rather than the productive and foreign-exchange earning sectors. The tourist plan never took off since, as you read in Chapter 6, most tourists in the Caribbean come from the USA, and Americans would hardly have been attracted to an island where the government favoured communist policies. Investors, both foreign and local, were cautious about investing in activities like manufacturing, for much the same reason. In August 1983, the Bishop administration signed an agreement with the International Monetary Fund (IMF) for financial assistance – an ironic necessity, since the IMF was typically seen by leftists as the symbol of all that was wrong with the capitalist and Western world.

There had always been internal rifts in the party and the IMF agreement exacerbated them. Two months later, Bishop was arrested and executed by the army, which set up a Revolutionary Military Council. The heads of CARICOM met in Port-of-Spain in Trinidad to discuss the crisis. Four years before, when the NJM had taken over the country, this regional body had issued a statement saying, 'the affairs of Grenada are for the people of that territory to decide'. This was intended as a message to Britain and the USA not to interfere in Grenada. At the 1983 meeting, it turned out that some Caribbean heads of government – those of Jamaica, Dominica and Barbados – had already told the Americans that they would support any action to remove the new government which had executed Bishop.

A week after Bishop was killed, the US invaded. The Governor-General, Sir Paul Scoon, was put in office by the Americans. A governing council was set up to run the country until an election could be held. The election, held in December 1984, was won by the New National Party headed by Herbert A. Blaize, who had led the government in the 1960s. The US military remained in the country until 1985.

The US invasion of Grenada served as a warning to other Caribbean leaders that the USA would not tolerate communism in the Caribbean, even on a small island. Only two Caribbean countries, Trinidad and Tobago, and Guyana, opposed the US invasion.

Activity 7.7 Find out more about the USA's invasion of Grenada. How long did it last? What impact did it have on the Grenadian economy and society?

Panama

> **FAST FACTS**
> - Panama is officially the Republic of Panama (in Spanish, the República de Panamá).
> - It is a Central American country which occupies the southernmost extension of the isthmus connecting with the north-western corner of South America, covering 75,517 square km.
> - It is a narrow, curved strip of land, bordered on the north (along a 1,160 kilometre coastline) by the Caribbean Sea, on the east by Colombia, on the south (along a 1,690 kilometre coastline) by the Pacific Ocean and on the west by Costa Rica.
> - The capital is Panama City.

Panama became independent from Spain in 1821 after Simón Bolívar cleared New Granada (present-day Ecuador, Colombia, Panama and Venezuela) of Spanish and loyalist forces, and voluntarily joined the Colombian union. Three attempts to secede from Colombia in the 1830s failed. This union was to affect US involvement in Panama in the 20th century.

US involvement in Panama really started in 1849, however, with the California gold rush. Gold had been discovered in that state, and thousands of people headed west, hoping to strike it rich by becoming prospectors. Since an overland route through the USA was very difficult, many of the prospectors chose to go through Panama, which sparked off a wave of prosperity in that country. The building of a transcontinental railroad was negotiated in 1845 with Colombia. The Bidlack-Mallarino Treaty of 1846, which came out of this deal, granted the USA the right to protect the line and free transit across the continent. The Panama railway, built by US investors, opened in 1855, and it alone was so profitable that an entire city, Colón, was built because of it. To ease transport further, construction of the Panama Canal was started.

Activity 7.8 Find out more about the California gold rush. How long did it last? How did it affect the development of the USA?

> **FAST FACTS**
> - Caribbean workers helped build the Panama Canal. Between 1900 and 1914, about 60,000 Barbadians went to Panama to work on the Canal and about 20,000 of them died during its construction.

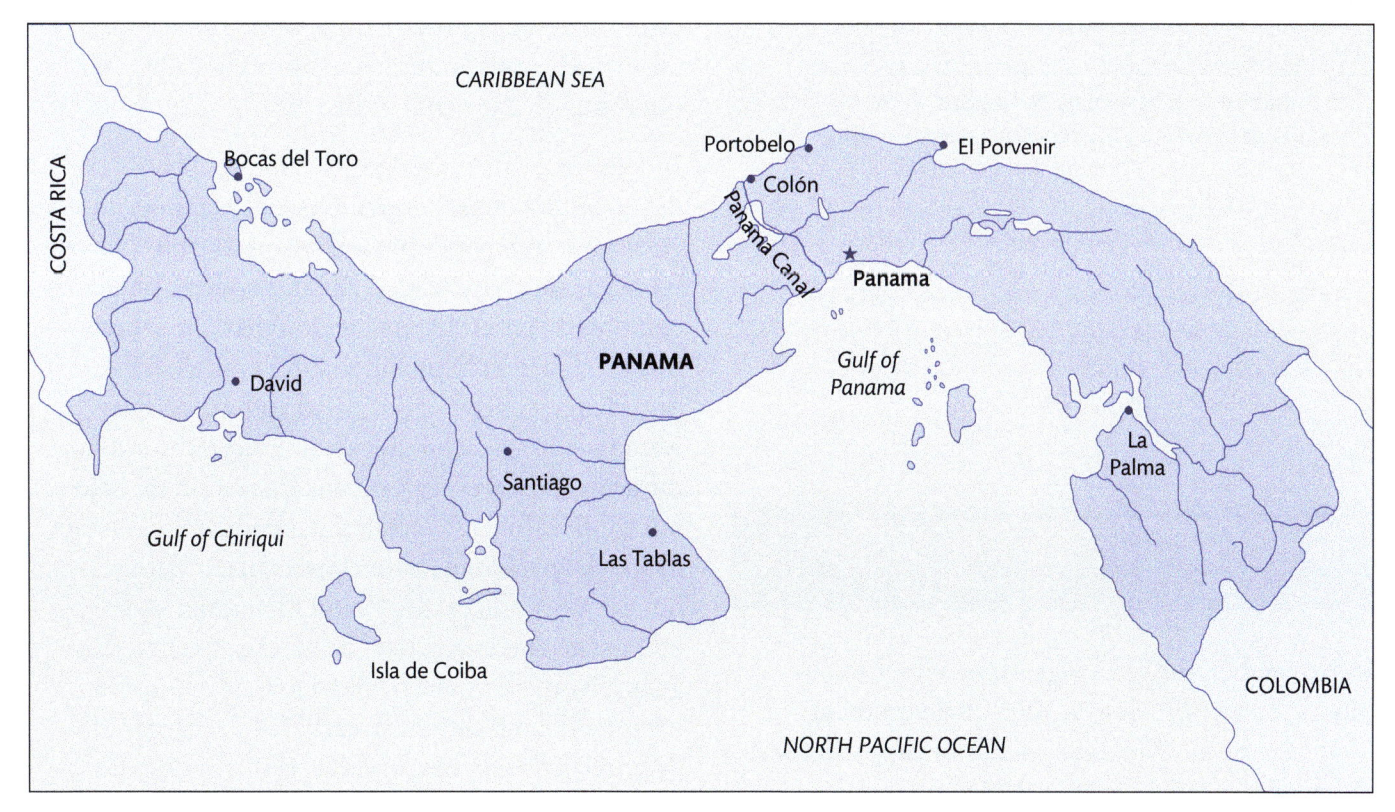

7.10 Panama

However, the sudden prosperity, as it usually does, brought social unrest. Between 1850 and 1900, Panama had 40 different administrations, 50 riots and 13 US interventions. The Americans wanted to keep control of the routes from Panama to California. In 1903, after the Colombian Senate put off ratifying a canal treaty, the US government led by President Theodore Roosevelt organized and financed a separatist movement, recognizing the Panamanian insurrection on 6 November. In other words, the USA effectively engineered a revolution in another country in order to protect its strategic interests. This was a main cause for distrust by Latin Americans of US foreign policy.

> **The Panama Canal (in Spanish, Canal de Panamá)**
> - It is a canal of the lake-and-lock type connecting the Atlantic and Pacific oceans through the narrow Isthmus of Panama in Central America.
> - Its length from deep water in the Atlantic to deep water in the Pacific is about 82 km.
> - It is one of the two most strategic artificial waterways in the world, the other being the Suez Canal; ships sailing between the east and west coasts of the USA, for example, can shorten their voyage by about 8,000 nautical miles by using the Panama Canal instead of rounding Cape Horn.
> - The first attempt to build the canal was in 1879, organized by Ferdinand de Lesseps, a French diplomat who had supervised excavation of the Suez Canal, who formed the Compagnie Universelle du Canal Interocéanique and began work in 1881 on cutting a sea-level channel through the isthmus. Poor planning, disease and accusations of fraud led to the collapse of the enterprise in 1889, and in 1894 the French company was reorganized as the Compagnie Nouvelle du Canal de Panama.

Separatist movement describes where a group of particular culture, ethnicity, religion, race, government or gender is kept separate from the larger group.

In November, the USA signed the Hay-Bunau-Varilla Treaty, which gave the US government control over the Panama Canal Zone in perpetuity. Work on the canal began in 1907 and the completed canal was opened in 1914. This new waterway changed US naval strategy, since US warships could now move quickly between the Atlantic and Pacific oceans, and this made it even more important to the USA that the Caribbean remain politically stable so the USA would have no problems defending the canal.

The new constitution gave the USA the right to send its army into Panama to quell disturbances. Political and economic unrest brought military interventions by the USA in 1908, 1912, 1918 and 1925.

After the Second World War, riots became frequent and there were increasing calls for the Americans to get out of Panama. Student protests against the regime of Ernesto de la Guardia (elected in 1956) and the USA led to the imposition of a state of siege in 1958. More disorders occurred during the first four months of 1959, and a march on Independence Day into the Canal Zone to raise the Panamanian flag was stopped by the police.

In 1968, the Panama National Guard staged a successful coup under Colonel Omar Torrijos Herrera. In 1977, a new treaty was signed, called the Panama Canal Treaty, which put the canal under Panama's jurisdiction, while the US government retained responsibility for the operation of the canal until 1999.

In 1989, the USA invaded Panama and overthrew the country's de facto ruler, General Manuel Antonio Noriega, commander of the Panama Defence Forces. Noriega, who had headed Panama's secret police, had once been a CIA operative. When the army's head resigned in September 1983 to pursue the presidency, control of the guard and the country went to Noriega, who quickly increased the size of the army, closed every media organization that did not support him and created paramilitary regiments to attack or assassinate his opponents. Custom houses, post offices, the Colón Free Zone and other state-run enterprises were taken over by the guard. Noriega was also linked to the Colombian drug-trafficking cartels. In early 1987, charges of drug-related activities, murdering of opponents and rigging of elections were made public against Noriega by the second-in-command of the National Guard, Roberto Díaz Herrera. In February 1988 in the US courts, Noriega was indicted on counts of drug trafficking and racketeering.

On 11 March, US President Ronald Reagan ordered sanctions against Panama, including the elimination of preferential trade and the withholding of canal fees. On 15 December 1989, the Noriega-led assembly of the Panamanian government declared war against the USA. The next day Panamanian soldiers killed an unarmed US marine officer dressed in civilian clothes.

The US government responded quickly. On 19 December, US President George Bush sent troops to Panama with orders to capture Noriega to face drug charges in the USA and to protect Americans in Panama. All resistance was quickly overcome by the US troops. Noriega was given refuge in the Vatican embassy in Panama, where he remained for 10 days, finally surrendering to the US army on 3 January 1990. He was then transported to Miami, tried and jailed.

> **Activity 7.9** Draw up a list of similarities and differences between the various interventions listed in this section.

Impact of the USA on the Anglophone Caribbean

> **Activity 7.10** Read this extract and answer the questions that follow.
>
> Extract from Selvon, S., *A Brighter Sun*, 1952
>
> 'The nearest Trinidad ever got to actual warfare was one dark night in 1942. An enemy submarine sneaked into the harbour and blasted two ships at anchor. The explosion shook the city. No one knew what it was about, but terror remained for a few days. A compulsory service bill was never proclaimed because there were sufficient volunteers.
>
> Later that year the western coast of the island was mined and entrances to the harbour closed to shipping and night sailings by coastal steamers shopped. By this time 15,000 people formally engaged in food production had either joined the forces or were working with the yanks. Foodstuffs were subsidized by the government to keep down prices. In a queue for bread at a baker's in George Street, a fight broke out between two men and one ran for the cutlass which a coconut vendor had stuck in his donkey cart. At least three marriages were hastened because the girls were pregnant. Tentative programmes of essential works were drawn up in anticipation of unemployment when work on the bases ceased. American authorities agreed to a methodical release of labour so as not to disturb the economic system. The sugar crop dropped to a low level because no one wanted to work in the fields again, but shipping difficulties prevented the export of the reduced quantity and the population was urged to consume more sugar. Steps were being taken to introduce rationing. A tiny island called Patos midway between the capital and the mainland of Venezuela was handed over to the Venezuelan Foreign Minister. Hooliganism increased.'
>
> **a** State two ways in which the war impacted Trinidad
> **b** Why do you think there was a queue for bread?
> **c** Why was unemployment anticipated?

Political effects

It may not be coincidental then that the countries the USA intervened the most with, such as Haiti, Cuba and the Dominican Republic, were the least democratic in the Caribbean. Puerto Rico is an exception to this rule, perhaps because the relationship there was based mainly on economic cooperation. Generally, the USA interfered more in the former Spanish and French colonies than the British ones.

Whereas civic and political organizations had begun to emerge in the British, French and Dutch colonies, the US engagements catalyzed the creation of authoritarian and militaristic leaders and groups. In the Dominican Republic, all senior officials were removed and replaced by US military officers.

In respect to the Anglophone Caribbean, the US presence was most fully felt during the Second World War, when the USA got 99-year leases for military bases in Trinidad, Guyana, Antigua,

St Lucia, Jamaica and the Bahamas. In Trinidad, the bases became a political issue in the 1950s, reaching a stage where Prime Minister Eric Williams led a protest march in 1960 for the USA to return the land to Trinidad and Tobago.

Generally, US political interference in the Anglophone territories was confined to the invasion of Grenada, though the USA takes the lead in helping the British government remove the leftist leader Cheddi Jagan in Guyana between 1961 and 1964. By the 1980s, the US opposition to communism and its demonstrated willingness to use force or aid to keep the Caribbean out of the hands of the USSR seemed to bear fruit. Prime ministers in Jamaica, Barbados, St Lucia and Dominica all aligned themselves with the USA, promising their citizens that such a relationship would have economic benefits for the islands. However, the 1980s was a period of economic recession and Caribbean countries had rising unemployment and inflation.

Historically, emigration from the region to the metropolitan countries has been one method through which Caribbean people have dealt with economic hardship. The USA has long been a preferred destination, with New York city being especially popular for Afro-Caribbeans. However, US government policy has always tried to restrict such immigrants. The Immigration Act of 1924 was based on race, trying to exclude Asians and Caribbeans by imposing a quota system based on the number of nationals already living in the USA. Only when the USA entered the Second World War were restrictions temporarily lifted since the country needed cheap labour at home as its troops went to fight. The US Manpower Act allowed Caribbean people short-term contracts to work in the USA, but this was repealed in 1952. In this same year, the USA passed the Immigration and Nationality Act, which retained the same quota system as the 1924 act. The 1952 act was changed in 1965, replacing quotas with seven new categories for allowing immigrants to the country, with family unification being the main criterion. In 1976, the US government added a preference for immigrants coming from countries in the Western hemisphere and also increased the number of immigrants allowed. By the 1980s, there were entire Caribbean communities in major cities such as New York, Miami and Washington, as well as in New Jersey and Connecticut.

Now that the Cold War has ended, the USA is less concerned about security in the Caribbean, but helping maintain political stability is still standard USA policy. This is shown by the US maintaining embassies in five Anglophone islands: the Bahamas, Barbados, Guyana, Jamaica, and Trinidad and Tobago. Cuba is no longer considered a serious threat. Caribbean leaders, now that they are unable to use the USSR as leverage for US aid, are now paying more attention to increasing trade within the region and attracting foreign investment from other countries, especially China.

US concerns in the region now centre around drug trafficking, particularly involving cocaine. This has made Caribbean governments pay more attention to drug-fighting initiatives than they otherwise might have. Since the 9/11 attacks in 2001, terrorism has become an additional security issue, with US attention being particularly focused on Guyana, and Trinidad and Tobago, because of the Muslim population in these countries.

Such issues, as well as others, have caused the USA to attach policy measures to loan, investment and trade agreements. As a result, several Caribbean countries have had to pass legislation to protect the environment and reduce official corruption. The USA has not abandoned the Monroe Doctrine, but the super-power now largely tries to pursue its objectives through economic and political methods, rather than through military force.

Activity 7.11 List the countries to which people from the Caribbean have migrated. How did emigration from the region affect these countries?

Economic effects

The economy of the USA has long had a strong influence on the fortunes of the Caribbean. In the financial depression of the 1880s, the failure of banks in New York and Boston caused the collapse of many plantations in the region. The wealthy elite of the Caribbean, especially those from Jamaica, Barbados and Trinidad, abandoned their homes and went to New York and Boston via the new steamships that plied the seas between the USA and the islands.

The USA remains the main trading partner for all Anglophone Caribbean countries. More than half of all exports from the region go to the USA and nearly one third of all imports are supplied from the USA. Also, US companies are the main investors in the Anglophone region, although Trinidad and Tobago, because of its oil and gas reserves, gets the largest amount of investment. Various Caribbean islands refine about 16% of the oil used by the USA and nearly half of the oil imported by the USA passes through the region. This brings extra revenue to the islands.

The US market also influences the underground economy in the Caribbean, mostly in respect to illegal narcotics such as cocaine and marijuana. Since these drugs are grown and processed in South America, and there is a high demand in the USA, the Caribbean islands serve as transhipment points. This trade affects the economy in several ways: hidden income, money laundering and social costs (through more expenditure on security, through official corruption and violent crime). However, because of the money spent in the 'war on terror' and the occupation of Iraq, the USA has also reduced expenditure on drug-trafficking initiatives in the region.

The Anglophone Caribbean has generally seen a growth in GDP over the past decades, but the region remains vulnerable to shifts on the world market, particularly in the prices of commodities (raw goods such as oil, bauxite, sugar and coffee). As the region is so dependent on its trading links with the USA, a downturn in the US economy has negative effects on all the Caribbean islands. Tourism is also very sensitive to a downturn in international economies.

Cultural effects

What are your favourite movies? What are your favourite songs? Chances are that, no matter what you answer, some of the films or music originate in the USA. As we mentioned at the start of this chapter, the USA is the most culturally dominant country in the Western world.

It is therefore a common complaint in the Anglophone Caribbean that people, especially young people, pay more attention to US culture than their own. They watch US movies and listen to US music. In the Dominican Republic, the US sport of baseball became popular with top players from the Dominican Republic getting valuable places on US baseball teams. This dominance of, for example, films, music and sport from another culture is sometimes referred to as 'cultural imperialism'.

Even our diet has changed because of American influence. US fast food franchises now have outlets in most Caribbean countries. As a result, many Caribbean people now regularly eat burgers, pizza, hotdogs, submarine sandwiches and other dishes which were irregular fare just 30 years ago. One consequence of this is that, just as in the USA where two out of every three people are overweight, obesity is becoming a health problem in the Caribbean.

Activity 7.12

- List two US fast food outlets in your country.
- Write the names of two US artists you are familiar with.
- State two ways in which you believe you and your friends are influenced by US culture.

However, even if this is so, it has not affected the cultural output from the Caribbean, which continues to produce reggae, calypso, soca, chutney and other indigenous musical forms. Jamaica produces a fairly steady output of movies. Many of the region's artistes depend on the diaspora Caribbean communities in the USA and in other parts of the world. This is not only because of the small economies within the region, but also because some arts products, such as film, can only be profitable if there is an audience of a certain size to patronize. In respect to food, the existence of US fast food outlets has not eradicated traditional dishes. On the contrary, entrepreneurs in some Caribbean territories have used 'creole' and ethnic dishes (Indian and Arabian in particular) to compete with the US fast food franchises.

Additionally, you should note that culture, however, does not refer only to creative products. It also encompasses values, attitudes and behaviour. Some Caribbean commentators have argued that Caribbean people have adopted the consumer lifestyle of Americans. The upper and middle classes, as well as higher-paid workers in the mineral industries, buy goods such as televisions and vehicles, as do Americans. Apart from this, most people from the Anglophone Caribbean do not have the same values as Americans. Caribbean people have more traditional values, where religion is important, the family is viewed as the most important social institution and the average person obeys those in authority. These are also the values of many Americans in the southern parts of the USA, but generally US attitudes towards family, religion and authority are very different from those of Caribbean people (see more on this in Chapter 9). Americans often move out of the family home as soon as they reach the age of 18, their constitution separates religion from state and their political system gives the president less power than prime ministers.

Activity 7.13

List the ways in which the USA influence is visible in your country in:

- food
- music
- fashion.

REVISION QUESTIONS

1 Examine the impact of the USA on any one named Caribbean territory. *(25 marks)*

2 a State two aspects of Fulgencio Batista's administration which the Cuban people did not like. *(4 marks)*

   b List three reasons why there was a revolution in Cuba in 1959. *(6 marks)*

   c Discuss two ways in which Fidel Castro attempted to improve the lives of Cubans. *(6 marks)*

   d Explain three reasons for the conflict between Cuba and the USA up to 1962. *(9 marks)*

   (Total = 25 marks)

Reference and recommended reading

- Dookham, I. *The US in the Caribbean*, London: Collins Caribbean, 1985
- Maingot, A. P. *The United States and the Caribbean*, London: Macmillan Press, 1994
- Selvon, S. *A Brighter Sun*, Essex: Longman, 1952
- Shepherd, V. and Beckles, H. *Freedoms Won: Caribbean emancipations, ethnicities and nationhood*, Cambridge: Cambridge University Press, 2006

8 Caribbean political development

This chapter will answer the following questions.
- What attempts were made to unify the British Caribbean up to 1985?
- How successful were these attempts?
- Why was the Federation of the West Indies established?
- What factors led to the failure of the Federation of the West Indies?
- Who were the key personalities involved in the Caribbean integration movement and how did they contribute to integration?
- What constitutional arrangements were made by the non English-speaking Caribbean territories as alternatives to independence?

Why does each Caribbean island have its own government? After all, even the largest islands have populations and land areas which are no bigger than a city in the USA or Europe. Some of the smaller islands would barely make a village in those countries, yet each island has its own parliament, flag, civil service and all the other trappings of government. In one view, this is wasteful and unnecessary. People who favour regional integration argue that, if the Caribbean was unified under one government, there would be more prosperity for the Caribbean people, it would be easier to go from one island to the next and the region would be more influential in the world, since the entire Caribbean would speak with one voice.

Such people sometimes cite the West Indies cricket team as an example of what the region would achieve if all the islands worked together. A team from Jamaica or Barbados would hardly even reach the World Cup but, because the West Indies draws on players from all islands, the team is a force to reckon with.

However, these arguments have never been able to persuade the political leaders in the islands to make integration a reality, even though nearly all of them say they are in favour of such an arrangement. Citizens of the larger territories, such as Jamaica and Trinidad, feel that a single Caribbean government would only benefit the smaller countries and drain the resources of the larger islands.

Activity 8.1 Would Caribbean integration benefit the people of the region? Would it benefit your territory specifically? Discuss with your class and draw up the pro's and con's of this debate.

In this chapter, we look at some of the attempts at putting several territories under one government and why such arrangements failed. You will also learn how most Caribbean countries moved from being colonies of the British Crown to independent governments and how actions by the Caribbean people influenced this change.

Imperialism the rule by more powerful countries over weaker ones as a result of invasion or occupation.

Early attempts at federation

'The overwhelming majority of West Indians have a sense of oneness – to them the West Indies is "home"… The outside world considers the West Indies a unit, and by imperial as well as local action the Caribbean area has been brought together in functional cooperation for a wide variety of purposes.'
Paul Knaplund, 1956

The idea that all the British Caribbean islands should be under one government has been around since the 19th century. It actually happened in 1871, with the Leeward Islands, but that arrangement came to an end early in the 20th century when a federation of all the British islands was proposed. Barbados and the Windward Islands had one governorship till 1885, then that was also dissolved in preparation for a larger federation. However, this proposed federation of the Leeward Islands, Windward Islands and Barbados sparked off riots in Barbados because the Barbadians did not feel this arrangement would benefit them, so the plan was abandoned. In 1882, a Royal Commission also recommended closer union. Nothing happened, though, and another Royal Commission in 1896 actually reached the opposite conclusion, seeing no benefit to federation or even a unified civil service.

In the 19th century, there was only minor integration, when St Kitts and Nevis joined, and when Tobago was linked to Trinidad in 1889. These two arrangements have lasted to the present day.

At the turn of the 19th to the 20th century, the British government was considering federating all its colonies throughout the Empire. This would have meant that the colonies would have more self-rule, and also be represented in Britain's parliament. In 1926, there was an Imperial

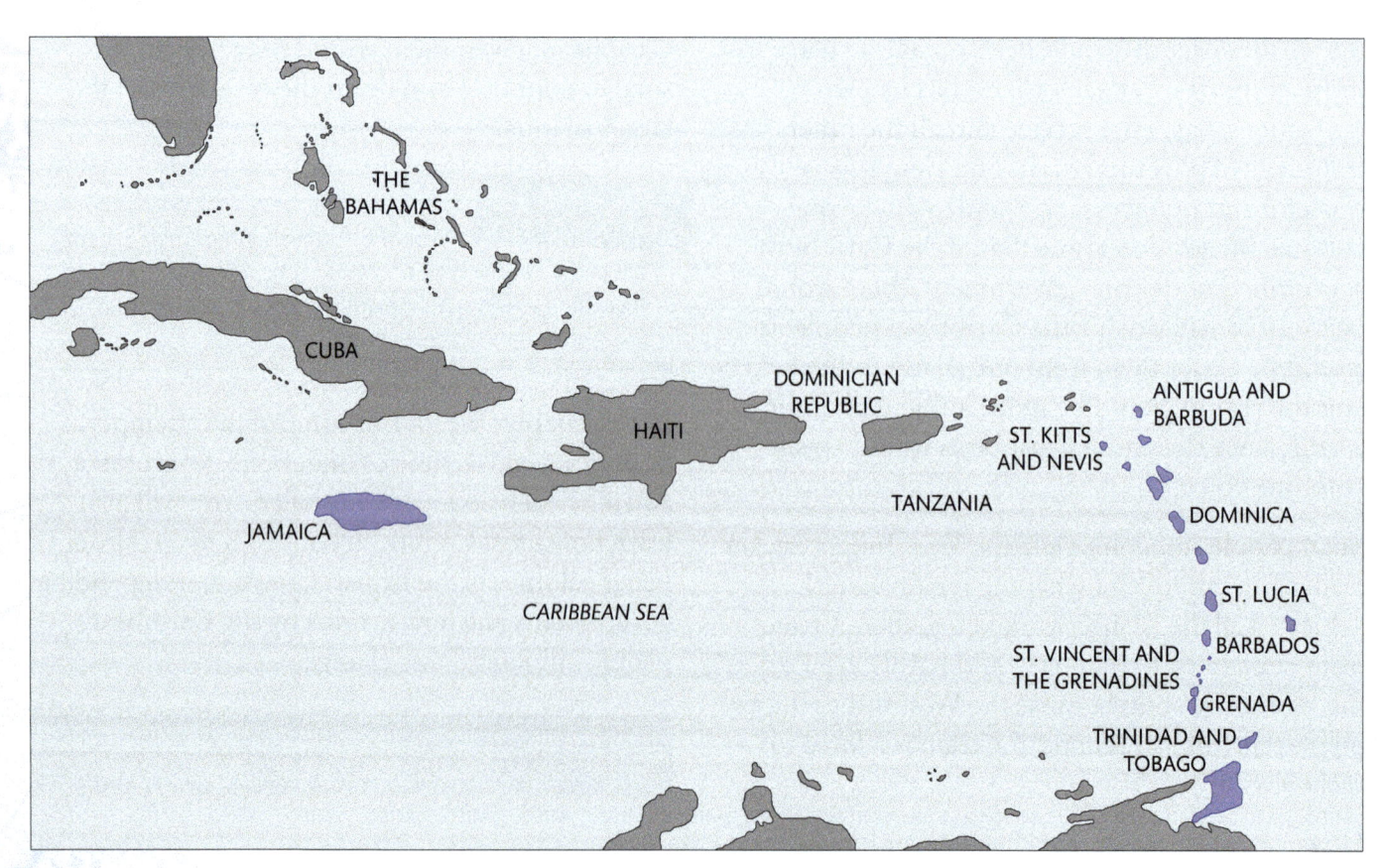

8.1 The Anglophone Caribbean region

Conference which debated the issue. In the end, however, both the 'Mother Country' and its colonies voted against such an arrangement. The British did not want its colonies influencing policies, and the colonies did not want the added responsibilities, such as raising their own revenues and having leaders elected instead of appointed, that came with a federal arrangement.

In the British Caribbean specifically, the legislatures on each island preferred to keep their own authority rather than share it in a federation and the difficulties of communication between the islands and financing also made them unwilling to integrate. In 1922, the Under-Secretary of State for the Colonies, Major Wood, said that federation would depend on popular support, but his opinion was that such support would not be given by the populace, especially in Barbados. He identified diversity of culture and economic organization, and difficulties of communication as the main barriers to federation. In 1931, there was a conference of governors on the issue. They failed to reach any agreement, however.

> **Early steps towards regional integration**
>
> **1904** – The Quarantine Conference led to the establishment of uniform quarantine laws and practices for region.
>
> **1932** – West Indian islands took over the imperial contribution for the Cane-Breeding Station, based in Barbados.
>
> **1933** – The Imperial College of Tropical Agriculture was set up in the Leeward and Windward islands. It replaced the 1898 Imperial Department of Agriculture.

> **Colonial regional organizations**
>
> The **Caribbean Commission** was established in 1942 to improve the economic and social well-being of the people of the Caribbean.
>
> The **Regional Economic Committee** was established to investigate different ways to achieve economic unity.
>
> The **Imperial Marketing Board** was set up to unify tariffs and other taxes in the different colonies.
>
> The **Advisory Council on Agriculture** was created so that information on scientific research and other matters related to the improvement of agriculture could be more easily distributed to farmers and the authorities in each colony.
>
> The **British West Indian Sugar Association** liaised with merchants and suppliers in the metropolitan countries and lobbied the governments on laws related to sugar exports.
>
> **University College of the West Indies** was established in 1948 as an external college of the University of London. Its main aims were to train personnel and conduct research. It went on to become the University of the West Indies in 1962.

Activity 8.2

Choose any one of the organizations mentioned above. Find out more about this organization. Use the following headings as a guide.

a When was the organization established?
b Why was it established?
c What are its main areas of work?
d How did it promote Caribbean integration?

You can present your research through either a PowerPoint presentation or a poster.

Even cooperation in specific areas ran into opposition. In 1933, for example, the British government proposed a joint agricultural department and a new colony made up of the Leeward and Windward islands. This suggestion was rejected by Grenada, which feared that this new department would sever the profitable agricultural arrangement Grenada had with Trinidad, since the new department would have taken over all research and marketing. When the Second World War started in 1939, the economic hardships brought on by the war led to bulk purchasing and bulk sale of commodities in the islands. This was a kind of regional cooperation which had never happened before. However, the Caribbean leaders did not see this as a formula for integration, but only as a temporary necessity caused by the war. So the bulk buying and selling stopped after the war ended in 1945 but, in the same year, meetings of the Associated Chambers of Commerce and the West Indian Conference in Barbados put federation on the front burner.

There was also an important conference in 1946, when the newly formed Caribbean Labour Congress discussed the issue, signing several resolutions about how a Caribbean federation should operate. In 1947, the Colonial Secretary invited the Bahamas, Barbados, British Guiana, British Honduras, Jamaica, the Leeward Islands, the Windward Islands, and Trinidad and Tobago to debate the issue. All the territories except the Bahamas voted in favour of the conference, which was held in Montego Bay in Jamaica. Delegates passed 14 resolutions, including a unified currency, the creation of commissions to examine customs unions and the unification of the region's civil services.

Customs union a government department responsible for taxes on all goods imported into a country.

The inclusion of Jamaica highlighted the problem of communications. Although air travel was expanding in the region, it was not commercially viable and it has never become so, with all regional air carriers being subsidized by their governments.

Roleplay

Imagine that you are a young West Indian man who has just completed studies in England in 1955, where you were exposed to ideas of Caribbean integration. Share these ideas with:

- former classmates who were also educated in England about five years before you
- your friends from the village where you grew up.

Even back in the 1940s and 1950s, steamship, and cable and radio facilitated communication between the Caribbean and the 'Mother Country', rather than inter-island contact.

Nationalism an ideology which holds that people's loyalty should be to their country, rather than their race, religion or any other identity.

During the Second World War, US bases were established in several British Caribbean islands. This was important, because the presence of the Americans aroused resentment, especially when Caribbean women began favouring the US soldiers, and this had the political effect of spurring calls for national independence. 'The establishment of American bases within the area was probably the single most important factor contributing to the development of West Indian nationalism,' noted one writer.

Activity 8.3

Read the calypso and answer the questions which follow.

Lyrics to Jean and Dinah 'Slinger Francisco – The Mighty Sparrow'

> Well, the girls in town feeling bad
> No more Yankees in Trinidad
> They going to close down the base for good
> Them girls have to make out how they could
> Well is now they park up in town
> In for a penny, in for a pound
> Yes, is competition for so
> Trouble in town when prices drop low.
> (Chorus)
> So when you bounce up Jean and Dinah
> Rosita and Clementina
> Round the corner posing
> Bet your life is something they selling
> And if you catch them broken
> You can get it all for nothing
> Don't make a row
> The Yankees gone and Sparrow take over now.

- Who are the 'Yankees'?
- What do you think they girls are selling?
- What happened when the 'Yankees' left?

This nationalist movement undermined the idea of a regional government. There were no strong economic reasons to push for integration, either. The products of islands competed with one another, rather than supporting one another – for example different islands produced sugar, rather than one producing sugar and another coffee. Flying fish was exported from Barbados to Jamaica, and Jamaican carrots were exported to Trinidad. Only rice from British Guiana was truly regional, and that was mainly because rice supplies from the Far East had been cut off by the war.

In the Windward Islands, the question of constitutional reform for local self-government took priority over federation. The Windward Islands Conference agreed that constitutional reform had to happen before federation with the Leeward Islands. A 1946 despatch from the Secretary of State for the Colonies recommended that both matters be discussed at the same time. He wanted 'a strong central government with wide powers over all matters of general administration'. This would have meant that the colonial and presidential councils would be changed into local councils and this never happened.

A commission was set up by the British government to examine the challenges of a federation of the British Caribbean territories. The Rance Report (named after the commission's chairman, Hubert Rance) was published in 1949. These were the report's main points.

- The purpose of federation was to ensure political independence.
- Federation alone would not solve the Caribbean's economic problems, but it was a necessary condition to do so.
- A strong central authority was needed, rather than delegation by other agencies.
- A federal authority would be responsible for public order, education and agriculture.

> 'We are pledged to guide colonial people along the road to self-government within the framework of the British Empire.'
> Secretary of State for the Colonies, 1942

A committee was then set up by the Caribbean leaders to decide whether the Caribbean governments should follow the report's recommendations. In the end, most of the commission's main principles were rejected by Caribbean leaders. This was because accepting them would have meant that these leaders would have had to reduce their authority, and perhaps risk losing elections if the federation policies were unpopular.

Universal adult suffrage the right to vote by all adults (usually defined as all people aged 18 years and over)

Groupwork

In preparation for this group work, each of you should prepare a list of points for and against federation. When you have done this, arrange a whole-class debate on whether the Caribbean islands should or should not federate. The class will then vote on the motion, in favour of or opposed to it, with the majority deciding the outcome.

As a result, the central (or federal) government was given few responsibilities. The committee argued that local organization was needed to administer public order, education and agriculture properly. The following decisions were taken by the committee.

- The federal government would be financed by 25% of customs duties from each territory.
- The federal government would see to external loans, while internal loans would be raised by both federal and the local units.
- There would be a two-chambered legislative body – a Federal House of Assembly and a Senate.
- Election would be by universal adult suffrage, which had already been granted in Jamaica and Trinidad.
- Senators would be nominated.
- Allocation of seats in the assembly would be by population size.
- Allocation of seats in the senate would be one per country.
- The Governor-General would appoint an executive.
- The executive would be made up of 14 members – eight appointed by the Federal Prime Minister, six by the Governor-General.
- The Governor-General would retain the power to block any laws relating to defence, public safety and order, federation, relations with foreign states, currency and divorce.

As you can see from some of these measures, Britain wanted to keep certain powers for itself. This was mainly because it was worried that universal adult suffrage in the Caribbean, which meant that even the poor and uneducated could now vote, might lead to bad choices.

These measures restricted the economic policies a federated British Caribbean could implement, particularly in respect to trade agreements with the non-Anglophone Caribbean territories, such as Cuba, Martinique, Puerto Rico and Suriname. The Governor-General's sweeping powers to appoint an executive also came in for criticism. Not only could he appoint senators, but he could prorogue (dismiss or dissolve) both the Senate and the House of Representatives at any time he chose. This meant that the Federation's Governor-General had all the powers that the governors had had during the time of slavery, whereas the core rationale for federation, from the Caribbean people's point of view, was greater autonomy. Indeed, these provisions in the Federal Constitution actually reduced the independence of countries such as Jamaica and Barbados, where the legislative assemblies, as you read in Chapter 5, had won significant authority for themselves.

> 'Colonial Office policy had always developed within a framework of moral relations; the responsibility of labour brought to the West Indies and the peculiar debt to the historical past of the West Indies had been stressed, for instance, in The Royal Commission of 1896 and again in that of 1938.'
> Lloyd Braithwaite, UWI Principal, 1956

The next major conference on federation was held over a two-week period, 13–30 April 1953, in London. This conference was intended to work out ways to implement the propositions agreed to by the federation committee and the Caribbean political leaders. As implementation was mainly a technical challenge, needing trained and experienced personnel, the Colonial Office was in charge of this part of the process.

The British government agreed to give £500,000 for the establishment of the federation. This was not enough in the view of the Caribbean leaders, who expected continued aid from Britain, and the delegates pressed for increased funding to set up the federation. Loans to finance the federation process were to be raised by individual territories, but the federal government would not take any of this money for first five years. This measure was intended to prevent the federal government from being able to tax the territories.

It had been recommended that membership in the federal legislature would exclude membership in the federal parliament. This proposal was rejected, allowing political leaders in individual territories also to be part of the federal government. The Caribbean leaders wanted this in order to prevent the federation officials from having any authority over them.

From the very start, the federation's powers were limited. A draft federal constitution was written, which among other clauses instituted almost total freedom of movement and goods. This caused controversy, but it was Trinidad which objected most strongly to the measure, since the island had always been a favoured destination for Caribbean immigrants, especially those from the smaller islands. Trinidadians were worried that federation would mean even more people from the small islands coming to live in their country. As a result, there was a separate conference on freedom of movement held in Trinidad. By contrast, the Barbados House of Assembly passed resolution stating that, 'This House stresses that freedom of movement for West Indians among the federated units of which they are native is essential to any scheme.' As a compromise, the Trinidad government relaxed restrictions on a immigrants. The provision was only temporary though, and the federal government would, at the end of five years, have been able to decide on all immigration regulations.

The final agreement was signed in London in 1956. For historical reasons, it was agreed that the proposed title, 'The British Caribbean Federation' would be replaced by 'The Federation of the West Indies'. The biggest difficulty was the customs union, which particularly affected Jamaica, because most of its revenues came from this source.

Eventually, it was decided that there would be an integrated trade policy and that a customs union, including internal free trade, would be introduced as soon as possible.

Apart from customs, conflict centred around two main points: independence versus continued authority of Colonial Office, and in which island to put the federal capital. A commission made up entirely of non-West Indians decided the second issue, although the final choice was up to the Standing Federation Committee whose members were all Caribbean. Although the other matters were settled, the location of the federal headquarters eventually caused the most argument. The commission had recommended Barbados. Trinidad was ruled out because of corruption and political instability, while Jamaica was considered too big.

However, the choice of Barbados was also opposed by Caribbean critics when the Standing Federation Committee met in 1957. They felt that the British bureaucrats preferred Barbados because it had remained a British possession, even keeping its Old Representative System, and because it had cooler sea breezes than the other two islands. The commissioners had said in their report that if Jamaica was chosen, the headquarters should be located in the hills. Tempers were heated by the fact that an Englishman filled the post of the Head of the Commission to establish the federation and that, on the day before the meeting, a European had been appointed as Chief Justice of the Supreme Court in the British Caribbean.

In January 1958, after 11 years of discussions, debates and conferences, the Federation of the

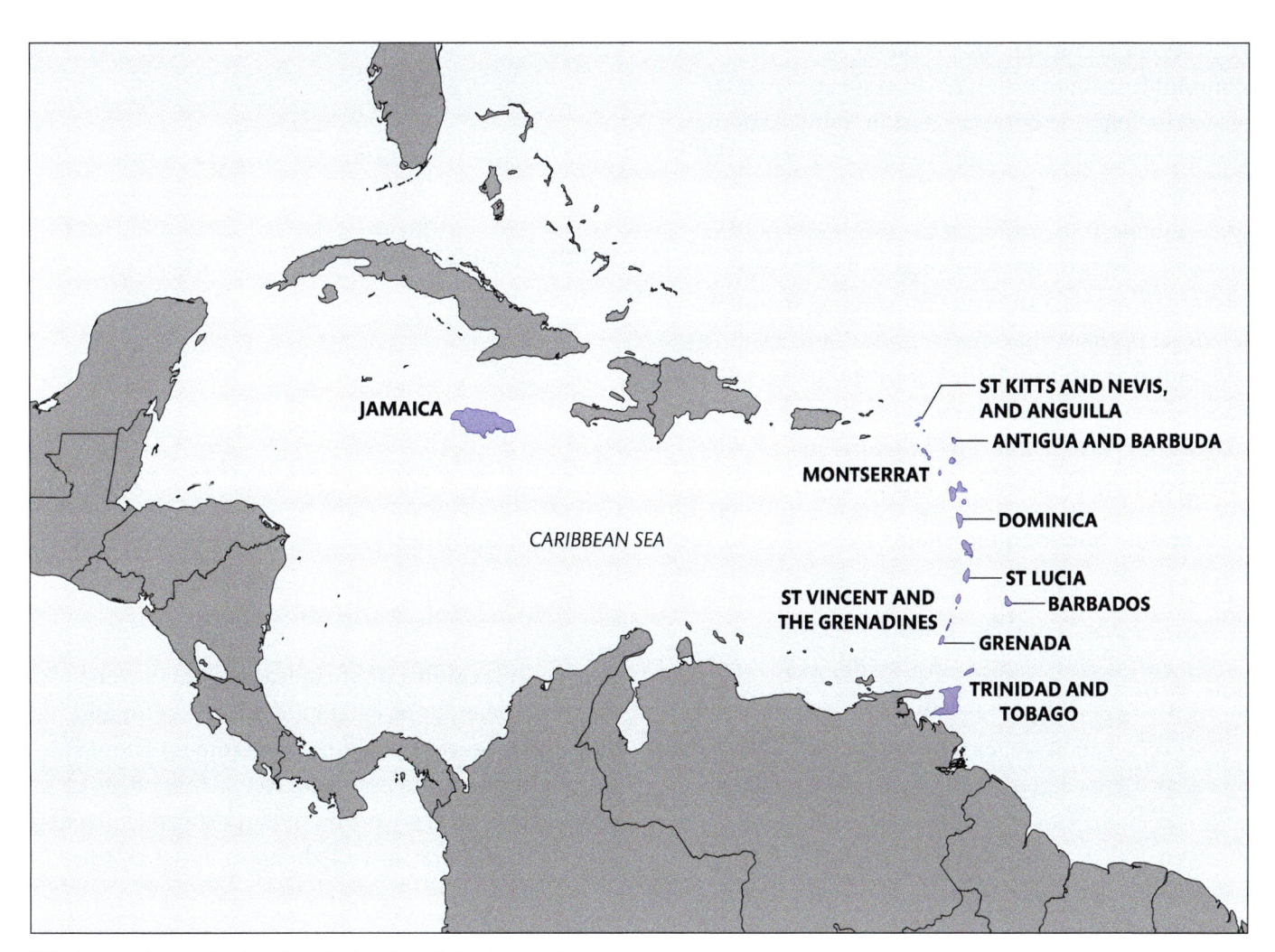

8.2 The member territories of the Federation of the West Indies

West Indies was finally formed. The capital was in Port-of-Spain and the Prime Minister was the Barbadian Grantley Adams. The Federation had 10 members. It lasted just four years, and was dissolved on 31 May 1962, after Jamaica withdrew following a referendum held in that island in September 1961.

Members of the Federation of the West Indies	
Antigua and Barbuda	Montserrat
Barbados	Jamaica
St Kitts and Nevis, and Anguilla	St Lucia
Dominica	Trinidad and Tobago
Grenada	St Vincent and the Grenadines

Many reasons have been given by various commentators for why federation failed. Some reasons are technical: the problems of communication between territories separated by sea, of having one currency and unifying customs duties. Some are political: the various leaders did not want to give any power to a regional government, it was difficult to coordinate public services across different islands and there was disagreement over the rules for electing members to a federal parliament. Some reasons for the failure of federation are cultural: the people in the various territories never really thought of themselves as Caribbean people, but only as Jamaicans, or Antiguans, or Grenadians and so on.

One commentator argued that:

> 'The Federation was less a colonial initiative than one inspired by British officials anxious to curtail the costs of empire for a weakened post-war Britain. The Federation was doomed to fail as an artificial creation that accurately represented neither the will of the majority nor the historical reality of the ties among the British West Indies.'

The coat of arms of the Federation of the West Indies

This coat of arms was used during the duration of the federation. The 10 circles on the shield represent the 10 territories which made up the federation. The British lion at the top of the shield represents the British government.

8.3 The Federation of the West Indies coat of arms (1958)

Another commentator said:

> 'Britain fostered a sense of division among its colonies as a way to enhance its control. There was little direct communication and trade among the colonies, as each dealt primarily with London. Significant disparities in the level of economic and political development among the British colonies also undermined efforts to promote a sense of cohesiveness and unity of purpose.'

Among the region's political leaders, there were different ideas about what federation was for and how much power the federal government should have. The two main concepts were a federation in which the central government had extensive powers over the members; and a federation in which the members had more independence to act, especially in economic policies. The first concept could not work for political reasons (the individual Caribbean leaders wanted to hold on to power), while the second could not work for economic reasons (once each territory was pursuing its own policies in respect to exchange rates, trade agreements and production, unity would be undermined).

These factors, in one way or another, led to the end of the Federation of the West Indies. But the failure also catalysed independence and nationalist movements, as many Caribbean leaders had seen federation mainly as a way to empower self-government in their territories.

Reasons for the break-up of the Federation of the West Indies

- The federal budget was insufficient.
- There was lack of popular support for the federation from the majority of the Caribbean people.
- There was disagreement among federal leaders.
- Jamaica, and Trinidad and Tobago, felt disillusioned by the idea of federation and were interested in full independence.
- The idea of a common 'Caribbean people' had not yet developed fully and each territory had its individual identity.

Activity 8.4 Number the reasons given above and place them in order of importance to the demise of the Federation of the West Indies, starting with the most important as number 1. Compare your order with that of another student in your class.

Activity 8.5 Read the verse of the calypso and answer the questions which follow.

'Caribbean Man' by Black Stalin

'You try with a federation
De whole ting get in confusion…
Mister West Indian politician
I mean yuh went to big institution
And how come you cyah unite 7 million.'

- Who is Black Stalin addressing in his calypso?
- State two reasons why the federation ended in 'confusion'.
- What does Black Stalin mean when he says 'yuh went to big institution'?
- Give three reasons why you think Caribbean politicians were unable to make the federation a successful one.

Protests and politics

We come now to the development of democracy in the British Caribbean. As in most parts of the world, this was not achieved without struggle, but in the West Indies there were only a few instances of violence on the road to self-government.

It was inevitable that the people in the Caribbean should begin to press for more and more freedom to rule themselves. As you have learned, this started even under slavery, when the Caribbean slaves defied the planters in several areas. After emancipation, this process continued and accelerated as mixed-race and black people reached positions of power, through wealth, professional qualifications and being members of the legislature. In Jamaica in 1884, for instance, all the members of the legislative council were white, but by 1910 there were five mixed-race and one black person out of the 14 officials.

In the early 20th century, widespread dissatisfaction with the economy led to more and more criticism of the British government and its treatment of the West Indies. The population was increasing rapidly and so was unemployment and underemployment. More and more people were also getting at least a primary school education and literacy levels were rising. This meant that more people could now formally express their criticisms of the British government, as well as claim that, because of their education, they should have more say in the politics of the colonies.

Labour organizations were a key part of this process. These first emerged during the period between the two world wars – that is, in the 1920s and 1930s. The formation of these organizations was partly impelled by shortages of basic commodities, such as food and housing, during the First World War. From 1918 to 1924, strikes and protests happened more and more often. In 1917, the oil and asphalt workers in Trinidad went on strike, as well as in 1919 and 1920. In Jamaica, workers held public marches and strikes in 1918 and 1924.

Caribbean workers started organizing themselves in labour organizations. Before 1918, all trade unions were illegal in the British Caribbean. In Britain, trade unions had been legalized in 1871, but this law did not extend to the colonies. In the early 1920s, the British Guiana Labour Union, which was led by a popular cricketer named Herbert Critchlow, unionized the mainly Afro-Caribbean dock workers and then expanded the union to include the Indian agricultural labourers. In Jamaica, Alexander Bustamante founded the Bustamante Industrial Union, while in Trinidad the Oilfield Workers Trade Union was formed, and the Manpower and Citizens Association in British Guiana.

In 1927, a Royal Commission was sent to British Guiana to examine the unrest taking place in the territory. The commission condemned the constitution on the ground that the government had never been able to govern. This system did not support effective trade or a good financial policy and it hampered the colony's efforts to get loans for development. The commission recommended that the colony's two legislative bodies be merged into one. However, this resulted in British Guiana in 1928 having less, rather than more, self-government.

Income tax was introduced in 1929. At this time, the only people allowed to vote were those who had house or land valued over US$480, or annual rent of over US$96, or annual income of over US$300. Voters also had to be able to read and write. The British commission recommended that these qualifications be lowered, so more people could vote, but the commission in British Guiana rejected this proposal in 1934, arguing that doing so would 'let in persons who by their lack of education (moral as well as mental) would be still more open to extraneous influences and less likely to exercise an independent judgement'.

In Trinidad, the Trinidad Workingmen's Association, led by a Trinidadian named Arthur Andrew Cipriani, arranged a successful strike by dockworkers in 1919, an action which led to sugar workers and others taking their own protest actions. In response to these protests in Trinidad, the government passed a trade union ordinance in 1932 which, for the first time, gave legal recognition to such bodies. However, the workers refused to register as trade unions under this new law because the Act did not allow peaceful protests. In 1933, in the capital city of Port-of-Spain, there was a small demonstration by unemployed people. In 1934, a larger demonstration, involving between 400 and 500 unemployed people, led to a commission of inquiry.

The Trinidad Workingmen's Association (TWA)

This organization was founded in 1897 by Alfred Richards. Its members were mostly lower middle class. Its first President was Walter Mills, a pharmacist, but the majority of the members were labourers and carpenters.

The TWA functioned as a trade union and a political pressure group but its main objective was to bring elective government to Trinidad and Tobago. It favoured constitutional reform and wanted the working classes to play a role in the government. It wanted to:

- improve working and sanitary conditions
- reduce taxes on foodstuffs and agricultural tools used by labourers
- improve transportation
- introduce saving banks.

The TWA acted as a pressure watchdog for the rights of the workers and kept a close watch on government policies, while attempting to get its members more politically involved.

Another important trade union leader in Trinidad was the Grenadian Tubal Uriah 'Buzz' Butler, who along with the Indian lawyer and communist activist Adrian Cola Rienzi organized a major strike among oil workers in 1937.

> **Roleplay**
>
> Imagine you are a labour leader in your country. You have the opportunity to address about 100 workers. Write a short speech convincing them to stay away from their jobs.

In Jamaica, the decline in the standard of living during the 1930s led to a major strike by sugar estate workers in 1938. This turned violent when they clashed with police, and the strike action spread to dock workers, banana employees and even public service employees. The strikes were all suppressed by the colonial authorities and resulted in 29 people being killed and 115 wounded.

In 1935 in St Kitts, protest by sugar workers was met with a military response from the government, with policemen firing on protesters, resulting in one death and eight people wounded. The British government also sent a warship with marines to patrol the island. In that same year in St Vincent, protests over new taxes again resulted in police action. One person was fatally shot and the British government again sent a warship. The riots lasted several days and a state of emergency was declared which lasted three weeks. A similar event happened in St Lucia, involving coal loaders, when the governor quickly mobilized the local militia and requested reinforcements from the British government, but in this case no one was killed. Table 8.1 lists protests that took place between 1935 and 1938.

However, it took the world economic depression of the 1930s and riots in the Caribbean territories for the British government to take Caribbean workers' demands seriously.

Table 8.1 Protest action 1935–38

Year	Island	Event
1935	St Kitts	Strike by sugar workers
1935	St Vincent	Demonstrations against customs duty hike
1935	British Guiana	Labour disputes on sugar plantations
1937	Trinidad	Strike by oil workers
1937	Barbados	General strike
1937	British Guiana	Uprising on sugar estates
1937	St Lucia	Strike by sugar workers
1937	Jamaica	Protests by sugar workers
1938	Jamaica	Strike by dockworkers

In 1938, largely because of these protest actions, a Royal Commission headed by Lord Alfred Moyne was appointed to analyse and report on the conditions causing unrest in the West Indies. The Moyne Commission's preliminary report recommended the creation of a West Indian welfare fund financed by the British government. This money would be used for educational, social and economic development. The report also recommended that the members of the legislative councils be restricted to three, the qualifications for membership reduced and adult suffrage be introduced.

The final report was submitted in 1940, just after the Second World War started. In British Guiana, the report emphasized the racial rift between Afro-Guyanese and Indo-Guyanese. It recommended increased democratization of government, and giving the right to vote to women and people who did not own land. In 1943, Governor Sir Gordon Lethem reduced property tax qualifications for holding office and made elected members a majority in the Legislative Council.

The Colonial Welfare and Development Act, which gave force to some of the recommendations was passed in 1940. Other important milestones occurred in 1944, when women were given the vote in Jamaica and Trinidad. In Barbados, this happened in 1942, and in 1951 in the Leeward and Windward Islands.

> **Quotes from the report of the Moyne Commission**
>
> **Agriculture:** 'The most obvious line of improvement is for the West Indies to produce more food for their own consumption. This is no new problem, though it has become more acute owing to the increase of population. The Royal Commission of 1897 approached it from another point of view and recommended the development of land settlement. It has not however been possible to reach a solution on these lines, partly for the reason I have just given that the peasant prefers to grow cash crops and partly because the general level of agricultural efficiency is extremely low.'
>
> **Finance:** 'Without British help it is beyond the power of the West Indian Colonies to achieve their own salvation. Everything possible has been done by officials and teachers, who have put up with lower scales of pay than elsewhere in the Colonial Empire and who have made gallant efforts to build up health, education, and other social services on hopelessly inadequate resources. The local revenues of these Colonies amount to less than 7 million a year, and it will be realized that the additional million pounds a year which the British Government has now promised for welfare work will enable great improvements to be made.'
>
> **Politics:** 'In spite of the social unrest however we found everywhere a striking loyalty to the British Crown and connection, and discontents are laid at the door of Colonial Office administration. This is perhaps a satisfactory fiction and reminds one of the tendency in many religions to divide phenomena between the opposite responsibilities of good and evil spirits, Downing Street here taking the diabolical part.'
>
> **Federation:** 'Although we have recommended considerable constitutional changes, we could not feel that the immediate grant of complete self-government based on universal suffrage, or the political federation of the whole of the scattered area would really touch the present difficulties. Unification of services wherever possible would clearly be of advantage, and we have recommended a practical test of how far federation can surmount the geographical difficulties in these widely dispersed communities by extending the federal system of the Leeward Islands so as to include the Windward group as well (Dominica, St Lucia, St Vincent, Grenada).'

Table 8.2 Political parties of the Caribbean

Decade formed	Country	Main political parties
1930s	Barbados	Barbados Labour Party, Democratic Labour Party
1930s	Jamaica	People's National Party, Jamaica Labour Party
1950s	St Lucia	United Workers Party, St Lucia Labour Party
1950s	St Vincent and the Grenadines	People's Political Party, St Vincent Labour Party
1950s	St Kitts and Nevis	St Kitts and Nevis Labour Party, People's Action Movement
1950s	Dominica	Dominica Labour Party, People's National Movement
1950s	Guyana	People's National Congress, People's Progressive Party
1950s	Trinidad and Tobago	People's National Movement, Democratic Labour Party
1960s	Antigua	Antigua Labour Party, Progressive Labour Movement

British Guiana obtained universal adult suffrage in 1952. Universal adult suffrage spurred the formation of political parties. However, many Caribbean political parties were formed out of the trade union movement. This is why nearly every party has the word 'labour' or 'people' in its title.

In Jamaica in 1942, Bustamante founded the Jamaica Labour Party. Before this, the People's National Party had been formed by Norman Manley in 1938. In 1939, a committee of the Legislative Council presented a draft constitution for the island. This proposed a small elective house, a nominated council and an executive committee to liaise between the governor and the legislature. However, the Colonial Office rejected this, in favour of a unicameral body with a large majority of elected members, with the governor's powers remaining the same.

Table 8.3 Political status of 27 Caribbean countries

Sovereign status	Countries
British dependency	Anguilla, Bermuda, British Virgin Islands, Montserrat, Turks and Caicos
Territory of the USA, France, Netherlands	US Virgin Islands, French Guiana, Aruba, Netherland Antilles
Territory of the USA, France	Puerto Rico, Guadeloupe, Martinique, St Martin
Independent	Bahamas, Antigua and Barbuda, Barbados, St Kitts and Nevis, St Lucia, Trinidad and Tobago, St Vincent and Grenadines, Jamaica, Grenada, Belize, Cuba, Suriname, Guyana, Haiti

Other important political parties were formed by Grantley Adams in Barbados and by Eric Williams in Trinidad. Many of the Caribbean political leaders in the 1950s and 1960s based their careers on nationalism and becoming independent countries. Table 8.3 shows the present political status of the Caribbean countries, including the non-Anglophone ones.

The political system in the Anglophone Caribbean is based on the British Westminster system (that is, a two-party state whose successful candidates make up a bicameral Parliament, with one chamber of elected members and another chamber of appointed members). However, although the institutions are formally the same as in Britain, the practice is different in the Caribbean. For example, Britain has had the same main two parties which contest elections for several centuries. In the Anglophone Caribbean between 1944 and 1991, 130 different political parties (some of them, however, with a membership of just a few people, sometimes less than 10) contested 101 elections in 10 countries. Of the 101 parties just 24 won elections on their own (that is, not in a coalition with other parties).

In most of the territories, power has changed hands between parties on several occasions. In Barbados and in Trinidad and Tobago such changes have occurred peacefully. In Jamaica, there has often been violence during elections although the outcome is accepted by politicians on either side. Between 1944 and 1998, administrations in Jamaica have changed 13 times, with the People's National Party winning in seven elections and the Jamaica Labour Party winning in six. In Barbados, shifts have happened 11 times, with the Democratic Labour Party winning six elections and the Barbados Labour Party winning five.

However, in some territories one political party has held power for a very long period. In Antigua the first change of government did not happen until 1971 when the Antigua Labour Party lost, and in Trinidad and Tobago the People's National Movement held office from 1956 to 1986.

Activity 8.6

CARIFTA was established on 15 December 1965. Its members were:

- Antigua and Barbuda
- Barbados
- Guyana
- Trinidad and Tobago
- Dominica
- Grenada
- St Kitts and Nevis, and Anguilla
- St Lucia
- St Vincent and the Grenadines
- Montserrat
- Jamaica
- Belize (then British Honduras)

The main aims of CARIFTA were to:

- promote trade among member countries
- increase the variety of goods and services available for trade among member countries
- remove tariffs and quotas on the goods produced and traded among member countries
- promote fair competition among members
- promote industrial development in the less-developed countries.

The manifesto of CARIFTA was redrafted in 1973 and it was changed to the Caribbean Common Market: CARICOM.

Do some research on CARIFTA. Specifically, find out three reasons why this organization failed.

Caribbean Community (CARICOM)

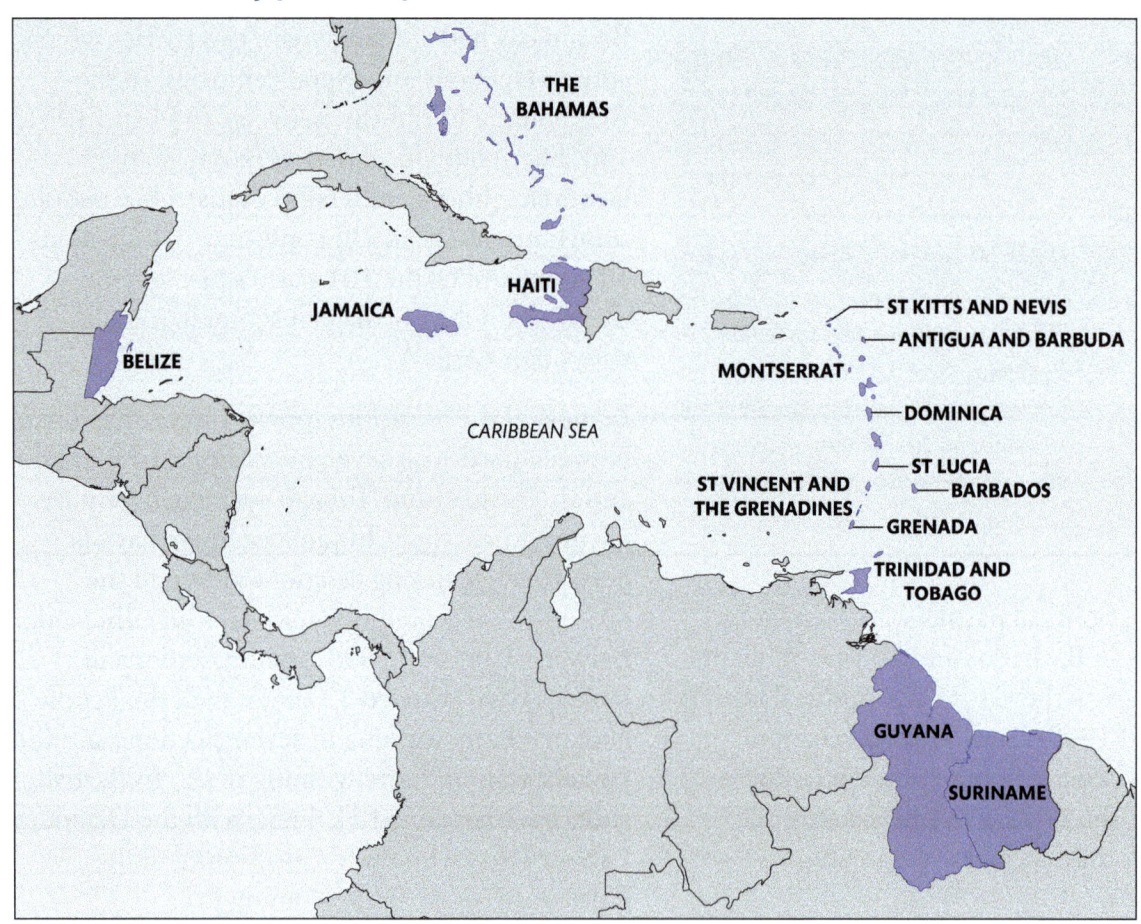

8.4 CARICOM members

CARICOM was established on 4 July 1973 by Commonwealth Caribbean leaders at the Seventh Heads of Government Conference. The main idea was to transform CARIFTA into a Common Market. Thus, they wanted to establish the Caribbean Community and the Common Market would be an integral part of this Caribbean Community.

The members of CARICOM are:

Antigua and Barbuda	Haiti
Jamaica	Belize
The Bahamas	St Lucia
Montserrat	Dominica
Barbados	St Vincent and the Grenadines
St Kitts and Nevis, and Anguilla	Grenada
Guyana	Suriname
Trinidad and Tobago	The Bahamas (not a member of the Common Market)

The main aims of CARICOM are to:

- allow for the free movement of labour and capital throughout the region
- coordinate and syncretize the region's agricultural, industrial and foreign policies
- improve living and work standards in the region
- promote sustainable development in the Caribbean
- ensure that the Caribbean countries can engage in positive competition
- internationally promote free trade and the free circulation of goods.

Activity 8.7

- Is your country a member of CARICOM today?
- Who is the head of CARICOM?
- State three ways in which CARICOM has benefited your country.
- State two ways in which your country has been important to CARICOM over the years.

> **Activity 8.8**
> Conduct research on V. C. Bird (both the father and the son). What have been the most significant contributions of the Birds to Antigua?

Women in politics

The role of women in Caribbean politics extends back to the days of slavery, from Nanny the Maroon leader with a girdle of knives who led runaway slaves in battle against the British, to Doña Maria de Maceo who is known as 'the mother of Cuba' for her role in the Ten Years' War.

In the 20th century, Caribbean women played important roles in getting the vote and other rights for Caribbean people. Luisa Capietillo, who was born in 1880 and died in 1922, was a labour activist in Puerto Rico who fought for equal rights for women. During the labour strikes of the 1930s, Capietillo and women from other territories played an important part in handling the trade unions' finances, as well as standing with the men in picket lines and joining protest marches. Despite this, trade unions in the region have remained a mostly male enclave.

Yet, unlike many other regions in the world, most women in the Caribbean have always been part of the labour force, with the percentages ranging from 68% of women in the Dominican Republic to 91% in Trinidad and Tobago.

In the latter part of the 20th century, Dame Nita Barrow of Barbados was perhaps the best-known Caribbean woman in international politics, representing her country at the United Nations between 1986 and 1990 and contesting for the post of UN Secretary-General while there. After this, she became the Governor-General of Barbados.

In electoral politics, Dame Eugenia Charles of Dominica became that country's and the Caribbean's first female Prime Minister in 1979. She was also the first female lawyer from the island, getting called to the bar in 1949. Charles was called 'the Iron Lady of the Caribbean' (Britain's first female Prime Minister, Margaret Thatcher, being the original 'Iron Lady'), and became known for her anti-Cuba position and, unlike many other Caribbean leaders, for not tolerating corruption. When the USA invaded Grenada, Charles featured prominently among the Caribbean leaders who supported the US action.

Janet Jagan, a US nurse, was the wife of Guyanese leader Cheddi Jagan. She was elected to the Parliament in 1970 and served as an MP for 27 years. She was appointed as President of Guyana after her husband died in 1997, a post she continued to hold after winning the general election in that year. However, she was able to serve for only two years before ill health led to her resignation. Jamaica's Portia Simpson Miller briefly led the People's National Party after winning party elections and was appointed Prime Minister in 2006, while Kamla Persad Bissessar from Trinidad and Tobago, who also emerged as leader in her party's elections, was elected Prime Minister in 2010.

> **Activity 8.9**
> Choose any one of the following female Caribbean leaders:
> - Janet Jagan
> - Kamla Persad Bissessar
> - Portia Simpson.
>
> Make a poster showing the leader's:
> - personal life
> - political achievements
> - contribution to the development of women in the leader's country and the wider Caribbean.

Political protests

Although most of the protest actions in the Anglophone Caribbean were rooted in trade unionism (issues related to salaries and working conditions), the region also has a history of unrest caused by electoral issues (dissatisfaction based on political outcomes). In the late 1960s and early

1970s, there were riots against the police in Montserrat, a secessionist movement from people living in the Rupununi savannah area in Guyana and military action by the British government in Anguilla when that island seceded from the St Kitts and Nevis association. Some other key political events involving mass protests were as follows.

- In Dominica in June 1979, the government was removed in a constitutional coup. A coalition of 28 groups opposed to the government was formed, made up of opposition politicians, trade unions, banana farmers, other farmers, small businessmen and members of churches. The supporters of this 'Committee for National Salvation' took to the streets, throwing stones at ministers' offices, and shutting down the island. The government resigned and elections were held in 1980 (delayed one year because of the damage caused by hurricane David) to legitimize the new administration.
- In St Kitts and Nevis in 1993, inconclusive election results caused street demonstrations. No party had won a clear majority. The St Kitts and Nevis Labour Party and the People's Action Movement had both won four seats, but the St Kitts and Nevis Labour Party claimed victory because it had received 54% of the votes while the People's Action Movement had gained 41%. However, the People's Action Movement formed a coalition with the Nevis Reformation Party, which had gained one seat of the three in the sister isle of Nevis. The protestors forced the government to hold new elections 10 months later. This time the St Kitts and Nevis Labour Party won seven of the eight St Kitts seats.
- A similar situation occurred in St Vincent in 1998, with the New Democratic Party winning eight of the 15 seats but just 45% of the total vote. The Unity Labor Party got just seven seats, but 55% of the popular vote. The opposition threatened to make the country ungovernable if fresh elections were not held within six to nine months. The government refused, saying it had won the election properly under the British Westminster system. This was true, since voting is by constituencies, so a party might win a majority of votes in most constituencies but, because there are more voters in some constituencies, still end up with not getting a majority of votes for the country as a whole. Two years later, the government passed a Pensions and Gratuities Bill which would have increased pensions for MPs and their spouses. This caused massive protests from teachers, nurses, prison officers and public servants, and these protests were supported by the Chamber of Commerce and the Caribbean Federation of Employers. The capital city was shut down, and business closed in support of the strikers. In response, the government tried to withdraw the legislation, but the opposition claimed that the Bill had been passed and could not simply be withdrawn. The opposition insisted that the Prime Minister had to resign, while the Prime Minister argued that, if he did, it would mean that the government had been removed by means other than elections. Eventually, both sides agreed to an early election in 2001.
- In Trinidad on 26 February 1970, 200 students at the University of the West Indies demonstrated to protest against Canadian racism, based on the arrests of Caribbean students at a Canadian university. This protest expanded into a movement headed by Black Power activists, with demonstrations lasting until April 21, when a state of emergency was declared by the government. Nine leaders of the movement were arrested for unlawful assembly, but 10,000 people came into the capital city on March 4, paralyzing all normal activity. Over the next few days, Molotov cocktails were thrown into the home of a government minister and several businesses were vandalized. On March 23, the Prime Minister Eric Williams addressed the nation to announce that he had fired one minister who had claimed that the Black Power activists were communists, and that special taxes would be levied on businesses to reduce unemployment. The demonstrations continued

and a general strike was planned for April 21 and 22. A state of emergency was declared and 15 leaders arrested. A section of the army mutinied, but the rebellious soldiers were contained by the coast guard, who arrested them. The government continued in office, and all the leaders, including the soldiers, were eventually freed after trial.

> **Activity 8.10** On a blank map of the Caribbean indicate the political status of the countries mentioned in Table 8.3 on page 203. Use a key and suitable colours or symbols.

Personalities behind the Federation of the West Indies

> **Activity 8.11** Select members of your class to represent each of the personalities described in this section. Imagine they are all having a discussion where they compare the causes they are fighting for and their successes.

> ### ARTHUR A. CIPRIANI
> (1875–1945)
>
> A man of European ancestry whose family owned cocoa estates, Cipriani became a champion of the working-class masses when he revived the Trinidad Workingmen's Association (TWA). Cipriani's social conscience was aroused when he served as an officer with the British West Indies Regiment in Egypt, where as a white West Indian he often had to defend the enlisted black men from racial prejudice. When he returned to Trinidad, he went up for elections to the Legislative Council in 1925, winning and holding his seat there until 1945. He also won the post of mayor of Port-of-Spain eight times. From his twin bases as a council member and head of the TWA, Cipriani was one of the earliest Caribbean voices pushing for West Indian federation.
>
> He criticized Crown Colony government as anti-democratic, calling it a 'glorified autocracy', and argued that this form of government did not serve the Caribbean people. He said that since all its members were nominated rather than elected they served the privileged class rather than the common man. 'Crown Colony officialdom tends to a close one, deaf, reserved, autocratic, independent, and sometimes indifferent to local opposition,' he stated in a memorandum to the 1938 Royal West Indian Commission. Cipriani campaigned for reforms that would benefit the working-class population, such as the right to trade unions, workmen's compensation, old-age pensions and a minimum wage. He wanted higher taxes on foreign-owned businesses and more local control of the economy. As federation was one of his core ideas, Cipriani helped make the movement for constitutional reform a regional one.

8.5 A statue of Arthur A. Cipriani

ALEXANDER BUSTAMANTE
(1884–1977)

A Jamaican trade unionist and politician, Bustamante was the person most directly responsible for the break-up of the Federation of the West Indies. The son of an Irish planter and an Indian-mixed mother, his birth name was Alexander Clarke, but he took the surname of a sea captain who befriended him during his youthful years in Spain. Bustamante spent most of his early adulthood in Europe and the USA, returning to Jamaica when he was 48 years old.

He formed the Bustamante Industrial Trade Union and became the foremost labour leader in Jamaica. In 1942, he was jailed for sedition because of his strong criticisms of the colonial system. After he was released, he formed a political party called the Jamaica Labour Party (JLP), which won the 1944 general election. He became the island's first Chief Minister in 1953, but lost the 1954 election.

When the Federation of the West Indies was formed in 1958, Bustamante immediately started campaigning for Jamaica to pull out. He was able to get the government to hold a referendum on the issue in 1961, in which a majority of the Jamaican electorate agreed that Jamaica should withdraw.

In 1962, the JLP won the general election and, under the new system of government, Bustamante became the island's first Prime Minister.

8.6 Britain's Princess Margaret dancing with Sir Alexander Bustamante, Jamaica 1962

THEOPHILUS ALBERT MARRYSHOW
(1885–1958)

A Grenadian journalist and politician, Marryshow founded a periodical called *The West Indian*. Through its pages, as well as personally by travelling often to the various islands, Marryshow campaigned for representative government for the colonies and federation.

He was elected to the Grenadian legislature in 1924, retaining his post until one year before his death. When the Federation of the West Indies was formed in 1958, his life-long work earned him a position as one of Grenada's two senators, but he died that same year. More than any other single figure, Marryshow is seen as the key Caribbean figure behind the Federation.

"I hope for the day when our islands linked together in an administrative and fiscal union the West Indian Dominion will take its place, small though it may be, in the glorious Empire"

GRANTLEY ADAMS
(1898–1971)

The first (and only) Prime Minister of the Federation of the West Indies, Adams was educated in Barbados and at Oxford University in England, where he studied law.

He returned to Barbados in 1925 and entered politics in the 1930s, getting elected to the House of Assembly in 1934. One of his first acts after being elected was trying, unsuccessfully, to get a law passed to make universal adult suffrage the basis for election to the assembly. At that time, property ownership was needed for someone to qualify as a voter. He was President of the Barbados Progressive League, which in 1938 became the Barbados Labour Party (BLP). In the 1940s, Adams was the main figure in Barbadian politics, and succeeded in changing the face of the island's governance by ending the dominance of the white merchant and land-owning group in the Electors Association. He argued that the Caribbean territories should have self-government because the region's people could manage their own affairs. 'West Indians have reached a stage of political maturity and educational development where they feel quite competent to assume full responsibility for the

8 Caribbean political development

8.7 Grantley Adams

administration of their territories,' he stated. Under his leadership, the BLP ended the dominance of the white merchants and planters in the assembly and helped win internal self-government for Barbados in 1958.

Adams was head of the government from 1946 to 1958, but never won an election after that.

WILLIAM DEMAS
(1929–98)

Considered one of the Caribbean's leading economists, Demas wrote several books and many essays on the economic challenges for regional integration. He was born in Port-of-Spain in Trinidad on November 14, 1929 and was educated at Tranquillity Boys' Intermediate Government School and Queen's Royal College. He won an Island Scholarship in 1947 and went on to study economics at Cambridge University in England. After teaching economics at McGill University, Canada, in 1966–67, he was appointed Head of the Carifta Secretariat.

8.8 William Demas

In 1974, he became President of the Caribbean Development Bank. He was also Chairman of the United Nations Development Committee. In 1988, he became Governor of the Central Bank of Trinidad and Tobago. One of his last major assignments on behalf of Caricom was to serve as Vice Chairman under Shridath Ramphal on The West Indian Commission, where he had the opportunity to advance his ideas further on developing the region's social, economic and political institutions.

In his book *Economics of Development in Small Countries*, Demas argued that integration was essential for the region's economic survival, since this was the best way to overcome the limits of size. He also argued that political integration would allow the Caribbean to have more influence on international affairs and, without such integration, the territories would be marginalized. Although his case for political integration was ignored by the region's politicians, his ideas on economic integration did serve as a foundation for CARIFTA in 1965, and its replacement CARICOM in 1973.

Demas received several honours during his lifetime, including the Humming Bird Medal (Gold), Guyana's Cacique Crown of Honour, Barbados's Companion of Honour, Colombia's Order of San Carlos and the Order of the Caribbean Community.

SHRIDATH RAMPHAL
(1928–)

An eminent lawyer and Caribbean figure, Ramphal was educated in Guyana, at the University of London and at Harvard Law School. He qualified as a lawyer in 1951. He worked in the legal department of the Guyanese government until 1961, when he was appointed Assistant Attorney-General of the Federation of the West Indies, an assignment which lasted one year.

He became the Attorney General of Guyana in 1965 and was knighted in 1970. In 1975, he became Secretary General of the Commonwealth and in 1989 Chancellor of the University of the West Indies. In 1991, Ramphal was appointed Chairman of the West Indian Commission, which travelled throughout the Anglophone Caribbean to hold talks with the Caribbean people on regional unification.

8.9 Shridath Ramphal

Alternatives to independence

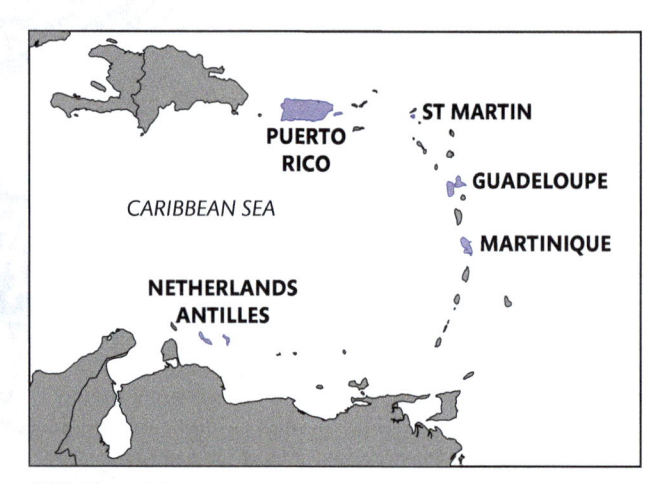

8.10 Map of the region

Metropole the parent state of a colony.

As Table 8.3 on page 199 shows, some Caribbean countries have chosen to remain politically linked to the metropoles which colonized them. In this section, we look at three different arrangements for these islands.

Puerto Rico

Puerto Rico is a commonwealth in free association with the USA. This means that its residents are US citizens. According to the constitution of 1952, the governor is equivalent to the prime minister in the British Caribbean countries. The governor is elected by a vote from citizens for a term of four years. The Puerto Rican parliament is divided into two bodies: a Senate of 27 members and a House of Representatives of 51 members. Members of both houses are elected for four-year terms. In addition, Puerto Rico is represented in the US Congress by a resident commissioner who is directly elected for a four-year term. Although the commissioner can make the island's views known to Congress, he or she cannot vote. The governor appoints all the judges and justices in Puerto Rico's judicial system, with the advice and consent of the Senate. The USA is responsible for the commonwealth's defence. As a commonwealth, Puerto Rico benefits from most US federal social and welfare programmes, but at a level lower than that of the US national averages.

Netherlands Antilles

Netherlands Antilles is a tripartite kingdom in which executive authority is vested in the sovereign of the Netherlands. The sovereign's authority is exercised by a governor nominated by the local government and appointed by the Crown. There is a Council of Ministers responsible to the Legislative Assembly, which is appointed by the governor. The assembly, called the Staten, has 22 members elected to four-year terms by popular vote. The islands are allotted members proportionally, with Curaçao having the largest number. In matters that affect the islands, central government makes all decisions and there are local governments for Curaçao, Bonaire and the northern group of islands. Only in international issues affecting the Netherlands does the metropolitan government exercise its authority.

Guadeloupe, Martinique and St Martin

Guadeloupe, Martinique and St Martin are départements of France, executive authority is represented by a commissioner and other officials, and there is an elected legislative council. There are smaller bodies called communes, each of which is administered by an elected municipal council. The islands are represented in the French National Assembly, in the French Senate and on the French Economic and Social Council. The courts in France have authority over the islands. There are two higher courts (grande instance), two lower courts (tribunaux d'instance), one administrative court and a commercial court.

REVISION QUESTIONS

1. Critically examine the factors which led to the break-up of the Federation of the West Indies. **(25 marks)**

2. Examine the reasons for the labour disturbances in the 1930s in the Caribbean. **(25 marks)**

3. a. State two reasons why attempts were made to unify various Caribbean territories. *(4 marks)*
   b. List two ways in which the British government attempted to unify Caribbean territories. *(3 marks)*
   c. Explain three problems which the British government faced in its attempts to unify Caribbean territories. *(9 marks)*
   d. Explain three problems which Caribbean governments faced in their attempts to unify their territories. *(9 marks)*
   (Total = 25 marks)

Recommended reading

- Demas, W. R. *Essays on Caribbean Integration and Development*, Kingston: Institute of Social and Economic Research, University of the West Indies, 1976
- Emmanuel, P. *Approaches to Caribbean Political Integration*, Cave Hill: University of the West Indies, 1987
- Shepherd, V. and Beckles, H. *Freedoms Won: Caribbean emancipations, ethnicities and nationhood*, Cambridge: Cambridge University Press, 2006

9 Caribbean society 1900–85

This chapter will answer the following questions.
- What was Caribbean society like during the period from 1900 to 1985?
- What was the economic condition of Caribbean people from 1900 to 1985?
- What was done to improve the socio-economic conditions of Caribbean people during this period?
- How did the various ethnic groups relate to each other?
- What were the major religious groups in Caribbean society and how did they change from the pre-1900 period to 1985?
- What changes were evident in recreational activities, art forms and communications?

In the last eight chapters, you have learned about the major events that happened in the Caribbean over the past five centuries. In this chapter, we will discuss how those events have created the kinds of societies we have today. By understanding your society, you can better understand yourself, because all of us are influenced by the history and the culture of the places we are born and grow up in.

Social and economic conditions

Infectious diseases diseases that are spread from one individual to another.

Non-communicable diseases diseases that are not spread through human contact.

In the past century, human beings have progressed more than in the past 100,000 years of our existence. People now live longer and are generally healthier. Fewer babies die at birth. Before the 20th century, the average life expectancy was 30 years. It is now 70 years in most parts of the world and significantly higher in developed nations. Whereas in the past people suffered and died from infectious diseases, the main causes of death now are non-communicable diseases, such as heart disease, diabetes and cancer. Poverty has been reduced more in the past 50 years than in the past five hundred – in fact, the average poor person today lives better than the average middle-class person three centuries ago and the average middle-class person now has far more possessions than the wealthy people of even a century ago. The only region in the world where this upward trend is not yet happening at the same level is sub-Saharan Africa and there are several other countries which have not had the same kind of advances experienced by most of the world. One Caribbean country – Haiti – is on this list, but the region as a whole has been part of this global progress.

In 1900, the total population of the Caribbean was 7 million; in 1960, it had risen three-fold to 21 million; and in 1985 it was 25 million. Table 9.1 shows the rate of growth in selected Caribbean countries for the latter part of the 20th century.

Table 9.1 Population growth 1960–98

Percentage growth	Country
Under 0.5	Barbados, Grenada, St Kitts, Montserrat
0.5–1	Suriname, St Vincent, Dominica, Antigua, Martinique
1–1.5	Trinidad and Tobago, Guyana, Jamaica, Guadeloupe, Netherland Antilles, Aruba, Puerto Rico, Cuba
2–2.5	Anguilla
2.5–3	Bahamas, Belize, British Virgin Islands, Dominican Republic
Over 3	Caymans, French Guiana, US Virgin Islands

Activity 9.1 Give three reasons why you think the population growth rate in the region is so varied. Compare your reasons with those given by a classmate.

Nonetheless, all the territories in the Anglophone Caribbean are still classified as developing countries, even though Barbados ranks high on the United Nations Human Development Index and Trinidad and Tobago is classified as a high-income nation. Unemployment and a wide gap between rich and poor are still the pattern in most Caribbean countries.

After the Second World War, as you read in Chapter 6, economic growth was based largely on the export of minerals and of agricultural products such as bananas and sugar, as well as tourism, while the manufacturing sector also expanded. However, all the sectors which had significant growth (except the banana industry) were foreign-owned. This means that, despite political independence, most important decisions affecting the region's economy were made in other, more developed nations. Not enough use was made of domestic natural resources, savings were too low, Caribbean entrepreneurs rare and technologies mostly imported.

Agriculture, the sector on which the Caribbean economy was founded, has become weaker throughout the 20th century, with most countries in the region importing food, from North and South America mainly, for both local and tourist consumption. In the 1960s, economist W. Arthur Lewis described agriculture as a 'dying industry' and, while the sector continues to provide some significant employment in the smaller territories and in Guyana, it remains underdeveloped because of a lack of mechanization and because agricultural produce is not used in food processing – both key measures to make the sector profitable.

Manufacturing also has been unable to become a significant driver of the Caribbean economies, mainly because the sector has remained heavily dependent on foreign money for investment, imported technology, and imported raw materials and components. Additionally, many of these foreign-owned manufacturing industries set up in the region only because they were allowed to avoid paying taxes for a certain period of time. This has meant that manufacturing spends as much foreign exchange as it earns, so it provides little or no advantage in trade. Similar weaknesses apply to the tourist industry.

Housing

The earliest Caribbean houses were called wattle huts which, demonstrating a West African building technique, had walls of braided twigs. In early times in Haiti, many houses were built from the royal palm trees, using the palm fronds for the roof and the trunks to make the walls. In later centuries, box-like houses painted brightly in blue, yellow and red became the dominant style.

In architecture, a fundamental principle is 'form follows function'. This means that buildings should be designed for effective use. Even if features are put in for aesthetic reasons (that is, to look attractive) these features, in a well-designed building, should have some purpose. When you look at houses, public buildings or office buildings in your country, you can examine whether the materials used or the ways, for example the roofs are designed, adhere to this principle.

By the 18th century, wood-shingled houses had become common. The walls of these houses were made with spider-like two-by-four planks pressed against a triangular roof. In the bigger houses, four-poster beds with mosquito nets were the usual furniture, along with mahogany side tables and mahogany rocking chairs with wicker seats. A unique piece of Caribbean furniture was the planter chair, which had a wicker seat, a round back and long arms that swung out so the planter could put up his legs while a servant pulled off his leather boots.

In the 19th century, cast iron was used to make the first kind of pre-fabricated houses, but these generated too much heat for the Caribbean climate. The influence of the colonial can be seen in many of the old buildings, such as St Nicholas's Abbey in Barbados, which has columns with a veranda, curved arches and four chimneys – a style which is totally inappropriate to the Caribbean in terms of scale or comfort. The houses in Barbados owed much to their British heritage, having Gothic lines and an enclosed veranda, but with delicate fretwork and rectangular shutters that were a Caribbean addition.

Activity 9.2

Find out about the Barbadian chattel house. How were these houses built? What was unique about them? How has this style of architecture influenced houses today?

At the start of the 20th century, more and more people began moving from the rural areas to the urban centres. Until this time, houses were rarely painted, but this became a more widespread practice between the two world wars. The urban movement started right after emancipation, mostly because there were jobs in the towns and cities that paid better, including work on the agricultural estates there. This movement, as it does in countries all over the world, created slums, as the newly arrived people constructed wattle huts (with woven tree branches and leaves), adobe (clay) houses or wooden shacks to live in.

In one settlement located just outside the capital city of Port-of-Spain in Trinidad, writes one historian:

'Laventille and East Dry River for the first time became thickly populated, creating over a century ago sub-standard housing which has continued from then till now, to provide accommodation for successive bands of displaced persons… So great was the exodus that five months later, by the end of December 1838, of the 22,359 former slaves, only a mere 8,000 were to be found on the estates.'

This trend sped up during the Second World War, because of the additional jobs provided by the Americans, and it continued after the war ended in 1945 because there were fewer jobs in the rural areas and more in the urban centres. By 1960, 40% of people in the Caribbean were living in urban centres. By the end of the 20th century, the ratio had increased to 59%. Different territories have different levels of urbanization. It is highest in Puerto Rico, the Bahamas and Martinique, where over 90% of the population live in towns and cities. More than 75% of the people in the US Virgin Islands, Suriname, Cuba and the Netherlands Antilles also live in the urban areas. The countries with largest numbers living in rural areas are Haiti, Grenada, Guyana, Montserrat, St Kitts and Nevis, and St Lucia

In 1950, only seven urban areas in the region had more than 100,000 people, but by 2008 there were 30 such cities in the Caribbean. This has caused significant housing problems in many countries.

Caribbean cities almost all had the same appearance when they were founded, based on Spanish custom. The cities were usually located on the coast and had a central plaza and a grid pattern of streets. All the most important buildings, from government offices to churches, were located around this plaza. Now, while these central districts still have the largest and most impressive buildings, the surrounding areas contain 'shanty towns', typical in many Caribbean cities.

As a general rule, most people in the urban areas live in brick or concrete dwellings, while in most rural areas wooden houses are dominant. Architectural styles have been influenced mainly by wealth and to some extent by culture. Caribbean countries have developed their unique architectural styles based on their historical cultures, the tropical climate and indigenous aesthetics. 'Creole' architectural features are those which have developed locally. Wooden jalousie shutters, for example, used to be a typical feature of houses, and are still common in the smaller islands. Features like porches are British Caribbean, but the woodwork of the eaves, which consists of frills and lacework, are purely local. Dormer windows (the kind that project vertically from a sloping roof) are a French Caribbean feature that help keep houses cool by circulating air under the roof. Houses were often built so their shuttered windows faced east to west, allowing the prevailing winds to cool them more efficiently. The middle classes live in concrete houses, designed along US or British styles, which are enclosed because of the temperate climate in those countries but which are unsuitable for the tropics. The upper classes also mimic this style to a large extent, but it is also among this set of very wealthy people that you will see houses designed for the Caribbean climate and landscape – that is, with high ceilings, large windows and a porch to take advantage of the breeze and allow the tropical heat to dissipate. Such houses use wood and stone in their construction and design, and may even have wooden louvres rather than glass windows.

Activity 9.3 Find photographs or illustrations of three different styles of houses in your country.

Table 9.2 Percentage ratios of the population in urban and rural areas in selected Caribbean countries

Countries with most urban population	%	Countries with most rural population	%
Puerto Rico	98	Montserrat	85
Martinique	98	Trinidad and Tobago	85
Bahamas	91	St Lucia	72
US Virgin Islands	95	St Kitts and Nevis	72

Generally speaking, the countries with the largest proportion of people in the urban areas have a more urgent need for housing. However, it is important to keep in mind how crowded each country is – that is, the ratio of land to population which tells us what the population density of the country is. On this basis, the most crowded Caribbean nation is Barbados, with a population density of 589 people per square kilometre. The least crowded is Suriname, which has three people per square kilometre. You should note, though, that most of Suriname and Guyana (which has four people per square kilometre) have large tracts of forest and swamp, which are difficult to inhabit.

> **What measures were implemented to improve the socio-economic conditions of Caribbean people during the period from 1900 to 1985?**
>
> - Social organizations developed: in the post-1930 period, after the Labour Riots, many groups and organizations were formed which provided assistance to people in impoverished areas. For example, public assistance, soup kitchens and homes for the poor and homeless were established.
> - Trade unions emerged from 1937 onwards which fought for better working conditions of labourers, higher wages and job security. The following is a list of trade unions which were established from 1937 onwards.
>
> **Barbados**
> Progressive League
> **St Vincent**
> Workingmen's Association
> **Jamaica**
> People's National Party
> Jamaica Workers' and Tradesmen's Union
> Jamaica United Clerks' Association
> **Trinidad and Tobago**
> All-Trinidad Sugar Estates and Factory Workers' Union
> Seamen and Waterfront Workers' Union
> Public Works Workers' Union
> Oilworkers' Trade Union

> Federated Workers' Union
>
> Transport and General Workers' Union.
>
> - Labour laws were developed to protect the rights of the workers. Laws pertaining to shorter working hours, workers' compensation, better working conditions, restrictions on child labour and social insurances were debated and put into effect.
> - Universal adult suffrage was introduced so individuals over the age of 18 had the right to vote.
> - In many territories, schools were constructed and primary school education was introduced. In others, secondary schools were built and more students had an opportunity to complete studies at secondary level.
> - The larger and/or richer territories such as Trinidad, Barbados and Jamaica started to build hospitals, highways and secondary roads, housing developments and sport facilities.
> - Welfare schemes, including free education and school meals in Barbados, were all very important in improving the socio-economic conditions of Caribbean people.

Cost of living

As you learned in Chapter 8, the rising cost of living was a key factor behind the protests and demonstrations in the 1930s in the British Caribbean. The government in the various countries tried to ease the burden by spending more on public services, such as education and health. In 1900, this expenditure was just US$7 per person, but by 1960 it had risen to US$69 per person.

The increase is not as much as it seems, however, because the price of goods and services would also have gone up in those 60 years. This is called inflation. A useful indicator of the cost of living is the inflation rate, which is the percentage by which prices rise from one year to the next. For example, if your pen costs $1 today and $2 next year, the inflation rate was 100% for your pen. For most of the second half of the 20th century, the Caribbean had an average inflation rate of between 3% and 5%. In other words, every year people were paying between 3% and 5% more for food, clothing, transport and so on. During the 1970s, this rate soared as high as 15–20% in many countries, because of a rise in world oil prices. Inflation affects poor people more seriously than the rich, because the poor spend a greater part of their income on necessities, such as food.

Another useful indicator is GDP per head. This looks at the amount of goods and services produced by a country, divided by the population. It is a crude indicator of how wealthy the country is. It is crude because it does not always tell you how well off all people are, since the distribution of wealth might be skewed, with most of it going to a small set of people. For example, Barbados has a higher standard of living than St Kitts and Nevis, even though the latter has a higher GDP per head. Table 9.3 lists the four richest and four poorest Caribbean countries based on GDP per head at the start of the 21st century.

Table 9.3 Wealthiest and poorest countries in the Caribbean based on GDP per head

	Country	GDP per head ($)
The four wealthiest Caribbean countries:	Bahamas	16,000
	St Kitts and Nevis	7,000
	Trinidad and Tobago	6,270
	Barbados	6,025
The four poorest Caribbean countries:	Cuba	2,535
	Suriname	1,775
	Guyana	807
	Haiti	427

Working conditions

If we take as our starting point the conditions of slavery, it is obvious that Caribbean people have much better working conditions at present than in the past. However, even if we compare conditions at the beginning of the 20th century with the situation now, most people are better off in their workplaces.

MARCUS GARVEY
(1887–1940)

9.1 Marcus Garvey

Marcus Garvey was born in St Ann's Bay, Jamaica. At the age of 14 he left school to work as an apprentice at a printing firm, where he led a strike for higher wages. He went on to become a leading political activist.

In 1914, Garvey founded the United Negro Improvement Association (UNIA), which became an important lobby group. Garvey pressured the British government over issues such as wages, civil liberties such as the right to strike, universal adult suffrage and land ownership for people of African descent in the Caribbean. The UNIA, trade unions and other civic groups all made gradual headway in winning such rights for ordinary workers.

Activity 9.4

Marcus Garvey was said to be a man ahead of his time. Find out more about Marcus Garvey and present your information either as a poster or a PowerPoint presentation. Use the following headings to guide you in your research.

a   Personal life
b   Education
c   Political and social/cultural activities
d   Accomplishments
e   Impact on Caribbean society.

The United Negro Improvement Association (UNIA)

9.2 Members of the United Negro Improvement Association (UNIA) founded by Marcus Garvey, parade in Harlem, New York City, 1924

Soon after Marcus Garvey established the Universal Negro Improvement Association (UNIA) in 1914, its membership increased rapidly and within three years it had established 30 branches and comprised over two million members. By 1920, the UNIA had over 1,000 branches in more than 40 countries. The majority of its branches were located in the USA and this country was also its operating base.

The UNIA was committed to the growth of 'black consciousness'; that is, a sense of identity among Africans. It promoted racial pride and the establishment of an independent black nation in Africa.

In 1917, *Negro World* was published. This journal promoted Garvey's ideas of African nationalism and African pride. It promoted the idea of the brotherhood of man and fatherhood of god. The UNIA's motto was 'One God! One Aim! One Destiny!'

> The UNIA collapsed in 1935 but during its lifespan it contributed immensely to the growth of an African identity and African pride. It also influenced the formation of other organizations and the ideas of Garvey, or 'Garveyism', spread throughout the world.

Most Caribbean countries now have a legally enforced minimum wage, but private companies generally offer workers wages which are equal to, or higher than, the stipulated amount. Most people now work an eight-hour day and 40-hour week, and have weekends and public holidays off work. Vacation time is also now written into law or company regulations. If people choose to work extra hours or days, they may be paid extra. Since the 1980s, many governments have also passed laws which prevent child labour. Maternity leave, even when not law, is granted by most employers.

While workers' rights still remain a contentious issue, the kind of authority wielded in the past by employers, which sparked off many of the protests of the 1930s, hardly exists now. Wage rates also remain a cause for concern, with the average person earning an income which supports a working-class, rather than a middle-class, lifestyle. However, trade unions have generally been able to wrest regular pay increases every three years or so, save in times of economic downturn.

> **Maternity leave in selected Caribbean countries**
>
> **Barbados**
>
> In Barbados, the Employment of Women (Maternity Leave) Act was passed in 1976. It stated the following.
>
> - Every employee, in addition to her annual holiday under the Holidays with Pay Act, is entitled to maternity leave upon delivering to her employer:
>   - **a** a certificate issued by a medical practitioner setting forth the expected date of her confinement; or
>   - **b** a certificate issued by a medical practitioner or a midwife setting forth the actual date of her confinement.
> - An employer may accept such other evidence in support of the entitlement of an employee to maternity leave as may be reasonable having regard to the circumstances of a particular case.
> - In order to qualify for a grant of maternity leave, an employee:
>   - **a** must by employed for at least 12 months by the employer from whom she requests such leave; and
>   - **b** is not entitled to maternity leave by the same employer on more than three occasions.
>
> **Jamaica**
>
> In Jamaica the Maternity Leave Act was passed in 1979. It stated the following.
>
> - The employer of a worker shall grant her leave, to be known as maternity leave, if that worker:
>   - **a** informs the employer that she is, or wishes to be, absent from work wholly or partly because of her pregnancy or confinement and that she intends to return to work with the employer
>   - **b** has been continuously employed by the employer for a period of not less than 52 weeks at the date on which her absence begins, or, being in seasonal employment, has been engaged by that employer in that employment for periods which amount to not less than 52 weeks during the five years immediately preceding that date; and
>   - **c** produces for the inspection of the employer, if the employer so requests, a certificate from a registered medical practitioner stating that it is necessary for the worker to be absent from work wholly or partly because of her pregnancy or confinement.
>
> **Trinidad and Tobago**
>
> In Trinidad and Tobago the Maternity Protection Act was passed in 1998. It stated the following.
>
> - A pregnant employee was entitled to:
>   - **a** leave of absence for the purpose of maternity leave
>   - **b** pay while on maternity leave
>   - **c** resume work after such leave on terms no less favourable than were enjoyed by her immediately prior to her leave.
> - Where an employee has proceeded on maternity leave and the child of the employee dies at birth or within the period of the maternity leave, the employee shall be entitled to the remaining period of maternity leave with pay.

> - Where an employee has not proceeded on maternity leave and:
>   a a premature birth occurs and the child lives, the employee is entitled to the full period of maternity leave with pay; or
>   b a premature birth occurs and the child dies at birth or at any time within 13 weeks thereafter, the employee is entitled to the full or remaining period of maternity leave with pay, as the case may be.
>
> An employee who is pregnant and who has, on the written advice of a qualified person, made an appointment to attend at any place for the purpose of receiving prenatal medical care shall, subject to this Act, have the right not to be unreasonably refused time off during her working hours to enable her to keep the appointment.

Unemployment

Up until the 1980s, unemployment was a major problem in all the Anglophone islands and, despite some improvement, it remains so today. In Jamaica unemployment averages between 20% and 30% of the workforce; in Barbados and in Trinidad and Tobago it is between 17% and 18%; and in the smaller islands more than 20% of the workforce are usually unemployed. In developed countries, the unemployment rate is usually below 10%.

> **Roleplay**
>
> Imagine that you are a man or woman living in one of the Caribbean territories in the late 1940s. You are the sole breadwinner in your family and you have just lost your job. State three ways in which this may affect you and your family. Make sure to specify whether you are male or female and the territory where you live. Explain one way in which you would cope in this situation.

Unemployment for women remains a cause for concern in many Caribbean countries, although historically female participation in the workforce has been relatively high. At the start of the 21st century, the average rate of unemployment for women in the Caribbean was 20%. This rate ranged from a high of 35% in French Guiana to a low of 8% in Aruba.

Health

The ultimate indicator of an improvement in health is whether people are living longer or not. In the Caribbean, life expectancy has risen significantly since 1900. At the start of the 20th century, average life expectancy was as low as 50 years in the Caribbean. Infectious diseases such as yellow fever, malaria, dysentery and tuberculosis shortened life expectancy. By the 1960s, with improved medical science and availability of health care, average life expectancy had increased to 60 years. Most Caribbean governments pay attention to providing good health care for their citizens, spending between 4% and 7% of their GDP on the health sector.

Now, the average Caribbean male can expect to live to 68 years of age, and the average Caribbean female to 73 years. Lifestyle diseases have become the main causes of death, such as cancer because of smoking, and heart attacks, strokes and diabetes because of poor diet and lack of exercise.

Aspects of social life

Ethnic or race relations

As it consists of developing countries, the Caribbean region is exceptional in having had few or no incidents of racial violence in the 20th century. The closest any country came to this was in Guyana under the Forbes Burnham regime, which from the 1960s to the early 1980s disenfranchised the Indo-Guyanese through rigged elections. Nor have there been widespread Afro-Caribbean attacks on white Caribbean people, even though there are pockets of historical resentment against a group seen to represent the former slave masters and who are still economically dominant in the region.

Nonetheless, some Caribbean territories have created their own versions of race prejudice. In Puerto Rico, for example, Dominicans are often resented, while in Haiti the mixed-race group is regarded as privileged. This should not be interpreted as the total lack of interaction among the groups, however. What is important to note is that during slavery a conscious attempt was made by those in the dominant white group to separate themselves from the non-white groups and that higher status was given to whites. This attitude has passed to the present Caribbean to some extent. That is, there are still communities where light-skin complexion is given higher status. This has seeped to some areas of employment, for example where customer service representatives are chosen because of their complexion.

Racial tensions have been expressed mostly in Guyana and in Trinidad and to some extent this is because of the presence of a larger percentage of people of Indian ancestry. In Trinidad, there is relatively similar percentages of African and Indian origin (approximately 40% each) and the rest of the society belongs to mixed groups. When all groups were free (when slavery was abolished and indentured labour ended) the two main ethnic groups had to compete for economic and political power and this led to some amount of tension between the groups. In recent times, this tension is seen mainly at election time. At no time did this tension turn into violence. Generally, both ethnic groups interact with each other on a daily basis in schools, places of employment, social activities and so on. In Guyana, the two ethnic groups have remained more separate from each other than in the case of Trinidad and Tobago. In both countries, race relations has had an impact on politics. Throughout the Caribbean, other minorities, especially those who are seen as economically successful, are often targets of resentment from the majority, although such emotions rarely go beyond rhetoric. These minority groups include Chinese in Trinidad, Jamaica, Guyana and Martinique; Syrian or Lebanese in Trinidad and Tobago, and the Dominican Republic; and Jews in Curaçao and Jamaica.

In general though, the Caribbean is an example where the logical expectations of history have been proved wrong. Anyone who looked at the violent past of the region might reasonably have expected that, once the enslaved Africans were freed, they might attack the whites eventually. At the very least, anyone looking at the past might have expected racial resentments to last well into the next few generations. However, while the Caribbean is a violent place, in that it has one of the highest murder rates in the world, group violence has not been a consequence of the region's history of oppression.

> **Plural societies**
>
> The concept of a plural society has often been used by historians and sociologists to explain why different groups co-exist in a community but do not integrate. In a plural society different ethnic groups keep their own identities, beliefs and traditions. In some Caribbean countries, there are many different ethnic groups who all co-exist but yet do not integrate; that is, they do not share each other's customs and traditions, inter-marry and so on. They live in the same country but identify themselves as separate, distinct groups. In other Caribbean countries, the various ethnic groups have inter-married and interacted so that there are no separate identities among them.

> **Groupwork**
>
> In a group of three or four people, consider the following situation.
>
> There are two teachers, one male and one female, of different ethnic groups. They go out often for lunch and socialize with each other on a regular basis. How do you think their co-workers would react if they were seen in each of the following towns:
> - Kingston, Jamaica
> - Bridgetown, Barbados
> - Georgetown, Guyana
> - Port-of-Spain, Trinidad?

Festivals and celebrations

The main festival which defines the Caribbean is the carnival. The best-known one takes place in Trinidad in February or March, depending on when Ash Wednesday falls. Equivalent carnivals take place in the other islands, but at different times of the year, such as May in St Vincent and August in Jamaica. Carnivals also have different lengths, with Cropover in Barbados lasting five weeks from

> **Divali**
>
> Divali is celebrated by Hindus. It is popularly referred to as the 'Festival of Lights'. Prior to this day, Hindus paint, clean and decorate their homes. They believe that the Goddess Lakshmi, who is worshipped as the giver of wealth and prosperity, will only enter a clean home. On Divali day they prepare feasts and invite friends to their homes to celebrate with them.
>
> They perform puja (prayers) to Lakshmi and light deeyas (small clay pots). A cotton wick is placed in the deeya, filled with oil and then lit. There are large public celebrations all over Guyana, and Trinidad and Tobago. In the weeks leading up to the Festival of Lights many businesses, other organizations, schools and temples hold celebrations.
>
> Divali is celebrated as a time of cleansing, purification and reflection on life. It is rooted in Indian tradition and Hindus celebrate Divali to commemorate the return of the god Ram to the city of Ayodhya after one year of exile in the forest. It is celebrated on the darkest night of the year according to the Hindu calendar and symbolizes the celebration of light over darkness and good over evil.

> **Eid-ul-Fitr**
>
> Eid-ul-Fitr is a festival celebrated by Muslims. It is celebrated at the end of the month of Ramadan. This is a month during which Muslims fast from sunrise to sunset, they practise self-control and engage in inner reflection. The month usually begins with the sighting of the new moon. At the end of this month of Ramadan, Muslims celebrate the end of fasting and they give thanks to Allah for helping them fast the previous month.
>
> They hold open-air worship in mosques and parks. They dress in new clothes and decorate their homes and invite friends over for celebratory meals. Eid-ul-Fitr is symbolic in that Muslims see it as a time to forgive others, to give to those less fortunate and to improve oneself through inner reflection and positive thoughts.

Activity 9.6 Write a letter to your friend in another Caribbean country, telling him or her how you celebrate Christmas in your country. Explain how you will spend the day. Describe the types of food that your family will make and anything that you will find only in your area, village or country.

July to August though there is only one day of masquerade, whereas the Trinidad carnival lasts two days, but carnival fetes begin from January. Carnivals are rooted in the slave experience and each festival is an indigenous celebration created out of each island's historical experience and French, British and African cultures.

Activity 9.5 Do research on carnival in your country and any one other country in the region. Where did carnival originate? How has carnival changed over the years? How does it benefit your country?

In Trinidad and Guyana in particular, the Indians have also brought their own cultural events. The main Hindu festival is Divali, or the Festival of Lights, which involves lighting wicks in small clay pots called deeyas and serving Indian food. The main Muslim festival is Eid-ul-Fitr which marks the ending of the fast held during the month of Ramadan. On this day, Muslims give alms to the poor and make special meals such as sawine.

Recreation and art forms

There are also other minor festivals, which are driven more by economic considerations than cultural impulses. Sailing is a popular activity in the region, especially for tourists, and there are several regattas, with the ones in Antigua and Grenada being the best known. Music festivals are also important and Jamaica's Reggae Sumfest in July attracts many visitors. Reggae is a music genre that first developed in Jamaica in the 1960's. Bob Marley is probably the most recognisable face of the genre and reggae has since spread to many countries across the world, often incorporating local instruments and fusing with other genres. Marley's music was heavily influenced by the social issues of his homeland, and he is considered to have given voice to the specific political and cultural situation of Jamaica at the time.

The average Caribbean person often relaxes by playing or watching sports, the two most popular being cricket and football.

9.3 Damian Marley performing at Sumfest in Montego Bay, Jamaica, 2009

West Indies cricket team

The West Indian cricket team, also known as the Windies, is a multi-national team representing 15 territories. The team orginated in the 1890's when the first sides were selected to play visiting English sides. The team played their first official international match in 1928, becoming the fourth Test nation. They first beat England at Lord's in 1950, and by the 1970's had a formidable reputation in international cricket.

9.4 The logo of the West Indies cricket team

Transport and communication

From oxen to horses to motor vehicles, the Caribbean has followed developments elsewhere in the world as it has modernized the islands' internal transport systems. However, the physical separation of the islands still poses problems, with no national or regional air carrier or boat service able to run at a profit. Every Caribbean country has at least one airport and several ports for ships.

Most of the territories now have good road networks, and land-line telephone as well as mobile cell networks. In the continental countries, such as Guyana and Suriname, vast swathes of territory remain unreachable save by small aircraft or river boats.

Means of transportation in the Caribbean

In the early years, travel was by:
- animal transportation – carts (drawn by horses, bulls, bison) – horseback
- vehicles – lorries, trucks, cars
- bicycles, scooters and motorcycles
- airplanes
- ferries, boats.

Present day transportation includes:
- vehicles – cars and trucks
- scooters and motorcycles
- ships
- airplanes – Caribbean Airlines (formerly known as British West Indian Airways) LIAT, Air Jamaica, Suriname Airways, Air Guyana, St Lucia Airline, Winair, Air Caraibes.

Activity 9.7 What was the transport network like in your country in the past?

How has its historical development affected the development of the Caribbean region?

Religious groups

Religions exist in all societies, but the form of any particular religion is shaped by many factors. History is one of the forces which determines religious practices. In the Caribbean, most of the world's major religions are represented, such as Christianity,

Hinduism and Islam. The last two are practised mainly in Trinidad and Guyana because of the large Indian populations in these countries. Christianity in the Caribbean can be divided into its different groups, such as Roman Catholic, Anglican, Methodist and Pentecostal. There are also religious groups which have been strongly influenced by African cultural traits. Some of these religions combine Christian and African rituals and beliefs and people practising them are found in Haiti, Cuba, the Dominican Republic, Puerto Rico and Trinidad. Table 9.4 lists these religions and their associated groups.

Apart from the Africanist religions, there are what are called revivalist religions. These are churches based on charismatic Protestant movements, mostly brought in from the USA. These churches are found throughout the Anglophone Caribbean. Then there are the groups which emphasize the magical aspects of religion, such as foretelling the future, healing through herbs and rituals, and divine revelations. These are found in Jamaica, Puerto Rico and Cuba. Another category is the one most directly influenced by the Caribbean's history of slavery: redemptionist religions, which emphasize regaining the African heritage and throwing off colonial influences. These are found mainly in Jamaica, although there are small groups in some of the other islands.

> **Roleplay**
>
> Imagine that one of your close friends has persuaded you to become a redemptionist. Now you want to get two other friends to become redemptionists. Prepare a short speech that you will give to them, outlining the reasons why they should join this religious group with you. Remember, you have to sound very convincing.

Table 9.4 Types of religion

Type of religion	Group
Africanist	Vodun, Santeria, Orisha, Shango
Revivalist	Pentecostal, Baptist, Seventh-Day Adventist, Shouters, Tie-Heads, Jordanites, Spirit Baptists, Cohortes
Magical	Myalism, Native Baptist, Spiritual Baptists, Espertismo, Karedecismo
Redemptionist	Rastafarianism, Nation of Islam
Eastern	Hinduism, Islam

9.5 Gros Islet Church in St Lucia

9.6 A Voodoo (Vodun) ceremony near Port-au-Prince, Haiti, December 2007

While all these religions draw on roots from other parts of the world, three can be categorized as native to the Caribbean in that their rituals and beliefs were developed in the region among the African population. These are Vodun, Santeria and Orisha. Their development was possible mainly through the Maroons who, when they ran away and formed their own communities, were able to practise freely the rituals they had brought with them from Africa. Santeria, for example, has elements from Nigerian Yoruba practices, while Vodun is based on rituals from Dahomey and Congo. The religions practised by the Amerindians in the Caribbean died out along with the natives.

> **Activity 9.8** Find out more about either Vodun, Santeria or Orisha. Make a poster depicting the main beliefs and celebrations of the religion you have chosen to research.

The extent to which Christianity is incorporated into these Africanist religions is a consequence of history and the policies practised by the different European governments. There is less African influence in the former British colonies, because the British did not try to convert the enslaved Africans to Anglicanism until the early 19th century. In the French territories, however, the Africans were exposed to Christian beliefs from the 16th century, and the Roman Catholic tradition, with its many saints, made that religion more compatible with the beliefs brought by the enslaved Africans. So from the start, African elements were woven into the French and Spanish Christian tradition.

In every territory, however, the fact that the Anglican and Catholic churches were the most wealthy and powerful provided strong motivation for people to join them. But the Methodist church also gained many members, mainly through post-emancipation efforts to win rights and resources for the former slaves. In the late 20th century, Pentecostal and Evangelical churches began gaining ground in the Caribbean. This movement is strongly linked to the evangelical movement in the USA, which was started in 1906 by Charles Parham (1872–1906) in the city of Los Angeles.

> **Roleplay**
> If you were a person of African or Indian ancestry, living in a Caribbean territory in the 1940s, why would you consider joining the Roman Catholic or Anglican churches?

After the British territories became independent in the 1960s, the Africanist religions slowly began to gain more adherents, mainly because the independence movement was linked to the search for ancestral roots. This ideology was part of the 1970 Black Power Revolution that you read about in Chapter 8.

Rastafarianism

Rastafarianism, which is the best-known religion from the Caribbean, started in Jamaica in the early years of the 20th century. The movement may be traced back to 1784. A US slave named George Liele was freed by his

9.7 Haile Selassie (1892–1975), Emperor of Ethiopia, 1930–74

by Marcus Garvey about a black messiah who would free all black people from oppression.

Rastafarianism in the Caribbean is characterized by:

- the colours red, green and gold, with red standing for the blood of the martyrs in the black struggle for liberation; gold representing the wealth of their African homeland and green symbolizing Ethiopia's beauty and lush vegetation
- consuming natural foods (foods that are not chemical-based)
- vegetarianism
- sporting dreadlocks
- a belief in peace and community-based economic activity.

Activity 9.9 How has Rastafarianism had an impact on Caribbean culture in relation to:

- song and music
- recreation
- dress
- food?

owner and then founded in Jamaica a church which he called the Ethiopian Baptist Church. This linked Christianity to Africa. Another important development was the founding of the Native Baptist Church by Alexander Bedward in 1891. Bedward claimed to have healing powers, that he was Jesus reborn and that white civilization would be destroyed after he and his followers ascended to heaven where, because they had suffered so much on Earth, they would be more exalted than white people.

This belief in redemption would become integral to the Rastafarian movement, which emerged in Jamaica shortly after 1930, when Haile Selassie became Emperor of Ethiopia. Selassie claimed to be the 225th descendant of the line of King David and the Queen of Sheba from the Bible. His enthronement was linked with a prophecy made

Islam

The first Muslims to enter the Caribbean came as enslaved Africans. Islamic conquerors had been present in Africa since the 10th century, and the Mandingo, Fulani and several other tribes had converted to Islam. Unfortunately, there are no detailed records about them or their religious practices in the Caribbean. So it was not until after emancipation, when the first set of Indian indentured labourers were brought to the Caribbean, that the Muslim religion became part of the recorded cultural landscape of the region. Islamic organizations such as the Anjuman Sunnat-ul-Jamaat Association (ASJA) were set up in the 1930s, and the Islamic Missionary Guild in 1960. Muslims are mostly represented among the Indians of Guyana and Trinidad. They make up about 7% of the Guyanese population and 6% of Trinidad's.

> **Basic tenets of Islam (known as The Five Pillars of Islam)**
>
> Shahadath – The belief that Allah (God) is the only god, and Muhammad is his messenger.
>
> Salat – Muslims must pray five times a day.
>
> Zakat – Muslims must give to those less fortunate than themselves.
>
> Sawm – Muslims must fast during the month of Ramadan. Pregnant women, sick Muslims and children are exempted from this.
>
> Hajj – A Muslim who can do so, must make a pilgrimage to Mecca at least once during his or her life.

A large number of Muslims in the Caribbean are also found in Jamaica, over 5,000 at present, though they make up less than 1% of the total population. Most of Jamaica's Muslims are of African descent, and their conversion has been influenced by US organizations such as the Nation of Islam (NOI). This organization, whose most famous member was Malcolm X, extended its influence in the Caribbean during the 1960s, when there were many social upheavals in the USA. The NOI's approach appealed because of its focus on social justice, racial pride and achieving prosperity for Africans.

Hinduism

The first Hindus started arriving in the region as soon as emancipation was declared, in 1838. Apart from a brief suspension between 1848 and 1851, the indentured labourers from India were brought in steadily. However, you should note that Hinduism has many different branches, so Hindus have different rituals and beliefs. Once in the Caribbean, however, Hindus were forced to adapt many of their ancient practices, since it was difficult to keep certain traditions among a relatively small group in a new environment.

> **What does 'Hindu' mean?**
>
> The word was really invented by the Muslim conquerors, since the inhabitants of the sub-continent did not call themselves Hindu. The term, as well as the country's name (India), came from 'Sindhu', which was the name of the main river in the Indus valley, the cradle of India's 5,000-year-old civilization. Hindus in India do not usually identify themselves by reference to Hinduism, but by caste, village, region and language.

For example, in India, people were defined by their caste. There were four main castes. Brahmins had the highest status, and made up the noblemen, the religious leaders and the philosophers. Then there were kshatriyas, who were the soldiers and administrators. The third caste was the vaishyas, who were merchants, farmers and so on. In the lowest caste were the sudras, who were labourers. Within all these were even more sub-castes in India, which determined the kind of work an individual was allowed to do, their status in society and even who they could marry. Naturally, on the Caribbean sugar estates where everyone did the same hard labour, and where there was a shortage of women, keeping such distinctions was quite impractical.

The Indians managed to preserve their religion, with only a minority being persuaded by the Christian missionaries and the colonial authorities to convert. In the 1890s in Trinidad, the East Indian Association was formed to preserve Hindu traditions and to protect the

9.8 Hindus putting up flags (jhandi) in front of their homes upon completion of a worship session (puja)

rights of Indians. Several different Hindu groups also sprang up, but the most influential was the Sanatan Dharma Maha Sabha (SDMS), which was formed in the 1950s. At the same time, Hindus were assimilated in territories where there were relatively few of them, such as Jamaica and St Vincent.

Although Hinduism cannot be considered a unified or homogenous religion, certain concepts are more or less common to all branches. One of the most important is dharma, which may be translated as truth, duty, righteousness, law and justice. Another is moksha, which means liberation from the cycle of birth and death (reincarnation) which Hindus believe all people go though until they are spiritually advanced.

Spiritual Baptists

This religion is a syncretism of Christianity and African doctrines, rites and rituals. Spiritual Baptists are found in large numbers in Trinidad, Barbados, St Vincent and Grenada. In the past, followers were referred to as 'Shouter Baptists' because of the loud clapping and singing associated with their prayer sessions. However, this term was used in a degrading manner and there has been a conscious attempt to use 'Spiritual Baptists' instead. In Trinidad, the Shouters Prohibition Ordinance was passed on 16 November 1917 by the colonial government. The government felt that the group disturbed the peace of the colony with its loud singing and clapping and, after numerous complaints by prominent citizens, it banned the religion. Years later, on 26 January 1996, Prime Minister Basdeo Panday granted the Spiritual Baptists a public holiday on 30 March in commemoration of their struggles and in celebration of their religious beliefs.

The religion is characterized as follows.

- Baptism – those who wish to join the Spiritual Baptists will attend prayers sessions regularly and participate in worship in preparation for the day when he or she is baptised. Baptism is symbolic in that it represents an invitation to follow God and shows the person's willingness to repent for all past sins and to lead a righteous life. During baptism, the person is immersed in water and this represents resurrection into a new life.
- Mourning – Spiritual Baptists' periods of mourning entails prayer sessions and meditation. This is one aspect of African custom which they kept in their practices.
- Prayer sessions – these are very vibrant occasions undertaken with much ceremony. They are sessions where the Spiritual Baptists give thanks to God. During these sessions they light candles, offer flowers and fruit, bread and cakes, for example. The philosophical idea is that the more you give, the more you will get in return or the richer you will be spiritually.
- Pilgrimage – this provides an opportunity for Spiritual Baptists to meet each other and to assemble as a larger group.

REVISION QUESTIONS

1 Read the passage below, then answer the questions that follow.

Rastafarians turned away from European customs. They believed in Africa and in black pride, and they worshipped Haile Selassie. Most Caribbean people viewed their lifestyle as different in the 1960s.

   a Give three reasons why Rastafarians turned away from European customs. *(9 marks)*
   b Give two reasons why Rastafarians worshipped Haile Selassie. *(8 marks)*
   c Describe two features of the Rastafarian lifestyle that most Caribbean people saw as 'different' up to 1962. *(8 marks)*

   (Total: 25 marks)
   CXC Past Paper, Basic Proficiency, May/June 2002

2 Read the passage below and answer the questions that follow.

'I saw before me then, even as I do now, a new world of black men, not peons, serfs, dogs, and slaves, but a nation of sturdy men making their impress [mark] upon civilization and causing a new light to dawn upon the human race.' Marcus Garvey, quoted in Hall, 1982, pg 126.

   a Explain why Marcus Garvey thought that the situation of blacks in Jamaica could be compared to that of peons, serfs and slaves. *(10 marks)*
   b Describe four measures taken by Marcus Garvey to improve the social and economic conditions of blacks. *(10 marks)*
   c Outline two ways in which individuals, groups or governments responded to Garvey and the Garvey movement. *(5 marks)*

   (Total: 25 marks)
   CXC Past Paper, General Proficiency, May/June 2003

3 Critically examine the reasons for the changes in the socio-economic positions of people in any one named Caribbean territory between 1950 and 1985. **(25 marks)**

4 'African religions underwent various changes in the Caribbean during the period 1900 to 1985.' Do you agree? **(25 marks)**

References and recommended reading

- Brereton, B. *Social Life in the Caribbean, 1838–1938*, London: Heinemann Educational Books, 1985
- Beckles, H. and Shepherd, V. *Freedoms Won: Caribbean emancipation, ethnicities and nationhood*, Cambridge: Cambridge University Press, 2006
- Gates, B. *Afro-Caribbean Religions*, London: Ward Lock Educational, 1980
- Hall, D. *The Caribbean Experience*, London: Heinemann Educational Books, 1982
- Slesin, S. *Caribbean Style*, New York: Clarkson Potter, 1998

10 The School-Based Assessment

This chapter will answer the following questions.
- What is a School-Based Assessment (SBA)?
- How do I write my SBA?
- Where do I get information for my SBA?
- How do I reference my sources?
- Which style should I use in my bibliography?

The CSEC® history School-Based Assessment (SBA) is a research paper which accounts for 21% of your final mark. It offers an ideal opportunity for you to work on a research paper at home and get as high a mark as possible, prior to entering the examination room. The SBA allows you to develop those skills that are critical to the study of history while working on a topic in which you are interested. It gives you a chance to research a topic of your choice under the supervision of your teacher. As a student, you may not be interested in all the topics you have to study for the examination, but you may have felt that one or more topics were more interesting than the others.

This is your opportunity to do more work on one of these topics. However, you do need to remember that your teacher might not want you to write an SBA on a topic he or she has not completed with you in class. Therefore, you might be limited to the topics which were actually taught in class. You can discuss this with your teacher. The SBA is an attempt on the part of the Caribbean Examinations Council (CXC) to 'individualize a part of the curriculum to meet the needs of students'. Through the SBA you are given an opportunity to chose one area of the syllabus and do more structured, intensive research on this specific area. This list sets out what you are required to do.

- Identify an area of research appropriate to either the core or a theme in the syllabus. You are also allowed to research an aspect of local history.
- Develop a rationale for selecting the particular area of research.
- Identify and evaluate both primary and secondary sources (see Step 3 on page 227).
- Analyse and interpret the information obtained from the sources, in relation to the research question.
- Make intelligent conclusions which are fully supported by the evidence.
- Present your findings in a well-written, acceptable paper.

Syllabus requirements

According to the CSEC syllabus, each student is required to submit one research paper. Therefore, even if students work in groups or research the same topic, every student has to submit his or her individual research paper. The syllabus requirements are as follows.

- The research paper must be between 1,200 and 1,500 words in length. It is important to know that papers that go beyond the word limit are penalized. Normally 10% of the student's mark

is deducted for papers which are above the required word limit.
- Each paper must include a bibliography, quotations and sources along with relevant illustrations (such as graphs, tables and photographs), references and appendices.
- The paper must be neatly presented (either typed or hand-written).

A step-by-step guide to writing the SBA

The CSEC history SBA requires a certain amount of intensive research and analytical writing. Here are some guidelines on how to progress with the SBA.

Step 1: Choosing a topic

This is probably the most difficult part of the process. Often it is very difficult to find a topic which is both interesting and possible to complete in a limited time.

You should take the following into consideration when choosing a topic.

- Can I get information for my topic?
- Where will I get information for my topic?
- Does it fit into the syllabus – that is, is it stated under one of the themes or core areas or is it some aspect of my local history?
- Will I be able to write my topic as a research question?
- Is it a topic I really want to work on?
- Will my teacher be able to help me with my topic? If not, will I get guidelines and assistance from someone else? This is important if you are choosing to investigate an aspect of local history.

The topic must be written as a research question. You should then be able to answer the research question. Your research question *must* include the specific topic and the time period.

The following are some examples of SBA topics and a research question (RQ) which can be framed from the topic.

Topic: The preservation of African culture in the Caribbean.
RQ: Why was it difficult to preserve African culture during the 16th and 17th centuries?

Topic: Indian indentured labour in the Caribbean.
RQ: Is there evidence to show that Indian indentureship (1845–1917) was another form of slavery?

Topic: The impact of the Haitian Revolution
RQ: What impact did the Haitian Revolution of 1781–1804 have on Haiti and the wider Caribbean?

Topic: European colonization of the 'New World'.
RQ: What was the impact of European colonization on the 'New World' in the 1500s?

Topic: Local history.
RQ: What is the origin and development of Charleston (replace with the name of your community, school, etc.)?

Once you write your topic as a research question, you will get a better idea of how easy or difficult it is to answer the question you have asked. Asking a question also gives you an idea of where to look for the answer and it encourages you to stick to the topic.

Step 2: Writing a thesis statement

Once you have chosen your topic, you will need to write your thesis statement. The thesis statement is a crucial part of your SBA. In fact, it might be said that the thesis statement is the most important part of your SBA as it defines both your topic and your argument. It is usually a single, simple sentence in your introduction which puts your entire SBA in context. It should be written as one simple sentence, to make your topic as clear as possible. It is usually written at the end of the first paragraph (the introduction). The thesis statement:

- helps to put the topic across in a simple, easy-to-read manner
- outlines the argument you will make in your SBA

- tells the examiner what to expect in the rest of your SBA
- acts as a guideline for your argument and helps to make your argument clearer.

The following are examples of thesis statements (TS) for the research questions given above.

Topic: The preservation of African culture in the Caribbean
RQ: Why was it difficult to preserve African culture during the 16th and 17th centuries?
TS: Colonial policies led to the decline of African cultural forms in Caribbean slave societies.

Topic: Indian indentured labour in the Caribbean
RQ: Is there evidence to show that Indian indentureship (1845–1917) was another form of slavery?
TS: Indian indentureship closely resembled another form of slavery.

Topic: The impact of the Haitian Revolution
RQ: What impact did the Haitian Revolution of 1781–1804 have on Haiti and the wider Caribbean?
TS: The Haitian Revolution had far-reaching consequences for Haiti and the wider Caribbean.

Topic: European colonization of the 'New World'.
RQ: What was the impact of European colonization on the 'New World' in the 1500s?
TS: European colonization of the 'New World' led to the destruction of the indigenous population.

Topic: Local history
RQ: What is the origin and development of Charleston (replace with the name of your community, school, etc.)?
TS: Charleston's (replace with the name of your community, school, etc.) history is important to our country and should therefore be preserved.

Step 3: Sourcing information

While many students have problems writing the thesis statement, some find that sourcing the information to write the SBA is the most difficult task. However, once you know where to go, finding information will not appear such a daunting task. When sourcing information you should focus on ensuring the following.

The information is relevant to your topic. You should only use information which is relevant to your work, so it is important that you start looking at sources which will give you information pertaining to the specific topic you are writing about. This will save you a lot of time – otherwise you will end up spending weeks reading books and articles which will not really give you substantial information for your SBA.

The time period is correct. Make sure the information you get is relevant to the time period about which you are writing. Here are some examples.

- If you are doing a SBA on the economic impact of Indian indentured labourers during the indentureship period, make sure your information does not go beyond 1917, as indentureship was ended in that year.
- If your SBA is on the impact of the Haitian Revolution on Haiti and the wider Caribbean up to 1810, then make sure the information you use does not go beyond 1810.

You are referring to important authors or studies. When you start researching a topic, it will help to find out who are the authors who have written on this topic and what are the main books. Then start your research by reading these works. The chances are that you will get all your main points for your SBA from these books. Then you can look for additional information in other works. Some books may also give further reading, a bibliography or a list of references – make sure you look at these as you might get an idea of other books or articles you can use.

Illustrations are used to enhance your work. Feel free to use illustrations in your SBA. This does not mean that you should fill your SBA with pages and pages of photographs, tables, charts and so on. It simply means that a few of these, used appropriately, will enhance your research paper. They should be integrated into your SBA or used within the SBA (where possible), being discussed within the main body.

For example, if you are doing a SBA on the impact of the Haitian Revolution on Haiti and the wider Caribbean, do not include 10 pictures of Toussaint L'Ouverture and his men fighting in battle. However, you may feel a picture of sugar plantations which were destroyed after the revolt would be appropriate because it gives a visual impression of exactly what you will talk about in the SBA.

Bibliographic information is accurately recorded. You have to cite all the sources that you use in your SBA. Therefore, it is important that you record the bibliographic information for each source (see Step 6 on page 232 for details). It is very important to note all the required details when you first use a source – too often students take information from a book or article and forget to take down the bibliographic information. When they realize that this information is missing, they waste time looking it up again, or may be unable to relocate the book or journal in question.

With the above in mind, here are some suggestions on where to look for information for your SBA.

- **The school library** is one of the first places you should look. Remember, it is likely that your group is not the first batch of students doing a SBA in that school. The library might have a collection of history textbooks and articles on various topics. It would help if you consult your school's librarian as soon as you choose your topic, to see what information the library has on that particular topic. The school's librarian might even be able to tell you where else to look for information.
- **Local and national libraries** can be approached once you have chosen your topic. Some of these libraries keep files on various topics and many of them have a separate section on Caribbean studies or West Indian references. Your librarian can guide you towards books on your topic or you can search the catalogues on your own.

When searching catalogues, look first for books or articles which deal with Caribbean history in general and then for those which deal with your specific topic. Remember, there might not be many books available on your specific topic but some of the general history books might include information on that topic so you should look at both.

- **The people in your community** can be particularly useful if you are working on an aspect of local or institutional history. In this case, you will use the books and articles to give you background information and you will get other supporting information from the people you will interview. For example, if you are doing an SBA on the history of your school, you might want to interview some older people in the community who attended that school, some past teachers and principals if they are still alive and other people who had a close relationship with the school. Remember to take notes or record interviews. Make arrangements to ask further questions as this may be necessary.

When collecting information you will need to focus on two main types of sources.

- **Primary sources** comprise sources which were produced at the time of the event. They are written by someone who experienced or witnessed the specific event you are writing about. They include documents which were produced at the time, such as diaries, memoirs, journals, letters, speeches, newspaper articles, photographs, drawings and audio-visual material.
- **Secondary sources** are the books and articles which are written using the information from primary sources; that is, authors will use the primary documents to reconstruct history and produce their own books and articles. Your textbooks are all secondary sources.

Step 4: Writing an essay plan

All essays must have an introduction, a body and a conclusion.

Introduction

A strong introduction shows that you already know what you are doing before you start to write. Try to limit your introduction to one paragraph. Do not exceed two paragraphs. The introduction could include some or all of the following.

- **What to expect:** your introduction should state what you will do in the essay. It should give the examiner a clear idea of what is to come. For example, you might state, 'This essay examines the decline of the indigenous populations in the Caribbean during the 16th century.'
- **Thesis statement:** your introduction will not be complete without this. As mentioned earlier, the thesis statement is crucial to your SBA.
- **Clarification of dates:** depending on the topic you have chosen you might need to specify the time period you are examining. For example, if you are looking at some aspect of the Haitian Revolution, you might need to state when the Haitian Revolution took place. Giving dates is also important for studies of institutions, places and so on. Some topics will not require a specific date but you might want to mention the time period, for example, the decline of the indigenous populations 'in the 16th century'.
- **Clarification of terms:** some topics might be better understood if various terms are clarified. These may be historic terms or some definitions which are important to your SBA. For example, in an SBA which examines the decline of the indigenous populations, you might want to clarify at the start which indigenous groups you are looking at or which European countries you will focus on in your SBA. Similarly, if your SBA examines the emergence and continuance of Vodun (Voodoo) in Dominica in the 18th century, then you will need to start by explaining what Vodun is.

Sample introduction

Topic: The impact of the Haitian Revolution on Haiti and the wider Caribbean.

TS: The Haitian Revolution had an impact on both Haiti and the wider Caribbean.

'The Haitian Revolution's multifarious impact on surrounding slave colonies and continents resulted in diverse ramifications such as the spawning of slave resistance, the opening of economic frontiers and the formulation of black and white diasporas.'[1]

This statement by David P. Geggus highlights some of the focal outcomes of the Haitian Revolution (1791–1804) on Haiti itself as well as, more expansively, on the Caribbean slave regions. It further supports the argument that the Haitian revolution had an impact on both Haiti and the wider Caribbean. This uprising in 18th century St Domingue transpired initially due to levels of unrest between the resident white planters and free coloureds but was ultimately triggered by the enslaved Africans' overwhelming desire for freedom and equality with both groups. During the period between instigation (22 August 1791) and culmination, the Haitian Revolution encompassed milestone success as well as historic failure. Despite these contrasting encounters, however, as the first successful rebellion among enslaved Africans in the Caribbean, there is no doubt that there was some effect on the colony itself as well as on neighbouring territories.

Reference
[1] Geggus, David P. The Impact of the Haitian Revolution in the Atlantic World, Carolina: University of Southern Carolina Press, 2001, pg 3

Body of the essay

The body is the main part of your SBA and it will be the largest part. In the body of your SBA you have to give historical evidence that supports what you were saying in the introduction. The following are important guidelines to follow when writing the body of your SBA.

- Develop each point in a new paragraph. You should have a sufficient number of points to answer your research question.
- Each new paragraph should start with a topic sentence which supports your thesis statement.

The rest of the paragraph should then support the paragraph's topic sentence, stating each point clearly and precisely.
- Each point must be developed in detail. This means that the point should directly give evidence to support the research question and the evidence given should be substantial enough to stand up in an argument.

Sample points

Topic: The impact of the Haitian Revolution on Haiti and the wider Caribbean.

TS: The Haitian Revolution had an impact on both Haiti and the wider Caribbean.

Point 1: The Haitian Revolution led to complete abolition of slavery in Haiti.

The complete abolition of slavery in St Domingue as well as the country's long awaited independence represented some of the most successful outcomes of the Haitian Revolution. By the end of 1798, both the Spanish and English forces were expelled from the colony under Toussaint L'Ouverture's administration and as a result, "some 100,000 persons within the west and north had achieved self-emancipation,"[2] with those in the south experiencing the same fate soon after. (A photograph of Toussaint L'Ouverture appears below for reference.)

Predictably, Toussaint's success was not short lived and, by 1800, the black general abolished slavery throughout the colony of St Domingue. Wasting no time as its newfound Governor, Toussaint soon seized Spanish Santo Domingo and, as in St Domingue, abolished slavery there. On the 1 January 1804, the tireless efforts of Toussaint and Dutty, among those of others, finally bore fruit as Jean-Jacques Dessalines, who succeeded Toussaint after the latter's death, successfully expelled the English, French and Spanish from St Domingue and ultimately declared the colony an independent nation.

Point 2: Various Caribbean territories benfited economically from the Haitian Revolution.

Several Caribbean colonies benefited economically from the Haitian Revolution. The USA, Cuba and Puerto Rico received the migratory planters of St Domingue and were able to use the skills of these émigrés to boost their economic success. The constant decline of St Domingue's coffee and sugar industries offered the opportunity of increased prosperity in these sectors in other regional colonies, as well. The British West Indian sugar industry experienced temporary success following the destruction of that of St Domingue – 'The shortage of sugar in Europe following the outbreak of the Haitian Revolution, favoured the British West Indies in the immediate post-Revolutionary years by increasing prices in the English and European markets.'[3] In Cuba, both the coffee and sugar industries thrived. There was a marked increase in coffee production which was expected since this was where many of the French coffee planters from St Domingue migrated to and, by the 1830s, there were some 50,000 slaves engaged in coffee production in Cuba. With regard to sugar production, 'The destruction of the Haitian economy had removed a major competitor from the sugar market,'[4] as it is recorded that pre-revolutionary St Domingue was the world's greatest supplier of sugar. Cuba, therefore, succeeded St Domingue as the most prosperous colony in the Caribbean.

References

[2] Shepherd, Verene and Beckles, Hilary. Liberties Lost, Cambridge: Cambridge University Press, 2007, pg 186
[3] Dookhan, Isaac. A Pre-Emancipation History of the West Indies, Collins: Longman Caribbean, 1988, pg 81
[4] Dookhan, pg 85

Illustration 1: Toussaint L'Ouverture

Conclusion

This is where you quickly remind the examiner of the points you have made and how they support your thesis statement, which answers the research question. A good way to remember how to write a conclusion is to ask yourself, 'What was the point I was trying to make?' You should take the following into consideration when writing your conclusion.

- Keep your conclusion short – one paragraph is sufficient.
- Summarize the main arguments that you made in the body of your SBA.
- You have the opportunity in the conclusion to make some final remarks which will strengthen your argument or remind the examiner of your original research question. Feel free to rewrite your thesis statement using different words if possible. This will remind the examiner of the argument you started off with in your introduction. New information should not be included in your conclusion.

> **Sample conclusion**
>
> In conclusion, the Haitian Revolution had an impact not only on Haiti, but also, more expansively, on the Caribbean. It marked a significant turning point in St Domingue's overall progress with the unfortunate occurrences of the exodus of the skilled white planters from the colony, the risen level of hatred among racial classes and, most ill-fatedly, the colony's severe economic downturn. Advantageous to St Domingue, however, was the emergence of exemplary black and coloured leaders such as Toussaint L'Ouverture, and, of greatest importance, the successful abolition of slavery in the colony. It is saddening, though, that even up to this very day, Haiti's potential has not been lived up to. The country that was once the 'pearl of the Caribbean' has never been able to restore its pre-revolutionary prosperity; an outcome of the Revolution that Haitians are still suffering from today and a factor that will continue to have a severe impact on their lives.

Step 5: Expanding on your points

Once you have an essay plan you will need to expand on each point to make a convincing argument. This is usually one part of the SBA where students experience some problems, but remember you will receive marks for analysis and interpretation. It is acceptable to rewrite your points a few times until your argument is convincing and you have analysed each point sufficiently. In fact, most teachers will not accept your first or even second draft as the final SBA. Some might even make you write five or six drafts of your research paper before they consider it as the final SBA. This can be helpful because it gives you the opportunity to work on your argument and to make sure your SBA is very analytical. Marks are also allocated for the standard of your writing. Correcting your own mistakes could increase your final score as every time you make such changes, your SBA will get better.

Answer the research question. As you expand on your points you need to keep asking yourself, 'Am I answering my research question?' Every point you make, every paragraph and sentence that you write must help to answer your research question. So, when you write a paragraph, ask yourself, 'Did I just write something which helps to answer my research question?' Asking yourself this question after each paragraph will help you achieve focus and decrease the possibilities of straying from the topic and writing irrelevant information.

Be analytical. At this level you are expected to write critically, that is, you need to analyse rather than just regurgitate information from your sources. You need to avoid narrative events and instead focus on examining these events. As you write, you should ask yourself, 'Am I supporting my thesis statement?' Your thesis statement presented your argument and you need to expand on your points to make your arguments clear and convincing.

Link the points you make. Group your points so that they flow rather than jump from one place to another. For example, if you are dealing with the impact of the Haitian Revolution on Haiti and the wider Caribbean, it might help to group your points under broader headings such as economic, social, political aspects and so on. By doing this, you will be able to organize your points so that they can be easily read and understood by the examiner. While it might be difficult to group the points into broader headings for all topics, it is important to remember that you should link points so that your paragraphs flow into each other.

Use data to support your argument. This shows that you did the research and you are familiar with the sources pertaining to your topic. Use facts to support everything that you have written. You may wish to put some of the information you got from your sources in the form of tables, charts, diagrams and so on. Make sure these are properly labelled and referenced though. An example is given in 10.2.

Use quotations to support your argument. This shows the examiner that you have done the research and you have read the sources. However, when using quotations be careful that these are not long and drawn out. Keep them short and make sure they are very relevant to the point you are making. Also, make sure they are properly referenced in a footnote or endnote (see Step 6).

Step 6: Referencing your sources

As you write your SBA, you will refer to many books, articles, online sources and maybe even interviews. The fact that you are using the information means that these sources are very important to your SBA. It is important that you reference these sources using endnotes or footnotes.

- Endnotes are written at the end of the research paper, listed alphabetically by author.
- Footnotes are found at the bottom of the page where source material appears. They start with a number which you also put against the source material you have quoted.

If you are directly quoting material, the page number it appears on in your source must be stated in the endnotes or footnotes. The following is a guideline on the format you might use for references to books and journal articles.

- **Books:** Richard Dunn. Sugar and Slaves: The Rise of the Planter Class in the English West Indies, 1624–1713, New York: Norton, 1994, pg 41.
- **Articles:** Rhoda Reddock. 'Freedom Denied: Indian Women and Indentureship in Trinidad and Tobago, 1845–1917', Economic and Political Weekly Vol. 20, No. 43 (Oct. 26, 1985), pg 80.

Step 7: Writing a bibliography

All the information you have used when doing your SBA must be properly cited in your bibliography. The bibliography tells the examiner what your sources were and where you got information for your SBA. Therefore, you have to list every single source, whether you quoted from them directly or not. Sometimes, you might look at books or articles and get ideas for your SBA, although you did not actually use the information. In this case, you are still required to cite the source. The bibliography is important because it:

- shows that you did research on the specific topic you chose for your SBA
- informs the examiner about the sources you have used for this research
- tells the examiner that you have a good idea of how to conduct research and how to use the information to write a research paper
- helps you to keep track of the sources that you used in your research – which will be useful if you have to research the same topic later on, maybe for another project, or for CAPE history.

History students, as part of modern studies, use the MLA format. MLA stands for Modern Language Association (of America). This organization developed a style of referencing which has been used for subjects in the humanities (history, social studies, language and literature, etc). As history students, you are required to follow the basic outline of the styles resented by the MLA. The following are examples.

Books

Burn, William. Emancipation and Apprenticeship in the British West Indies. New York: Johnson Reprint Corp., 1970.

Articles

Smith, James Patterson. 'The Liberals, Race, and Political Reform in the British West Indies, 1866–1874.' The Journal of Negro History 79. 2 (1994): 131–46.

- Make sure you put the title of the article in inverted commas ('…') and you underline the title of the journal.
- It is very important to put the journal's volume, issue number and/or series in addition to the year, as many journals will publish volumes and issues more than once in the same year.

Websites

'Slavery and negotiating freedom', The National Archives, http://www.nationalarchives.gov.uk/caribbeanhistory/slavery-negotiating-freedom.htm, June 1st 2010.

- Some websites might not have the name of the authors or even the title of the article, so you will only be able to give the URL and the date on which you accessed the information.
- You need to remember to put the date on which you accessed the information because websites are updated and the information might change over days or months. If you have not confirmed when you found the information, the examiner checks the site and the information you have referred to is not there, this will question the credibility of your entire SBA.

Presentation

- The paper should be neatly hand-written or typed. If it is typed, then lines must be double-spaced.
- Try to put your essay in a folder. It makes it look more organized and professional. Remember, your SBA might be chosen as a sample for closer examination by CXC. If this happens, you want to know that you submitted an essay that not only reads well, but also looks neat and organized.
- Make sure your margins are wide enough so that if you put your SBA in a folder, parts of the words are not hidden by the folder on the left-hand side. Set your margins at 2 cm to allow enough space.

Marking scheme

CXC provides very structured guidelines to teachers on how to mark the SBA. Thus, marks are allocated for specific areas. The SBA is geared towards examining both knowledge and the communication of knowledge.

According to the *Mark Scheme for Research Projects*, marks are allocated in the following manner.

CRITERIA	
1. Identify an Area of Research (2 marks)	
• Area of research clearly identified	2 marks
• Area of research not clearly identified	1 mark
2. Develop a Rationale (3 marks)	
• Rationale for selecting area of research full developed	3 marks
• Satisfactory development of rationale	2 marks
• Limited development of rationale	1 mark

continued

CRITERIA	
3. Collection of Data (8 marks)	
• Excellent use of sources	7-8 marks
• Good use of sources	5-6 marks
• Satisfactory use of sources	3-4 marks
• Weak use of sources	1-2 marks
4. Analysis and Interpretation (6 + 4 = 10 marks)	
a • Excellent analysis of data	5-6 marks
• Satisfactory analysis of data	3-4 marks
• Weak analysis of data	1-2 marks
b • Conclusions are fully supported by the data	4 marks
• Conclusions are partially supported by the data	2-3 marks
• Conclusions are minimally supported by the data	1 mark
5. Presentation and Documentation (6 + 6 = 12 marks)	
a • Excellent language skills	5-6 marks
• Satisfactory language skills	3-4 marks
• Weak language skills	1-2 marks
b • Excellent use of the conventions for writing a research paper	5-6 marks
• Satisfactory use of the conventions for writing a research paper	3-4 marks
• Weak use of the conventions for writing a research paper	1-2 marks
TOTAL	**35 marks**

Index

A

abolition 91
  amelioration proposals 102–5
  British naval action 95–6
  campaign by abolitionists 91–4
  Cuba 148
  economic factors 108
  French slave trade 98–102
  Haitian Revolution 95
  political factors 107
  racism 105, 114
  response from planters 96
  social factors 106–7
  Spanish abolition 97–8
Adams, Grantley (1898–1971) 194, 199, 205
Adams, John Quincy 168
Adams, Tom 166
Africa 20, 29, 36
  disease 38–9
African cultural forms 61–2
African slave trade 32, 33, 34, 35, 36–8
  ecological factors 38–9
  economic factors 40–1
  geographical factors 38
  technological factors 39–40
  see also trans-Atlantic slave trade
African-Americans 128
African-Caribbean-Pacific Group (ACP) 143
Agricultural Revolution 35
agriculture 34–5, 139, 209
  bananas 30, 34, 138, 141, 150–1
  bitters 152
  cocoa 34–5, 55, 57, 138, 151–2
  coffee 28, 32, 34, 35, 55, 57, 137, 151
  conuco cultivation 15
  diversification 150, 152–3, 159
  fruit 152
  indigenous peoples 12–13, 19–20
  livestock 30, 34, 151
  rice 151, 190–1
Akara 80

aluminium 141
Aluminum Company of America (Alcoa) 161
Aluminum Company of Canada (Alcan) 161
America *see* USA
American Civil War 98
American cultural forms 185–6
American Revolution 47, 56
American War of Independence 167
Anglophone Caribbean 128
  economy 140, 162
  impact of USA 183–6
Angostura Bitters 152
Anti-Slavery Society 125
Antigua 28, 61, 115, 124
  Antigua Sail Week 154
apprenticeship system 114–15, 116
Arabian slave trade 41
Arawaks 10, 12, 16
archaeology 6, 7, 8, 9
architecture 18, 29
  housing 209–11
art forms 217–18
  indigenous peoples 17–18
Aruba 29
Asia 7, 21, 32
Atta 80, 81
Aztecs 7, 27, 29, 56

B

Báez, Buenaventura 176–7
Bahamas 7, 12, 23, 24, 61
Balaguer, Joaquin 178
Balfour, Arthur 168
bananas 30, 34, 138, 141, 150–1
Banwari Man 7
Barbados 16, 28, 55, 65
  Barbados Slave Code 1661 67, 68, 69
  Cropover 216–17
  emancipation 115, 116, 118, 124
  maternity leave 214
  mixed groups 66

  revolt 1676 78
  sugar production 50–1
Barrancoids 10
Barrow, Nita 201
Basdeo, Panday 223
Batista, Fulgencio 169–70, 171
bauxite 137, 138, 141
Bedward, Alexander 221
Belize (British Honduras) 9, 56
Biassou, Jorge 87
Bishop, Maurice 179, 180
Bissessar, Kamla Persad 201
Blaize, Herbert 166, 180
Bolívar, Simón 181
Bonaparte, Napoleon (1769–1821) 97, 98, 99, 100
Booker McConnell 161
Bosch, Juan 177–8
brain drain 141, 176
Britain 27, 28, 29, 31, 56, 57, 58, 165
  abolition 91–6, 98, 99–100, 106–7, 107–8, 108–10
  amelioration proposals 102–5
  economic policies and sugar production 119–21
  Emancipation Act 110–16
  Imperial Conference on colonies 1926 188–9
  Navigation Laws 46–7
  Parliament 134, 199
  slave laws 66–7
  slave trade 39, 44, 45–6, 47, 48
British Guiana 118, 123, 124, 127
  Royal Commission 1927 196
British Petroleum 160
British West Africa Squadron 95–6
Burke, Edmund 106
Bush, George 183
Bussa 81
Bustamante, Alexander (1884–1977) 196, 198, 204
Butler, Tubal Uriah 'Buzz' 197
Buxton, Sir Thomas 92, 95

235

C

caciques (chiefs) 13–14, 16–17, 18
calinda stick fighting 61
calypso 61, 75, 195
cannibalism 17, 19, 24–5
Capietillo, Luisa 201
capitalism 171
car assembly plants 158
Caribbean Basin Initiative 166
Caribbean Labour Congress 190
Caribs 10, 16, 17, 24–5, 29
CARICOM 141, 143, 152, 155, 180, 200
CARIFTA 199
Carlyle, Thomas 121–2
carnivals 216–17
Caroni Ltd 146
Carter, Jimmy 165
Casimiroids 6, 7, 10
cassava 13, 16, 19–20
Castro, Fidel 170–2, 173
Central America 9
Central Intelligence Agency (CIA) 172, 182
Charles, Dame Eugenia 166, 201
China 20, 21, 125
    Chinese labour 128
chocolate 11, 57
Christianity 20, 21, 30, 31, 59, 72, 96, 115, 218, 220
    British missionaries 103–4
    English Reformation 106–7
    social cohesion 133
Christophe, Henri 178
Ciboneys 13
Cipriani, Arthur A. (1875–1945) 196, 203
city-states 32
Clarkson, Thomas 93, 101
cocoa 34–5, 55, 57, 138, 151–2
coconuts 30, 34
coffee 28, 32, 34, 35, 55, 57, 137
    Blue Mountain 151
Cold War 171, 173
Coleridge, Samuel Taylor 106
Columbus, Christopher (1451–1506) 7–8, 14, 16, 19
    voyages 20–5
commodities 137–8
communications 190, 218
Communism 165, 171, 172, 174, 180
commutation 127
concubinage 78
Condorcet, Nicolas 74

conquistadores 25, 29
corn 20, 28
Cortés, Hernan 57
cost of living 212
cotton 15, 16, 30, 34, 55, 56, 57–8, 109, 137, 138
Cowper, William 93
Creole 62
cricket 187, 217, 218
Critchley, Herbert 196
crops 13, 16, 19–20
    Africa 36, 41
    main crop economy 138, 150–1
    peasant farmers 133
cruise ships 153, 154
Cuba 6, 7, 8, 12, 24, 25, 28, 30, 61, 201
    abolition 97, 98, 100
    Agrarian reform Law 172
    Bay of Pigs invasion 172
    Chinese labour 128
    sugar industry 146–50
    uprisings 65
    War of Independence (1895–98) 149
Cumina 61
Curaçao 216

D

da Gama, Vasco 34, 39
dance 61, 75, 79–80
Darwin, Charles 74
Davis, Cain 81
de la Guardia, Ernesto 182
De Las Casas, Bartolomé 29, 31
de Maceo, Doña Maria 201
Demas, William (1929–98) 205
Demerara Bauxite Company Limited (Demba) 161–2
democracy 177, 195, 197–8
Denmark 29, 56
Dessalines, Jean-Jacques 87
Devil's Island 6
Diderot, Denis 74
disease 9, 17, 28–9, 215
    Africa 38–9
    migrant labour 125, 126, 127, 129, 130
    social and economic conditions 208
Divali 217
dollar diplomacy 168
Dominica 16, 24, 29, 57, 115
Dominican Republic 8, 12
    race relations 216
    USA 176

Dookhan, Isaac 68
Drake, Frances 27–8
drumming 75–6, 79
Dutch *see* Netherlands
Dutty, Boukman 87
Duvalier, Francis 'Papa Doc' 179
Duvalier, Jean-Claude 'Baby Doc' 179
dyes 34–5

E

Earth 20, 21
East India Company (EIC) 46, 107
economy 137
    agriculture 150–3
    commodities 137–8
    competition between Caribbean islands 138, 190–1
    diversification 138, 150
    economic categories of Caribbean territories 139–40
    economic performance 140–1
    five factors affecting Caribbean economy 138
    food production 139
    foreign debt 141
    foreign ownership 138
    imports and exports 140
    incomes 140
    industrialization 155–6, 157–60
    information processing 139
    natural disasters 141
    offshore financial services 139
    percentage of labour force by sector 1945 139
    production system 138
    regional integration 138
    remittances 140
    social and economic conditions 208–9
    tourism 153–5
    unemployment 140, 141
    volatile world markets 141
    see also social and economic conditions
education 156, 195
Eid-ul-Fitr 217
emancipation *see* post-emancipation
Emancipation Act 110–14
    apprenticeship system 114–15, 116
    stipendiary magistrates 115–16
emasculation 76
encomienda system 30
England *see* Britain
Enlightenment 31

Equiano, Olaudah 49
Eratosthenes 21
Estrada Palma, Tomás 169
Europe 20–2, 32
    impact of the New World 25–8
    manufactured goods 39–40
European Economic Community (EEC) 143
examination 5
export processing zones (EPZs) 139
exports 138

F

Federation of the West Indies 193–5
    Adams, Grantley (1898–1971) 194, 205
    Bustamante, Alexander (1884–1977) 204
    Cipriani, Arthur A. (1875–1945) 203
    Demas, William (1929–98) 205
    Marryshow, Theophilus Albert (1885–1958) 204
    Ramphal, Shridath (1928–) 206
Ferdinand and Isabella of Spain 20
festivals and celebrations 216–17
First Maroon War (1729–39) 84
First World War (1914–1918) 168, 196
floods 141
food production 139
Forbes Burnham, Linden 161, 215
France 27, 28, 29, 31, 47, 56, 57, 96, 165
    abolition 98–102, 110
    amelioration proposals 105
    Code Noir 67–8
    slave laws 66, 67, 72
    slave trade 41, 44, 46, 47, 48
Francklyn, Washington 81
Francophone Caribbean 128
free trade 142
free villages 133–4
French Guiana 6, 127
French Revolution 74, 85, 87, 58, 95, 98, 110
fruit 138
Furnivall, J.S. 132

G

Gairy, Eric 179, 180
Garvey, Marcus (1880–1940) 213, 221
gas 141, 160
Germany 29, 39, 165
Goethe, Johannes Wolfgang von 96

gold 30, 39, 137
    Gold Rush 1849 181
Gomes, Fernão 34
Gómez, José Miguel 169
Gonave Island 15
good neighbour policy 168
government 187
    alternatives to independence 206–7
    colonial regional organizations 189
    Crown Colony government 134–5
    development of democracy 195, 197–8
    economic policies 140
    federation attempts 188, 189, 190, 191
    Federation of the West Indies 193–5
    federation proposals 191–3
    income tax 196
    Moyne Commission 197–8
    nationalism 190
    political parties 198–9
    political protests 201–3
    regional cooperation 189–90
    Royal Commission 1982 188
    St Kitts and Nevis 188
    Trinidad and Tobago 188
Grant, Ulysses S. 176–7
Great Britain *see* Britain
Great Depression 144, 177
Greater Antilles 6, 24, 25, 29
Grenada 16, 27, 29, 116
    USA 179
Griggs, Nanny 81, 201
gross domestic product (GDP) 175, 212, 215
gross national product (GNP) 175
Guadeloupe 24, 27, 47, 80
    government 207
    sugar 110
Guatemala 12
Guevara, Che 170
Guyana 6, 9, 20, 115, 116, 218
    bauxite 160–2
    race relations 216

H

Haiti 8, 12, 65
    coffee 57
    cotton 58
    race relations 215
    USA 178–9
Haitian Revolution 28, 74, 61, 84–5, 95
    causes 85–6
    impact 89–90

    timeline 88–9
Hartley, David 93
Harvey, Thomas 122
Hawkins, John 45
Hay-Bunau-Varilla Treaty 182
health 215
Henry the Navigator (1394–1460) 33–4
Herrera, Omar Torrijos 182
Herrera, Roberto Díaz 183
Heureaux, Ulises 177
Hinduism 217, 219, 222–3
Hispaniola 8, 12, 13, 24, 25, 28, 30, 80
history 4, 64
    Caribbean history 4
    passing examination 5
    studying history 4–5
Holland *see* Netherlands
housing 209–11
Hume, David 73, 74
hurricanes 141

I

immigration 125–6
    contract stipulations 130–1
    effects of immigration on society 132
    effects of immigration on sugar industry 131
    immigration from Africa 127–8
    immigration from China and Madeira 128
    immigration from Europe 126–7
    immigration from India 129–31
    shipping 130
Incas 7, 29, 56
India 19, 20, 21, 23, 32, 125
    Indian labour 129–31
indigenous peoples 6–17
    agriculture 12–13, 15, 19–20
    architecture 18
    art forms 17–18
    canoes 15, 19
    economic organization 15
    impact of Europeans 28–30
    impact on Europeans 30–1
    oppression 9, 30
    religion 14, 18–19
    science 19
indigo 34
Industrial Revolution 28, 35, 56, 58, 104, 107, 120
    synopsis 109
industrialization 155–6
    bauxite 156, 160–2
    effects 157–60

industrialization by invitation 158, 175
oil 156, 160
oil and gas 160
screwdriver industries 156
urbanization 162
women's employment 162
inflation 212
International Monetary Fund (IMF) 141, 180
Islam 217, 219, 221–2

J

Jackey 81
Jagan, Cheddi 184, 201
Jagan, Janet 201
Jamaica 8, 12, 14, 25, 28, 30, 48, 61, 65
bauxite 160–1
coffee 57, 151
Consolidated Slave Law 1816 102
emancipation 115, 116, 118, 122, 123
labour movements 197
Maroons 83–4, 122
maternity leave 214
minerals 161
missionaries 103–4
mixed groups 66, 75
race relations 216
reggae 155, 217
James Nourse Shipping Company 130
Jean Francois (Papillion) 87
Jessel Securities 161, 162
Johnson, Dr Samuel 93
Johnson, Lyndon 178
joint-stock companies 46

K

Kalinagos 10, 14, 15, 16–17, 19, 20
Kennedy, John F. 173
Kofi (Cuffy) 80
Kruschev, Nikita 172, 173

L

L'Ouverture, Toussaint 85, 86, 87
labour organizations 195–7
language 8–9, 24, 61, 62, 128
Le Jeune 70, 84–5
Leeward Islands 7, 14
Lesser Antilles 6, 12, 16, 17, 24, 28, 29
Lewis, W. Arthur 143, 144, 157–8, 158–9, 159–60, 175, 209

Liele, George 221
life expectancy 215
Ligon, Richard 66, 67
livestock 30, 34, 151
Locke, John 46, 72–3
logwood 34, 55, 56
Lomé Convention 146

M

mahogany 55, 56
maize 13, 20
Malcolm X 222
Malta 29
mangoes 30, 34
Manley, Norman 198
Mansfield judgement 93
manufacturing 156, 158–60, 139, 209
Europe 39–40
Marley, Bob 217
Maroons 83–4, 122, 201
Marryshow, Theophilus Albert (1885–1958) 204
Martinique 27, 47, 48, 57
government 207
race relations 216
slave rebellions 105
sugar 110
Mayans 7, 10–12, 15, 16, 17, 18, 19, 20, 57
mercantilism 46–7, 119
Mexico 27, 28
Middle East 32
migration 6–7, 9–10
Miller, Portia Simpson 201
mineral extraction 139
molasses 55, 145
Monroe Doctrine 164, 168, 178, 184
Montesquieu, Charles 72
Morgan, Henry 28
Moyne Commission 197–8
mulattos 58, 59, 86, 125
music 61, 79–80
calypso 61, 75, 195
jazz 155
reggae 155, 217
tourism 153, 155
Myal 61

N

National Gas Company 160
nationalization 158, 161–2
nature tourism 153–4

Netherlands 27, 28, 29, 41, 44
slave trade 41, 46, 48
Netherlands Antilles 206–7
Nevis 28
Nicaragua 7
Noriega, Manuel Antonio 182–3

O

oil 137, 138, 141
Old Representative System 134–5, 193
oranges 30, 34
Organisation for Economic Cooperation and Development (OECD) 153
Orisha 61, 75, 220
Ortoiroids 6–7, 10
Ostionoids 7, 10, 12

P

Panama 28
Panama Canal 178, 181, 182
USA 181
Pané, Ramón 24
Papacy 25–7
Parham, Charles (1872–1906) 220
peasantry 123, 124
contribution to Caribbean society 132–3
Peru 28
philosophers 72–4
piracy 27–8, 56
Pitt, William, the Younger 106
plantation economy 50–1
plantation organization 51–3
categories of enslaved Africans 53
plantation society 58–60
plural societies 132, 216
political parties 198–9
Grenada 179–80
Puerto Rico 174
women in politics 201
population 7–8, 50
population density 50
population growth 209
slave populations 65
urban and rural areas 211
Portugal 21, 25–7, 96
Portuguese labour 127
slave trade 33–4, 35, 41, 44, 45, 47, 48
post-emancipation 118
attitudes to labour after 1838 121–4
effects of immigration on society 132

effects of immigration on sugar industry 131
government 134–5
immigration 125–6
immigration from Africa 127–8
immigration from China and Madeira 128
immigration from Europe 126–7
immigration from India 129–31
impact of free villages 133–4
peasant farmers 132–3
wage rates in the 1840s 124
pottery 10, 11, 15, 17
privateers 27
Puerto Rico 7, 12, 13, 19, 28, 30, 40
government 206
race relations 215
USA 174–6

Q
Quakers 93, 94, 106
Quamina 82
quotas 142

R
racism 105, 114, 215–16
Ramphal, Shridath (1928–) 206
Ramsay, Reverend James 93, 96–7
Rance Report 191
Ranger 81
Rastafarianism 220–1
Reagan, Ronald 165–6, 183
recreation 217–18
Reid, Basil 25
religion 14, 18–19, 20, 218–20
African cultural forms 61
types of religion 219
revision questions
abolition 117
Caribbean economy 1875–1985 163
Caribbean political development 207
indigenous peoples 31
post-emancipation 136
revolt 90
slavery 63
social and economic conditions 224
USA in the Caribbean 1776–1985 186
revolt 64–6
Barbados 1816 (Easter Rebellion) 81
Berbice 1763 80–1
dance and music 79–80
Demerara 1823 82
dress 79
Haitian Revolution 84–90
insurrectionary resistance 79, 80–3
Jamaica 1831 (Christmas Rebellion) 82
marronage 83–4
non-insurrectionary resistance 77–8
proportion of revolts in selected English colonies 83
slave revolts 1733–1791 66
women 78–9
Reynolds Bauxite Company 161, 162
rice 151, 190–1
Rienzi, Adrian Cola 197
Roach 81
Roosevelt, Franklin D. 179
Roosevelt, Theodore 165, 166, 168, 182
Rousseau, Jean-Jacques 74
Royal African Company (RAC) 43, 46, 73
rum 54–5, 145

S
Saladoids 7, 10
San Salvador 24
Santeria 61, 220
Santo Domingo 7, 19
São Tomé 80
Schoelcher, Victor 101–2
School-Based Assessments (SBAs) 225
choosing a topic 226
expanding on your points 231–2
marking scheme 233–4
presentation 233
referencing your sources 232
sourcing information 227–8
syllabus requirements 225–6
writing a bibliography 232–3
writing a thesis statement 226–
writing an essay plan 229–31
science 19
Scoon, Sir Paul 180
Seaga, Edward 166
Second Maroon War (1795–96) 84
Second World War (1939–1945) 165, 175, 183, 189–90, 209
Selassie, Haile 221
Selvon, S. *A Brighter Sun* 183
settlements 13
Sharp, Granville 92–3
Sharpe, Samuel 82
silver 9, 28
slave laws 66–70
ideological and psychological control 71–5
physical control 70
socio-cultural control 75–6
women 76–7, 78–9
slave names 58, 39
slave populations 65
slavery 35–6, 91
chattel slavery 41
freedom 75
Smith, Adam 46, 74, 108, 119
Smith, John 81, 82
social and economic conditions 208–9
cost of living 212
ethnic or race relations 215–16
health 215
housing 209–11
improvements 211–12
unemployment 215
wealthiest and poorest countries 212
working conditions 213–14
social structure of plantations 58–60
socialism 171, 179
Society for the Gradual Abolition of Slavery 102, 104, 116
Somerset, James 93
South America 6–7, 9, 10
Spain 8, 25–7, 28, 29, 56, 57, 96
abolition 97–8
Cuba 148, 149, 165, 168
Dominican Republic 177
Panama 181
Puerto Rico 174
Siete Partidas 67, 68
slave laws 66, 67, 72
slave trade 45
spices 20–1, 32, 152
Spiritual Baptists 223
St Domingue (Haiti, Santo Domingo) 55, 61, 66, 77
St Kitts 28, 50, 115, 118, 124
St Lucia 16, 27, 57, 116
Jazz Festival 155
St Martin 207
St Vincent 16, 27, 29, 216
stipendiary magistrates 115–16, 122
Strong, Jonathan 92–3
Sturge, Joseph 122
subsidies 142

sugar 16, 28, 30, 32, 34, 35, 40, 137
   beet sugar 110, 118–19, 142
   Cuban sugar industry 146–50
   East India Company (EIC) 107, 108–9
   effects of immigration on sugar industry 131
   Industrial Revolution 109–10
   molasses 55, 145
   plantation economy 50–3
   problems affecting the industry 1838–54 118–21
   problems of the sugar industry 1875–1985 142–5
   processing 53–4
   rum 54–5, 145
   solving industry's problems 145–6
   sugar production 1831–42 119–21
Suriname 211, 218
Sweden 29
syncretism 61, 223

T

Tainos 8, 10, 12–15, 16, 17, 18–19, 20, 23, 24, 25
tariffs 142
tea 28, 32, 34, 35
technology 19, 39–40
Ten Years' War (1868–78) 148, 201
Thatcher, Margaret 201
Thistlewood, Thomas 70
Thomas, John Jacob (1840–89) 62
timber 56
tobacco 15, 32, 34, 35, 55, 56
Tobago 27, 214–15
   car assembly plants 158
   Carnival 155
   oil 141
   race relations 216
Toscanelli, Paolo dal Pozzo 21
tourism 138, 141, 153–5
trade 32–4
trans-Atlantic slave trade 41–3
   arrival in the Caribbean 48–9
   Hawkins, John 45
   middle passage 47–8

   numbers of people transported 41, 42
   rise and fall in the price of slaves 1793–1820 97
   Royal African Company 46
   slave forts 43–5
   see also African slave trade
transport 218
Treaty of Cateau-Cambresis 27
Treaty of Tordesillas 26
Trinidad 6–7, 8, 29, 57, 118, 123, 124
   car assembly plants 158
   Carnival 155, 216, 217
   cocoa 57
   cotton 58
   gas 160
   labour movements 196–7
   maternity leave 214–15
   oil 141, 160
   race relations 216
Trinidad and Tobago National Petroleum Marketing Company 160
Trinidad Leaseholds 160
Trinidad Workingmen's Association (TWA) 196
Troumassoids 10
Trujillo, Rafael 177

U

unemployment 140, 141, 209, 215
Union of Soviet Socialist Republics see USSR
United Fruit Company 151
United Kingdom see Britain
United Nations Human Development Index 209
universal adult suffrage 191–2, 198
Universal Negro Improvement Association (UNIA) 213–14
USA 28, 29, 57, 96
   abolition 97, 98, 105
   British Caribbean in the 18th century 167–8
   Cuba 165, 168–70, 173–4
   Cuba and Castro 170–2, 173
   Cuban Missile Crisis 172–3

   cultural impact on Anglophone Caribbean 185–6
   Dominican Republic 165, 176–8
   economic impact on Anglophone Caribbean 184–5
   Great Depression 144, 177
   Grenada 179–80
   Haiti 178–9
   historical development 164–6
   immigration 184
   intervention policy 168
   Monroe Doctrine 166
   Panama 165, 181–3
   political impact on Anglophone Caribbean 183–4
   Puerto Rico 174–6
USSR 165, 166, 167, 171, 172
   Cuban Missile Crisis 173

V

Vásquez, Horacio 177
Venezuela 6, 7, 10, 165
Virgin Islands 12, 14
Vodun (voodoo) 61, 220

W

Wedgwood, Josiah 106
West India Royal Commission 150
wheat 28
Wilberforce, William 91, 92, 94, 95, 96, 101
Wilhelm II of Germany 165
Williams, Eric 183–4, 199, 202
   Capitalism and Slavery 108
Windward Islands 6, 10, 16, 57
women 76–7, 78–9, 162
   politics 201
   suffrage 197–8
working conditions 213–14
Wray, John 82

Y

yachting 154
Yoruba 61, 62, 220